John Nodin

The British duties of customs, exise, &c. Containing

An account of the net sums payable on all goods imported, exported, or carried

coastwise

John Nodin

The British duties of customs, exise, &c. Containing
An account of the net sums payable on all goods imported, exported, or carried coastwise

ISBN/EAN: 9783337713324

Printed in Europe, USA, Canada, Australia, Japan

Cover: Foto ©ninafisch / pixelio.de

More available books at **www.hansebooks.com**

OF

CUSTOMS, EXCISE, &c.

CONTAINING

AN ACCOUNT OF THE NET SUMS PAYABLE

ON ALL

GOODS IMPORTED, EXPORTED, OR CARRIED COASTWISE;

AND THE

NET DRAWBACKS TO BE REPAID ON DUE EXPORTATION,
Including the Seffion of Parliament ending June the 10th, 1791.

ALSO THE SEVERAL

BOUNTIES AND ALLOWANCES

Upon certain Articles of MERCHANDISE exported and imported;

Arranged under the particular Branches of

CUSTOMS AND EXCISE:

And following the Article SALT in the CUSTOMS, are inferted the

DUTIES PAYABLE UPON BRITISH MADE SALT
Under the Management of the Commiffioners of that REVENUE,

WITH THE

DRAWBACK ALLOWED THEREON WHEN DULY EXPORTED.

ALSO

TABLES of the DUTIES of PACKAGE and SCAVAGE,
Payable in the Port of London to the CITY of LONDON by ALIENS:

WITH NOTES,

Explaining the various REGULATIONS of IMPORTATION and EXPORTATION
upon a Principle of ready INFORMATION.

By JOHN NODIN,
OF LEADENHALL STREET, AGENT;
LATE OF THE CUSTOM-HOUSE, LONDON.

LONDON:

PRINTED FOR J. JOHNSON, NO. 72, ST. PAUL'S CHURCH YARD;
AND G. G. J. AND J. ROBINSON, PATERNOSTER ROW.

M.DCC.XCII.

TO THE

MERCHANTS AND TRADERS

IN GENERAL.

IMPRESSED with a Defire of communicating, in the moſt uſeful Manner, more general Information to the Commercial Intereſt reſpecting the DUTIES, DRAWBACKS, ALLOWANCES, BOUNTIES, and LAWS, which relate to EXPORTATION and IMPORTATION than has hitherto been given in fimilar Publications, this Collection is reſpectfully fubmitted by

Their moſt obedient

Leadenhall Street, London,   humble fervant,
31ſt Dec. 1791.

JOHN NODIN.

GENERAL DIRECTIONS

FOR

IMPORTATION.

Goods of the Growth, Production, or Manufacture of Africa, America, or Asia, can only be imported into Great Britain from thence, or from the Parts where they are, usually have been, or can only be first shipped for Transportation, in British built Ships legally navigated, of which the Master, and three fourths of the Mariners at the least, are British Subjects; or in Ships of the Built of the Countries of which the Goods are the Growth, Production, or Manufacture, navigated by the Master and three fourths of the Mariners at the least, Subjects of the States from which the same are imported.

These Goods can only be so imported from each of those Quarters of the Globe directly: the Growth, Production, or Manufacture of Africa, cannot be imported from America, Asia, or Europe, and *vice versa*; nor can any Growth or Production of Africa, America, or Asia, manufactured in Foreign Parts, except in the Country or Place of which they are the Growth or Production, be imported into Great Britain, except the Goods hereafter particularly specified, and those of the Spanish or Portuguese Dominions, or Plantations, which may be imported from Spain, Portugal, the Western Islands called the Azores, Madeira, or the Canaries respectively, in British Ships; but the Goods of the Dominions or Plantations, of either of those two Sovereigns, cannot be imported from any Port or Place belonging to the other Sovereign.

By the Expression legally navigated or imported, whenever it occurs, is to be understood, that British and British built Ships, must be navigated by a British Master, and three fourths of the Mariners at the least, British Subjects, and Foreign built Ships must be of the Built of the Country of which the Goods are the Growth, &c. navigated by the Master, and three fourths of the Mariners at the least, Subjects of that State from whence the same are and can be imported, and so remaining during the whole Voyage.

In case of Death of the Mariners, or absolute Necessity by Seamen quitting the Ship in Foreign Parts, or by unavoidable Necessity at Sea, taking in other Mariners to save the Ship and Cargo from being lost, upon Proof being made of any of those Circumstances occurring, the Commissioners of the Customs may dispense with the Restrictions in the several Acts of Navigation.

In case it shall be found necessary to declare War against any Foreign Power, his Majesty may, if he shall judge it requisite, by Proclamation, permit Trading Ships and Privateers to be navigated by three fourths Foreign Seamen. 13 Geo. II. Chap. 3. Sect. 4. One fourth to be his Majesty's native or naturalized

Subjects

Subjects of Great Britain (sudden Death, Hazard, and Casualties of War, and the Seas excepted).

Goods may not be put on board Ships of War except for the sole Use of the Ship; but after they have been put on board, to be subject to the same Regulations as other Merchandise in Merchant Ships.

Goods of the Growth, Production, or Manufacture of Europe, may be imported into Great Britain in British, or British built Ships legally navigated, or in Ships of the Built of any Country or Place in Europe, belonging to the Sovereign or State in Europe, legally navigated, of which the Goods are the Growth, Production, or Manufacture respectively, or of such Ports where the said Goods can only be, or are most usually first shipped for Transportation. 27 Geo. III. Chap. 19.

British built, includes Ships built in Great Britain, Ireland, and the British Plantations, or Prize Ships legally condemned; each Description wholly owned by British Subjects, navigated and registered according to Law.

Irish Ships are entitled to the same Privileges and Advantages as British Ships under the same Regulations.

Timber of any Sort, Masts, Boards, Salt, Pitch, Tar, Rosin, Hemp, Flax, Raisins, Figs, Prunes, Olive Oils, Corn, Grain, Sugar, Pot Ashes, Wines, Vinegar, Spirits called Aqua Vitæ, or Brandy Wine, the Growth, Production, or Manufacture of Europe, may now be imported from any Port in Europe in British, or British built Ships, or in Ships the Built of any Country or Place in Europe, belonging to or under the same Sovereign or State in Europe, as the Country of which such Goods are the Growth, Production, or Manufacture, or from such Ports where the same can only be, or are most usually first shipped for Transportation.

Goods of the Streights, Levant Seas, and East India Goods, may be imported from the usual Places of lading in British Ships; except Raw Silk and Mohair Yarn, which can be brought only from the Dominions of the Grand Seignior, or from Malta, Ancona, Venice, Messina, Genoa, Leghorn, and Marseilles, if landed at either of those Places for the Purpose of opening and airing only, and re-shipped on board the same Ship from which they were landed.

Goods of the Growth of the Dominions of the Emperor of Morocco, not lying to the South of Mogadore, may be imported from Gibraltar as from the Place of the Growth, &c. in British or British built Vessels legally navigated, or in Ships belonging to the Empire of Morocco.

The Empire of Morocco comprehends the Kingdoms of Morocco, Fez, Tafilet, Suz, and the Province of Dara; Mogadore is a Port of the Kingdom of Morocco to the Atlantic Ocean, lying South from, and the nearest Place of Trade to Cape Cantin. Suz and Dara lie to the South of Mogadore, so that this Description of the Dominions of the Emperor, not lying to the South of Mogadore, includes Part of Morocco, Fez, and Tafilet. Santa Cruz is a Port of Morocco to the South of Mogadore. Algiers, Tunis,
and

and Tripoli, are individual States of Barbary, said to be under the Protection of the Grand Seignior, and lie to the North East of Mogadore.

Any Sort of unmanufactured Wood, being the Growth and Product of America (except Masts, Yards, and Bowsprits), may be imported into Great Britain directly from any Part of America, in British Vessels navigated according to Law, free of Duty if a due Entry be made thereof, expressing the Quantity and Quality, and being landed in the Presence of the proper Officer, otherwise to be liable to Duty. 11 Geo. III. Chap. 41. Sect. 1, 2.

Any Goods of the Growth, Produce, or Manufacture of Jersey, Guernsey, Sark, and Alderney, may be imported by the Inhabitants of the said Islands into Great Britain free of Duty, upon Oaths of the Growth, &c. before the Magistrate of the said Islands respectively, and Certificates from the Governors, Lieutenant-Governors, or Deputy-Governors, or Commanders in Chief, by the 3 Geo. I. Chap. 4. Sect. 5. but by the 5 Geo. I. Chap. 18. Salt imported from any of those Islands is subject to the same Duty as any Foreign Salt imported.

Coarse printed Callicoes, and other prohibited East India Piece Goods, Arrangoes, Cowries, and Tea, may, by Licence from the Lords of the Treasury, be imported for the African Trade, &c. when the East India Company have not a sufficient Quantity of any of those Sorts of Goods to supply the Demand.

Cotton Wool of any Sort, may be imported from any Part or Place whatsoever, in British built Ships legally

legally navigated, free of Duty; and being legally imported in any other Ships, is subject to a Duty of one Penny per Pound Weight.

Cinnamon, Cloves, Nutmegs, and Mace, may, by Licence of the Commissioners of the Customs, be imported from Ports of Europe; the Cinnamon in Bales containing 70 lb. each, the Cloves, Nutmegs, and Mace, in Casks containing 300 lb. each.

Oil of Cinnamon, Oil of Cloves, Oil of Mace, and Oil of Nutmegs, may be imported from Places not of their Growth.

Persian Goods may be brought through Russia by the Russia Company.

Indico and Cochineal may be imported into Great Britain from any Port or Place whatever, in British Ships, or in Ships belonging to any Kingdom or State in Amity with Great Britain. *N. B.* For a limited Time, this being one of the Laws which are continued for fixed Periods; but observe, that to be exempt from Duty, the same must be legally imported, otherwise it will be subject to a Duty of 6d. per lb. Continued by 29 Geo. III. Chap. 55. to Sept. 29, 1795, and to the End of the then next Session of Parliament.

Bullion, Gold, Silver, or Jewels, may be imported from any Place in any Ships.

Lobsters and Turbots may be imported freely by any Persons whatever, in any Ships whatever.

Gum Senega may be imported from Europe by British Subjects in British built Ships, upon Payment of the Duty.

No Currants, nor Goods of the Turkish or Ottoman Dominions,

Dominions, can be imported into Great Britain or Ireland, except in British built Ships, or in Ships of the Built of the Country of which they are the Growth, Production, or Manufacture, or of the Port from whence the same can only be, or are most usually shipped.

Goods of Muscovy, Russia, or the Dominions of the Sovereign thereof, are not to be imported except in British or Irish Ships, or in Ships of the same Country with the Goods.

Goods may not be imported or exported in the Packet-Boats (except by Permission of the Commissioners of the Customs).

Tobacco can only be imported into Great Britain from the British Plantations, Colonies, Islands, or Territories in America, from some Port or Place within the United States of America, from the Plantations or Dominions of Spain or Portugal, or from Ireland, and under the Rules, Regulations, Restrictions, and Provisions of the several Acts of Parliament in Force at, and prior to, the 10th October 1789, and from and after the 10th October 1789.

Goods wrecked, or in Danger of being wrecked, are excepted from all the Restrictions of Importation or Exportation.

The Orders of his Majesty in Council regulate the Importations of Merchandise from the United States of America, to authorize which an Act passes every Session of Parliament; and the Trade with the United States of America will probably continue under that Regulation until there shall be a Commercial Treaty between Great Britain and thofe States: the laft Order of Council, dated 1ft April 1791, is therefore recited from Page 9 to 16, and when any Goods from the States of America have Duties and Regulations impofed thereon by Parliament, the fame are fpecified under the feveral Articles in Table A; but it will be always neceffary to refer to the laft Order of Council in the London Gazette refpecting the Importation or Exportation of the Articles therein mentioned from and to the United States of America.

See the Account of Goods prohibited to be imported into or exported from Great Britain, fpecified in Table K, under the feveral Circumftances of Prohibition.

It will be found in the following Tables, that all Goods and Merchandife imported pay Duties by Gauge, Meafure, Tale, or Weight, the Quantities being afcertained by the proper Officers at the Waterfide; and as the exact Quantity of any Goods liable to Duty by the Gauge, Meafure, or Weight, cannot be accurately afcertained before they are landed, it is an immemorial Cuftom and Practice, to make a fair Entry of a Quantity fhort of the Whole eftimated to be imported, upon which the Duty is received; and after the Goods have been examined, and the whole Quantity charged by the Officers, the Duties are to be paid upon the remaining Quantity. Thefe two Acts of the Merchant produce from the Collector, Comptroller, and Examiner, Certificates of the Payment of thofe Duties, which authorize the examining Officers to deliver the Goods to the Merchant, and are called

Prime

Prime Entries and Poft Entries. All Goods or Merchandife which pay Duty by Tale, the Merchant is fuppofed to know the exact Quantity, therefore no Second or Poft Entry is permitted for any fuch Goods after they have been unfhipped with Intent to land; and if by Examination the Quantity is found to be greater than the Duties have been paid for before they they were unfhipped, the Surplus is by Law and long eftablifhed Cuftom forfeited, but the Commiffioners of the Cuftoms and Excife have a Power to relieve in all Cafes where it fhall be made appear to their Satisfaction that there was not any Intention of Fraud. In thofe Inftances where the Merchant is doubtful of the Quality or Quantity of the Goods, which frequently occur, the Law has permitted him to take out a Bill of View or Sight, and the Officers then afcertain the Quantity of the different Sorts of Goods, which they make a Return of to the Collector upon the Bill of Sight, and the Merchant is to declare of what Country they are the Growth, Production, or Manufacture.

The Acts of the 23d of Geo. III. Chap. 39. 24 Geo. III. Chap. 2. which give his Majefty Powers to regulate the Trade between the Subjects of his Majefty's Dominions and the Inhabitants of the United States of America, and the Trade and Commerce of this Kingdom with the Britifh Colonies and Plantations in America with refpect to certain Articles therein mentioned, are referred to by the *Order of Council, dated at the Court at St. James's, the 1ft Day of April* 1791, which then declares: And whereas the Powers given by the faid recited Acts were extended to the Trade

and

and Intercourse between this Kingdom and the British Colonies and Plantations in America, so far as the same might relate to Iron, Hemp, and Sail Cloth, and other Articles of the Produce of any Place bordering on the Baltic which might be exported from this Kingdom; which Acts are by subsequent Acts continued until the 5th of April 1792. His Majesty doth thereupon, by and with the Advice of his Privy Council, hereby order and declare, that any unmanufactured Goods and Merchandises, the Importation of which into this Kingdom is not prohibited by Law *(except Tobacco, for which Provision is herein after made, and except Oil made from Fish or Creatures living in the Sea, and Blubber, Whale Fins, and Spermaceti)*, and any Pig Iron, Bar Iron, Pitch, Tar, Turpentine, Rosin, Pot Ash, Pearl Ash, Indico, Masts, Yards, and Bowsprits, being the Growth or Production of any of the Territories of the United States of America, may be imported directly from thence into any of the Ports of this Kingdom, either in British built Ships owned by his Majesty's Subjects, and navigated according to Law, or in Ships built in the Countries belonging to the United States of America, or any of them, and owned by the Subjects of the said United States, or any of them, and whereof the Master and three fourths of the Mariners at least, are Subjects of the said United States, or any of them; and may be entered and landed in any Port of this Kingdom, upon Payment of such Duties as the like Sorts of Goods or Merchandise are or may be subject and liable to, if imported in British built Ships, owned by his Majesty's Subjects, and navigated

vigated according to Law, from any British Island or Plantation in America, *notwithstanding such Goods or Merchandise, or the Ships in which the same may be brought, may not be accompanied with the Certificates or other Documents heretofore required by Law.*

And it is further ordered, that all other Goods and Merchandise not herein before enumerated or described, the Importation of which into this Kingdom is not prohibited by Law (except Snuff, for which Provision is herein after made, and also Oil made from Fish, or Creatures living in the Sea, and Blubber, Whale Fins, and Spermaceti), being the Growth, Production, or Manufacture of any of the Territories of the said United States of America, may be imported from thence into this Kingdom in British or American Ships, owned and navigated as herein before required, upon Payment of such Duties of Customs and Excise as are payable on the like Goods and Merchandise, upon their Importation into this Kingdom from Countries not under the Dominion of his Majesty, according to the Schedule and Tables marked A, D, and F, annexed to the 27th of Geo. III. Chap. 13. or by any other Laws in Force, passed subsequent to the said Act touching the Duties contained in the said Schedule and Tables marked A, D, and F. And in Cases where different Duties are imposed upon the like Goods, imported from different Countries, not under the Dominion of his Majesty, then that such Goods shall be imported upon the lowest Duties which by the said Schedule and Tables marked A, D, and F, are required to be paid on the Importation of any such Goods

from

from any European Country not under the Dominion of his Majesty.

And his Majesty is hereby further pleased to order, that all such Goods and Merchandise shall be entitled to the same Drawbacks as are allowed upon the Exportation of the like Goods and Merchandise when exported from this Kingdom, according to the said Schedule and Tables marked A, D, and F, annexed to the beforementioned Act of the 27 Geo. III. Chap. 13. or according to any other Law in Force passed subsequent to the said Acts touching Drawbacks. And it is hereby further ordered, that there shall be allowed and paid the same Drawbacks and Bounties on Goods and Merchandise exported from this Kingdom to the Territories of the said United States, or any of them, as are, or may hereafter be allowed by Law, upon the Exportation of the like Goods or Merchandise to any of the Islands, Plantations, or Colonies belonging to the Crown of Great Britain in America: And it is hereby further ordered, that there shall be allowed and paid the same Drawbacks upon the Exportation of any Sort of Foreign Hemp or Foreign Iron exported from this Kingdom into any British Colony or Plantation in America, or into the Territories of the United States of America, or any of them, as are, or may hereafter, be allowed by Law, upon the Exportation of the like Sort of Hemp or Iron to other Foreign Parts; and all such Drawbacks and Bounties respectively, shall be allowed and paid in the same Manner, and under the same Rules, Regulations, and Forfeitures, in all Respects, as such Drawbacks and Bounties are

allowed

allowed and paid, or are subject and liable to by Law.

And his Majesty is hereby further pleased to order, that *any Tobacco*, being the Growth or Production of any of the Territories of the said United States of America, *may be imported in British or American Ships*, owned and navigated as herein before required, upon Payment of the same Duties as Tobacco imported by British Subjects from any British Colony or Plantation, is, or may hereafter be subject to: And that any Snuff, being the Production or Manufacture of any of the said Territories, may be imported in Manner before mentioned, upon Payment of such Duties as Snuff, being the Production or Manufacture of Europe, imported from Europe, is, or hereafter may be subject to, and may be warehoused and again exported; subject respectively, nevertheless, to all and singular the Regulations of the Acts of the 29 Geo. III. Chap. 68. and the 30 Geo. III. Chap. 40.

And his Majesty is further pleased to order, that any Rice, being the Growth or Production of any of the Territories of the United States of America, which shall be imported directly from thence into any of the Ports of this Kingdom, in Manner above mentioned, may, upon the Importer paying down, in ready Money, the Duty of Eightpence the Hundred Weight, being Part of the Duties now payable upon the Importation of Rice, be landed and warehoused (except as herein after excepted), under his Majesty's Locks, in such Warehouses as shall be approved of for that Purpose by the Commissioners of his Majesty's Customs,

toms, or any Four or more of them, upon the Importer's own Bond for Payment of the Remainder of the Duties, due and payable for such Rice, within Eighteen Months, according to the Net Weight and Quantity of such Rice at the Time it shall be so landed; but it is his Majesty's Pleasure nevertheless, that upon the Importation of any Rice into the Port of London, Bristol, Portsmouth, Cowes, Liverpool, Lancaster, Falmouth, Poole, Whitehaven, Hull, Greenock, and Port Glasgow, or either of them, in the Manner herein before expressed, the Importer shall be at Liberty to enter and land the same without Payment of any Duty whatever; in which Case such Rice shall be warehoused, under the joint Locks of his Majesty and the Proprietors, in such Warehouse or Warehouses as shall be approved of for that Purpose by the Commissioners of his Majesty's Customs, or any Four or more of them, in that Part of Great Britain called England, and any Three or more of them, in that Part of Great Britain called Scotland; every Expence attending which Warehousing shall be borne by the said Proprietors; and that such Proprietor or Proprietors, or his or their known Agent, shall, from Time to Time, at all seasonable Hours, as Occasion may require, have free Access to such Warehouses, in the Presence of some proper Officer of the Customs, for the Purpose of skreening and shifting the Rice, to prevent its receiving Damage. And that if any Rice, which shall be so imported from the Territories of the said United States into any of the Ports above mentioned respectively, and warehoused as aforesaid, shall be taken out of the Warehouses

houses wherein the same shall be secured under the joint Locks of his Majesty and the Proprietors, as aforesaid, for Home Consumption, the full Duties due and payable by Law upon the Importation of such Rice into this Kingdom for Home Consumption, shall, previously to its being taken out of such Warehouses, be paid to the Collector of his Majesty's Customs at the Ports where such Rice shall be so warehoused; but that such Proprietor, if he intends to export such Rice, shall have Liberty to export the same from such Warehouses respectively, under the usual Regulations, without Payment of any Duty whatever: And that if any Rice, which shall have been imported into any Port of this Kingdom not herein before specially named, and shall have been warehoused upon the Importer's Bond, in Manner aforesaid, shall, within the Time herein before mentioned, be taken out of the Warehouse wherein it shall have been so secured, to be exported directly from thence, the Bond entered into for the Payment of the said Duties thereon shall be discharged and cancelled, by Debenture or Debentures made out and passed in the usual Manner, for the Quantity or Qualities of Rice duly exported. And if any Rice imported into any Port of this Kingdom, not herein before specially named, and warehoused in Manner aforesaid, shall be taken out of any such Warehouse for Home Consumption, the Remainder of the Duties due and payable by Law, shall, previously to its being taken out of such Warehouse, be paid to the Collector of his Majesty's Customs at the Port where such Rice shall be so warehoused.

And

And the Right Honourable the Lords Commissioners of his Majesty's Treasury, and the Lords Commissioners of the Admiralty, are to give the necessary Directions herein, as to them may respectively appertain. Signed STEPHEN COTTRELL.

By the 27 Geo. III. Chap. 13. called the Consolidation Act, the Duties of Package, Scavage, Balliage, or Portage, or any other Duties, are to continue as heretofore payable to the Mayor and Commonalty, and Citizens of London, or to any City or Town Corporate within the Kingdom of Great Britain, the Prisage of Wines, the Duty called Butlerage, the Duty of Twelvepence per Chaldron on Sea Coal exported from Newcastle upon Tyne, are also continued, and all Persons, Bodies Politick or Corporate, are to continue to enjoy any special Privilege or Exemption to which they were entitled by Law. Sect. 1.

From and after the 10th May 1787, the several Duties of Customs and Excise, payable upon Merchandise imported or carried Coastwise, and the several Drawbacks allowed upon Exportation to cease, except the Duties or Licences formerly payable to the Excise; and, in lieu thereof, the several Duties are to be payable, and the several Drawbacks to be allowed as specified in the Tables A, B, C, D, E, and F; but Goods not liable to Duty before 10th May 1787, are to be permitted to be entered Duty free, unless particularly charged in any of the Tables.

No Drawbacks to be allowed unless the Goods are properly entered for Exportation, and actually shipped
within

within three Years from the Time of Importation, which is to be taken from the Date of the Report of the Ship inwards; nor unlefs claimed within two years from the Time of fhipping, and not to extend to any Port or Place of Export to which a Drawback was not before allowed.

All the Regulations, Reftrictions, Penalties, and Forfeitures to which any Goods were fubject upon Importation or Exportation, or with refpect to any Duties of Excife, are to continue in Force unlefs fpecially altered.

Bonds for Security of Duties permitted to be taken as heretofore, except the Duties on Coals, which are to be paid in ready Money without Difcount.

All Goods imported into Great Britain to be landed (except Diamonds, Jewels, Pearls, precious Stones, and Bullion, frefh Fifh Britifh taken, imported in Britifh built Ships, Lobfters and Turbots, however taken or imported), whether liable to Duty or not, muft be regularly entered and landed in the Prefence of the proper Officer, who is to examine the fame, and not deliver them out of his Cuftody until he has taken a particular Account of the Quantity and Species of the Goods.

Eaft India Goods not fpecifically and particularly rated in Table A, are to be liable to the Duties and Drawbacks in Table B, and the Value to be taken by the grofs Price at the Company's public Sales.

Any Goods imported, which are not by Law exempt from Duty and not rated in Table A, are to be liable to the Duties and Drawbacks fpecified in Table D.

C ‘ The

The Value of Goods imported is to be ascertained by the Declaration of the Merchant or his Agent, which Declaration is to be equally binding as an Oath; and if the Goods are judged to be undervalued by the examining Officers, they may take them to the King's Warehouse for the Benefit of the Crown, within eight Days from the landing in London or Leith, and within fifteen Days from the landing in any other Ports in Great Britain; four Commissioners of the Customs being authorized to direct the Receiver-General to pay the Importer the Value so ascertained, with the Addition of Ten *per Cent.* thereon, and also the Duties paid on Importation, but without any further Allowance for ⟨Freight⟩ or other Charges, which Payment is to be made within fifteen Days if the Value exceeds twenty Pounds, and without Delay if the Value does not exceed twenty Pounds.

Goods chargeable with Duty according to the Value thereof upon Exportation, the Value is to be ascertained by the Declaration of the Exporter or his Agent, which is to be equally binding as his Oath; and if it shall appear to the proper Officers upon Examination, that the Goods are undervalued, he may detain the same in like Manner, and under the same Regulations as are directed to be pursued with Goods subject to Duty at Value upon Importation; and the Exporter or Proprietor is to be paid the said Value, together with Ten *per Cent.* Addition thereon, and the Duty paid on the Entry for Exportation, without any further Allowance on any Account whatever, within fifteen Days after the Goods shall have been detained.

From

From the 10th of May 1787, to the 10th of May 1800, the Articles enumerated in Tables C and F, being the Produce of the European Dominions of the French King, may be imported from thence upon Payment of the Duties therein specified, and French Wine in Bottles or Flasks, as well for Sale as for private Use, in British built Ships, or in French built Ships, legally navigated.

The Rules, Orders, Directions, and Regulations annexed to the two Books of Rates of the 12 Cha. II. and 11 Geo. I. are repealed, except those Parts re-enacted in this Act of 27 Geo. III. Chap. 13. Sect. 1, 32, 33, and 34, which comprise the Rules 13, 18, 19, 22, 24, and 25, annexed to the 12 Cha. II. Chap. 4. inserted in Page 23 to 26, for the Information of the Merchants, and Officers.

Fresh Fish of every Kind or Sort whatever, caught or taken in any Part of the Ocean by the Crews of Vessels built in Great Britain, Ireland, the Islands of Jersey, Guernsey, or Man, or in any of the Territories now belonging, or which did belong at the Time of building such Vessels, or which may hereafter belong to, or be in the Possession of his Majesty, his Heirs and Successors, and wholly belonging to and owned by his Majesty's Subjects, usually residing in Great Britain, Ireland, Islands of Guernsey, Jersey, or Man, navigated and registered according to Law, may be imported into Great Britain in Ships built, owned, navigated, and registered as aforesaid, free of Duty. Sect. 32.

If any Goods (except Wine, Tobacco, Raisins, and Currants) shall receive any Damage by Salt Water or otherwise, during the Course of the Voyage after such Goods shall have been shipped in Foreign Parts, and before the same shall have been unshipped or discharged from the Ship in which they shall have been imported into Great Britain, any Two principal Officers of the Customs, of which the Collector shall be one (the Proof of such Damage being first ascertained in the Manner heretofore required by Law), shall have Power to choose Two indifferent Merchants experienced in the Value of such Goods, who, upon viewing the same, shall certify and declare upon their corporal Oaths, first administered by the said Officers, what Damage such Goods have received, and how much the same are lessened in their true Value according to such Damage in relation to the Duties set on them in Table A; and thereupon the proper Officers shall make a just, reasonable, and proportionable Allowance to the Merchant, by Way of Return or Repayment, out of the Duties which shall have been actually paid for the same. Sect. 33.

Goods are to continue to be laden and unladen at the Times and Places now allowed by Law, the Officers of the Customs respectively, are to attend the lawful Hours, and the Fees established by Law to the Officers of the Customs are not to be altered, varied, or increased in any Respect, but the same are respectively to continue as heretofore. Sect. 34.

All special Allowances in the Duties of Excise particularly directed by any Act of Parliament in force before 10th May 1787, are to be continued.

The Allowances, Bounties, and Drawbacks of Excife, are in Table F.

The Bounties on Goods exported, which have not been liable to the Duties of Excife, are in Table G.

The Duty of Scavage, as fpecified in Table H, is payable to the City of London by Aliens, and the Sons of Aliens, importing any Merchandife into the Port of London in any Ships whatever, and by Britifh Subjects importing in Foreign Ships, Wines of the Growth of France or Germany, Mafts, Timber, or Boards, Foreign Salt, Pitch, Tar, Rofin, Hemp, Flax, Raifins, Figs, Prunes, Olive Oils, all Sorts of Corn or Grain, Sugar, Pot Afhes, Spirits commonly called Brandy Wine or Aqua Vitæ, Wines of the Growth of Spain, the Iflands of the Canaries or Portugal, Madeira or Weftern Iflands, and all the Goods of the Growth, Production, or Manufacture of Mufcovy or Ruffia.

The Duty of Package, as fpecified in Table I, is payable to the City of London by Aliens, and the Sons of Aliens, exporting any Merchandife from the Port of London in any Ships whatever.

Table K contains a Lift of Goods prohibited to be imported into or exported from Great Britain, whether circumftantially or abfolutely, arranged under the different Circumftances of Prohibition.

Table L contains an account of the Quantities of Corn and other Articles which may be exported in one Year to certain Places, for the Ufe and Suftenance of the Inhabitants thereof, from certain Ports, by the 31 Geo. III. Chap. 30.

Then follow a Wine Table for the Port of London,

and a Wine Table for the other Ports of Great Britain, shewing the several Duties of Customs and Excise payable upon any Sort of Wine imported either in British built Ships, or in Foreign Ships, from one Gallon to a Tun; also the several Drawbacks allowed upon Exportation of any Sort of Foreign Wine to any Place whatever, by which the Merchant may readily see the Duties he has to pay, and the Drawbacks he has to receive; and for the other Duties payable upon Importation, see the Note following Wine in Table A.

By the 28 Edw. III. Chap. 13. and 20 Rich. II. Chap. 4. Ships freighted towards England or elsewhere, are not to be compelled to come to any Port of England, nor here to abide against the Will of the Masters and Mariners of the same, or of the Merchants whose the Goods be; and if such Ships come of their own good Will or otherwise, to any Port in England, Part of their Merchandise may be delivered and the Duties paid, and the Ships be permitted to proceed with the Remainder where the Masters and Mariners, or Merchants, please, without Custom thereof to be paid, and if any set Disturbance, he shall incur a grievous Forfeiture to the King according to the Trespass.

The first Rule annexed to the Book of Rates of the 12 Char. II. does not appear to have been re-enacted by the 27 Geo. III. Chap. 13. therefore it seemed necessary to refer to the above Acts of Edw. III. and Rich. II. in order to elucidate this Situation of Commerce, which must frequently arise in different Ports of the Kingdom, and to transcribe the first Rule verbatim, it still continuing the Practice in the first Port where

where a Ship arrives, for the Master to declare upon Oath the Contents of the Ship's Lading, what Part of the same is intended to be landed there, and to what other Port or Ports, the Remainder, being particularly specified, is intended to be carried.

Rule 1.

Every Merchant shall have free Liberty to break Bulk in any Port allowed by the Law, and to pay Custom and Subsidy for no more than he shall enter and land, provided that the Master or Purser of every such Ship shall first make Declaration upon Oath, before any two principal Officers of the Port, of the true Content of his Ship's Lading; and shall likewise after declare, upon his Oath, before the Customer, Collector, Comptroller, or Surveyor, or Two of them, at the next Port of this Kingdom where his Ship shall arrive, the Quantity of the Goods landed at the other Port where Bulk was first broken, and to whom they did belong.

Rules annexed and referred to in the 12 Char. II. Chap. 4. which are re-enacted by the 27 Geo. III. Chap. 13.

Rule 13.

That the Merchants trading in the Port of London have free Liberty to lade and unlade their Goods at any the lawful Quays, and Places of shipping and landing of Goods, between the Tower of London and London Bridge, and between Sun Rising and Sun Setting, from the tenth Day of September to the tenth Day of March; and between the Hours of six of the Clock in the Morning, and fix of the Clock in the Evening, from the tenth Day of March to the tenth Day of September, giving Notice thereof to the respective Officers appointed to attend the lading and unlading of Goods: and such Officer as shall refuse, upon due calling, to be present, he shall forfeit for every Default five Pounds, the one Moiety unto the King, and the other Moiety to the Party grieved and suing for the same.

Rule 18.

The Officers who sit above in the Custom House of the Port of London, shall attend the Service of their several Places from nine to twelve of the Clock in the Forenoon; and one Officer, or one able Clerk, shall attend with the Book in the Afternoon, during such Time as the Officers are appointed to wait at the Water Side, for the better deciding of all Controversies that may happen concerning Merchants Warrants: all other the Officers of the Out Ports shall attend every Day in the Custom House of every respective Port, for Dispatch of Merchants and Shippers, between the Hours of nine of the Clock and twelve in the Morning, and two and four of the Clock in the Afternoon.

Rule 19.

Every Merchant making an Entry of Goods, either inwards or outwards, shall be dispatched in such Order as he cometh; and if any Officer, or his Clerk, shall, either for Favour or Reward, put any Merchant, or his Servant duly attending, by his Turn, or otherwise delay any Person so duly attending, and making his Entries aforesaid, to draw any other Reward or Gratuity

from

from him than is limited in the Act for Tonnage and Poundage, and this Book; if the Master Officer be found faulty herein, he shall, upon Complaint to the chief Officers of the Custom House, be strictly admonished of his Duty; but if the Clerk be found faulty therein, he shall, upon Complaint to the said chief Officers, be presently discharged of his Service, and not be permitted to sit any more in the Custom House.

The RULES 20, and 21, respecting Duties payable to the City of London, or any other City, Town, or Corporation of Great Britain, being particularly re-enacted in the first Section of the 27 Geo. III. Chap. 13. are therefore omitted, being recited in the Abstract of that Act, in Page 16.

RULE 22.

N. B. As Section 34, of the 27 Geo. III. Chap. 13. recited in Page 20, relates to the Attendance of the Officers, this Rule is transcribed verbatim.

The Under Searchers, or other Officers of Gravesend, having Power to visit and search any Ship outward bound, shall not, without just and reasonable Cause, detain any such Ship, under Colour of searching the Goods therein laden, above three Tides after her Arrival at Gravesend, under Pain of Loss of their Office, and rendering Damage to the Merchant or Owner of the Ship. And the Searcher, or other Officer of the Custom House in any of the Out Ports, having Power to search and visit any Ship outward bound, shall not, without just and reasonable Cause, detain any such Ship under Colour of searching the Goods therein laden, above one Tide after the said Ship is fully laden and

ready

ready to set Sail, under Pain of Loss of the Office of such Offender, and rendering Damage to the Merchant and Owner of the Ship.

RULE 24.

For avoiding all Oppression by any of the Officers of the Customs in any Port of this Kingdom, in exacting unreasonable Fees from the Merchant, by Reason of any Entries, or otherwise touching the shipping and unshipping of any Goods, Wares, and Merchandise; it is ordered, that no Officer, Clerk, or other belonging to any Custom House whatsoever, shall exact, require, or receive any other, or a greater Fee, of any Merchant or other whatsoever, than such as are, or shall be established by the Commons in Parliament assembled: if any Officer, or other, shall offend contrary to this Order, he shall forfeit his Office and Place, and be for ever after incapable of any Office in the Custom House.

RULE 25.

All Fees appointed to be paid unto the Customer, Comptroller, Surveyor, or Surveyor General, in the Port of London, for any Cocket or Certificate outwards, shall be paid altogether in one Sum to that Officer from whom the Merchant is to have his Cocket or Certificate above, in the Custom House; and after the Merchant has duly paid his Custom and Subsidy, and other Duties above, in the Custom House, as is appointed in this Book of Rates, he is to be Master of, and keep his own Cocket or Certificate until he shall ship out his Goods so entered; when he is to deliver the same to the Head Searcher, or his Majesty's Under Searcher

Searcher in the Port of London, or other Ports, together with the Mark and Number of the Goods.

> The Importance of the Port of London in the Confideration of the Commerce of Great Britain, has induced the Author to infert the Names of the lawful Quays, Wharfs, &c. the Regulations refpecting them, or the fhipping and landing of Goods in the Port of London as fet forth in his Majefty's Commiffion, affigning, appointing, and allowing the fame in purfuance of the Acts of the 1 Eliz. Chap. 11. and 13 and 14 Char. II. Chap. 11.

1. BREWER'S QUAY, bounded on the Eaft with Tower Dock, containing from Eaft to Weft 73 Feet, and in Breadth from the River of Thames northward, 40 Feet in the narroweft Place.
2. CHESTER'S QUAY, containing from Eaft to Weft 51 Feet, and from the River of Thames northward, 40 Feet in the narroweft Place.
3. GALLY QUAY, containing from Eaft to Weft 101 Feet, and from the River of Thames northward, 40 Feet in the narroweft Place.
4. WOOL DOCK, containing from Eaft to Weft 61 Feet, and from the River of Thames northward, 40 Feet in the narroweft Place.
5. CUSTOM HOUSE QUAY, containing from Eaft to Weft 202 Feet, befides fix Feet more at the Eaft End thereof, betwixt that and Wool Dock, being a common Sewer arched over; and from the River of Thames northward, all the Extent of Ground which fhall

shall not be employed or used in the building of his Majesty's Custom House, and Offices thereunto belonging.

But the Stone Stairs on the West Side thereof, containing 15 Feet in Breadth, is declared to be a Place for Wherries and Passengers, and fetching of Water only, and not for any Goods or Merchandise.

6. PORTER'S QUAY, containing from East to West 103 Feet, and from the River of Thames northward, 40 Feet in the narrowest Place.

7. BEAR QUAY, containing from East to West 62 Feet 4 Inches, and from the River of Thames northward, 40 Feet in the narrowest Place.

8. SAB'S DOCK, excluding the Stairs there (which are hereby declared no lawful Place of shipping or landing of Goods or Merchandise), containing from East to West 30 Feet, and from the River of Thames northward, 40 Feet.

9. WIGGON'S QUAY, containing from East to West $52\frac{1}{2}$ Feet, and from the River of Thames northward, 40 Feet in the narrowest Place.

10. YOUNG'S QUAY, containing from East to West 46 Feet four Inches, and from the River of Thames northward, 40 Feet in the narrowest Place.

11. RALPH'S QUAY, containing from East to West 81 Feet, and from the River of Thames northward, 40 Feet in the narrowest Place.

12. DICE QUAY, containing from East to West 111 Feet, and from the River of Thames northward, 40 Feet, and if the Stairs on the east Side thereof be

taken

taken away, and the Paſſage leading thereunto be laid into the ſaid Quay, then to contain ſix Feet more from Eaſt to Weſt, and northward from the River of Thames, the ſaid Paſſage to contain 40 Feet; but in the mean Time the ſaid Stairs are declared unlawful for the landing, lading, or ſhipping of Goods or Merchandiſe.

13. SMART's QUAY, at the ſouth End thereof, containing from Eaſt to Weſt 27 Feet two Inches, and extending northward along the Side of Billingſgate Dock 176 Feet ſix Inches; and in all other Parts extending from the ſaid Dock eaſtward 40 Feet.

14. SOMER's QUAY, containing from Eaſt to Weſt, and including the Paſſage leading to the Stairs on the eaſt Side thereof, 73½ Feet, and from the River of Thames northward, 40 Feet; but the Place where the ſaid Stairs now ſtand is hereby declared to be no lawful Place of landing or ſhipping of Goods and Merchandiſe until the Stairs be taken away.

15. LYON QUAY, containing from Eaſt to Weſt 36 Feet nine Inches, and from the River of Thames, northward, 40 Feet; but no Stairs, as formerly, to be erected thereupon or thereunto.

16. BUTTOLPH WHARF, containing from Eaſt to Weſt 78 Feet, and from the River of Thames northward, 40 Feet, in the narroweſt Place.

17. HAMMOND's QUAY, containing from Eaſt to Weſt 23 Feet, and from the River of Thames northward, 40 Feet.

18. GAUNT's QUAY, containing from Eaſt to Weſt 31 Feet, including the ſmall Stairs on the eaſt Side thereof,

thereof, and from the River of Thames northward, 40 Feet; but the Stairs are hereby declared unlawful for shipping, lading, or landing of Goods or Merchandise.

19. COCK'S QUAY, containing from East to West 40 Feet eight Inches, and from the River of Thames northward, 40 Feet in the narrowest Place.

20. One Place betwixt Cock's Quay and Fresh Wharf, commonly called Part of Fresh Wharf, containing from East to West 25 Feet, including the Stairs at the east Side thereof, and northwards from the River of Thames, 40 Feet in the narrowest Place; but the said Stairs are hereby declared unlawful for shipping or landing of Goods.

21. FRESH WHARF, containing from East to West 115 Feet, and from the River of Thames northward, 40 Feet in the narrowest Place.

22. BILLINGSGATE, containing from North to South $171\frac{1}{2}$ Feet, and in Breadth from East to West 40 Feet, to be a common open Place, for the landing or bringing in of Fish, Salt, Victuals, or Fewel of all Sorts, and all Native Materials for building, and for Fruit (all manner of Grocery excepted), and for carrying out the same, and for no other Wares or Merchandise. And if the Lord Mayor and Aldermen of the City shall think fit to fill up any Part of the said Dock, at the north End thereof, not exceeding 40 Feet in Length, the same Ground, so filled up, may have the same Privilege as the Rest of the Wharf before prescribed.

BRIDGE HOUSE in Southwark may be allowed as a

Place convenient for the landing of any Kind of Corn, bought or provided for the Provision or Victualling of the City, and not upon any private or particular Person's Account, and for no other Goods or Merchandise.

It may be lawful for any Person to ship or lade into any Ship or Vessel, on the River of Thames, bound over Seas, and lying between London and Woolwich, any of the Goods or Merchandise hereafter mentioned, viz. Horses, Coals, Beer, ordinary Stores for building, Fish taken by any of his Majesty's Subjects, Corn or Grain, provided that the Customs and Duties of such Goods be duly paid, and Cockets or other lawful Warrants passed for the same, and delivered to the Searcher, or One of his Majesty's Under Searchers, and shipped in the Presence of some of them, and in the Presence of a Deputy, to such Persons as shall be appointed from Time to Time to manage or receive the Customs in the Port of London, and not otherwise.

It may be lawful for any Person or Persons to unship and lay on Land, Deal Boards, Balks, and all Sorts of Masts and great Timber, at any Place of the River of Thames betwixt Westminster and Limehouse Dock; provided the Owners of such Goods do first pay or compound for the Custom and other Duties, and declare the Place at which they will land them (before they unship any of the Goods) to the Officers or Farmers of the Customs thereof, for the Time being, and receive Sufferance or Permission from them so to do;

and

and that they unship none of the said Goods but in the Presence of a Waiter or Officer appointed thereunto, unless by a special Licence of the said Officers or Farmers of the Customs for the Time being; otherwise the said Goods to be liable to Forfeiture according to Law.

It may be lawful for the Owners or Possessors of the several Wharfs, called Lyon Quay, Somer's Quay, Dice Quay, and Sab's Dock, to fill up or wharf over, and enlarge into the River of Thames, so much as will make the Front of their Wall or Campshot range equally with the adjoining Quays or Wharfs.

If any of the Houses or Buildings be intended for Warehouses upon the Wharf, or hereafter so employed, the two Upper Stories and Garrets of the said Houses to be made, and from Time to Time continued, with glazed Windows.

The Number of Cranes upon the said several Wharfs to be at the Election of the Owners or Possessors of the Ground, provided they exceed not the Dimensions following, viz. a single Crane with one Wheel, 12 Feet in Breadth, and a double Crane with two Wheels, 20 Feet, and each of them in Depth or Length, from the Wall or Campshot, 21 Feet at the most; and that the said Cranes, as well single as double, be kept open and free for common Passage from the Ground to the Floor under the Wheels, without any other Inclosure, Partition, Separation, or Hindrance by Posts or Spurs, than the necessary Posts and Timbers which support the same at both Ends, and that the open Height of the said Crane be at least 10½ Feet

from

from the Ground to the Floor under the Wheels, that Carts and Carriages may freely pafs under them.

It fhall not be lawful for any Perfon to build any Outfets, Jets, Penthoufes, Warehoufe, Rooms, Lodging, or any Manner of Pofts, Sheds, or Buildings, contiguous or annexed to the faid Cranes, or any Part of the open Wharf of 40 Feet in Breadth, defcribed as aforefaid, more than what is convenient about the Cranes for the Wheels to work in and upon, and fufficient Covering thereunto, not exceeding the Height, Breadth, and Length aforefaid. And for further Ornament, thofe Cranes to be laid in Oil, and coloured blue, and in the Front thereof towards the Thames, be placed the King's Arms, painted and fet in an Efcutcheon or other Frame, with a decent Moulding about it, of at leaft $4\frac{1}{2}$ Feet Diameter.

That all the Paffages, Lanes, or Cartways, leading to the faid Quays or Wharfs, from Thames Street, and every of them, be made of the Breadth of 11 Feet at the leaft; but if any was of a larger Breadth or Dimenfion heretofore, this fhall not be conftrued or meant to leffen or ftreighten it, but that it continue at the ancient or larger Dimenfion.

The feveral Quays and Wharfs defcribed and allowed to be free Places for fhipping and landing of Goods and Merchandife, as aforefaid; and which, according to the Tenor of the faid Act of Parliament for rebuilding the faid City, is, and ought to be left open and free at the Diftance of 40 Feet from the Water Side, fhall not be feparated or divided one from another by any Houfe, Wall, Pale, Poft, Rail, or other Impediment

Impediment whatsoever, but only by mere Stones or Marks in the Pavement, for the Distinction of Property, and not otherwise.

If any Wharfinger or Owner of any of the Wharfs or Grounds allowed for shipping, lading, or landing of Goods or Merchandise, as aforesaid, do not conform to the present Form, Rules, and Method hereby prescribed and directed for their Wharfs, Cranes, or Buildings, or hereafter shall discontinue or alter the same, or make new Encroachments thereupon, after public Notice given by any Three or more of the principal Officers or Farmers of his Majesty's Customs, by fixing up a Writing under their Hands, upon the Wharf where the Fault shall be committed, declaring the Offence, and limiting a Day and Time for the Amendment thereof; which if not amended and performed accordingly, that then such Wharf or Crane, shall from thenceforward be no more reputed, or taken to have the Benefit or Privilege as a lawful Place of shipping, lading, or landing of Goods or Merchandise, but to be thenceforward utterly debarred thereof, unless restored by his Majesty's special Warrant, and nevertheless, the said Buildings, Alterations, and Encroachments to be demolished and removed as the Law in that Case hath directed.

If at any Time it shall seem reasonable to the principal Officers or Farmers of the Customs for the Time being, and consistent with his Majesty's Service, to give Sufferance or Permission for the shipping, lading, or landing of any Goods or Merchandise, at any other Place or Places, or in any other Manner than is herein before

before nominated and advised, or assigned to be lawful Quays and Wharfs, it shall and may be lawful for them so to do; and such Sufferance and Permission shall be good and warrantable, without any Forfeiture or Advantage to be taken against the Goods so landed, notwithstanding any Thing herein before declared to the contrary.

Whosoever shall accept of, or from henceforward employ any of those Quays or Wharfs by virtue of such Concessions, to the Use of shipping, lading, or landing of Goods or Merchandise, it is to be understood, and it is declared to be with this Covenant and Condition, that they perform all and singular the Orders, Assignments, and Appointments which on their Parts and Behalfs is before declared to be performed and done, and not otherwise.

The several Wharfingers or Possessors of any of the said Quays or Wharfs, or their Servants, shall not suffer to stand or remain upon their Wharfs or Passages leading to them from Thames Street, any more than such Cars or Carts as shall be immediately called to load or take up Goods, Wares, or Merchandise there.

To prevent all future Differences and Disputes touching the Extent and Limits of The Port of London, and the many Frauds and Abuses which have been acted and committed, as well upon and within the River of Thames, as without the Mouth thereof upon the Sea, the said Port is declared to extend, and be accounted from the Promontory or Point called the North Foreland in the Isle of Thanet, and from thence northward in a supposed right Line, to the opposite

Promontory or Point called the Naes, beyond the Gunfleet, upon the Coaſt of Eſſex, and ſo continued Weſtward through the River of Thames, and the ſeveral Channels, Streams, and Rivers falling into it, to London Bridge; ſaving the uſual and known Right, Liberty, and Privilege to the Ports of Sandwich and Ipſwich, and either of them, and the known Members thereof, and of the Cuſtomers, Comptrollers, Searchers, and their Deputies, of and within the ſaid Ports of Sandwich and Ipſwich, and the ſeveral Creeks, Harbours, and Havens to them, or either of them reſpectively belonging, within the Counties of Kent or Eſſex; but that every Part and Place of the River Thames, and the Sea within the Limits and Bounds aforeſaid, not included or belonging to the ſaid Ports of Sandwich or Ipſwich, or the ſeveral Creeks, Harbours, or Havens, to them, or One of them reſpectively belonging, within the ſaid Counties of Kent or Eſſex, ſhall be deemed and taken to be within, and Part and Parcel of the Port of London.

No further or other Paſſages to be made or enlarged to the Wharfs, or any Part of the River of Thames from Thames Street, within the Limits aforeſaid, other than the ancient and common Paſſages to the ſame.

The propofed Cuftom Houfe Reform, refpecting the Abolition of Fees not having yet taken Place, the following Order of the Commons in Parliament affembled, figned by E. Turner, by virtue of an Order of the Houfe of Commons, dated the 17th May 1662, remains in Force.

WHEREAS in and by an Act of this prefent Parliament, intitled, An Act for confirming of public Acts, an Act therein, intitled, A Subfidy granted to the King of Tonnage and Poundage, and other Sums of Money payable upon Merchandife exported and imported, was confirmed; by which Act fo confirmed, it is, amongft other Things, enacted and ordained, that during the Continuance of that Grant, where the Goods exported or imported amount to the Value of five Pounds or more, the Cuftomer and Collectors, and all others his Majefty's Officers in the feveral Ports, fhall take and receive fuch Fees (and none other) as were taken in the fourth Year of the late King James, until fuch Time as the faid Fees fhould be otherwife fettled by Authority of Parliament.

And whereas alfo, amongft the Rules, Orders, and Directions annexed to the Book of Rates, ratified and confirmed by the aforefaid Act, it is ordered and directed, that for the avoiding of all Oppreffions by any of the Officers of the Cuftoms in any Port of this Kingdom, in exacting unreafonable Fees from the Merchant, by reafon of any Entries, or otherwife touching the fhipping or unfhipping of any Goods, Wares, or Merchandife, it is ordered that no Officer, Clerk, or other belonging to any Custom House whatsoever, shall exact, require, or receive any other or greater Fee of any Merchant, or other whatsoever, than such as are or shall be established by the Commons in Parliament assembled. And if any Officer or other shall offend contrary to this Order, he shall forfeit his Office and Place, and be for ever after incapable of any Office in the Custom House.

In Prosecution of which said several Clauses in the Act and Book of Rates beforementioned, and for the Settlement and Certainty of all the aforesaid Fees, for Satisfaction, as well of Merchants and others, as of the Officers, what Fees are to be paid and received for any Cause, Matter, or Thing whatsoever, for or concerning the Importation or Exportation, shipping, landing, or entering of any Ships, Goods, Wares, or Merchandise, of what Nature, or in what Kind soever; it is ordered and declared by the Commons in Parliament assembled, that the several and respective Fees and Allowances, mentioned in a Schedule or Table of Fees relating to the Port of London, and the Members and Creeks thereunto belonging (and none other), shall be paid to the Officers and others employed, and to be employed in and about his Majesty's Customs in the Port aforesaid, and are by the Authority aforesaid settled and confirmed.

And be it further ordered and declared by the Authority aforesaid, that the Fees and Allowances hereby intended, are set down, mentioned, and expressed in a Schedule or Table of Fees, intitled, Fees and Allowances due and payable to the Officers of his Majesty's
Customs

Customs and Subsidies in the Port of London, and the Members and Creeks thereunto belonging, and subscribed with the Hand of Sir Edward Turner, Knight, now Speaker of the House of Commons in Parliament assembled; and every particular Clause therein mentioned and contained, shall be and remain as effectual to all Intents and Purposes, as if the same were included and particularly expressed within the Body of this Order: and in case any Merchant, Master of a Ship, or other Person or Persons whatsoever, shall refuse to pay all or any of the Fees hereby ordered or intended, that in such Case it shall and may be lawful for all and every Officer and Officers to make stay of every Bill of Entry, Cocket, or other Warrant, that shall be tendered or given in for passing of any Ships, Goods, or Merchandise whatsoever, exceeding the Value of five Pounds in the Book of Rates, for which the Fees shall be detained and denied to be paid, as aforesaid.

And be it further ordered and ordained, that Copies or Transcripts of this Order and Table of Fees shall be made and set up in public View in the Custom House in London, and in all other Offices and Places where the said Fees, or any of them, are to be paid or received.

A BREVIATE of the Fees of his Majesty's Officers of the Customs and Subsidies in the Port of London, payable by the before written Order of the House of Commons.

For the Officers of the Petty Customs outwards.

	£.	s.	d.
For a Cloth Cocket by British Freemen of London, paid to the principal Officers and their Clerks	0	2	6
For a Stranger's Cocket, or Unfreemen	0	3	2
For a Cloth Certificate, by British or Strangers	0	2	8
For a Ship's Entry crossing the Seas	0	1	8
For a Ship's Entry to the Streights, Canaries, or Western Islands	0	4	4
For clearing of Ships, and examining the Books	0	2	6
For every Indorsement	0	0	4
For making a Bond to the King's Majesty's Use	0	0	6
For every Entry in the Certificate Book	0	0	2

Subsidy outwards.

For every Ship's Entry within the Levant, or beyond the Streights Mouth, to the Officers and their Clerk	0	4	4
For every Ship's Entry going to any other Foreign Parts	0	1	8
For every Ship's Entry going to the Out Ports, and for a Coast Cocket and Bond	0	4	9

	£.	s.	d.

For clearing of every Ship paſſing to Foreign Parts, and examining the Ship's Contents - - - 0 2 6

For every Britiſh Cocket, by Freemen - 0 2 6

For every Stranger's Cocket, or Unfreemen of London - - - 0 3 4

For every Certificate, upon Warrant from his Majeſty, or the Lord Treaſurer, paying no Duties - - - 0 4 4

For Indorſement of all Warrants and Licences - - - 0 0 8

For a Foaring Bill - - - 0 2 0

For diſcharging a Bond, and filing the Certificate - - - 0 0 4

For making a Certificate of Return - 0 2 0

For a Debenture for Repayment of Half Subſidy, &c. to the principal Officers 2s; to the Searchers 6d; for the Oath 2d; examining 4d; caſting up and paying the Money 8d; in all - - - 0 3 8

For making and entering a Certificate to let paſs - - - - 0 0 6

For a Bill or Ticket to the Lord Mayor for Corn, Victuals, and other Proviſions - 0 0 4

Petty Cuſtoms inwards.

For every Stranger's Warrant inwards. See *Subſidy inwards*, Page 42.

For taking every Bond - - 0 0 6

For every Bill at Sight - - 0 2 0

	£.	s.	d.
For discharging every Bond	- 0	0	6
For every great Employment	- 0	2	6

Subsidy inwards.

For every Warrant by British Freemen of London, to the principal Officers, the King's Waiters, and Registers	- 0	2	6
For every Warrant for Strangers	- 0	4	6
or Unfreemen	- 0	3	2
For every Certificate of Foreign Goods coming from the Out Ports to London	- 0	2	4
For Goods sent by Sea, by the Importer thereof, to any of the Out Ports from London	- 0	1	0

All the Rest of the Fees under the Title of Subsidy inwards, are single, and paid to particular Persons. See the Table of Fees payable to particular Officers in the Port of London, Page 45.

Great Customs.

For a Cocket for Calve Skins, to the Officers and Packer	- 0	3	6
For Wools, Woolfells, Skins, and Hides	- 0	3	0
For a Bond to his Majesty's Use	- 0	1	0
For filing the Return	- 0	0	6
For a Return and Discharge outwards	- 0	3	4

Fees inwards and outwards concerning the Clerks.

For every Bill of Portage	- 0	1	0
For a Second or Parcel Cocket outwards	- 0	0	6

The

The Packer. } All these are reckoned together with the former Entries.
The King's Waiters for the three first Articles.
Regifters of the King's Warrants.

All other Fees in the Table not herein before comprifed (except only Two concerning the Act of Navigation.) } See the Table of thofe particular Fees.
The Fees of the Chief Searcher, and his Majefty's five Under Searchers at London, and two at Gravefend, are fingle, and do not admit Abbreviation.

For all Goods not paying twenty Shillings Cuftom, whether in or out, there fhall be but Half Fees taken.

All Goods under the Value of five Pounds in the Book of Rates, fhall pafs without Payment of any Fees.

Coin and Bullion inwards; } Pafs without Warrant or Fee.
Precious Stones, Jewels, and Pearls outwards;

The Merchants fhall pay for all Goods opening that fhall be fhort entered above 10s. Cuftoms.

The Merchants fhall pay for weighing of all Goods that fhall be fhort entered above 20s. Cuftoms.

The Merchants not to be at any Charge if duly entered.

No Britifh Merchant that fhall have Goods of his own to be landed out of one Ship or Veffel, at one Time (although the Receipt of the Subfidy be diftributed

into

into feveral Offices), fhall be charged to pay any more or other Fees than for a fingle Entry.

Goods in Partnerfhip to pafs as if the Proprietors were one fingle Perfon.

Fifh by Britifh, in Britifh Shipping or Veffel, inwards or outwards, or along the Coaft, to pay no Fees.

Foreign Coin and Bullion inwards, may be landed by any Perfon without Warrant or Fee.

Poft Entries inwards to pafs without Fee, under five Shillings; if above five Shillings, and under forty Shillings, then Sixpence: but if the Cuftom to be paid exceed forty Shillings, then it fhall pay the full Fees as was paid for the firft Warrant.

Whereas fome Societies and Companies of Merchants do trade in a joint Stock, and enter the whole Lading and Cargo of a Ship inwards, in one fingle Entry, when the Adventurers therein concerned are many, the Officers and Waiters may take and receive fuch Gratuity as the faid Company fhall hereafter voluntarily confent to pay unto them; any Thing in this Order or Table of Fees, or any other Act or Provifion to the contrary, notwithftanding.

FEES and ALLOWANCES due and payable to particular Officers in the Port of London, not mentioned in the foregoing Tables.

Subsidy inwards.

To the Collector.

	£.	s.	d.
For making a Bond to his Majesty's Use	0	0	6
For every Oath administered by the Collector	0	0	2
For a Shipper's Entry, with the particular Contents, viz. from the East Indies	0	2	6
From the Streights	0	2	6
From Spain, Portugal, and the West Indies, or British Plantations	0	2	0
From Dunkirk or France	0	1	0
From Flanders, Holland, Ireland, or any eastern or northern Parts	0	1	0
For every Ship or Vessel less than twenty Ton	0	0	8

For every Stranger's Ship's Entry to pay double Fees.

For every Certificate of Foreign Goods imported to be shipped out free of Subsidy, Eighteenpence; which is understood, Sixpence for the Search, although several Ships, and Twelvepence for the Certificate	0	1	6
If the Goods be under the Value of twenty Pounds, according to the Book of Rates, the Merchant is to pay for the Certificate, in all, but	0	0	6

For

	L.	s.	d.
For examining and comparing every Debenture with the original Certificate	0	0	4
For cafting up the Sum, and keeping an account of every Debenture, and paying the Money	0	0	8
For every Bale, Pack, Trufs, Cheft, Cafe, or other Package, brought into the King's Warehoufe, to be allowed to the Officer when the Merchant is fhort entered, above five Shillings, to be paid to the proper Officer, Twopence.			

Fees to be paid to the Clerks.

	Cuftomer.			Comptroller.			Surveyor.		
	£.	s.	d.	£.	s.	d.	£.	s.	d.
For every Bill of Portage	0	0	6	0	0	3	0	0	3
For a Second or Parcel Cocket outwards	0	0	2	0	0	2	0	0	2

To the King's Majefty's Waiters, being in number Eighteen.

Received at the Waterfide by the faid King's Waiters, and others attending; to be divided as formerly.

	L.	s.	d.
For a Bill of Store or Portage for any Thing above ten Shillings Cuftom	0	1	0
For a Bill of Sight, Bill of Sufferance, or any other imperfect Warrant	0	1	0
For Wools, Woolfells, Leather, Hides, and prohibited Goods, from the Out Ports by Cocket	0	1	0

To the Usher of the Custom House.

	L.	*s.*	*d.*
For every Oath administered by the King's Officers outwards - - -	0	0	2

The FEES of the Chief Searcher and of the five Under Searchers in the Port of London.

Duties between the Chief Searcher, and his Majesty's five Under Searchers that attend at London.

		L.	*s.*	*d.*
For every Ship that passeth into Foreign Parts.	Spain, Portugal, the Streights, West Indies, Guinea, or the Western Islands -	0	6	0
	East Indies - -	0	10	0
	All other British Ships into Foreign Parts -	0	4	0
	For every Stranger's Ship or Bottom - -	0	6	8

Duties of his Majesty's five Under Searchers that attend at London.

		L.	*s.*	*d.*
British and Aliens.	For every Certificate for shipping out Goods formerly imported -	0	2	0
	But if the Half Subsidy to be received back amounts but to 40 s. then	0	1	0

Duties of his Majesty's five Under Searchers that attend at London.

		£.	s.	d.
	Pipe, Puncheon, or Butt	0	0	4
	Hogshead or Bag	0	0	2
	Tin, the Block or Barrel	0	0	1
	Beer Eager, Wood of all Sorts, Copperas, Alum, and such gross Goods, the Ton	0	0	4
	Corn, the Last; Sea Coal, the Chalder; Beer, the Ton	0	0	2
	Lead, the Fodder	0	0	2
To be paid by British and Aliens for Goods that pay Subsidy, and pass out by Cocket or Warrant.	The Maund, Fatt, or Pack	0	0	6
	The Bundle, Bale, Chest, or Case	0	0	3
	Raisins and Figs, the twenty Frails or Barrels	0	0	3
	Butter, and such Goods, the Barrel	0	0	2
	For every Coast Certificate or Cocket	0	1	0
	Transires for the Coast, free.			
	For every Horse, Mare, or Gelding	0	1	0
	For certifying every Debenture for receiving back Half Subsidy, &c.	0	0	6
	For every Piece of Ordnance	0	1	0

Duties of his Majesty's five Under-Searchers that attend at London.

		£.	s.	d.
To be paid by British and Aliens for Goods that pay Subsidy, and pass out by Cocket or Warrant.	For the Indorsement of every Cocket	0	1	0
	For every Certificate out of their Books of Goods lost at Sea, taken by Pirates, or returned, whereby so much may be shipped Custom free	0	1	0
	For every Bill of Sufferance or Store, above ten Shillings in the Book of Rates	0	1	0
	If under	0	0	6
	The Fardle, or Truss, by British, of three Hundred Weight or upwards	0	0	6
	Woollen Cloth, the Bale, not exceeding five Cloths, or three Hundred Weight, Stuffs, Bays, or Says	0	0	3
Merchant Strangers, Unfreemen of London, or such as ship on Strangers Ships or Vessels	the Fardle or Truss	0	1	0
	the Bale	0	0	6

The Fees of his Majesty's two Searchers at Gravesend.

	£.	s.	d.
For every Ship that passeth over the Seas for Spain, Portugal, Streights, the West Indies, Guinea, or the Western Islands	0	6	0
For every Ship to the East Indies	0	10	0
For all other Ships into Foreign Parts	0	4	0
For every Stranger's Ship or Bottom	0	8	0
For every Ship having a Coast Cocket	0	0	4
For Passengers outwards, not being Merchants or Mariners	0	0	6

IN this Work all the Articles are placed alphabetically in Table A, except Drugs, Hides, Linen, Seeds, Skins, Wood, and all Articles made of Wood, *which being very numerous in their several Classes, it appeared to be more eligible for immediate Reference to arrange them under these respective Titles.*

Hair *and* Wool *are placed alphabetically according to the distinguishing Character,* viz. *Camel's Hair under Letter* C, *Beaver Wool under Letter* B, *and in like Manner all the other Descriptions of Hair and Wool.*

The Conditions, Regulations, and Restrictions under which various Merchandise may be imported free of Duty, or circumstantially, by the several Acts of Parliament now in Force, are explained in a short Note immediately following the Article, sufficient to give the necessary Information, without entering so much into Detail as to disturb the easy Reference intended for the several Duties to be paid, or for the several Allowances, Bounties, and Drawbacks to be received; which has been done in this Manner from the Expectation that Experience will prove it a better Way thus to quote Part of the Acts, than either to refer to Marginal Notes, Index, or the several Acts regulating the Importation or Exportation of those Goods.

TABLE A.

Being a Schedule of the Net Duties payable on the *Importation* into this Kingdom of certain Goods, Wares, and Merchandife, therein enumerated; and of the Drawbacks to be allowed on the Exportation thereof from this Kingdom.

Alfo of the Net Duties payable on the *Exportation* of Goods, Wares, and Merchandife from this Kingdom.

And likewife of the Net Duties payable on Goods, Wares, and Merchandife, brought or carried *Coaftwife* or from Port to Port within this Kingdom.

By the 28 Geo. III. Chap. 27. all Goods of the Growth, Produce, or Manufacture of the European Dominions of the States General of the United Provinces, legally imported (except Linens) are to pay the fame Duties as fet forth in Table C, or the loweft Duties which are payable on Importation from any other Foreign Country or State in Europe, and are to be allowed the fame Drawbacks upon Exportation from Great Britain as the like Goods are allowed.

By the 30 Geo. III. Chap. 26. the like Drawback of the Duties of Cuftoms and Excife is to be paid or allowed to the Exporters of Goods to the Settlement of Yucatan in South America as is now allowed on the Exportation of fuch Goods to the Britifh Colonies or Plantations in America.

TABLE A.

INWARDS.

	Duty.			Drawback.		
	£.	s.	d.	£.	s.	d.
Agates rough, small as a Bean, the Hundred Dozen	0	3	0	0	2	8
large, the Piece	0	0	1½	0	0	1
Alderney, Guernsey, Jersey, and Sark. Any Goods of the Growth, Produce, or Manufacture of those Islands may be imported by the Inhabitants of the said Islands into Great Britain free of Duty, under the Certificate of the Governor, Lieutenant-Governor, Deputy-Governor, or Commander in Chief, by the 3 Geo. I. Chap. 4; but Salt by the 5 Geo. I. Chap. 18. is made subject to the same Duty as any Foreign Salt imported into Great Britain. The 27 Geo. III. Chap. 13. Sect. 8. not referring to the Excise Duties in Table F, and there not being any Notes under the Articles therein specifically rated, the Duties of Excise will be payable on all the Articles as therein named, when imported from those Islands.						
Ale, the Barrel containing 32 Gallons	0	6	8	0	6	0
Subject also to the Duty of Excise.						
Almonds, viz. Jordan, the Hundred Weight	2	6	3	2	3	3
Of any other Sort (except Bitter Almonds), the Hundred Weight	1	3	2	1	1	8

(55)

		£	s	d	£	s	d
Almonds, Bitter	-	0	14	0	0	9	4
Alum, Roniſh or Roch, the Hundred Weight	-	0	3	0	0	2	0
Amber, the Pound	-	0	1	3	0	1	1
imported by the Eaſt India Company, the Pound	-	0	1	5	0	1	3
Beads, the Pound	-	0	4	5	0	4	2
Anchovies, the Barrel containing 16 Pounds of Fiſh	-	0	2	1	0	1	10
N.B. One Third is allowed for Pickle and Salt, exclufive of the Weight of the Package.							
Anniſeeds, the Hundred Weight	-	1	3	2	1	1	8
Annotto, the Pound	-	0	0	1½	0	0	0
By the 8 Geo. I. Chap. 15. Sect. 10. Annotto is admitted free of Duty if legally imported, regularly entered, and landed.							
+ Apples, the Buſhel	-	0	2	4	0	0	4
dried, the Buſhel		0	3	0	0	4	0
Archelia, or Orchelia, the Hundred Weight	-	0	3	1	0	0	0
By the 8 Geo. I. Chap. 15. Sect. 10. Archelia is admitted free of Duty, if legally imported, regularly entered, and landed.							
Argoil, the Hundred Weight	-	0	2	7	0	0	0
By the 8 Geo. I. Chap. 15. Sect. 10. Argoil is admitted free of Duty, if legally imported, regularly entered, and landed.							
Arrack, imported by the Eaſt India Company, the Gallon	-	0	0	9	0	0	8
Subject alfo to the Duty of Excife.							

E

TABLE A.

INWARDS.

	Duty. £. s. d.	Drawback. £. s. d.
Ashes, viz.		
Pearl Ashes, the Hundred Weight	0 2 3	0 0 0
Pot Ashes, the Hundred Weight	0 2 3	0 0 0
By the 24 Geo. II. Chap. 51. Sect. 1 to 3. Pot and Pearl Ashes made in and imported from his Majesty's Colonies in America into Great Britain, permitted free of Duty, if legally imported, duly entered, and examined by the proper Officers, and accompanied by a Certificate under the Hands and Seals of the Collector, Comptroller, and Naval Officer, or any Two of them, at the Port in America where the Ashes shall have been shipped, and also upon Oath being made by the Master, or Person taking Charge of the Vessel, before the Collector, Comptroller, or chief Officer of his Majesty's Customs of the Port of Importation, that the said Casks, Parcels, and Goods, contained in such Certificate, are the same as were taken on board in America, otherwise to be liable to the Payment of Duty.		
Soap Ashes, the Hundred Weight	0 0 7	0 0 0
Weed Ashes, the Hundred Weight	0 0 7	0 0 0
Wood Ashes, the Hundred Weight	0 0 7	0 0 0

(57)

	£	s	d
Bacon, the Hundred Weight - - -	2	7	0		2	6	4
By the 5 Geo. III. Chap. 1. the 8 Geo. III. Chap. 9. and 16 Geo. III. Chap. 8. salted Bacon, Beef, Butter, and Pork, allowed to be imported into Great Britain from Ireland free of Duty.							
Balls, viz. Washing Balls, the Pound -	0	0	6		0	0	0
Bandstring Twist, the dozen Knots - -	0	2	3		0	0	2
N. B. By established Practice, the Knot is charged at 32 Yards.							
Barilla, the Hundred Weight -	0	5	3		0	5	0
Barley hulled, or Pearl Barley, the Hundred Weight	0	8	10		0	6	0
See Barley under the Title Corn and Grain.							
Basket Rods, the Bundle not exceeding three Feet in Circumference at the Band	0	1	6		0	1	4
Baskets, viz. Handbaskets, the Dozen -	0	0	9		0	0	8
Bast or Straw Hats or Bonnets, each Hat or Bonnet not exceeding 22 Inches in Diameter, the Dozen -	0	2	9		0	2	6
Bast or Straw Hats or Bonnets, each Hat or Bonnet exceeding 22 Inches in Diameter, the Dozen -	0	5	6		0	5	0
Bast Platting, or other Manufacture of Bast to be used in or proper for making Hats or Bonnets, the Pound	0	1	10		0	1	8
Bast Ropes, the Hundred Weight -	0	1	10		0	0	0
Battery, the Hundred Weight - -	2	5	2		2	0	8
Bay-berries, the hundred Weight	0	4	8		0	0	0

TABLE A.

INWARDS.

	Duty. £. s. d.	Drawback. £. s. d.
Beef from Ireland, falted, free of Duty by the 5 Geo. III. Chap. 1. the 8 Geo. III. Chap. 9. and 16 Geo. III. Chap. 8.		
Beer, viz. Spruce Beer, the Barrel containing 32 Gallons N. B. Subject alfo to the Duty of Excife.	0 12 0	0 11 0
of all other Sorts, the Barrel containing 32 Gallons N. B. Subject alfo to the Duty of Excife.	0 6 8	0 6 0
Bell-Metal, the Hundred Weight	0 7 4	0 6 6
Berries for Dyers Ufe, not otherwife enumerated, the Hundred Weight	0 11 0	0 0 0
Beftials.		

By the 5 Geo. III. Chap. 43. Sect. 11. Beftials may be imported from the Ifle of Man by the Inhabitants thereof into Great Britain free of Duty, by a Certificate from the Governor, Lieutenant-Governor, Commander in Chief, or chief Magiftrates, that Oath has been made before him or them, in the Prefence of the Officer of the Cuftoms of the Port where the Beftials fhall be fhipped, that they are the Produce of the Ifle of Man, which Certificate is to exprefs the Number of Beftials, and the Officer of the Cuftoms is to atteft the fame; the Mafter of the Veffel alfo making Oath at the Port of

Importation before the Collector, or other principal Officer of the Customs, that the Beasts are the same that were taken on board by virtue of the Certificate produced, otherwise to be liable to Duties, Penalties, and Forfeitures, as heretofore. Any other Goods the Growth, Manufacture, or Produce of the Isle of Man, except Woollen Manufactures, Beer, and Ale, may be imported into Great Britain free of Duty, under the like Restrictions, but not to extend to any Foreign Goods, in Part or fully manufactured in the Isle of Man, except Linen Manufactures made of Hemp or Flax not the Growth of the Island; and the same Bounty is allowed on the re-export from Great Britain of Linens the Manufacture of the Isle of Man, as is allowed upon British and Irish Linens by the 29 Geo. II. and under the same Regulations.

Bever Wool, free of Duty.

	£	s	d	£	s	d
cut and combed (except combed in Russia, and imported from thence in British built Ships), the Pound	0	16	6	0	0	3
Birds, viz. Singing Birds, the Dozen	0	2	6	0	2	8
Biscuit or Bread, the Hundred Weight	0	1	10	0	1	8
Blacking, the Hundred Weight	0	17	8	0	15	8
Black Lead, the Hundred Weight	0	6	3	0	4	5
Bladders, the Dozen	0	0	14¼	0	0	1

TABLE A.

INWARDS.

	Duty. £. s. d.	Drawback. £. s. d.
Blubber, Fish Oil, or Train Oil, of Foreign Fishing, the Tun containing 252 Gallons	18 3 0	13 13 0
of British Fishing, viz. of Greenland and Parts adjacent, the Tun containing 252 Gallons	1 15 3	1 11 3
of Greenland and Parts adjacent, taken by any Shipping belonging to his Majesty's Colonies or Plantations, and imported in such Shipping, the Tun containing 252 Gallons	0 15 5	0 12 5
of Greenland and Parts adjacent, taken by any Shipping belonging to his Majesty's Colonies or Plantations, and imported in Shipping belonging to Great Britain, the Tun containing 252 Gallons	0 12 2 1 6 5	0 10 7 0 1 3
of Newfoundland, and like Sort, the Tun containing 252 Gallons		
of Newfoundland, and like Sort, taken by Shipping belonging to any of his Majesty's Colonies or Plantations, and imported in such Shipping, the Tun containing 252 Gallons	0 13 3	0 10 2
of Newfoundland, and like Sort, taken by Shipping belonging to any of his Majesty's Colonies or Plantations, and imported in Shipping belonging to Great Britain, the Tun containing 252 Gallons	0 9 11	0 8 5

By the 26 Geo. III. Chap. 26. Oil or Blubber of Fish, or Creatures living in the Sea, and Seals Skins, caught and taken on the Banks and Shores of the Island of Newfoundland and Parts adjacent, wholly by his Majesty's Subjects, carrying on the said Fishery from his Majesty's European Dominions, and usually residing in the said Dominions; Oath being made before the Collector or other chief Officer of the Customs, by the Master of the Ship importing the same, that the said Oil or Blubber, or Seals Skins, were so caught and taken, or that they were purchased as aforesaid; in which Case of Purchase, a Certificate by the Naval Officer, or, if no Naval Officer, by the Commander of any of his Majesty's Ships on that Station, is to be produced by the Master of the Ship to the Collector or other chief Officer of the Customs, may be imported free of Duty.

The 26 Geo. III. Chap. 41. Sect. 14 and 15, allows to be imported into Great Britain free of Duty, until the 25th of December 1791, Blubber or Oil of Whales, Whale Fins, Seal Oil or Seal Skins, or any other Produce of Seals, or other Fish or Creatures taken or caught in the Greenland Seas or Davis's Streights, or in the Seas adjacent, by British Subjects usually residing in Great Britain, Ireland, Guernsey, Jersey, or Man, in British built Ships, owned by British Subjects usually residing in the Places beforementioned, Oath being made by the Master and Mate of the Ship importing

TABLE A.

INWARDS.

	Duty. £. s. d.	Drawback. £. s. d.

Blubber, Fish Oil, or Train Oil, of British Fishing, in British built Shipping, British owned, and British navigated, caught in any Part of the Ocean by the Crew of the Ship, may be imported free of Duty.

The 26 Geo. III. Chap. 50. Sect. 2, and 5, requires that the Ship fitted and cleared out from a Port of Great Britain, Ireland, Guernsey, Jersey, or Man, did appear by her Register to be British built, wholly owned by his Majesty's Subjects usually residing in some Part of the said Dominions, navigated by a Master and three fourths of the Mariners at the least, his Majesty's Subjects usually residing as aforesaid; or if the Ship shall clear from any Port of Great Britain, then such Ship may be navigated by Persons not being his Majesty's Subjects, but being Protestants, who have heretofore been employed in carrying on the Fishery to the Southward of the thirty-fixth Degree of South Latitude, who shall at the Time of the Ship clearing out, on board which they shall serve, make Oath or Affirmation, before Two of the principal Officers of the Customs of
the same, that the said Articles were caught and taken as aforesaid. The Greenland Seas and Davis's Streights to be deemed to extend to the Latitude of 59′. 30″. North, and no farther.

the Port in Great Britain from which the Ship shall clear out, if it be their first Voyage, that they have already established, or that it is their Intention to establish themselves and their Families in Great Britain as Inhabitants thereof, and Subjects of his Majesty, and if it shall be their Second or any subsequent Voyage, that they have actually established themselves and their Families as aforesaid, in Great Britain.

By Sect. 9. Upon the Importation into Great Britain of any Oil or Head Matter, taken in the Seas to the Southward of the thirty-fixth Degree of South Latitude, the Master, Mate, and Two of the Mariners of the Ship, shall make Oath before Two or more of the principal Officers of the Customs at the Port of Importation, from what Port, and the Time when such Ship cleared out; and that all such Oil or Head Matter so imported, is the Produce of One or more Whale or Creature living in the Seas, actually taken and killed by the Crew of such Ship only, at the Times and in the Latitudes respectively mentioned and set down in the Log Book.

By Sect. 23. All Oil, Head Matter, or other Produce of Fish or Creatures living in the Seas, caught and taken as required by this Act, also all Whale Fins and Skins of Seals so caught and taken, and all Oil, Head Matter, or other Produce of Whales or other Crea-

TABLE A.

INWARDS.

	Duty. £. s. d.	Drawback. £. s. d.

tures living in the Seas, Fins of Whales, and Skins of Seals, taken and caught in any Part of the Ocean, by the Crew of any Ship built in Great Britain, Guernsey, Jersey, or Man, wholly owned by his Majesty's Subjects usually residing therein respectively, and navigated in Manner aforesaid, shall upon Importation into Great Britain be admitted to Entry, and landed without Payment of any Duty whatever.

N.B. By the 28 Geo. III. Chap. 20. Sect. 3, and 10. Every Ship which shall sail or pass to the Eastward of the Cape of Good Hope, or to the Westward of Cape Horn, or through the Streights of Magellan, is obliged to have a Licence from the East India and South Sea Companies, and may pass to the Eastward of the Cape of Good Hope as far as the Equator Northward, and as far as fifty-one Degrees of Longitude East from London; to the Westward of Cape Horn, or through the Streights of Magellan, as far as the Equator Northward, and as far as one hundred and eighty Degrees of Longitude West from London, and no further. All Oil, Head Matter, or other Produce of Fish or other Creatures living in the Seas, taken by the Crew of any Ship fitted and cleared

(65)

	£ s d	£ s d
out under the Directions of this Act for the additional Premiums upon Importation into Great Britain to be admitted to Entry, and landed without Payment of any Duty.		
Books bound, the Hundred Weight	0 19 3	0 0 0
unbound, the Hundred Weight	0 8 10	0 0 0
Borargo, the Pound	0 0 4	0 0 3
Bottles of Earth or Stone, the Dozen	0 1 2	0 1 0
of Glass, viz.		
covered with Wicker, the Dozen Quarts	0 12 0	0 7 7
full or empty, the Dozen Quarts	0 4 5	0 0 0
French, for every £.100 of the Value	12 0 0	0 0 0
N. B. During the Commercial Treaty with France. of French European Green Glass, when imported in British built, or French European built Ships, an additional Duty, the Hundred Weight	0 4 0¼	0 0 0
N. B. This last mentioned Duty is not limited to the Duration of the Commercial Treaty.		
For the Excise Duties on Glass, see Table F.		
Bowls or Buckets of Wood, the Dozen	0 0 11	0 0 10
Boxes, viz.		
Nest Boxes, the Gross containing twelve Dozen Nests, each Nest containing eight Boxes	0 13 3	0 11 8

(66)

TABLE A.

INWARDS.

	Duty. £ s. d.	Drawback. £ s. d.
Boxes, viz.		
Pill Boxes, the Grofs containing twelve Dozen Nefts, each Neft containing four Boxes	0 1 4½	0 1 3
Sand Boxes, the Grofs containing twelve Dozen Boxes	0 4 5	0 3 11
Bracelets, or Necklaces of Glafs, the Grofs containing twelve Bundles or Dickers, each Bundle or Dicker containing ten Necklaces	0 3 8	0 3 6
Brandy, of any Country or Place, the Gallon	0 0 9	0 0 8
Brafs or Copper Wire, not otherwife enumerated, the Hundred Weight	2 12 3	2 9 0
Brafs, Powder of, for Japanning, the Ounce	0 0 2	0 0 1½
Bread or Bifcuit, the Hundred Weight	0 1 10	0 1 8
Bricks, the Thoufand	0 7 2	0 6 8
Bridges Thread, the Dozen Pounds	0 9 11	0 8 9
Brimftone, the Hundred Weight	0 6 8	0 6 6

The 23 Geo. III. Chap. 77. allows the Drawback of the whole Duties of Cuftoms paid upon the Importation of Brimftone and Salt Petre ufed and confumed in making Oil of Vitriol, the Maker having entered his Name and Place of Abode with the Collector of the Cuftoms of the Port or Diftrict within which his Work is carried on, fpecifying in the Entry the Articles upon which the Draw-

(67)

back is to be claimed, at least one Year before making his Claim, producing a Certificate from the Collector or Comptroller of the Customs where the Brimstone or Salt Petre was imported, that the Duties charged thereon had been paid, and making Oath at the End of the Year from the Entry of his Name and Place of Abode, or within six Months thereafter, which is confirmed by the Note following this Article in Schedule A, 27 Geo. III. Chap. 13.

Bristles, viz.					
dressed, the Dozen Pounds	—	0 2 9	0 2 6		
dressed of Muscovy or Russia, imported in a Foreign Ship, the Dozen Pounds	—	0 2 11	0 2 6		
rough or undressed, the Dozen Pounds	—	0 1 4½	0 1 3		
rough or undressed of Muscovy or Russia, imported in a Foreign Ship, the Dozen Pounds	—	0 1 6	0 1 3		
Brooms, viz. Flag Brooms or Whisk Brooms, the Dozen	—	0 0 1¼	0 0 1		
Buckets of Wood, the Dozen	—	0 0 11	0 0 10		
Bugle, viz.					
Great Bugle, the Pound	—	0 1 7	0 1 6		
Great Bugle to be warehoused, the Pound	—	0 0 1	0 0 0		
Great Bugle so warehoused, when taken out of such Warehouse to be used in this Kingdom, the Pound	—	0 1 6	0 0 0		
Small or Seed Bugle, the Pound	—	0 2 7	0 2 5		

F 2

TABLE A.

INWARDS.

	Duty. £. s. d.	Drawback. £. s. d.
Bugle, viz.		
Small or Seed Bugle to be warehoused, the Pound	0 0 2	0 0 0
Small or Seed Bugle so warehoused, when taken out of such Warehouse to be used in this Kingdom, the Pound	0 2 5	0 0 0

The 5 Geo. III. Chap. 30. permits any Bugles to be imported upon Payment of the Low Duties, being immediately secured in Warehouses appointed by the Commissioners of the Customs, subject to the same Regulations on Exportation as East India Goods prohibited to be worn and used in Great Britain are now liable; but if not exported, or the full Duties paid within five Years, the Commissioners of the Customs may sell the same publicly by Auction, and after applying the Money arising from the Sale, first in Discharge of the full Duties and Expences of Sale, the Overplus, if any, is to be paid to the Proprietor or Importer.

N. B. Upon a Demand of the Excise Duties on Glass by the Commissioners of Excise in 1787 on Bugle imported, it was determined by the Lords of the Treasury, that Bugle should not be liable to the Duty of Excise upon Glass.

Bullion or Foreign Coin of Gold or Silver, Duty free.

Bull-Rushes, the Load containing sixty-three Bundles	—	0	4	5	0	3	11
Burrs for Mill-stones, the Hundred containing five Score	—	0	11	0	0	9	9
Butter, the Hundred Weight	—	0	2	6	0	2	2
The 5 Geo. III. Chap. 1. 8 Geo. III. Chap. 9. and 16 Geo. III. Chap. 8. permit the Importation of all salted Butter, Bacon, Beef, and Pork into Great Britain from Ireland, free of Duty.							
Cables tarred or untarred, the Hundred Weight	—	0	8	6	0	0	0
Cable Yarn, the Hundred Weight	—	0	8	6	0	0	0
Calicoes, plain white, imported by the East India Company, the Piece	—	0	5	3	0	5	0
By the 4 and 5 William and Mary, Chap. 5. Sect. 11. the Piece of Calico of one Yard and a Quarter in Breadth, or under, not to exceed ten Yards in Length, above that Breadth not to exceed six Yards in Length, if exceeding those Lengths, to be charged according to the respective Lengths of ten Yards and six Yards.							
And besides for every £.100 Value of such Calicoes at the gross Price the same shall be publicly sold at the Sales of the United East India Company	—	16	10	0	0	0	0
The Drawback upon the further Duty of £.16 10 0, per £.100, if exported to Africa	—				16	10	0
if exported to the British Colonies or Plantations in America	—				11	15	0

TABLE A.

INWARDS.

	Duty. £ s. d.	Drawback. £ s. d.
The Drawback upon the further Duty of £.16 10 0, per £.100, if exported to any Parts or Places beyond the Seas (except to Africa or the British Colonies or Plantations in America)	—	14 10 0
if exported to any Parts or Places beyond the Seas (except to Africa or the British Colonies or Plantations in America), if the said Goods shall have been printed, stained, painted, or dyed in this Kingdom	—	16 10 0
Calves Velves to make Rennet, the Hundred Weight	0 5 6	0 5 0
Camels Hair, the Pound	0 0 8	0 0 7
Candles, viz.		
of Tallow, the Hundred Weight	1 12 8	0 0 0
of Sperma Cœti, the Pound	0 1 4	0 0 0
of Wax, the Pound	0 1 8	0 0 0
of Wax, imported by the East India Company, the Pound	0 1 9	0 0 0
Candles imported in any Package containing less than 224 lb. net, forfeited, and £.50 by the Master of the Ship importing the same; must be stowed openly in the Hold of the Ship. 23 Geo. II. Chap. 21. Sect. 7.		
Candlewick, the Hundred Weight	1 12 8	1 8 0

Cane, Chip, or Horse Hair Hats or Bonnets, each Hat or Bonnet not exceeding 22 Inches in Diameter, the Dozen	-	0	3	6	0	3	1½
Ditto, exceeding 22 Inches in Diameter, the Dozen	-	0	7	0	0	6	3
By 10 Geo. III. Chap. 43. Sect. 6. to be imported into London only in Bales or Tubs containing each 75 Dozen Hats or Bonnets, and in Ships exceeding 50 Tons Burthen, otherwise forfeited.							
Cane, Bast, Chip, Horse Hair, Straw Platting, or other Manufacture thereof, to be used in or proper for making Hats or Bonnets, the Pound	-	0	1	10	0	1	8
By 10 Geo. III. Chap. 43. Sect. 6. to be imported into London only in Bales or Tubs containing each 224 Pounds Weight at the least, of such Platting or other Manufacture, and in Ships exceeding 50 Tons Burthen, otherwise forfeited.							
Canes, viz.							
Reed-Canes, the Thousand	-	0	11	0	0	9	9
Walking Canes, the Thousand	-	1	18	6	1	17	3
Walking Canes, imported by the East India Company, the Thousand	-	2	1	3	2	0	0
Rattans, the Thousand	-	0	16	6	0	15	3
Rattans, imported by the East India Company, the Thousand	-	0	19	3	0	18	0
Capers, the Pound	-	0	0	2	0	0	1
N. B. One third Part allowed for Pickle and Weight of Package inclusive.							
Cards, viz. Playing Cards, the Dozen Packs		1	1	0	0	0	0

TABLE A.

INWARDS.

	Duty £ s. d.	Drawback £ s. d.
Carmenia Wool, the Pound - - -	0 0 8	0 0 7
imported by the East India Company, the Pound	0 0 9	0 0 8
Carpets, viz.		
of Persia, imported by the East India Company, the square Yard	1 4 9	1 3 7
of Turkey, containing four Yards square or upwards, the Carpet	2 4 0	2 0 0
of Turkey, containing less than four Yards square, the Carpet -	0 8 3	0 7 6
Casks empty, the Ton - - - -	0 8 3	0 7 6
Catlings, the Gross containing twelve Dozen Knots - -	0 2 6	0 2 2
Cattle. By 5 Geo. III. Chap. 10. and 16 Geo. III. Chap. 8. Cattle of all Sorts are allowed to be imported from Ireland into Great Britain free of Duty.		
Caviare, the Hundred Weight - - - -	0 4 5	0 3 11
Cheese, not of Ireland, the Hundred Weight - -	0 1 6	0 0 0
Cherries, the Hundred Weight - - -	0 4 5	0 3 11
Chip Hats or Bonnets, liable to the same Duty and Restrictions as Cane, &c. as beforementioned.		
Chip, Manufactures of, liable to the same Duty and Restrictions as Cane, &c. as beforementioned.		

(73)

Commodity		£	s	d		£	s	d
Chryſtal, in broken Pieces for Phyſical Uſes, the Pound	—	0	0	3		0	0	2
Beads, the Thouſand	—	0	13	3		0	11	8
Cider, the Tun containing 252 Gallons	—	6	3	3		5	3	3
N. B. Subject alſo to the Duty of Exciſe.								
By the 3 Geo. I. Chap. 4. Cider, being the Produce of Guernſey, Jerſey, Alderney, or Sark, may be imported by the Inhabitants of the ſaid Iſlands into Great Britain free of the Duty of Cuſtoms.								
Cinabrium, or Vermilion, the Pound	—	0	0	7		0	0	$4\frac{1}{2}$
imported by the Eaſt India Company, the Pound	—	0	0	7		0	0	$4\frac{1}{2}$
Cinnamon, the Pound	—	0	4	5		0	0	0
imported by the Eaſt India Company, the Pound	—	0	4	5		0	4	0
Citron Water, the Gallon	—	0	5	8		0	5	1
Cloths, viz. all Manner of Woollen Cloths, the Yard	—	1	17	5		1	13	1
Cloves, the Pound	—	0	2	8		0	2	5
imported by the Eaſt India Company, the Pound	—	0	2	8		0	2	5
Coals, the Chalder containing thirty-ſix Buſhels Winchester Meaſure	—	1	1	0		0	0	0
Cochineal, the Pound	—	0	0	6		0	0	0
By the 8 Geo. I. Chap. 15. free of Duty if legally imported, regularly entered, and landed.								
Cocoa Nuts, viz.								
of the Produce of any Britiſh Colony or Plantation in America, the Hundred Weight	—	0	13	9		0	13	9

TABLE. A.

INWARDS.

	Duty. £. s. d.	Drawback. £. s. d.
Cocoa Nuts, viz. of the Produce of any other Country or Place, the Hundred Weight - - -	0 13 9	0 12 6

The 10 Geo. I. Chap. 10. Sect. 26. allows Coffee, Cocoa Nuts, or Tea, to be warehoused at Importation, upon paying the Low Duties, and the Remainder of the Duties to be paid before taken out for Home Consumption. The 6 Geo. III. Chap. 52. allows British Coffee to be imported free of Duty into any British Colony or Plantation in America, to be warehoused, and if exported to Great Britain, or to some other British Colony or Plantation in America within twelve Months, and Foreign Coffee to be imported free of Duty, into any British Colony or Plantation on the Continent of America, if exported from thence within twelve Months, and no other than the Low Duty to be paid on Importation of such British Coffee or Foreign Coffee into Great Britain directly, provided the same be warehoused; if taken out for Home Consumption, to be liable to the same Duties as Coffee imported by the 10 Geo. I. Chap. 10. or the same

Regulations as directed by that Act, if taken out for Exportation; and by the 10 Anne, Chap. 26. Sect. 45. the Commissioners of the Customs are impowered to allow all Stones, Dirt, and Trash found among Coffee warehoused, to be destroyed at the Request of the Importers or Buyers.						
of the Produce of any British Colony or Plantation in America, on Importation to be secured in Warehouses, the Hundred Weight - - - -	0	1	3	0	1	3
of the Produce of any other Country or Place, on Importation to be secured in Warehouses, the Hundred Weight -	0	1	3	0	0	0
being on Importation been secured in Warehouses, when taken out of such Warehouse for Home Consumption, the Hundred Weight - - -	0	12	6	0	0	0
N. B. Cocoa-Nuts are also subject to the Inland Duty of Excise.						
Coffee of the Produce of any British Colony or Plantation in America, the Hundred Weight - - -	1	18	6	1	18	6
of the Produce of any other Country or Place, or imported by the East India Company, the Hundred Weight -	1	18	6	1	15	0

See the Explanatory Note and Reference following Cocoa Nuts. By the 5 Geo. III. Chap. 43. Coffee imported in any Package containing less than 112 lb. net, is forfeited.

(76)

TABLE A.

INWARDS.

	Duty. £. s. d.	Drawback. £. s. d.
By the 13 Geo. III. Chap. 73. British Plantation Coffee imported in the Husk to have an Allowance of one seventh Part on every hundred Pounds Weight.		
Coffee of the Produce of any British Colony or Plantation in America, on Importation to be secured in Warehouses, the Hundred Weight	0 3 6	0 3 6
Coffee of the Produce of any British Colony or Plantation in America, on Importation to be secured in Warehouses, the Hundred Weight having on Importation been secured in Warehouses, when taken out of such Warehouse for Home Consumption, the Hundred Weight	1 15 0	0 0 0
N.B. Coffee is also subject to the Inland Duty of Excise.		
Comfits, the Pound	0 0 6	0 0 5
Concy Wool, the Pound	0 0 1¾	0 0 0
Copper, viz.		
Ore, the Hundred Weight	0 0 9	0 0 7
unwrought, viz. Copper Bricks, Rose Copper, Copper Coin, and all Cast Copper, the Hundred Weight	0 10 6	0 10 3
unwrought, viz. Copper in Plates, the Hundred Weight	0 16 0	0 15 9
part wrought, viz. Bars, Rods, or Ingots, hammered or raised, the Hundred Weight	2 0 2	1 17 2

(77)

		£	s	d	£	s	d
Copperas, Green, the Hundred Weight	-	0	1	8	0	0	0
Blue, the Hundred Weight	-	0	2	4	0	0	0
White, the Hundred Weight	-	0	4	8	0	0	0
Coral, White or Red, for Physical Uses, in Fragments, the Pound	-	0	0	3	0	2	0
imported by the East India Company, the Pound	-	0	0	3	0	2	0
whole, unpolished, the Pound	-	0	1	6	0	0	0
imported by the East India Company, the Pound	-	0	1	6	0	1	0
whole, polished, the Pound	-	0	3	0	0	1	0
imported by the East India Company, the Pound	-	0	3	0	0	2	0
Beads, the Pound	-	0	4	5	0	2	0
Cordage, tarred or untarred, the Hundred Weight	-	0	8	6	0	4	0
N. B. By the 25 Geo. III. Chap. 56. All Foreign Cordage belonging to a Ship owned by his Majesty's Subjects resident in Great Britain, or any of the British Colonies, is to pay Duty, and be reported by the Master, standing and running Rigging excepted.							
Cordial Waters, the Gallon	-	0	2	10	0	2	7
Subject also to the Duty of Excise.							
Cork, the Hundred Weight	-	0	3	8	0	3	3
Corks, ready made, the Grofs containing twelve Dozen	-	0	0	6	0	0	5

TABLE A.

INWARDS.

	Duty £. s. d.	Drawback £. s. d.
Corn and Grain, viz. from the 15th November 1791.		
Barley, whenever the District Price at the Port of Importation shall be under 25s. per Quarter, the Quarter containing 8 Bushels	1 2 0	0 0 0
whenever the District Price at the Port of Importation shall be at or above 25s. per Quarter, but under 27s. per Quarter, the Quarter containing 8 Bushels	0 1 3	0 0 0
whenever the District Price at the Port of Importation shall be at or above 27s. per Quarter, the Quarter containing 8 Bushels	0 0 3	0 0 0
Beans, whenever the District Price at the Port of Importation shall be under 34s. per Quarter, the Quarter containing 8 Bushels	1 2 0	0 0 0
whenever the District Price at the Port of Importation shall be at or above 34s. per Quarter, but under 37s. per Quarter, the Quarter containing 8 Bushels	0 1 6	0 0 0
whenever the District Price at the Port of Importation shall be at or above 37s. per Quarter, the Quarter containing 8 Bushels	0 0 3	0 0 0
Beer or Big, whenever the District Price at the Port of Importation		

(79)

	£	s.	d.		£	s.	d.
shall be under 25 s. per Quarter, the Quarter containing 8 Bushels	0	0	0		1	2	0
whenever the District Price at the Port of Importation shall be at or above 25 s. per Quarter, but under 27 s. per Quarter, the Quarter containing 8 Bushels	0	0	0		0	1	3
whenever the District Price at the Port of Importation shall be at or above 27 s. per Quarter, the Quarter containing 8 Bushels	0	0	0		0	0	3
Indian Corn and Maize, whenever the District Price of Barley at the Port of Importation shall be under 25 s. per Quarter, the Quarter containing 8 Bushels	0	0	0		1	2	0
whenever the District Price of Barley at the Port of Importation shall be at or above 25 s. but under 27 s. per Quarter, the Quarter containing 8 Bushels	0	0	0		0	1	3
whenever the District Price of Barley at the Port of Importation shall be at or above 27 s. per Quarter, the Quarter containing 8 Bushels	0	0	0		0	0	3
Oats, whenever the District Price at the Port of Importation shall be under 17 s. per Quarter, the Quarter containing 8 Bushels	0	0	0		0	6	7

TABLE A.

INWARDS.

	Duty. £. s. d.	Drawback. £. s. d.
Corn and Grain, viz.		
Oats, whenever the District Price at the Port of Importation shall be at or above 17s. but under 18s. per Quarter, the Quarter containing 8 Bushels	0 1 0	0 0 0
whenever the District Price at the Port of Importation shall be at or above 18s. per Quarter, the Quarter containing 8 Bushels	0 0 2	0 0 0
Oat-Meal, whenever the District Price at the Port of Importation shall be under 16s. per Boll of 140 lb. Avoirdupoise, or 128 lb. Scots Troy, the Boll	0 8 0	0 0 0
whenever the District Price at the Port of Importation shall be at or above 16s. but under 17s. per Boll as beforementioned, the Boll	0 1 0	0 0 0
whenever the District Price at the Port of Importation shall be at or above 17s. per Boll as beforementioned, the Boll	0 0 6	0 0 0
Pease, whenever the District Price at the Port of Importation shall be under 34s per Quarter, the Quarter containing 8 Bushels	1 2 0	0 0 0
whenever the District Price at the Port of Importation shall be		

at or above 34s. but under 37s. per Quarter, the Quarter containing 8 Bushels - - - - 0 1 6 0 0 0

whenever the District Price at the Port of Importation shall be at or above 37s. per Quarter, the Quarter containing 8 Bushels - - - - 0 0 3 0 0 0

Rye, whenever the District Price at the Port of Importation shall be under 34s. per Quarter, the Quarter containing 8 Bushels - - - 1 2 0 0 0 0

whenever the District Price at the Port of Importation shall be at or above 34s. but under 37s. per Quarter, the Quarter containing 8 Bushels - - 0 1 6 0 0 0

whenever the District Price at the Port of Importation shall be at or about 37s. per Quarter, the Quarter containing 8 Bushels - - - - 0 0 3 0 0 0

Wheat, whenever the District Price at the Port of Importation shall be under 50s. per Quarter, the Quarter containing 8 Bushels - - - 1 4 3 0 0 0

whenever the District Price at the Port of Importation shall be at or above 50s. but under 54s. per Quarter, the Quarter containing 8 Bushels - - 0 2 6 0 0 0

whenever the District Price at the Port of Importation shall be at or above 54s. per Quarter, the Quarter containing 8 Bushels - - - - 0 0 6 0 0 0

TABLE A.

INWARDS.

	Duty. £. s. d.	Drawback. £. s. d.
Corn and Grain, viz.		
Wheat Flour and Meal, whenever the District Price of Wheat at the Port of Importation shall be under 50s. per Quarter, the Hundred Weight containing 112 Pounds -	0 6 6	0 0 0
whenever the District Price of Wheat at the Port of Importation shall be at or above 50s. but under 54s. per Quarter, the Hundred Weight containing 112 Pounds -	0 1 6	0 0 0
whenever the District Price of Wheat at the Port of Importation shall be at or above 54s. per Quarter, the Hundred Weight containing 112 Pounds -	0 1 0	0 0 0

N. B. When Wheat, Wheat Meal or Flour, Rye, Pease, Beans, Barley, Beer or Bigg, Oats or Oat Meal, Indian Corn or Maize, is permitted by the Parliament of Ireland to be imported from Great Britain into Ireland at the Prices beforementioned taken Quarterly, the following Duties shall be paid upon Importation into Great Britain *from Ireland, the Province of Quebec, the other British*

(83)

	o	o	o	o	o	o	o	o
	o	o	o	o	o	o	o	o
	o	o	o	o	o	o	o	o

Colonies or Plantations in North America (and from other Foreign Countries the respective Duties beforementioned), after the Expiration of three Calendar Months from the Notification by Order of his Majesty in Council, published in the London Gazette, of such Act having passed in the Parliament of Ireland, and during the Continuance of such Act, or any other Act there passed to the same Purport and Effect, viz.

Barley, whenever the District Price at the Port of Importation shall be under 24s. per Quarter, the Quarter containing 8 Bushels - - - 1 2 0
whenever the District Price at the Port of Importation shall be at or above 24s. but under 26s. per Quarter, the Quarter containing 8 Bushels - - - 0 1 3
whenever the District Price at the Port of Importation shall be at or above 26s. per Quarter, the Quarter containing 8 Bushels - - - 0 0 3

Beans, whenever the District Price at the Port of Importation shall be under 32s. per Quarter, the Quarter containing 8 Bushels - - - 1 2 0
whenever the District Price at the Port of Importation shall be at or above 32s. but under 35s. per Quarter, the Quarter containing 8 Bushels - - - 0 1 6
whenever the District Price at the Port of Importation shall be at or above 35s. per Quarter, the Quarter containing 8 Bushels - - - 0 0 3

G 2

TABLE A.

INWARDS.

	Duty. £. s. d.	Drawback. £. s. d.
Corn and Grain, viz. from Ireland, Quebec, or the British Colonies or Plantations in North America, after the Notification of his Majesty in Council beforementioned.		
Beer or Bigg, whenever the District Price at the Port of Importation shall be under 24 s. per Quarter, the Quarter containing 8 Bushels - - - -	1 2 0	0 0 0
whenever the District Price at the Port of Importation shall be at or above 24 s. but under 26 s. per Quarter, the Quarter containing 8 Bushels - -	0 1 3	0 0 0
whenever the District Price at the Port of Importation shall be at or above 26 s. per Quarter, the Quarter containing 8 Bushels - - -	0 0 3	0 0 0
Indian Corn or Maize, whenever the District Price of Barley at the Port of Importation shall be under 24 s. per Quarter, the Quarter containing 8 Bushels -	1 2 0	0 0 0
whenever the District Price of Barley at the Port of Importation shall be at or above 24 s. but under 26 s. per Quarter, the Quarter containing 8 Bushels - -	0 1 3	0 0 0

whenever the District Price of Barley at the Port of Importation shall be at or above 26s. per Quarter, the Quarter containing 8 Bushels	0	0	0	0	0	0	3
Oats, whenever the District Price at the Port of Importation shall be under 16s. per Quarter, the Quarter containing 8 Bushels	0	0	0	0	0	6	7
whenever the District Price at the Port of Importation shall be at or above 16s. but under 17s. per Quarter, the Quarter containing 8 Bushels	0	0	0	0	0	1	0
whenever the District Price at the Port of Importation shall be at or above 17s. per Quarter, the Quarter containing 8 Bushels	0	0	0	0	0	0	2
Oat Meal, whenever the District Price at the Port of Importation shall be under 15s. per Boll of 140 lb. Avoirdupois, or 128 lb. Scotch Troy, the Boll	0	0	0	0	0	8	0
whenever the District Price at the Port of Importation shall be at or above 15s. but under 16s. per Boll as beforementioned, the Boll	0	0	0	0	0	1	0
whenever the District Price at the Port of Importation shall be at or above 16s. per Boll, as beforementioned, the Boll	0	0	0	0	0	0	2

TABLE A.

INWARDS.

Corn and Grain, viz. from Ireland, Quebec, or the British Colonies or Plantations in North America, after the Notification of his Majesty in Council beforementioned.

	Duty. £. s. d.	Drawback. £. s. d.
Pease, whenever the District Price at the Port of Importation shall be under 32 s. per Quarter, the Quarter containing 8 Bushels	1 2 0	0 0 0
whenever the District Price at the Port of Importation shall be at or above 32 s. but under 35 s. per Quarter, the Quarter containing 8 Bushels	0 1 6	0 0 0
whenever the District Price at the Port of Importation shall be at or above 35 s. per Quarter, the Quarter containing 8 Bushels	0 0 3	0 0 0
Rye, whenever the District Price at the Port of Importation shall be under 32 s. per Quarter, the Quarter containing 8 Bushels	1 2 0	0 0 0
whenever the District Price at the Port of Importation shall be at or above 32 s. but under 35 s. per Quarter, the Quarter containing 8 Bushels	0 1 6	0 0 0
whenever the District Price at the Port of Importation shall be at or above 35 s. per Quarter, the Quarter containing 8 Bushels	0 0 3	0 0 0

(87)

	£	s.	d.
Wheat, whenever the District Price at the Port of Importation shall be under 48 s. per Quarter, the Quarter containing 8 Bushels	1	4	3
whenever the District Price at the Port of Importation shall be at or above 48 s. but under 52 s. per Quarter, the Quarter containing 8 Bushels	0	2	6
whenever the District Price at the Port of Importation shall be at or above 52 s. per Quarter, the Quarter containing 8 Bushels	0	0	6
Wheat Meal and Flour, whenever the District Price of Wheat at the Port of Importation shall be under 48 s. per Quarter, the Hundred Weight containing 112 Pounds	0	6	6
whenever the District Price of Wheat at the Port of Importation shall be at or above 48 s. but under 52 s. per Quarter, the Hundred Weight containing 112 Pounds	0	2	6
whenever the District Price of Wheat at the Port of Importation shall be at or above 52 s. per Quarter, the Hundred Weight containing 112 Pounds	0	0	6

N. B. Subject to a Duty of 2 d. per Last of ten Quarters, to be paid to the Corn Inspector.

TABLE A.

INWARDS.

By the 31 Geo. III. Chap. 30. All Corn, under the Direction of this Act, is to be measured by the Winchester Bushel, and eight such Bushels are to be deemed a Quarter.

Barley ground, Beans ground, Beer or Bigg ground, Indian Corn or Maize ground; Malt made of Barley, Beer or Bigg, of Indian Corn or Maize, of Oats, of Rye, or of Wheat; Pease ground, and Rye ground, are prohibited to be imported under Forfeiture, and of the Ship, Furniture, Tackle, and Apparel, in which it is imported.

Wheat, Wheat Meal or Flour, Rye, Pease, Beans, Barley, Beer or Bigg, Oats or Oat Meal, Indian Corn or Maize, may be imported into any Town or Port having a Collector and Comptroller of the Customs, or into any other Port that shall be approved by his Majesty in Council, to be warehoused under the joint Locks of the King and the Importer, at the Expence of the Importer, under the Care and Inspection of the Commissioners of the Customs, without Payment of any Duty; with Liberty to screen, turn, and take any Care of it Necessity shall require, in the Presence of an Officer of the Customs.

If delivered out to be used in this Kingdom, to pay at the Time of

	Duty.			Drawback.		
	£.	s.	d.	£.	s.	d.

taking out, the Duties payable on that Sort of Corn imported into that Port from any Foreign Country whatever, and also in Addition, the highest of the two low Duties payable upon the like Sort of Corn, and it is to be measured out from the Warehouses.

If taken out for Exportation, or to be carried Coastwise, as permitted by this Act, Security is to be given for the due Exportation or Landing at the Port to which it is to be carried.

N.B. When the Parliament is not sitting, if the average Price of any Sort of Corn or of Oat Meal, taken from the Returns of the whole Kingdom, is higher than the Price at or above which Foreign Corn is allowed to be imported (not from Ireland, Quebec, or the British North American Colonies), at the low Duties, the King in Council may permit generally the Importation of any Sort of Corn, &c. on the lowest Duties then payable, and such Permission shall continue in Force three Months from the Date of the Order of Council made for that Purpose.

The Maritime Counties of England divided into Districts in the following Manner, including the Cities and Towns which are Counties of themselves.

1 District, The City of London, the Counties of Essex, Kent, and Sussex; and the Exportation and Importation of Corn, Grain, Flour, and Meal

TABLE A.

INWARDS.

		Duty. £. s. d.	Drawback. £. s. d.
	Duties, &c. within that District, to be regulated by the Prices of the several Sorts taken at the Corn Exchange in Mark Lane, in the City of London.		
2 District,	The Counties of Suffolk and Cambridge; to be regulated by the Prices of the several Sorts taken at Ipswich, Woodbridge, Sudbury, Hadleigh, Stowmarket, Bury Saint Edmunds, Beccles, Bungay, Lowestoft, Cambridge, Ely, and Wisbeach.		
3 District,	The County of Norfolk; to be regulated by the Prices of the several Sorts taken at Norwich, Yarmouth, Lynn, Thetford, Watton, Wymondham, East Dereham, Harleston, Holt, Aylesham, Fakenham, and Walsingham.		
4 District,	The County of Lincoln, East and North Ridings of the County of York, with the Town and County of Kingston upon Hull; to be regulated by the Prices of the several Sorts taken at Lincoln, Gainsborough, Glamfordbridge, Louth, Boston, Sleaford, Stamford, Spalding, York, Bridlington, Beverly, Howden, Hull, Whitby, and New Malton.		
5 District,	The Counties of Durham and Northumberland, and Town of Berwick upon Tweed; to be regulated by the Prices of the several Sorts		

taken at Durham, Stockton, Darlington, Sunderland, Barnard Castle, Wolsingham, Belford, Hexham, Newcastle upon Tyne, Morpeth, Alnwick, and Berwick upon Tweed.

6 District, The Counties of Cumberland and Westmoreland; to be regulated by the Prices of the several Sorts taken at Carlisle, Whitehaven, Cockermouth, Penrith, Appleby, and Burton.

7 District, The Counties of Lancaster and Chester; to be regulated by the Prices taken at Liverpool, Ulverstone, Lancaster, Preston, Ormskirk, Warrington, Manchester, Bolton, Chester, Nantwich, Macclesfield, and Stockport.

8 District, The Counties of Flint, Denbigh, Anglesea, Carnarvon, and Merioneth; to be regulated by the Prices of the several Sorts taken at Holywell, Mold, Denbigh, Wrexham, Tymawr, Llangollan, Beaumaris, Llannerchymed, Amlwch, Carnarvon, Pwhelli, Conway, Bala, Corwen, and Dolgelly.

9 District, The Counties of Cardigan, Pembroke, Carmarthen, and Glamorgan; to be regulated by the Prices of the several Sorts taken at Cardigan, Lampeter, Aberystwith, Pembroke, Fishguard, Haverfordwest, Carmarthen, Llandilo, Kedwilly, Swansea, Neath, and Cowbridge.

10 District, The Counties of Gloucester, Somerset, and Monmouth, and City of Bristol; to be regulated by the Prices of the several Sorts taken

TABLE A.

	Duty. £. s. d.	Drawback. £. s. d.

INWARDS.

at Gloucester, Cirencester, Tetbury, Stow on the Wold, Tewkſbury, Taunton, Wells, Bridgewater, Frome, Wellington, Monmouth, Abergavenny, Chepſtow, Pontypool, and Briſtol.

11 Diſtrict, The Counties of Devon and Cornwall; to be regulated by the Prices of the ſeveral Sorts taken at Exeter, Barnſtaple, Plymouth, Totneſs, Taviſtock, Kingſbridge, Truro, Bodmin, Launceſton, Redruth, Helſtone, and Saint Auſtell.

12 Diſtrict, The Counties of Dorſet and Hants; to be regulated by the Prices of the ſeveral Sorts taken at Blandford, Bridport, Dorcheſter, Sherborne, Lyme Regis, Wareham, Wincheſter, Andover, Baſingſtoke, Fareham, Goſport, Newport, Ringwood, Southampton, and Portſmouth.

The Exportation and Importation of Corn, Grain, Flour, and Meal, Duties, &c. within that Part of Great Britain called Scotland, to be regulated in each of the Diſtricts by the Prices of the ſeveral Sorts taken at the Places hereafter mentioned.

13 Diſtrict, The Counties of Fife, Kinroſs, Clackmannan, Stirling, Linlithgow, Edinburgh, Haddington, Berwick, Roxburgh, Selkirk, and

Peebles, by the Prices taken at the County Towns of the several Counties beforementioned, for all Sorts of Corn by the Winchester Bushel, and for Oat Meal by the Boll of 128 lb. Scotch Troy, or 140 lb. Avoirdupois.

14 District, The Counties of Dumfries, Wigton, and Air, and the Stewartry of Kircudbright, at the County Towns of the several Counties, as beforementioned for the 13th District.

15 District, The Counties of Argyle, Dumbarton, Lanerk, Renfrew, and Bute; at Glasgow in the County of Lanerk, at Paisley in the County of Renfrew, and at the County Towns in the other several Counties, as beforementioned for the 13th District.

16 District, The Counties of Orkney and Shetland, Caithness, Sutherland, Ross, Inverness, Cromarty, Nairn, Elgin, Banff, Aberdeen, Kincardine, Forfar, and Perth; at Thurso in the County of Caithness, and at the County Towns in the other several Counties, as beforementioned for the 13th District.

Cotton Wool, of the British Plantations, Duty free. — 0 0 0
not of the British Plantations, the Pound — 0 0 1
The 6 Geo. III. Chap. 52. Sect. 20 and 21. permits the Importation of Cotton Wool into Great Britain free of Duty, from any Place whatsoever, in British built Ships legally navigated, if regularly entered and landed, otherwise to be liable to Duty. 0 0 0¾

TABLE A.

INWARDS.

	Duty.			Drawback.		
	£.	s.	d.	£.	s.	d.
Cotton Yarn, the Pound	0	0	3½	0	0	3
imported by the East India Company, the Pound	0	0	3½	0	0	3
The 18 Geo. III. Chap. 56. permits the Importation of Cotton Yarn the Manufacture of Ireland, directly from thence into Great Britain, free of Duty, if the Master brings with him a Certificate as directed, and makes Oath before the Collector or other principal Officer at the Port of Importation, that the Packages and Goods are those taken on board by virtue of the Certificate.						
Cow or Ox Hair, the Hundred Weight	0	8	3	0	7	6
Cucumbers pickled, the Gallon	0	0	9	0	0	7½
Culm, the Chalder containing 36 Bushels Winchester Measure	0	15	9	0	0	0
Currants, imported in a British built Ship, the Hundred Weight	1	3	4	1	1	9
imported in a Foreign Ship, the Hundred Weight	1	4	10	1	1	9
By the 23 Geo. III. Chap. 11. not to be imported otherwise than loose in Hogsheads or Casks, containing each five Hundred Weight net, of Currants, under the Penalty of Forfeiture, and also the Packages.						
Cuttle Bones, the Thousand	0	5	11	0	5	3
Cynders, the Chalder containing 36 Bushels Winchester Measure	0	10	6	0	0	0

Dates, the Hundred Weight	-	2	6	3	
Diamonds, Pearls, Rubies, Emeralds, and all other precious Stones and Jewels, Duty free.					
By the 6 Geo. II. Chap. 7. All Diamonds, Pearls, Rubies, Emeralds, and all other precious Stones and Jewels, are to pass inwards without any Warrant or Fee, in like Manner as they pass outwards, and free from any Duty to his Majesty; and any Person may import or export the same in any Ship whatever, but not to affect the Duty payable to the East India Company for such as shall be imported from within the Limits of their Charter, nor to alter any of their Privileges, Profits, or Advantages.					
Dice, for every Pair	-	0	12	6	
Dimity, viz. Plain White Dimity, imported by the East India Company, the Yard	-	0	1	6	0 1 5
And besides, for every Hundred Pounds of the true and real Value thereof according to the gross Price at which the same shall be publicly sold at the Sales of the United Company of Merchants of England trading to the East Indies	-	16	10	0	
The Drawback of the last mentioned Duty of sixteen Pounds ten Shillings, to be allowed on the Exportation of such Dimity, shall be for every Hundred Pounds of the true and real Value thereof according to the gross Price which such Goods shall have been					

TABLE A.

INWARDS.	Duty. £ s. d.	Drawback. £ s. d.
Dimity, if publicly sold at the Sales of the United Company of Merchants of England trading to the East Indies, viz.		
if exported to Africa	—	16 10 0
if exported to the British Colonies or Plantations in America	—	11 15 0
if exported to any Parts or Places beyond the Seas (except to the British Colonies or Plantations in America) if the said Goods shall have been printed, stained, painted, or dyed in this Kingdom	—	16 10 0
if exported to any Parts or Places beyond the Seas (except to Africa or the British Colonies and Plantations in America) if the said Goods shall be exported from this Kingdom without having been printed, stained, painted, or dyed therein	—	—
Down, the Pound	0 0 6	0 0 5
of Muscovy or Russia, imported in a Foreign Ship, the Pound	0 0 7	0 0 5
Drillings. See Linen.		
Drugs, viz.		
Acacia, the Pound	0 0 9	0 0 6
Acorus, the Pound	0 0 2	0 0 1½
Adianthum Album, the Pound	0 0 2	0 0 1½
Nigrum, the Pound	0 0 1½	0 0 1

(97)

Item	£	s	d	£	s	d
Agaric, the Hundred Weight	0	4	8	0	0	0
Agnus Castus Seeds, the Pound	0	0	3	0	0	2
Alkermes Confectio, the Ounce	0	0	8	0	0	5½
———— Syrup, the Pound	0	1	0	0	0	8
Alkanet Roots, the Pound	0	0	3	0	0	2
Aloes Epatica, the Pound	0	0	6	0	0	4
———— imported by the East India Company, the Pound	0	0	6	0	0	4
Succotrina, the Pound	0	1	2	0	0	9
———— if not imported directly from the Place of its Growth, the Pound	0	3	6	0	2	4
———— imported by the East India Company, the Pound	0	1	2	0	0	9
Alumen Plume, the Pound	0	0	1	0	0	0¼
Ambergris, Black or Grey, the Ounce Troy	0	2	0	0	1	4
———— imported by the East India Company, the Ounce Troy	0	2	0	0	1	4
Ambra Liquida, the Pound	0	2	6	0	1	8
Ameos Seeds, the Pound	0	0	2	0	0	1½
Amomi Seeds, the Pound	0	0	2	0	0	1½
Anacardium, or Cashew Nuts, the Pound	0	0	9	0	0	6
Angelica, the Pound	0	0	2	0	0	1½
Antimonium Crudum, the Hundred Weight	0	4	8	0	0	0
———— Præparatum or Stibium, the Pound	0	0	1	0	0	0¾
Aqua-Fortis, the Hundred Weight	0	4	8	0	0	0

H

(98)

TABLE A.

INWARDS.

	Duty. £ s. d.	Drawback. £ s. d.
Drugs,		
Argentum Sublime or Quickſilver, the Pound	0 0 8	0 0 6
imported by the Eaſt India Company, the Pound	0 0 8	0 0 6
Ariſtolochia, the Pound	0 0 3	0 0 2
Arſenic, White or Yellow, or Roſalgar, the Hundred Weight	0 4 8	0 0 0
Aſarum Roots, the Pound	0 0 3	0 0 2
Aſpalthus, the Pound	0 0 2	0 0 1½
Aſſa-Fœtida, the Pound	0 0 3	0 0 2
if not imported directly from the Place of its Growth, the Pound	0 0 9	0 0 6
imported by the Eaſt India Company, the Pound	0 0 3	0 0 2
Auriculæ Judæ, the Pound	0 0 3	0 0 2
Baccæ Alkakengi, the Pound	0 0 3	0 0 2
Balauſtium, the Pound	0 0 3	0 0 2
Balſam Artificial, the Pound	0 1 6	0 1 0
imported by the Eaſt India Company, the Pound	0 1 6	0 1 0
Canada Balſam, the Pound	0 0 3	0 0 2
Copaivæ or Copaiba, the Pound	0 0 9	0 0 6
Natural, the Pound	0 1 6	0 1 0

(99)

Item	£	s	d
Barbadoes Tar, the Pound	0	1	0¼
Barley hulled, or Pearl Barley, the Hundred Weight	0	0	0
Bayberries, the Hundred Weight	0	6	0
Bdellium, the Pound	0	0	0
— if not imported directly from the Place of its Growth, the Pound	0	0	2
— imported by the East India Company, the Pound	0	0	6
Ben-album, or Rubrum, the Pound	0	0	2
Benjamin, the Pound	0	0	3½
— imported by the East India Company, the Pound	0	0	4
Bezoar Stones of the West Indies, the Ounce Troy	0	0	4
— imported by the East India Company, the Ounce Troy	0	0	6
Bitumen Judaicum, the Pound	0	0	8
Bolus Communis or Armoniacus, the Hundred Weight	0	1	1½
Verus or fine Bole, the Pound	0	0	4
Borax in Paste or unrefined, the Pound	0	2	1½
— imported by the East India Company, the Pound	0	0	2
refined, the Pound	0	0	2
— imported by the East India Company, the Pound	0	0	8
Calamus, the Pound	0	0	8
Cambogium or Gutta Gambe, the Pound	0	0	1½
	0	0	4

TABLE A.

INWARDS.

	Duty. £. s. d.	Drawback. £. s. d.
Drugs,		
Cambogium or Gutta Gambæ, imported by the East India Company, the Pound	0 0 6	0 0 4
Camphire, refined, the Pound	0 0 8	0 0 5½
— if not imported directly from the Place of its Growth, the Pound	0 2 0	0 1 4
— imported by the East India Company, the Pound	0 0 8	0 0 5½
— unrefined, the Pound	0 0 4	0 0 2¼
— if not imported directly from the Place of its Growth, the Pound	0 1 0	0 0 8
— imported by the East India Company, the Pound	0 0 4	0 0 2¼
Cancrorum Oculi, the Pound	0 0 6	0 0 4
Cantharides, the Pound	0 1 0	0 0 8
— imported by the East India Company, the Pound	0 1 0	0 0 8
Capita Papaverum, the Thousand	0 1 8	0 1 1
Cardamoms, the Pound	0 0 9	0 0 6
— imported by the East India Company, the Pound	0 0 9	0 0 6
Carlina, the Pound	0 0 3	0 0 2

(101)

		£	s.	d.		£	s.	d.
Carpo-Balsamum, the Pound	—	0	0	0	—	0	0	6
Carrabe or Succinum, the Pound	—	0	0	0	—	0	0	2
Carraway-Seeds, the Hundred Weight	—	0	5	3	—	0	0	4
Carthamus-Seeds, the Pound	—	0	0	0	—	0	0	$1\frac{1}{2}$
Caffia-Buds, imported by the East India Company, the Pound	—	0	0	0	—	0	0	$2\frac{5}{4}$
Fistula, the Pound	—	0	0	0	—	0	0	2
imported by the East India Company, the Pound	—	0	0	0	—	0	0	c
Lignea, the Pound	—	0	0	0	—	0	0	$2\frac{1}{4}$
imported by the East India Company, the Pound	—	0	0	0	—	0	0	$2\frac{3}{4}$
Castor-Oil, the Gallon	—	0	2	4	—	0	0	4
Castoreum, or Beaver's Cods, the Pound	—	0	0	1	—	0	0	4
Cerussa, the Hundred Weight	—	0	2	7	—	0	1	8
Cetrach, the Pound	—	0	0	4	—	0	0	2
Chamæpitys, the Pound	—	0	0	0	—	0	0	$1\frac{1}{2}$
Chelæ Cancrorum, the Pound	—	0	0	0	—	0	0	$0\frac{3}{4}$
China-Roots, the Pound	—	0	0	0	—	0	0	$3\frac{1}{2}$
if not imported directly from the Place of their Growth, the Pound	—	0	1	3	—	0	0	10
imported by the East India Company, the Pound	—	0	0	5	—	0	0	$3\frac{1}{2}$
Cinabrium or Vermilion, the Pound	—	0	0	7	—	0	0	$4\frac{1}{2}$
imported by the East India Company, the Pound	—	0	0	7	—	0	0	$4\frac{1}{2}$
Cinnabaris-Nativa, the Pound	—	0	1	0	—	0	0	8

(102)

TABLE A.

INWARDS.

	Duty. £. s. d.	Drawback. £. s. d.
Drugs,		
Ciperus, the Hundred Weight —	0 7 4	0 4 11
Citrago, the Pound —	0 0 3	0 0 2
Civet, the Ounce Troy —	0 2 0	0 1 4
Coculus Indiæ, the Pound —	0 0 5	0 0 3½
if not imported directly from the Place of its Growth, the Pound —	0 1 3	0 0 10
imported by the East India Company, the Pound —	0 0 5	0 0 3½
Colophonia, the Hundred Weight —	0 3 3	0 2 2
Coloquintida, the Pound —	0 0 6	0 0 4
if not imported directly from the Place of its Growt', the Pound —	0 1 6	0 1 0
imported by the East India Company, the Pound —	0 0 6	0 0 4
Columbo-Root, imported by the East India Company, the Pound —	0 0 6	0 0 4
Copperas Blue, the Hundred Weight —	0 2 4	0 0 0
White, the Hundred Weight —	0 4 8	0 0 0
Coral, in Fragments, and other Coral, fee rated under Letter C.		
Coriander Seeds, the Hundred Weight —	0 4 5	0 2 11
Cornu-Cervi Calcinatum, the Pound —	0 0 3	0 0 2

(103)

	£	s	d		£	s	d
Cortex-Cariophyllorum, the Pound	0	0	2		0	0	1½
Elatheriæ, the Hundred Weight	0	9	6		0	6	4
Guaiaci, the Hundred Weight	0	13	3		0	8	10
Limonum, vel Aurantiorum, the Pound	0	0	1		0	0	0¾
Peruvianus, the Pound	0	0	9		0	0	6
Simarouba, the Pound	0	0	3		0	0	2
Tamarifci, the Pound	0	0	2		0	0	1½
Winteranus, the Pound	0	0	2		0	0	1½
Coftus Dulcis et Amarus, the Pound	0	0	4		0	0	2¾
imported by the Eaft India Company, the Pound	0	0	4		0	0	2¾
Cowitch, the Pound	0	0	4		0	0	2¾
Cream of Tartar, the Hundred Weight	0	4	8		0	0	0
Cryftal in broken Pieces for phyfical Ufes, the Pound	0	0	3		0	0	2
Cubebs, the Pound	0	0	2		0	0	1½
imported by the Eaft India Company, the Pound	0	0	2		0	0	1½
Cummin Seeds, the Hundred Weight	0	7	4		4	11	
Cufcuta, the Pound	0	0	3		0	0	2
Cyclamen or Panis Porcinus, the Pound	0	0	3		0	0	2
Daucus Creticus, the Pound	0	0	3		0	0	2
Diagredium, or Scammony, the Pound	0	2	6		0	1	8
if not imported directly from the Place of its Growth, the Pound	0	7	6		0	5	0

(104)

TABLE A.
INWARDS.

		Duty. L. s. d.	Drawback. L. s. d.
Drugs, Diagredum, or Scammony, imported by the East India Company, the Pound	—	0 2 6	0 1 8
Dipamus Leaves, the Pound	—	0 0 3	0 0 2
Roots, the Pound	—	0 0 3	0 0 2
Doronicum, the Pound,	—	0 0 6	0 0 4¼
Eboris Rafuræ, the Pound	—	0 0 1	0 0 0¼
Eleborus, the Pound	—	0 0 1½	0 0 1
Epithymum, the Pound	—	0 0 3	0 0 2
Essence of Lemons, the Pound	—	0 2 0	0 1 4
Euphorbium, the Pound	—	0 0 2	0 0 1½
Fechia Brugiata, the Hundred Weight	—	0 3 0	0 2 0
Fennel-Seeds, the Pound	—	0 0 1½	0 0 1
Fenugreek, the Hundred Weight	—	0 3 4	0 2 3
Flores-Chamœmeli, the Pound	—	0 0 1½	0 0 1
Meliloti, the Pound	—	0 0 1½	0 0 1
Folium Indiæ, the Pound	—	0 0 6	0 0 4
imported by the East India Company, the Pound	—	0 0 6	0 0 4
Fox Lungs, the Pound	—	0 0 8	0 0 5½

		£	s.	d.	£	s.	d.
Frankincense, the Hundred Weight	—	0	4	8	0	3	2 1/2
Galanga, the Pound	—	0	0	2	0	0	1 1/2
if not imported directly from the Place of its Growth, the Pound	—	0	0	6	0	0	4
imported by the East India Company, the Pound	—	0	0	2	0	0	1 1/2
Galbanum, the Pound	—	0	0	4	0	0	2 3/4
if not imported directly from the Place of its Growth, the Pound	—	0	1	0	0	0	8
imported by the East India Company, the Pound	—	0	0	4	0	0	2 1/4
Gentiana, the Pound	—	0	0	1	0	0	0 1/4
Ginfang, the Pound	—	0	0	8	0	0	5 1/2
Grains of Guinea. See in G.							
Grana-Tinctorun, the Pound	—	0	0	9	0	0	6
Granadilla-Peruviana, the Pound	—	0	0	9	0	0	6
Guinea Pepper, the Pound	—	0	0	3	0	0	2
Gum-Animi, the Pound	—	0	0	3	0	0	2
imported by the East India Company, the Pound	—	0	0	3	0	0	2
Arabic or Gum-Senega, the Hundred Weight	—	0	0	6	0	0	0
imported by the East India Company, the Hundred Weight	—	0	0	6	0	0	0
Senega imported from Europe, the Hundred Weight	—	0	12	11	0	0	0

The 25 Geo. II. Chap. 32. permits the Importation of Gum-Senega

(106)

TABLE A.

INWARDS.

	Duty. £. s. d.	Drawback. £. s. d.
Drugs, from Europe by British Subjects, in British built Ships, but the Rate is placed as above, in the Consolidation Act, 27 Geo. III. Chap. 13, Schedule A, without any Reference.		
Cashew Gum, the Growth or Production of his Majesty's West India Islands, including the Bahama and Bermuda Islands, may be imported in British Ships upon the same Duty as Gum-Arabic, by the 30 Geo. III. Chap. 28.		
Gum-Armoniac, the Pound - - - -	0 0 4	0 0 2¾
—— if not imported directly from the Place of its Growth, the Pound - - -	0 1 0	0 0 8
—— imported by the East India Company, the Pound	0 0 4	0 0 2¼
Carannæ, the Pound - - - - -	0 0 9	0 0 6
Copal, the Pound - - - - -	0 0 8	0 0 5½
Elemi, the Pound - - - - -	0 0 2½	0 0 1½
—— imported by the East India Company, the Pound	0 0 2½	0 0 1½
Guaiaci, the Pound - - - - -	0 0 9	0 0 6
Hederæ, the Pound - - - - -	0 0 9	0 0 6
Lac, viz. Cake Lac, the Pound - - -	0 0 1	0 0 0¼

Description	£	s	d	£	s	d	£	s	d
imported by the East India Company, the Pound	0	0	1	0	0	0	0	0	0¼
Shellac or Seed-Lac, the Pound	0	0	2	0	0	0	0	0	1½
imported by the East India Company, the Pound	0	0	2	0	0	0	0	0	1½
Sticklac, the Pound	0	0	1	0	0	0	0	0	0
By the 8 Geo. I. Chap. 15. Sect. 10. Gum Sticklac may be legally imported free of Duty, if regularly entered and landed.									
Gum-Opoponax, the Pound	0	0	4	0	1	0	0	0	11
if not imported directly from the Place of its Growth, the Pound	0	0	4	0	4	0	0	2	8
imported by the East India Company, the Pound	0	0	4	0	1	0	0	0	11
Sandrake or Juniperi, the Hundred Weight	0	0	0	0	7	0	0	4	8
Sarcocolla, the Pound	0	0	4	0	0	0	0	0	2¼
if not imported directly from the Place of its Growth, the Pound	0	0	4	0	0	0	0	0	8
imported by the East India Company, the Pound	0	0	4	0	0	0	0	0	2¼
Serapinum or Sagapenum, the Pound	0	0	4	0	0	0	0	0	2¼
if not imported directly from the Place of its Growth, the Pound	0	0	4	0	1	0	0	0	8
imported by the East India Company, the Pound	0	0	4	0	0	0	0	0	2¼
Tacamahaca, the Pound	0	0	9	0	0	0	0	0	6
Tragacanth, the Pound	0	0	3	0	0	0	0	0	2

(108)

TABLE A.

INWARDS.

Drugs,	Duty £ s. d.	Drawback £ s. d.
Gum-Tragacanth, if not imported directly from the Place of its Growth, the Pound	0 0 9	0 0 6
imported by the East India Company, the Pound	0 0 3	0 0 2
Hermodactilus, the Pound	0 0 3	0 0 2
Horns of Harts or Stags, the 100 Horns	0 6 8	0 4 5
Hypocistis, the Pound	0 0 5	0 0 3½
Jalop, the Pound	0 0 9	0 0 6
Incense or Olibanum. See Olibanum.		
Ireos, the Hundred Weight	0 14 0	0 9 4
Isinglass, the Pound	0 0 0¼	0 0 0
Jujubes, the Pound	0 0 2	0 0 1½
Juniper-berries, the Hundred Weight	0 4 5	0 3 3
Labdanum or Lapodanum, the Pound	0 0 3	0 0 2
if not imported directly from the Place of its Growth, the Pound	0 0 9	0 0 6
Lapis-Calaminaris, the Hundred Weight	0 3 8	0 0 0
imported by the East India Company, the Hundred Weight	0 3 8	0 0 0

Item	£	s	d	£	s	d
Contrayervæ, the Ounce	0	0	6	0	0	9
— imported by the East India Company, the Ounce	0	0	6	0	0	9
Hæmatitis, the Pound	0	0	1½	0	0	2
Hibernicus, the Hundred Weight	0	4	0	0	6	4
Hyacinthi, the Pound	0	0	2	0	0	6
Judaicus, the Pound	0	0	4	0	0	3
Lazuli, the Pound	0	0	4	0	0	6
— imported by the East India Company, the Pound	0	0	4	0	0	6
Magnetis, the Pound	0	0	2	0	0	3
Nephriticus, the Pound	0	0	4	0	0	6
Oftiocolla, the Pound	0	0	1½	0	0	2
Rubinus, the Pound	0	0	2	0	0	3
Sapphirus, the Pound	0	0	2	0	0	3
Smaragdus, the Pound	0	0	2	0	0	3
Spongiæ, the Pound	0	0	2	0	0	3
Topazi, the Pound	0	0	2	0	0	3
Tutiæ, the Pound	0	0	2	0	0	3
— imported by the East India Company, the Pound	0	0	2	0	0	3
Lavender-Flowers, the Pound	0	0	2¼	0	0	4
Leaves of Roses, the Pound	0	0	2	0	0	3
— of Violets or Flowers, the Pound	0	0	1½	0	0	2
Lentiles, the Pound	0	0	0½	0	0	0½

(110)

TABLE A.

INWARDS.

	Duty. £ s. d.	Drawback. £ s. d.
Drugs, Lignum-Aloes, the Pound	0 0 6	0 0 4
Afpalthum, the Pound	0 0 2	0 0 1½
imported by the East India Company, the Pound	0 0 2	0 0 1½
Nephriticum, the Pound	0 0 6	0 0 4
Rhodium, the Hundred Weight	0 7 0	0 4 8
Litharge of Gold, the Hundred Weight	0 0 10	0 0 7
of Silver, the Hundred Weight	0 0 8	0 0 5½
Lupines, the Hundred Weight	0 2 4	0 1 7
Lyntificus or Xylobalfamum, the Pound	0 0 3	0 0 2
Madder-Roots, the Hundred Weight	0 4 8	0 0 0
By the 8 Geo. I. Chap. 15. Sect. 10. Madder-Roots may be legally imported free of Duty, if regularly entered and landed.		
Manna, the Pound	0 0 6	0 0 4
imported by the East India Company, the Pound	0 0 6	0 0 4
Marmelade, the Pound	0 0 3	0 0 2
Maftich Red, the Pound	0 0 3	0 0 2
if not imported directly from the Place of its Growth, the Pound	0 0 9	0 0 6

(111)

	£	s	d
imported by the East India Company, the Pound	0	0	3
White, the Pound	0	0	6
if not imported directly from the Place of its Growth, the Pound	0	1	0
imported by the East India Company, the Pound	0	0	6
Mechoacana, the Pound	0	0	6
Mercury-Precipitat, the Pound	0	0	9
Sublimat, the Pound	0	0	9
Millium-Solis, the Pound	0	0	2
Mirobolanes-Condited, the Pound	0	0	2
if not imported directly from the Place of its Growth, the Pound	0	0	6
if imported by the East India Company, the Pound	0	0	2
Dry, the Pound	0	0	1
if not imported directly from the Place of its Growth, the Pound	0	0	3
imported by the East India Company, the Pound	0	0	1
Mithridate Venetiæ, the Pound	0	1	6
Mother of Pearl Shells rough, the Pound	0	0	4
imported by the East India Company, the Pound	0	0	4

	£	s	d
	0	0	2
	0	0	4
	0	0	0
	0	0	4
	0	0	4
	0	0	6
	0	0	6
	0	0	$1\frac{1}{2}$
	0	0	$1\frac{1}{2}$
	0	0	4
	0	0	$1\frac{1}{2}$
	0	0	$0\frac{1}{4}$
	0	0	2
	0	1	$0\frac{1}{2}$
	0	0	$0\frac{1}{2}$
	0	0	$2\frac{1}{4}$
	0	0	$2\frac{1}{4}$

(112)

TABLE A.

INWARDS.

	Duty. £. s. d.	Drawback. £. s. d.
Drugs, Musk, the Ounce Troy -	0 2 0	0 1 4
imported by the East India Company, the Ounce Troy	0 2 0	0 1 4
Myrrha, the Pound -	0 0 6	0 0 4
if not imported directly from the Place of its Growth, the Pound	0 1 6	0 1 0
imported by the East India Company, the Pound	0 0 6	0 0 4
Myrtle-Berries, the Pound -	0 0 2	0 0 1½
Nardus-Celtica, or Spica Romana, the Hundred Weight	0 9 4	0 6 2
Nitrum, the Pound -	0 0 5	0 0 3½
Nutmegs Condited, the Pound,	0 0 10	0 0 7
imported by the East India Company, the Pound	0 0 10	0 0 7
Nux de Ben, the Pound	0 0 2	0 0 1½
Cupressi, the Pound	0 0 2	0 0 1½
Indica, each	0 0 1	0 0 0¾
Vomica, the Pound	0 0 1½	0 0 1
Oil of Almonds, the Pound	0 0 3	0 0 2
of Amber, the Pound	0 0 6	0 0 4
Oleum-Anisi, the Pound	0 1 6	0 1 0

Oil of Bay, the Hundred Weight	—	—	0	0	5	10
Oleum-Cariophyllorum, the Pound	—	—	0	0	1	8
By the 19 Geo. III. Chap. 48. Oleum-Cariophyllorum, Oleum Cinnamoni, Oil of Mace, and Oleum Nucis Muscatæ Liquidum, may be imported from Places not of the Growth.						
Oleum-Carui, the Pound	—	—	0	0	0	4
Cinnamomi, the Ounce Troy	—	—	0	1	0	0
Juniperi, the Pound	—	—	0	0	0	4
Oil of Mace, the Pound	—	—	0	0	0	11
Oleum Nucis Muscatæ Liquidum, the Pound	—	—	0	1	0	4
Origani, the Pound	—	—	0	0	0	10
Palmæ, the Hundred Weight	—	—	0	0	4	8
Petroleum, the Pound	—	—	0	0	0	2
Oleum Rhodii, the Pound	—	—	0	0	3	4
Oil of Rosemary, the Pound	—	—	0	0	0	6
Oleum Sassafras, the Pound	—	—	0	0	0	8
Oil of Spike, the Pound	—	—	0	0	0	$2\frac{3}{4}$
Oleum Thymæ, the Pound	—	—	0	0	0	10
Oil of Turpentine, the Pound	—	—	0	0	0	$0\frac{1}{4}$
Oleum Vitrioli, the Pound	—	—	0	0	0	$0\frac{1}{4}$
Oil, viz. Chemical Oils not otherwise enumerated, the Pound	—	—	0	0	0	5

(114)

TABLE A.

INWARDS.

	Duty £. s. d.	Drawback £. s. d.
Drugs, Oil, viz. Orange, Jessamine, and Perfumed Oils, not otherwise enumerated, the Pound	0 1 6	0 1 0
Olibanum or Incense, the Hundred Weight if not imported directly from the Place of its Growth, the Hundred Weight	1 1 0	0 14 0
imported by the East India Company, the Hundred Weight	3 3 0	2 2 0
Opium, the Pound	1 1 0	0 14 0
if not imported directly from the Place of its Growth, the Pound	0 1 6	0 1 0
imported by the East India Company, the Pound	0 4 6	0 3 0
Orange Flower Ointment, the Pound	0 1 6	0 1 0
Water, the Gallon	0 0 6	0 0 4
Origanum, the Pound	0 1 0	0 0 8
Orpiment or Auripigmentum, the Hundred Weight	0 0 1½	0 0 1
imported by the East India Company, the Hundred Weight	0 8 9	0 5 10
Pearl beaten, the Ounce Troy	0 8 9	0 5 10
Pellitory, the Pound	0 0 6	0 0 4
Pepper Long, the Pound	0 0 1	0 0 0¾
	0 0 2½	0 0 1½

(115)

	£	s	d
Piony Seeds, imported by the East India Company, the Pound	0	0	$1\frac{1}{2}$
——— the Pound	0	0	1
Pistachias or Nux Pistachiæ, the Pound	0	0	2
——— if not imported directly from the Place of its Growth, the Pound			
Pix Burgundiæ, the Hundred Weight	0	6	9
Polypodium, the Pound	0	6	4
Folium Montanum, the Pound	0	0	1
Pomegranate Peels, the Hundred Weight	0	4	$1\frac{1}{2}$
Pompholix, the Pound	0	0	8
Poppy Seeds, the Pound	0	0	1
Prunelloes, the Pound	0	0	$1\frac{1}{2}$
Psyllium, the Pound	0	0	3
Radix Bistortæ, the Hundred Weight	0	4	$1\frac{1}{2}$
Castiminar, the Pound	0	0	8
Radix Contrayervæ, the Pound	0	0	4
——— imported by the East India Company, the Pound	0	0	6
Enulæ Campanæ, the Hundred Weight	0	6	4
Fringii, the Pound	0	0	$1\frac{1}{2}$
Esulæ, the Pound	0	0	$2\frac{1}{2}$
Hypocacuana, the Pound	0	1	8

	0	0	$1\frac{1}{2}$	0	0	$1\frac{1}{2}$
	0	0	1	0	0	1
	0	0	2	0	0	2
	0	0	6			
	0	4	2	0	4	$0\frac{3}{4}$
	0	0	1	0	0	$0\frac{1}{4}$
	0	0	1	0	0	2
	0	0	1	0	0	2
	0	0	$2\frac{3}{4}$			
	0	3	4			
	0	0	4	0	4	2
	0	0	1	0	1	$1\frac{1}{2}$

(116)

TABLE A.

INWARDS.

Drugs,	Duty. £. s. d.	Drawback. £. s. d.
Radix Mei Athamantici, the Pound	0 0 1½	0 0 1
Phu, the Pound	0 0 1½	0 0 1
Scorcionera, the Pound	0 0 3	0 0 2
Seneca, the Pound	0 0 2	0 0 1½
Serpentariæ, the Pound	0 0 9	0 0 6
Tormentillæ, the Hundred Weight	0 3 2	0 2 1
Red Lead, the Hundred Weight	0 3 8	0 2 5
Retina Jalapii, the Pound	0 3 2	0 2 1
Scammonii, the Pound	0 3 2	0 2 1
Rhabarbarum or Rhubarb, the Pound	0 1 6	0 1 0
imported by the East India Company, the Pound	0 1 6	0 1 0
Rhinehurst, the Hundred Weight	0 6 4	0 4 2
Rofalgar. See Arsenic.		
Saccharum Saturni, the Pound	0 0 3	0 0 2
Saffron, the Pound	0 2 6	0 1 8
Sago, the Pound	0 0 3	0 0 2
imported by the East India Company, the Pound	0 0 3	0 0 2
Sal Alkali, the Pound	0 0 6	0 0 4

(117)

	£	s	d	£	s	d
Ammoniacum, the Hundred Weight	0	4	8	0	0	0
By the 8 Geo. I. Chap. 15. Sect. 10. Sal Ammoniacum may be legally imported free of Duty, if regularly entered and landed.						
Gem, the Hundred Weight	0	4	8	0	0	0
By the 8 Geo. I. Chap. 15. Sect. 10. Sal Gem may be legally imported free of Duty, if regularly entered and landed.						
Prunellæ, the Pound	0	0	2	0	0	1½
Succini, the Pound	0	1	2	0	0	9
Tamarisci, the Pound	0	1	2	0	0	9
Tartari, the Pound	0	0	3	0	0	2
Vitrioli, the Pound	0	0	3	0	0	2
Volatile Ammoniaci, the Pound	0	0	6	0	0	4
Volatile Cornu Cervi, the Pound	0	0	6	0	0	4
Salep, the Pound	0	0	3	0	0	2
if not imported directly from the Place of its Growth, the Pound	0	0	9	0	0	6
Sandracha. See Gum Sandrake.						
Sanguis Draconis, the Pound	0	0	8	0	0	5½
if not imported directly from the Place of its Growth, the Pound	0	2	0	1	0	4
imported by the East India Company, the Pound	0	0	8	0	0	5½

TABLE A.

INWARDS.

	Duty £.	s.	d.	Drawback £.	s.	d.
Drugs,						
Sanguis Hirci, the Pound - - - -	0	0	2	0	0	1½
Sarsaparilla, the Pound - - - -	0	0	8	0	0	5½
Sassafras Wood or Roots, the Hundred Weight - -	0	2	4	0	1	7
Saunders Red, the Hundred Weight - - -	0	4	8	0	0	0
By the 8 Geo. I. Chap. 15. Sect. 10. Red Wood may be legally imported free of Duty, if regularly entered and landed; and Red Saunders is called Red Wood.						
Saunders White, the Pound - - - -	0	0	3	0	0	2
Yellow, the Pound - - - - -	0	0	3	0	0	2
imported by the East India Company, the Pound	0	0	3	0	0	2
Scammony. See Diagredium.				0	0	0¾
Scincus Marinus, each - - - -	0	0	1	0	0	0¾
Scordium, the Pound - - - - - -	0	0	1	0	0	0¾
Sebestines, the Pound - - - -	0	0	2	0	0	1½
Seeds for Gardens, the Pound - - - -	0	0	1½	0	0	1
Seler Montanus, the Pound - - - -	0	0	1½	0	0	1
Semen Cucumeris, Cucurb, Citrol, Melon, the Pound - -	0	0	1½	0	0	1
Sena, the Pound - - - - -	0	0	6	0	0	4

if not imported directly from the Place of its Growth, the Pound - - - 0 1 6 0 1 0

imported by the East India Company, the Pound - - 0 0 6 0 0 0

Sperma Cœti, coarse and oily, the Hundred Weight - 0 17 8 0 11 9

The 26 Geo. III. Chap. 41. Sect. 14 and 15. permits to be imported into Great Britain free of Duty, until the 25th December 1791, any Produce of Seals, or other Fish or Creatures taken or caught in the Greenland Seas or Davis's Streights, or in the Seas adjacent, by British Subjects usually residing in Great Britain, Ireland, Guernsey, Jersey, or Man, in British built Ships owned as above, upon Oath by the Master and Mate of the Ship importing the same, that the said Produce was caught as aforesaid. The Greenland Seas and Davis's Streights deemed and taken to extend to the Latitude of 59 Degrees 30 Minutes North, and no further. The 26 Geo. III. Chap. 50. Sect. 2, 5, 9, and 23, permits to be imported into Great Britain without Payment of any Duty whatever, all Oil, Head Matter, or other Produce of Fish or Creatures living in the Seas, caught and taken in any Part of the Ocean by the Crew of any Ship built in Great Britain, Ireland, Guernsey, Jersey, or Man, wholly owned by British Subjects usually residing therein respectively, navigated and cleared out as required by this Act, from one of

(120)

TABLE A.

INWARDS.

	Duty. £ s. d.	Drawback. £ s. d.
Drugs, the above Places, and upon Oath by the Master, Mate, and Two of the Mariners of the Ship importing the same, that the said Articles are the Produce of one or more Whales or Creatures living in the Seas, actually taken and killed by the Crew of such Ship only, at the Times and in the Latitudes respectively set down in the Log Book.		
Sperma Cœti fine, the Pound - - -	0 0 8	0 0 5½
Spikenard, the Pound - - -	0 1 4	0 0 11
imported by the East India Company, the Pound	0 1 4	0 0 11
Spiritus Cornu Cervi, the Pound - -	0 0 8	0 0 5½
Vitrioli, the Pound - - -	0 0 1	0 0 0¼
Sponge, the Pound - - -	0 0 9	0 0 6
if not imported directly from the Place of its Growth, the Pound - - - -	0 2 3	0 1 6
Squilla, the Hundred Weight - -	0 2 6	0 1 8
imported by the East India Company, the Hundred Weight	0 2 6	0 1 8
Squinanthum, the Pound - - -	0 0 4	0 0 2¼

(121)

		£	s	d	£	s	d
Stavesacre, if not imported directly from the Place of its Growth, the Pound	-	0	0	0	0	1	8
Stechados, the Hundred Weight	-	0	0	0	1	8	10
Storax Calamita, the Pound	-	0	0	0	0	0	1½
if not imported directly from the Place of its Growth, the Pound	-	0	0	0	0	0	6
Storax Liquida, the Pound	-	0	0	0	0	2	6
imported by the East India Company, the Pound	-	0	0	0	0	3	6
if not imported directly from the Place of its Growth, the Pound	-	0	0	0	0	0	2¾
Succus Liquoritiæ, the Hundred Weight	-	0	0	0	1	8	8
Sulphur Vivum, the Hundred Weight	-	0	0	0	0	8	8
Talc Green, the Pound	-	0	0	0	0	0	0
White, the Pound	-	0	0	0	0	4	5
Tamarinds, the Pound	-	0	0	0	0	0	1½
imported by the East India Company, the Pound	-	0	0	0	0	0	1½
Tapioca, the Pound	-	0	0	0	0	0	1½
Tartarum Vitriolatum, the Pound	-	0	0	0	0	0	1½
Terra Japanica, the Pound	-	0	0	0	0	3	2
Lemnia, the Pound	-	0	0	0	0	4	2¼
Sigillata, the Pound	-	0	0	0	0	6	4
		0	0	0	0	6	4

TABLE A.

INWARDS.

	Duty. £. s. d.	Drawback. £. s. d.
Drugs,		
Thlaspii Semen, the Pound	0 0 2	0 0 1½
Tornsal, the Hundred Weight	0 4 8	0 0 0
Treacle common, the Pound	0 0 4	0 0 2¼
of Venice, the Pound	0 1 6	0 1 0
Turbith, the Pound	0 1 0	0 0 8
if not imported directly from the Place of its Growth, the Pound		
imported by the East India Company, the Pound	0 3 0	0 2 0
Turbith Thapsiæ, the Pound	0 1 0	0 0 8.
Turmeric, the Pound	0 0 5	0 0 3½
imported by the East India Company, the Pound	0 0 2	0 0 1¼
Turpentine common, the Hundred Weight	0 0 2	0 0 1½
of Venice, Scio, or Cyprus, the Pound	0 2 3	0 1 6
of Germany or of any other Place not otherwise enumerated, the Hundred Weight	0 0 4	0 0 2¼
Varnish, the Hundred Weight	0 12 9	0 8 6
Verdigrease common, the Pound	0 8 9	0 5 10
crystallized, the Pound	0 0 3	0 0 0
	0 1 0	0 0 0

(123)

Item	£	s	d
Viſcus Quercinus, the Pound	0	0	7
Vitriolum Romanum, the Pound	0	0	1½
— if not imported directly from the Place of its Growth, the Pound			
Umber, the Hundred Weight	0	0	4
Ungulæ Alcis, the 100 Hoofs	0	2	11
White Lead, the Hundred Weight	0	2	2
— imported by the Eaſt India Company, the Hundred Weight	0	2	11
Worm Seeds, the Pound	0	2	11
— if not imported directly from the Place of its Growth, the Pound	0	0	4
— imported by the Eaſt India Company, the Pound	0	1	0
Zedoaria, the Pound	0	0	4
— if not imported directly from the Place of its Growth, the Pound	0	0	4
— imported by the Eaſt India Company, the Pound	0	1	0
	0	0	4

Many of the Drugs enumerated by the 27 Geo. III. Chap. 13, being at this Time little in Uſe, or ſcarcely ever imported, a Liſt of thoſe of that Deſcription is inſerted after Table L, the Engliſh Name where it could be obtained, and an Account of

(124)

TABLE A.

INWARDS.

what Quarter of the Globe they are produced in, with the View of cautioning the Merchant against an illegal Importation.

	Duty. £. s. d.	Drawback. £. s. d.
Earthen Ware, viz.		
Flanders Tiles to scour with, the Thousand	0 12 2	0 11 2
Galley Tiles, the Foot square	0 0 3	0 0 2½
Paving Tiles not exceeding ten Inches square, the Thousand	1 9 9	1 8 3
Tiles exceeding ten Inches square, the Thousand	2 6 3	2 4 9
Pan Tiles, the Thousand	2 12 10	2 8 10
Eels, viz. Quick Eels, the Ship's Lading	4 13 6	3 18 6
Eggs, the Hundred containing six Score	0 0 5	0 0 4
Elephants Teeth, the Hundred Weight	1 6 5	1 4 5
imported by the East India Company, the Hundred Weight	1 10 10	1 8 10
Elks Hair, the Hundred Weight	0 8 3	0 7 6
Emeralds, and all other precious Stones and Jewels, Duty free.		
Emery Stones, the Hundred Weight	0 1 10	0 1 7
of Turkey, imported in a Foreign Ship, the Hundred Weight	0 1 11	0 1 7
Enamel, the Pound	0 3 4	0 1 6
Essence of Lemons, the Pound	0 2 0	0 1 4

(125)

Estridge Wool, imported in a British built Ship, Duty free.						
imported in a Foreign Ship, the Hundred Weight	—	0	7	9	0	7	0
Feathers, viz.							
Feathers for Beds, the Hundred Weight	—	1	6	5	1	3	5
of Muscovy or Russia imported in a Foreign Ship, the Hundred Weight	—	1	8	1	1	3	5
Ostrich or Estridge Feathers dressed, the Pound	—	0	8	10	0	7	10
undressed, the Pound	—	0	4	5	0	3	11
N. B. One third Part allowed for Quills of undressed.							
Figs, imported in a British built Ship, the Hundred Weight	—	0	12	10	0	12	0
imported in a Foreign Ship, the Hundred Weight	—	0	13	4	0	12	0
Fish, viz.							
Anchovies, the Barrel containing 16 Pounds of Fish	—	0	2	1	0	1	10
Eels, viz. Quick Eels, the Ship's Lading	—	4	13	6	3	18	6
Oysters, the Bushel	—	0	0	6	0	0	0
Stock-Fish, the 120	—	0	2	1	0	1	4
Sturgeon, the Keg	—	0	3	4	0	2	11
Fish caught and taken by British Subjects.							

See the Abstract of the 27 Geo. III. Chap. 13, preceding Table A, which includes all the Regulations of that Act called the Consolidation Act, respecting the Duties of Customs and Excise; and for

(126)

TABLE A.

INWARDS.

	Duty. £. s. d.	Drawback. £. s. d.
the particular Exemption from Duty of Fresh Fish caught by British Subjects, see Section 32 there explained fully.		
Lobsters and Turbots may be imported freely by any Persons whatever, in any Ships whatever.		
Flannel, the Yard	0 0 7	0 0 6
Flax, viz.		
dressed, imported in a British built Ship, the Hundred Weight	5 4 6	4 17 0
dressed, imported in a Foreign Ship, the Hundred Weight	5 8 8	4 17 0
rough or undressed, imported in a British built Ship, the Hundred Weight	0 4 10	0 4 7
imported in a Foreign Ship, the Hundred Weight	0 5 1	0 4 7

By the 7 and 8 William III. Chap. 39, any Sorts of Hemp or Flax, and all the Production thereof, as Thread, Yarn, and Linen, of the Growth and Manufacture of Ireland, may be imported directly from thence into England free of Duty, by the Natives of England or Ireland; the Master or chief Officer of the Vessel importing the same, bringing with him Certificates from the chief Officer or Officers of the Port in Ireland where such Goods are laden, expressing the Marks, Number, Tale, or Weight of the Species in each

Bale or Parcel mentioned in the Bills of Lading, with the Names and Places of Abode of the Exporters from Ireland, the Names and Places of Abode of the Persons that shall have sworn the Goods thereinmentioned to be of the Growth and Manufacture of the Kingdom, where and to whom consigned in England; and also the Master or chief Officer of the said Ship, on arrival in England, making Oath that the said Bales, Parcels, and Goods therein contained, are the said Bales, Parcels, and Goods taken on board by virtue of those Certificates.

By the 4 Geo. II. Chap. 27, rough or undressed Flax may be legally imported into Great Britain free of Duty, if regularly entered and landed, otherwise to be subject to the Duties.

By the 16 Geo. II. Chap. 26. Sect. 6. the Oath of the Exporter or other Person swearing such Goods were of the Growth of Ireland is dispensed with, provided the other Requisites of the 7 and 8 William III. Chap. 39, are pursued.

Flint Stones for Potters, the Ton containing 20 Hundred Weight	-	0	1	0	0	0	0
Flocks, the Hundred Weight	-	0	8	10	0	7	10
Frize of Ireland, the Yard	-	0	0	6	0	0	5
Furriers Waste fit only for making Glue, the Hundred Weight	-	0	5	0	0	0	0

TABLE A.

INWARDS.

	Duty. £ s. d.	Drawback. £ s. d.
Garnets, viz.		
rough, the Pound —	0 4 5	0 3 11
imported by the East India Company, the Pound	0 5 6	0 5 0
cut, the Pound —	0 13 3	0 11 9
imported by the East India Company, the Pound	1 9 9	1 8 3
Galls, the Hundred Weight	0 4 5	0 0 0
By the 8 Geo. I. Chap. 15. Sect. 10. Galls may be legally imported free of Duty, if regularly entered and landed.		
Geneva, the Gallon —	0 0 9	0 0 8
Ginger, of the British Plantations, the Hundred Weight	0 11 0	0 10 6
not of the British Plantations, the Hundred Weight	1 8 0	1 6 0
Green, the Pound —	0 0 6	0 0 4
imported by the East India Company, the Pound	0 0 6	0 0 4
N. B. Green Ginger, is Ginger preserved in Syrup.		
Glass, viz. Beads. See Bugle.		
Bottles. See Bottles.		
Broken, fit only to be re-manufactured, the Hundred Weight	0 1 3	0 1 0
Glovers Clippings, fit only to make Glue, the Hundred Weight	0 1 4½	0 1 3
Glue, the Hundred Weight —	0 4 5	0 3 11

(129)

Goats Hair, viz.						
Carmenia Wool, the Pound	–	–	–	–	0	0
imported by the East India Company, the Pound	0	0	8	0	0	7
By the 24 Geo. III. Sess. 2. Chap. 21. Sect. 6. any Duties whatever payable upon any Goats Hair or Turkey Goats Wool, imported into Great Britain, to cease and determine from the 20th August 1784.	0	0	9	0	0	8
Grain or Scarlet Powder, the Pound	–	–	–	–	–	–
of Seville in Berries, and Grains of Portugal or Rotta, the Pound	0	0	9	0	0	7
Grains, viz. Guincy Grains, the Pound	0	0	4½	0	0	3½
Graves, for Dogs, the Hundred Weight	0	0	2	0	0	1½
K Grease.	0	0	11	0	0	10
By the 7 Geo. III. Chap. 12. Grease may be legally imported from any Place into this Kingdom free of Duty, if duly entered and landed; continued by 26 Geo. III. Chap. 53. and 29 Geo. III. Chap. 55. to 25th March 1791, or at any Time thereafter before the End of the then next Session of Parliament.						
Greenland Seas.						
See the Notes following Blubber.						
Grogram Yarn, the Pound	–	0	0	8	0	0	7
Guernsey.						
See the Note after Alderney.						

(130)

TABLE A.

INWARDS.

	Duty.			Drawback.		
	£.	s.	d.	£.	s.	d.
Guiney Grains, the Pound —	0	0	2	0	0	1½
Gunpowder, viz. Corn Powder, the Hundred Weight	1	15	3	1	11	3
Serpentine Powder, the Hundred Weight —	1	2	0	0	19	6
Hair Powder, the Hundred Weight —	5	5	8	0	0	0
By 3 Geo. I. Chap. 4. and 20 Geo. III. Chap. 52. it is denominated Hair Powder made of Starch, or other Powder that will ferve for the fame Ufes as Starch; to be imported in Packages containing 224 lb. each, net Weight, otherwife forfeited.						
Hams are confidered to be Bacon.						
Handbafkets, the Dozen —	0	0	9	0	0	8
Hare's Wool, the Pound —	0	0	1	0	0	0
Harp Strings, the Grofs containing twelve Dozen Knots —	0	2	6	0	0	2
Hats, viz.						
Baft or Straw Hats or Bonnets, each Hat or Bonnet not exceeding 22 Inches in Diameter, the Dozen -	0	2	9	0	2	6
each Hat or Bonnet exceeding 22 Inches in Diameter, the Dozen -	0	5	6	0	5	0

(131)

	£	s.	d.	£	s.	d.
Chip, Cane, or Horse-hair Hats or Bonnets, each Hat or Bonnet not exceeding 22 Inches Diameter, the Dozen	0	3	6	0	3	1½
Chip, Cane, or Horse-hair Hats or Bonnets, each Hat or Bonnet exceeding 22 Inches in Diameter, the Dozen	0	7	0	0	6	3
By 10 Geo. III. Chap. 43. Sect. 6. to be imported into London only, in Bales or Tubs containing each 75 Dozen Hats or Bonnets, and in Ships exceeding 50 Tons Burthen, otherwise forfeited.						
Hay, the Load containing 36 Trusses, each Truss being 56 Pounds made of, or mixed with, Felt, Hair, Wool, or Beaver, the Hat	2	4	0	1	19	0
Head Matter; under what Circumstances it may be imported free of Duty, see the Notes following Blubber.	0	11	0	0	10	0
Heath for Brushes, the Hundred Weight	0	4	5	0	3	11
Hemp, viz.						
dressed, imported in a British built Ship, the Hundred Weight	2	4	0	1	19	0
imported in a Foreign Ship, the Hundred Weight	2	6	9	1	19	0
rough or undressed, imported in a British built Ship, the Hundred Weight	0	3	8	0	3	4
imported in a Foreign Ship, the Hundred Weight	0	3	11	0	3	4
By the 7 and 8 William III. Chap. 39, any Sorts of Hemp or Flax, and all the Production thereof, as Thread, Yarn, and Linen, of the Growth and Manufacture of Ireland, may be imported di-						

K 2

TABLE A.

INWARDS.

rectly from thence into England free of Duty; which see fully explained by the Note following Flax.

By the 8 Geo. I. Chap. 12. Hemp of the Produce of the British Plantations in America may be lawfully imported into this Kingdom free of Duty, after the 24th June 1722.

Hides, viz.

	Duty. £. s. d.	Drawback. £. s. d.
Cow or Ox Hides in the Hair, the Piece -	0 0 9	0 0 8
By the 9 Geo. III. Chap. 39. raw or undressed Hides of any Cattle whatsoever (except of Horses, Mares, or Geldings), Calves Skins or Goats Skins, raw or undressed, from Ireland or the British Colonies or Plantations in America, may be imported free of Duty, if regularly entered and landed, otherwise subject to Duty; continued by the 21 Geo. III. Chap. 29. and 27 Geo. III. Chap. 36. until 1st June 1791, and to the End of the then next Session of Parliament.		
Cow or Ox Hides, tanned, the Pound - - -	0 0 5	0 0 8
of Horses, Mares, or Geldings, in the Hair, the Piece -	0 0 9	0 0 0
tanned, the Pound -	0 0 5½	0 0 0
Indian Hides undressed, the Piece - - -	0 1 2	0 1 0½

(133)

		£ s. d.	£ s. d.
Lofh Hides, the Pound	-	0 0 0 10	0 0 0
Mufcovy or Ruffia Hides tanned, the Pound	-	0 0 0 8	0 0 0
Hones, the Hundred containing 5 Score	-	0 0 11 0	0 0 10
Honey, the Barrel containing 42 Gallons	-	0 8 10 0	0 7 10
N.B. Twelve Pounds Avoirdupois Weight allowed to be a Gallon of Honey.			
Hoops of Iron for Cafks, the Hundred Weight of Wood for Coopers, the Thoufand	-	0 11 5	0 0 0
Hops, the Hundred Weight	-	0 5 11	0 5 3
Horns of Cows or Oxen, the Hundred containing 5 Score	-	5 18 10	0 4 4
of Harts or Stags. See Drugs.		0 1 10	0 1 8
Horn-Tips, the Hundred, containing 5 Score	-	0 0 7	0 0 6
Horfe Hair, the Pound	-	0 0 9	0 0 8
Horfes, Mares, or Geldings, the Horfe, Mare, or Gelding	-	2 4 0	1 19 0
By the 5 Geo. III. Chap. 10. and 16 Geo. III. Chap. 8. all Sorts of Cattle are allowed to be imported from Ireland into Great Britain free of Duty.			
Human Hair, the Pound	-	0 2 0	0 0 7
Hungary Water, the Gallon	-	0 2 10	0 2 0

Jerfey, Ifland of.
See the Note after Alderney.

K 3

(134)

TABLE A.

INWARDS.

	Duty.			Drawback.		
	£.	s.	d.	£.	s.	d.
Jet, the Pound - - - - - -	0	0	9	0	0	8
Beads, the Pound - - - -	0	1	5	0	1	3
Jewels, free of Duty.						
Incle unwrought or Short Spinnel, the Pound	0	0	3½	0	0	0
wrought, the Dozen Pound -	0	9	4	1	5	4
Indian Corn. See Corn.						
Indigo, the Pound - - - -	0	0	6	0	0	0
By the 8 Geo. I. Chap. 15. Sect. 10. Indigo may be legally imported free of Duty, if regularly entered and landed.						
Ink for Printers, the Hundred Weight - -	0	8	10	0	7	10
Irish Wool, combed or uncombed, free of Duty.						
Iron, viz.						
in Bars or unwrought, of Ireland, the Ton -	1	10	10	1	7	4
of Muscovy or Russia, imported in a British built Ship, the Ton -	2	16	2	2	12	8
of Muscovy or Russia, imported in a Foreign Ship, the Ton -	3	9	1	2	12	8
not of Ireland or of Muscovy or Russia, imported in a British built Ship, the Ton -	2	16	2	2	12	8

not of Ireland or of Muscovy or Russia, imported in a Foreign Ship, the Ton	-	3	7	2	2	12	8
of Ireland, slit or hammered into Rods, the Hundred Weight	-	0	4	5	0	3	11
drawn or hammered less than ¼ of an Inch square, the Hundred Weight	-	0	9	11	0	9	5
of Muscovy or Russia, slit or hammered into Rods, and Iron drawn or hammered less than ¾ of an Inch square, imported in a British built Ship, the Hundred Weight	-	0	9	11	0	9	5
slit or hammered into Rods, and Iron drawn or hammered less than ¾ of an Inch square, imported in a Foreign Ship, the Hundred Weight	-	0	10	3	0	9	5
of any other Country, slit or hammered into Rods, and Iron drawn or hammered less than ¾ of an Inch square, the Hundred Weight	-	0	9	11	0	9	5
Hoops for Casks, the Hundred Weight	-	0	11	5	0	0	0
Ore, the Ton	-	0	2	9	0	2	6
Old broken and old cast Iron, the Ton	-	0	13	9	0	12	6
Pig Iron from the British Plantations, the Ton	-	0	5	6	0	5	0
Wire, the Hundred Weight	-	2	17	9	2	14	0

By the 23 Geo. II. Chap. 29. and 30 Geo. II. Chap. 16. Bar and Pig Iron are allowed to be imported into Great Britain from his

TABLE A.

INWARDS.

His Majesty's Colonies in America free of Duty, if accompanied by a Certificate from the Governor, Lieutenant-Governor, Collector, or Comptroller of the Customs, Naval Officer, or any Two of them, and being stamped with a Mark, denoting the Place or Colony where made; and Oath being made by the Master or commanding Officer of the Ship importing the same, that it is the Iron mentioned in the Certificate, otherwise to be subject to Duty.

	Duty. £. s. d.	Drawback. £. s. d.
Isinglass, the Pound	0 0 0½0	0 0 0
Juice of Lemons, the Tun containing 252 Gallons	3 10 5	3 6 5
Limes, the Gallon	0 0 3	0 0 2½
Juniper Berries, the Hundred Weight	0 4 5	0 3 3
Ivory, the Pound	0 2 3	0 2 0
Kelp, the Ton	0 16 6	0 15 0
Lace, viz.		
Bone Lace of Thread, the Dozen Yards	0 17 8	0 15 8
Lambs Wool, Duty free.		
Lamp Black, the Hundred Weight	1 15 3	1 13 3

(137)

Lard, the Pound	-	0	0	1	0	0	0
By the 7 Geo. III. Chap. 12. Hogs Lard may be legally imported from any Place into this Kingdom free of Duty, if duly entered and landed; continued by the 26 Geo. III. Chap. 53. and 29 Geo. III. Chap. 55. to 25th March 1791, or at any Time thereafter before the End of the then next Session of Parliament.							
Latten, viz.							
Black, the Hundred Weight	-	0	13	3	0	12	3
Shaven, the Hundred Weight	-	1	2	0	1	0	4
Wire, the Hundred Weight	-	2	13	0	2	9	8
Lawns. See Linen.							
Lead Ore, the Ton	-	0	17	8	0	15	8
Black, the Hundred Weight	-	0	6	8	0	4	5
Red, the Hundred Weight	-	0	3	8	0	2	5
White, the Hundred Weight	-	0	4	5	0	2	11
imported by the East India Company, the Hundred Weight	-	0	4	5	0	2	11
Leaves of Gold, the 100 Leaves	-	0	1	2	0	1	0
Lemons, the Thousand	-	0	4	5	0	3	11
Juice of, the Tun containing 252 Gallons	-	3	10	5	3	6	5
pickled, the Tun containing 252 Gallons	-	1	15	3	1	13	3
Lime Juice, the Gallon	-	0	0	3	0	0	2½

TABLE A.

INWARDS.

	Duty. £ s. d.	Drawback. £ s. d.
Linen, viz.		
Alexandria or Turkey plain, not exceeding one Yard in Width, the Ell	0 0 7	0 0 6
exceeding one Yard in Width, the Ell	0 0 10	0 0 9
Calicos, viz.		
plain White Calicos imported by the East India Company, the Piece	0 5 3	0 5 0
N.B. No Piece of Calico of the Breadth of one Yard and one Quarter, or under, shall exceed in Length ten Yards; and no Piece of Calico above that Breadth shall exceed six Yards; and if any Piece of Calico shall exceed those Lengths, the same shall be charged according to the respective Lengths of ten Yards and six Yards for each Piece, and shall pay Duty for the same in that Proportion for any greater or lesser Quantity. See 4 and 5 William and Mary, Chap. 5. Sect. 11.		
Calicos, and besides, for every £.100 of the true and real Value of such Goods according to the gross Price at which the same shall be publicly sold at the Sales of the United Company of Merchants of England trading to the East Indies	16 10 0	0 0 0
The Drawback of the last mentioned further Duty of £.16:10s.		

to be allowed on the Exportation of such Goods, shall be for every £.100 of the true and real Value thereof, according to the gross Price at which such Goods shall have been publicly sold at the Sales of the United Company of Merchants of England trading to the East Indies, viz.

	£	s.	d.
Calicos, if exported to Africa	16	10	0
if exported to the British Colonies or Plantations in America	11	15	0
if exported to any Parts or Places beyond the Seas (except to the British Colonies or Plantations in America), if the said Goods shall have been printed, stained, painted, or dyed in this Kingdom	16	10	0
if exported to any Parts or Places beyond the Seas (except to Africa or the British Colonies or Plantations in America), if the said Goods shall be exported from this Kingdom without having been printed, stained, painted, or dyed therein	14	10	0

Bricks and French Lawns to be secured in Warehouses for Exportation, the Half Piece, containing 6½ Ells — 0 0 6

2 Geo. II. Chap. 32. and 7 Geo. III. Chap. 43. Cambrics and French Lawns may, by Licence of the Commissioners of the Customs, be imported in Bales, Cases, or Boxes, co-

TABLE A.

	Duty. £. s. d.	Drawback. £. s. d.
INWARDS.		
vered with Sack Cloth or Canvas, each of which to contain 100 Whole Pieces, or 200 Demy or Half Pieces, in British Ships, into the Port of London only, to be secured in Warehouses for Exportation; but no Cambrick or Lawn whatsoever is to be imported from Ireland into any Part of Great Britain until the Importation of Cambricks and French Lawns into Ireland shall be prohibited by Law.		
For the Regulations respecting the Importation of French European made Cambricks and Lawns for Home Consumption, until the 10th May 1800, see the Note after the Duty on them in Table C; and for the Duty payable on Exportation to his Majesty's Colonies in America, after having been secured in Warehouses as directed by the 32 Geo. II. Chap. 32. and 7 Geo. III. Chap. 43. see Table A, outwards.		
Linen, viz.		
Canvas, viz.		
Heffens Canvas, or Dutch Barrass, the 120 Ells -	1 7 0	1 5 3
Packing Canvas, Guttings, Spruce, Elbing, or Queensborough Canvas, the 120 Ells -	0 18 2	0 16 11

(141)

Poldavies, the Bolt containing 28 Ells	-	0	8	9	0	0	0
Damask Tabling, of the Manufacture of Holland, or any other of the United Provinces, viz.						
not exceeding 1 Ell ⅛ in Breadth, the Yard	-	0	5	4	0	4	10
above 1 Ell ⅛, and under 2 Ells in Breadth, the Yard	-	0	6	2	0	5	8
of the Breadth of 2 Ells or upwards, and under 3 Ells, the Yard	-	0	7	0	0	6	6
of the Breadth of 3 Ells or upwards, the Yard	-	0	10	4	0	9	10
of Ireland. See Irish Cloth.						
of Russia. See Russia Linen.						
of Silesia making, or of any other Place not otherwise enumerated, the Yard	-	0	1	3	0	1	1½
Damask Towelling and Napkining of the Manufacture of Holland, or any other of the United Provinces, the Yard	-	0	1	11	0	1	8
of Ireland. See Irish Cloth.						
of Russia. See Russia Linen.						
of Silesia making, or of any other Place not otherwise enumerated, the Yard	-	0	0	5	0	4	4½
Diaper Tabling of the Manufacture of Holland, or any other of the United Provinces, viz.						
not exceeding 1 Ell ⅛ in Breadth, the Yard	-	0	2	5	0	2	2

TABLE A.

INWARDS.

	Duty. £. s. d.	Drawback. £. s. d.
Linen, viz.		
Diaper Tabling of the Manufacture of Holland, or any other of the United Provinces, viz.		
above 1 Ell ⅛ in Breadth, and under 2 Ells, the Yard	0 2 10	0 2 6
of the breadth of 2 Ells or upwards, and under 3 Ells, the Yard	0 3 2	0 2 10
of the Breadth of 3 Ells, or upwards, the Yard	0 4 8	0 4 4
Diaper Tabling of Russia. See Russia Linen.		
of Silesia making, or of any other Place, not otherwise enumerated, the Yard	0 1 1	0 0 11
Diaper Towelling and Napkining of the Manufacture of Holland, or any other of the United Provinces, the Yard	0 0 10	0 0 8
of Ireland. See Irish Cloth.		
of Russia. See Russia Linen.		
of Silesia making, or of any other Place not otherwise enumerated, the Yard	0 0 5	0 0 4½
Drillings and Packduck, the 120 Ells	2 5 4	2 4 4
Flanders and Holland Linen plain, not otherwise enumerated, viz.		
not exceeding 1 Ell ⅛ in Breadth, the Ell	0 1 4	0 1 2

above 1 Ell ⅛, and under 2 Ells in Breadth, the Ell	-	0	1	7	0	1	5
of the Breadth of 2 Ells or upwards, and under 3 Ells, the Ell	-	0	1	9	0	1	7
of the Breadth of 3 Ells or upwards, the Ell	-	0	2	7	0	2	5

German, Switzerland, East Country (except Russia), and Silesia Cloth, plain, viz.

above the Breadth of 31½ Inches, and not exceeding 36 Inches, the 120 Ells	3	1	5	2	16	5
above 36 Inches in Breadth, the 120 Ells	4	14	5	4	9	5
not above 31½ Inches in Breadth, the 120 Ells	1	4	7	1	2	7

Hinderlands, Brown, viz.

under 22½ Inches in Breadth, the 120 Ells	0	16	5	0	15	1
above 22½ Inches, not exceeding 36 Inches in Breadth, the 120 Ells	0	12	4	0	11	4
exceeding 36 Inches in Breadth, the 120 Ells	2	5	4	2	4	4

By the 7 and 8 William III. Chap. 39. Linen of the Manufacture of Ireland (except Cambricks or Lawns, which by the 7 Geo. III. Chap. 43. are prohibited to be imported from Ireland until the Importation of Cambricks and French Lawns into Ireland shall be prohibited by Law), not being chequered, striped, printed, painted, stained, or dyed, may be imported free of Duty. For the Regulations, see the Note after Flax.

(144)

TABLE A.

INWARDS.

	Duty. £. s. d.	Drawback. £. s. d.
Linen, viz.		
Lawns, viz.		
Silesia and all other Lawns plain (except Lawns of the Manufacture of the European Dominions of the French King), not bleached in Holland, the Piece not exceeding 8 Yards in Length	0 3 1	0 2 10
Silesia and all other Lawns plain (except Lawns of the Manufacture of the European Dominions of the French King), bleached in Holland, the Piece not exceeding 8 Yards in Length	0 3 10	0 3 7
French, see the Duty in Table C, and the Regulations following Cambricks under the Head of Linen in Table A.		
Oil Cloth, not exceeding Yard Wide, the Ell	0 0 4	0 0 3
exceeding Yard Wide, the Ell	0 0 7	0 0 6
Packduck and Drillings, the 120 Ells	0 5 4	0 4 4
Russia Linen, plain, viz.		
Towelling and Napkining of the Manufacture of Russia, not exceeding 22½ Inches in Breadth, imported in a British built Ship, the 120 Ells	0 15 5	0 14 2

Towelling and Napkining of the Manufacture of Ruffia, not exceeding 22½ Inches in Breadth, imported in a Foreign Ship, the 120 Ells	0	16	1	0 14 2
Narrow Ruffia Linen, not otherwise enumerated, not exceeding 22½ Inches in Breadth, imported in a British built Ship, the 120 Ells	0	16	5	0 15 1
Narrow Ruffia Linen, not otherwise enumerated, not exceeding 22½ Inches in Breadth, imported in a Foreign Ship, the 120 Ells	0	17	2	0 15 1
Linen Cloth and Diaper of Ruffia, not otherwise enumerated, exceeding 22½ Inches in Breadth, and not exceeding 31½ Inches, imported in a British built Ship, the 120 Ells	1	4	7	1 2 7
Linen Cloth and Diaper of Ruffia, not otherwise enumerated, exceeding 22½ Inches in Breadth, and not exceeding 31½ Inches, imported in a Foreign Ship, the 120 Ells	1	5	8	1 2 7
Linen Cloth and Diaper of Ruffia, not otherwise enumerated, exceeding 31½ Inches in Breadth, and not exceeding 36 Inches, imported in a British built Ship, the 120 Ells	1	16	11	1 13 11
Linen Cloth and Diaper of Ruffia, not otherwise enumerated, exceeding 31½ Inches in Breadth, and not exceeding 36 Inches, imported in a Foreign Ship, the 120 Ells	1	18	6	1 13 11

(146)

TABLE A.

INWARDS.

	Duty. £. s. d.	Drawback. £. s. d.
Linen, viz.		
Ruffia Linen Cloth and Diaper of Ruffia, not otherwife enumerated, exceeding 36 Inches in Breadth, and not exceeding 45 Inches, imported in a British built Ship, the 120 Ells	3 9 11	3 6 11
Linen Cloth and Diaper of Ruffia, not otherwife enumerated, exceeding 36 Inches in Breadth, and not exceeding 45 Inches, imported in a Foreign Ship, the 120 Ells	3 11 6	3 6 11
Linen Cloth and Diaper of Ruffia, not otherwife enumerated, exceeding 45 Inches in Breadth, imported in a British built Ship, the 120 Ells	4 14 5	4 9 5
Linen Cloth and Diaper of Ruffia, not otherwife enumerated, exceeding 45 Inches in Breadth, imported in a Foreign Ship, the 120 Ells	4 17 2	4 9 5
Sail Cloth, or Sail Duck of Holland or of any other of the United Provinces, not exceeding 36 Inches in Breadth, the 120 Ells	2 3 1	0 0 0
Sail Cloth, or Sail Duck of Holland or of any other of the United Provinces, exceeding 36 Inches in Breadth, the 120 Ells	3 16 1	0 0 0
Sail Cloth, or Sail Duck of Ruffia, not exceeding 36 Inches in Breadth, imported in a British built Ship, the 120 Ells	2 1 9	0 0 0

(147)

Sail Cloth, or Sail Duck of Ruſſia, not exceeding 36 Inches in Breadth, imported in a Foreign Ship, the 120 Ells	2	3	1
Sail Cloth, or Sail Duck of Ruſſia, exceeding 36 Inches in Breadth, imported in a Britiſh built Ship, the 120 Ells	3	14	9
Sail Cloth, or Sail Duck of Ruſſia, exceeding 36 Inches in Breadth, imported in a Foreign Ship, the 120 Ells	3	16	1
Sail Cloth, or Sail Duck, not otherwiſe enumerated, not exceeding 36 Inches in Breadth, the 120 Ells	2	1	9
Sail Cloth, or Sail Duck, not otherwiſe enumerated, exceeding 36 Inches in Breadth, the 120 Ells	3	14	9
Sail Cloth, or Canvas, of the Manufacture of Ireland, on which the Bounty of 4ᵈ the Yard has been there granted, being of the Value of 14ᵈ the Yard or upwards, the Yard	0	0	4
Sail Cloth, or Canvas, of the Manufacture of Ireland, on which the Bounty of 2ᵈ the Yard has been there granted, being of the Value of 10 the Yard, and under the Value of 14ᵈ the Yard, the Yard	0	0	2

By the 23 Geo. II. Chap. 32. no Canvas or Sail Cloth is to be imported from Ireland into this Kingdom but in whole or entire Bolts or Pieces; and if the Loops or double Threads of the Bolts or Pieces, Part of the Warp at the Middle of that End of the Web laſt in Weaving, ſhall be cut off, ſuch Sail Cloth or Canvas ſhall be deemed to have received the

TABLE A.

INWARDS.

	Duty. £. s. d.	Drawback. £. s. d.
Linen, viz.		
Bounty, or if the same shall be stamped with an Impression importing the Payment of the Bounty.		
By the Orders of the Commissioners of the Customs, all Linen weighing above 17 Ounces $\frac{6}{15}$ths the Yard square, is to pay Duty as Sail Cloth; which is said to be in consequence of a Verdict in Trinity Term 1745, respecting two Pieces of Broad Russia Linen: but if any such Linen shall be subject to a higher Duty than is payable for Sail Cloth, this will not be deemed an Exemption from that Duty.		
Sheets old, the Piece	0 0 6	0 0 5
Spanish or Portugal Linen plain, viz.		
not exceeding 36 Inches in Breadth, the Ell	0 0 5	0 0 4½
exceeding 36 Inches in Breadth, the Ell	0 0 8	0 0 7½
Turkey or Alexandria plain,		
not exceeding one Yard in Width, the Ell	0 0 7	0 0 6
exceeding one Yard in Width, the Ell	0 0 10	0 0 9
Linseed.		

			l.	s.	d.		l.	s.	d.
By the 3 Geo. I. Chap. 7. Sect. 38. Linseed may be imported into this Kingdom by any Person free of Duty.									
Liquorice Juice, the Hundred Weight	-	-	1	8	0	-	0	2	0
Powder, the Hundred Weight	-	-	2	12	1	-	2	11	1
Root, the Hundred Weight	-	-	1	8	10	-	1	8	0
Litharge of Gold, the Hundred Weight	-	-	0	0	10	-	0	0	7 ½
of Silver, the Hundred Weight	-	-	0	0	8	-	0	0	0
Litmus, the Hundred Weight	-	-	0	3	4	-	0	0	0
By the 8 Geo. I. Chap. 15. Litmus may be legally imported free of Duty, if regularly entered and landed.									
Lobsters.									
By the 1 Geo. I. Stat. 2. Chap. 18. Sect. 10. Lobsters may be imported freely by any Persons whatever, in any Ship whatever, free of Duty.									
Lutestrings or Catlings, the Gross containing twelve Dozen Knots	-	-	0	2	6	0	0	2	2
Mace, the Pound	-	-	0	4	0	-	0	3	8
imported by the East India Company, the Pound	-	-	0	4	0	-	0	3	8
Madder, the Hundred Weight	-	-	0	4	8	-	0	0	0
Roots, the Hundred Weight	-	-	0	4	8	-	0	0	0
By the 8 Geo. I. Chap. 15, Madder and Madder Roots may be legally imported free of Duty, if regularly entered and landed.									

TABLE A.

INWARDS.

	Duty. £. s. d.	Drawback. £. s. d.
Maize. See Corn.		
Man, Isle of.		
By the 5 Geo. III. Chap. 43, Goods, &c. the Growth, Produce, or Manufacture of the Isle of Man may be imported directly from thence free of Customs. See the Note after Bestials.		
Maps, the Map	0 0 6	0 0 0
Marble. See Stones.		
Mares, the Mare	2 4 0	1 19 0
By the 5 Geo. III. Chap. 10. and 16 Geo. III. Chap. 8. all Sorts of Cattle may be imported from Ireland into Great Britain free of Duty.		
Marmelade, the Pound	0 0 3	0 0 2
Mats of Russia, viz.		
imported in a British built Ship, the Hundred containing five Score	0 11 0	0 9 9
imported in a Foreign Ship, the Hundred containing five Score	0 11 9	0 9 9
Matting of Barbary or Portugal, the Yard	0 0 5	0 0 4½
Matting the Yard, is for each Breadth and running Measure; if se-	0 0 2	0 0 1½
of Holland, the Yard		

(151)

veral Breadths of Matting are fewed together for a particular Floor, fubject to a Duty of $27\frac{1}{2}$ per Cent. on the Value.

Meal. See Corn.					
Mead, the Hogfhead containing 63 Gallons	—	—	0	8 10	0 7 10
Medlars, the Bufhel	—	—	0	2 4	0 0 4
Melaffes, viz.					
of and from the Britifh Plantations in America, the Hundred Weight	—	—	0	3 0	0 2 8
not of and from the Britifh Plantations in America, the Hundred Weight	—	—	0	11 9	0 11 5
Metal, viz.					
Leaf (except of Leaf Gold) the Packet containing 250 Leaves prepared for Battery, the Hundred Weight	—	—	0	0 2	0 $1\frac{1}{2}$
			1	11 11	1 8 11
Metheglin, the Hogfhead containing 63 Gallons	—	—	0	8 10	0 7 10
Millboards. See Pafteboards, under Wood.					
Mohair Yarn or Camel Yarn, the Pound	—	—	0	0 7	0 0 6
Morels, the Pound	—	—	0	0 2	0 1 0
Mofs, viz.					
Rock Mofs for Dyers Ufe, the Ton containing twenty Hundred Weight	—	—	0	5 0	0 0 $2\frac{3}{4}$
Mother of Pearl Shells rough, the Pound	—	—	0	0 4	0 0 $2\frac{1}{4}$
imported by the Eaft India Company, the Pound			0	0 4	0 0 $2\frac{1}{4}$

L 4

TABLE A.

INWARDS.

	Duty. £. s. d.	Drawback. £. s. d.
Mum, the Barrel containing 32 Gallons — N. B. Subject also to the Duty of Excise; and one Gallon in Ten allowed for filling up.	0 9 10	0 7 10
Neats Tongues, the Dozen of Ireland, salted, free of Duty by the 5 Geo. III. Chap. 1. 8 Geo. III. Chap. 9. and 16 Geo. III. Chap. 8.	0 1 0	0 0 0
Necklaces of Glass, or Bracelets, the Groce containing twelve Bundles or Dickers, each Bundle or Dicker containing ten Necklaces	0 3 8	0 3 6
Nutmegs, the Pound	0 2 0	0 1 10
imported by the East India Company, the Pound	0 2 0	0 1 10
condited, the Pound	0 0 10	0 0 7
imported by the East India Company, the Pound	0 0 10	0 0 7
Nuts, viz.		
Chesnuts, the Bushel	0 1 5	0 1 3
Small Nuts, the Bushel	0 0 9	0 0 8
Walnuts, the Bushel	0 0 6	0 0 5
Oak Bark (when allowed to be imported), the Hundred Weight	0 0 1	0 0 0

By the 12 Geo. III. Chap. 50. Oak Bark is allowed to be imported when the Price shall be ten Pounds or upwards, for the Load of Hatch Bark, containing forty-five Hundred Weight; or when the Price of Oak Bark in the Rinds shall be two Pounds ten Shillings or upwards, for the Load of Rinds containing thirty Yards, when the same are set three Rinds thick, with 2 Skirts and a Cover, delivered at the Buyers Warehouses in the City of London, or within the weekly Bills of Mortality. Every Person living as aforesaid, purchasing five Loads of Hatch Bark, or twenty Loads of Oak Bark Rinds as beforementioned, is to deliver in an Account thereof to the Clerk of the Tanners Company, who is to keep a Register of the same, which shall and may be inspected at all convenient Times by any Person without any Fee, and when the Average Price of one Month of either of those Barks shall appear to be as aforesaid, three or more Purchasers of the said Bark may, and they are required to certify to the Lord Mayor of London, or any two of the Aldermen thereof, the average Price for one Month preceding, and to which they are to make Oath; and the Clerk of the Tanners Company is also to make Oath to the Truth of the Entries of the Accounts delivered in to him, whereupon the said Mayor or Aldermen are to sign the same, and deliver the same as soon as conveniently may be to the Collector or Receiver of his

TABLE A.

INWARDS.

	Duty. £ s. d.	Drawback. £ s. d.

Majesty's Customs at the Port of London, who is to publish the same in the London Gazette; from and after which Publication, no more than one Penny per Hundred Weight is to be paid on the Importation of any Oak Bark into Great Britain. After which Time, when it shall appear by Publication in the London Gazette, that one Hundred Loads of Hatch Bark, or three Hundred Loads of Rind Bark, have been purchased under the beforementioned Prices, no Oak Bark shall be imported; but any Orders bona fide given during the Time it was allowed to be imported, upon sufficient Proof to the Collector of the Customs, such Oak Bark shall be imported and entered upon the said Duty. Oak Bark imported when the Price of Hatch Bark is under ten Pounds, or Oak Bark in the Rinds under two Pounds ten Shillings the Load as aforesaid, is forfeited, and a Penalty on the Importer of twenty Pounds for each Load imported. Continued by the 24 Geo. III. Chap. 26. and 30 Geo. III. Chap. 18. from that last Act for five Years, and to the End of the then next Session of Parliament.

	Duty £ s. d.	Drawback £ s. d.
Oaker, the Bushel	0 2 0	0 1 9
Oakham, the Hundred Weight	0 2 3	0 2 0

(155)

Oil, viz.							
Sallad Oil, imported in a British built Ship, the Gallon	-	0	1	1	0	1	0
imported in a Foreign Ship, the Gallon	-	0	1	2	0	1	0
Ordinary Oil of Olives, imported in a British built Ship, the Tun containing 252 Gallons	-	7	0	9	6	4	9
imported in a Foreign Ship, the Tun containing 252 Gallons	-	7	9	8	6	4	9
Rape and Linseed Oil, the Tun containing 252 Gallons	-	24	4	0	22	9	0
Oil of Hemp Seed, or any other Seed Oil, not otherwise enumerated, the Tun containing 252 Gallons	-	13	4	0	12	14	0
Train Oil, or Blubber, or Fish Oil, of Foreign Fishing, the Tun containing 252 Gallons	-	18	3	0	13	13	0
Train Oil, or Blubber, or Fish Oil, of British Fishing, viz.							
of Greenland and Parts adjacent, the Tun containing 252 Gallons	-	1	15	3	1	11	3
of Greenland and Parts adjacent, taken by any Shipping belonging to his Majesty's Colonies or Plantations and imported in such Shipping, the Tun containing 252 Gallons	-	0	15	5	0	12	5
of Greenland and Parts adjacent, taken by any Shipping belonging to his Majesty's Colonies or Plantations and imported in Shipping belonging to Great Britain, the Tun containing 252 Gallons	-	0	12	2	0	10	7

(156)

TABLE A.

INWARDS.

	Duty. £. s. d.	Drawback. £. s. d.
Oil, viz. Train Oil, or Blubber, or Fish Oil, of British Fishing, viz. of Newfoundland and like Sort, the Tun containing 252 Gallons	1 6 5	1 3 5
of Newfoundland and like Sort, taken by Shipping belonging to any of his Majesty's Colonies or Plantations and imported in such Shipping, the Tun containing 252 Gallons	0 13 3	0 10 2
of Newfoundland and like Sort, taken by Shipping belonging to any of his Majesty's Colonies or Plantations and imported in Shipping belonging to Great Britain, the Tun containing 252 Gallons	0 9 11	0 8 5

By the 26 Geo. III. Chap. 41. and Chap. 60. Oil, or Blubber of Whales, Seal Oil, Head Matter, or other Produce of Seals, Whales, or other Fish or Creatures living in the Seas, taken or caught in any Part of the Ocean, under certain Conditions, Regulations, and Restrictions, may be imported into Great Britain without paying any Duty; which fee fully explained in the Notes following Blubber.

See the Duties on the several Oils drawn from Minerals or Vegetables under the Title of Drugs.

N.B. 7½ Pounds Avoirdupois Weight allowed to be a Gallon of Oil.

Oil Cloth, not exceeding Yard Wide, the Ell	—	0	0	4	0	0	3
exceeding Yard wide, the Ell	—	0	0	7	0	0	6
Olives, the Hogshead containing 63 Gallons	—	1	15	3	1	11	3
Onions, the Bushel	—	0	0	3	0	0	2½
Oranges and Lemons, the Thousand	—	0	4	5	0	3	11
Orange Flower Ointment, the Pound	—	0	0	6	0	0	4
Water, the Gallon	—	0	1	0	0	0	8
Orchal, the Hundred Weight	—	0	6	4	0	0	0
By the 8 Geo. I. Chap. 15. Sect. 10. Orchal may be legally imported free of Duty, if regularly entered and landed.							
Orchelia, or Archelia, the Hundred Weight	—	0	3	1	0	0	0
By the 8 Geo. I. Chap. 15. Sect. 10. Orchelia may be legally imported free of Duty, if regularly entered and landed.							
Orsedew, the Dozen Pounds	—	0	6	0	0	5	3
Ostrich or Eltridge Feathers dressed, the Pound	—	0	8	10	0	7	10
undressed, the Pound	—	0	4	5	0	3	11
Outnal Thread, the Dozen Pounds	—	0	17	8	0	16	2½
Oysters, the Bushel	—	0	0	6	0	0	0

(158)

TABLE A.

INWARDS.

By the 27 Geo. III. Chap. 13. Sect. 32. Fresh Fish of every Kind, caught by the Crews of British built Ships, may be imported in British built Ships free of Duty.

	Duty. £. s. d.	Drawback. £. s. d.
Packthread, the Hundred Pounds	0 13 3	0 11 9
Pails of Wood or Kits of Wood, the Dozen	0 1 10	0 1 8
Painters Colours of all Sorts, not otherwise enumerated, the Pound	0 0 2	0 0 1½
Paper, viz.		
Atlas, ordinary, the Ream	1 8 10	0 0 0
Fine, the Ream	2 5 2	0 0 0
Bastard, or double Copy, the Ream	0 5 4	0 0 0
Blue Royal, the Ream	0 8 6	0 0 0
Blue Paper, for Sugar Bakers, the Ream	0 7 1	0 0 0
Brown Paper, the Bundle containing 40 Quires	0 2 11	0 0 0
Brown Cap, the Ream	0 4 11	0 0 0
Cap, viz.		
Fool's Cap, Fine, the Ream	0 6 2	0 0 0
Second, the Ream	0 5 4	0 0 0
Genoa Fool's Cap, fine, the Ream	0 4 7	0 0 0

(159)

	£	s	d
——— second, the Ream	0	3	9
German Fool's Cap, the Ream	0	3	9
Fine Printing Fool's Cap, the Ream	0	3	9
Second ordinary Printing Fool's Cap, the Ream	0	3	4
Cartridge Paper, the Ream	0	5	9
Chancery double, the Ream	0	5	0
Crown, viz.			
Fine Genoa Crown the Ream	0	4	7
Second Genoa Crown, the Ream	0	3	9
German Crown, the Ream	0	3	9
Fine Printing Crown, the Ream	0	3	9
Second ordinary Printing Crown, the Ream	0	3	4
Demy, viz.			
Demy Fine, the Ream	0	13	6
Second, the Ream	0	11	0
Genoa Demy, Fine, the Ream	0	6	9
Second, the Ream	0	5	11
German Demy, the Ream	0	5	11
Printing Demy, the Ream	0	6	2
Elephant, Ordinary, the Ream	0	12	3
Fine, the Ream	1	5	4
Fool's Cap. See Cap Paper.			

TABLE A.

INWARDS.

	Duty. £. s. d.	Drawback. £. s. d.
Paper, viz.		
Imperial Fine, the Ream	2 5 2	0 0 0
Second Writing, the Ream	1 16 11	0 0 0
Lombard, viz. German Lombard, the Ream	0 3 9	0 0 0
Medium, viz.		
Medium Fine, the Ream	0 16 2	0 0 0
Second Writing Medium, the Ream	0 12 11	0 0 0
Genoa Medium Fine, the Ream	0 10 5	0 0 0
Second, the Ream	0 9 1	0 0 0
Post, viz.		
Small Post, the Ream	0 5 1	0 0 0
Fine Large Post, weighing fifteen Pounds per Ream, or upwards, the Ream	0 8 7	0 0 0
Fine Large Post, weighing under fifteen Pounds per Ream, the Ream	0 7 9	0 0 0
Pot, viz.		
Fine Genoa Pot, the Ream	0 3 4	0 0 0
Second Genoa Pot, the Ream	0 3 4	0 0 0
Ordinary Pot, the Ream	0 3 4	0 0 0

(161)

		£ s d	£ s d
Superfine Pot, the Ream	—	0 5 4	0 0 0
Second Fine Pot, the Ream	—	0 4 7	0 0 0
Pressing Paper, the Hundred Weight	—	0 12 10	0 0 0
Royal, viz.			
Royal Fine, the Ream	—	1 5 4	0 0 0
Super Royal Fine, the Ream	—	1 11 11	0 0 0
Second Writing Royal, the Ream	—	1 1 3	0 0 0
Super Royal, the Ream	—	1 5 4	0 0 0
Genoa Royal Fine, the Ream	—	0 14 5	0 0 0
Second, the Ream	—	0 13 1	0 0 0
Fine Holland Royal, the Ream	—	0 14 5	0 0 0
Second Fine Holland Royal, the Ream	—	0 11 0	0 0 0
Ordinary Royal, the Ream	—	0 7 9	0 0 0
Parchment, the Dozen containing twelve Sheets	—	0 4 9	0 0 0
Pearls, Diamonds, and all other Jewels and precious Stones, free of Duty.			
Pears, the Bushel			
dried, the Bushel	—	0 1 5	1 3 0
Pelts. See Skins.			
Pepper, on Importation by the East India Company, to be warehoused, the Pound	—	0 0 9	0 8 0
when taken out of such Warehouse for Home Consumption, the Pound	—	0 0 0½	0 0 0
Pound	—	0 0 6	0 0 0

M

TABLE A.

INWARDS.

By the 8 Ann, Chap. 7. Sect. 7 and 8. to be imported into London only, and the Duties for Home Consumption to be paid by the Buyers of the Importers when taken out of the Warehouse; if exported, Security is to be given by the Importers or Buyers that it shall not be relanded; and it may be sifted or garbled in the Warehouses to make it merchantable.

By the 10 Ann, Chap. 26. Sect. 45. at the Request of the Importers or Buyers, the Commissioners of the Customs are impowered to destroy Dirt or Trash found among Pepper.

	Duty. £. s. d.	Drawback. £. s. d.
Pepper,		
Guinea Pepper, the Pound — — —	0 0 3	0 0 2
Long Pepper, the Pound — — —	0 0 2½	0 0 1½
imported by the East India Company, the Pound	0 0 2½	0 0 1½
Perry, the Tun containing 252 Gallons — —	8 8 0	7 7 0
N. B. Subject also to the Duty of Excise.		
Pewter, Old, the Hundred Weight — —	0 13 9	0 12 6
Pickled Cucumbers, the Gallon — —	0 0 9	0 0 7½
Pickles of all Sorts, not otherwise described and enumerated, the Gallon	0 0 9	0 0 7
Pictures of four Feet Square or upwards, the Picture	3 11 6	0 0 0

imported by the East India Company, the Picture	3	17	0
Pictures of two Feet Square, and under four Feet Square, the Picture imported by the East India Company, the Picture	2	7	8
Pictures under two Feet Square, the Picture imported by the East India Company, the Picture	2	11	4
Pimento, of the British Plantations, the Pound	1	3	10
———— not of the British Plantations, the Pound	1	5	8
Pistachias, or Nux Pistachiæ, the Pound	0	0	$2\frac{3}{4}$
	0	0	$5\frac{1}{2}$
	0	0	2
Pitch, if not imported directly from the Place of its Growth, the Pound	0	0	6
——— not being the Product of any of the Dominions or Plantations of the Crown of Great Britain, viz.			
imported in a British built Ship, the Last containing 12 Barrels, each Barrel not exceeding $31\frac{1}{2}$ Gallons	0	12	5
imported in a Foreign Ship, the Last containing 12 Barrels, each Barrel not exceeding $31\frac{1}{2}$ Gallons	0	13	1
——— of the Product of any of the Dominions or Plantations of the Crown of Great Britain, the Last containing 12 Barrels, each Barrel not exceeding $31\frac{1}{2}$ Gallons	0	11	0
Plaster of Paris, the Hundred Pounds	0	1	1
Platting or other Manufacture of Bast, Straw, Chip, Cane, or Horse-hair, to be used in or proper for making Hats or Bonnets, the Pound	0	1	10

TABLE A.

INWARDS.

To be imported into the Port of London only, in Ships of 50 Tons Burthen, and in Packages containing each 224 lb. Weight net. 10 Geo. III. Chap. 43. Sect. 6.

	Duty. £. s. d.	Drawback. £. s. d.
Plate of Silver ungilt, the Ounce Troy -	0 2 2	0 0 0
imported by the East India Company, the Ounce Troy	0 3 3	0 0 0
part gilt, the Ounce Troy -	0 2 4	0 0 0
imported by the East India Company, the Ounce Troy - - -	0 3 7	0 0 0
gilt, the Ounce Troy - - -	0 2 6	0 0 0
imported by the East India Company, the Ounce Troy - - -	0 3 10	0 0 0
Plate wrought of Gold, the Ounce Troy - - -	1 10 0	0 0 0
imported by the East India Company, the Ounce Troy	2 7 8	0 0 0
Plate battered, fit only to be re-manufactured. See Bullion, Duty free; being so deemed.		
Plumbs, dried, the Pound - - -	0 0 3	0 0 2¼
Polonia Wool, Duty free.		
Pomegranates, the Thousand -	0 8 10	0 7 10
Pomegranate Peels, the Hundred Weight -	0 4 8	0 0 0
Pork, from Ireland.		

		£	s.	d.		£	s.	d.
Salted, free of Duty, by the 5 Geo. III. Chap. 1. the 8 Geo. III. Chap. 9. and 16 Geo. III. Chap. 8.								
Potatoes, the Hundred Weight	—	0	3	8	—	0	3	3
Pots, viz. Melting Pots for Goldsmiths, the Hundred	—	0	0	7	—	0	0	6
Powder of Sago. See Sago Powder.								
Brass for Japanning, the Ounce	—	0	0	2	—	0	0	1½
viz. Hair Powder, the Hundred Weight	—	0	5	8	—	0	0	0
See the Note following Hair Powder.								
Precious Stones, free of Duty.								
Prints, viz. Paper Prints, the Piece	—	0	0	6	—	0	0	0
Prunes, the Hundred Weight	—	0	12	5	—	0	8	3
Prunelloes, the Pound	—	0	0	3	—	0	0	2
Puddings or Sausages, the Pound	—	0	0	3½	—	0	0	3
Quills, viz. Goose Quills, the Thousand	—	0	0	6	—	0	0	5
Swan Quills, the Thousand	—	0	2	0	—	0	1	8
Quinces, the Hundred containing five Score	—	0	1	10	—	0	1	7

Rags old, old Ropes or Junks, or old Fishing Nets, fit only for the making Paper or Pasteboard.
By the 11 Geo. I. Chap. 7. Sect. 10. may be imported into this Kingdom without paying any Duty, if due Entry thereof be made

(166)

TABLE A.

INWARDS.

in the same Manner and Form, expressing the Quantities and Qualities of the said Goods, as heretofore practised, and being landed in the Presence of the proper Officer; upon Failure of these Conditions the Goods to be liable to Forfeiture.

	Duty. £. s. d.	Drawback. £. s. d.
Raisins, of the Sun, imported in a British built Ship, the Hundred Weight	0 18 8	0 17 6
imported in a Foreign Ship, the Hundred Weight	0 19 1	0 17 6
Smyrna, imported in a British built Ship, the Hundred Weight	0 11 5	0 10 10
imported in a Foreign Ship, the Hundred Weight	0 11 8	0 10 10
Lexia, imported in a British built Ship, the Hundred Weight	0 8 0	0 7 8
imported in a Foreign Ship, the Hundred Weight	0 8 1	0 7 8
Faro, imported in a British built Ship, the Hundred Weight	0 8 0	0 7 8
imported in a Foreign Ship, the Hundred Weight	0 8 1	0 7 8
Lipra or Belvidere, imported in a British built Ship, the Hundred Weight	0 8 3	0 7 11
imported in a Foreign Ship, the Hundred Weight	0 8 5	0 7 11
Denia, and all other Raisins not otherwise enumerated, imported in a British built Ship, the Hundred Weight	0 7 1	0 6 10
imported in a Foreign Ship, the Hundred Weight	0 7 2	0 6 10
Rape of Grapes, the Tun containing 252 Gallons	5 8 11	4 8 11

(167)

		£ s. d.	£ s. d.
Cakes, or Cakes made of Rape Seed. Under the 15 Geo. III. Chap. 34. all Rape Cakes, or Cakes made of Rape Seed, commonly used for the Purpose of Manure, may be imported from Ireland Duty free.			
Rattans, the Thousand	—	0 16 6	0 15 3
imported by the East India Company, the Thousand	—	0 19 3	0 18 0
Red Lead, the Hundred Weight	—	0 3 8	0 2 5
Wool, Duty free.			
Reeds, viz. Reed Canes, the Thousand	—	0 11 0	0 9 9
Rennet, the Gallon	—	0 0 2¼	0 0 2
Rice, the Hundred Weight	—	0 7 4	0 7 4
imported by the East India Company, the Hundred Weight	—	0 8 10	0 8 10
of the Growth and Production of any of the British Plantations in America, imported for the Purpose of Exportation into the Ports of Plymouth, Exeter, Poole, Southampton, Chichester, Sandwich, and Glasgow, and the Members thereunto belonging, and into the Ports of Bristol, Liverpool, Lancaster, and Whitehaven, the Hundred Weight	—	0 0 8	0 0 0
By the 5 Geo. III. Chap. 45. and 12 Geo. III. Chap. 60. Rice so imported for the Purpose of Exportation, the Importer of such Rice shall give Notice to the Collector and Comptroller of any of the Ports beforementioned wherein the Ship shall arrive, of his Inten-			

M 4

TABLE A.

INWARDS.

	Duty. £. s. d.	Drawback. £. s. d.
tion to export the whole Cargo of such Rice immediately in the same Ship to Foreign Parts, and the Master of such Ship shall so report his Cargo accordingly; and the Importer of such Rice shall give Bond, with one or more sufficient Securities, in double Value of the Rice so imported, for the Payment of the remaining Duties within sixty Days from the Date of such Bond, for all such Rice as shall be landed out of any Ship so entered and reported; which Bond shall be vacated and discharged upon Payment of the remaining Duties within the Time before limited, or upon the said Rice being duly reshipped and exported. See the King's Order in Council, Page 13, preceding Table A.	—	—
Rock Moss, for Dyers Use, the Ton containing twenty Hundred Weight	0 5 0	0 0 0
Ropes new. See Cordage.		
old. See Rags.		
Rosa Solis, the Gallon	—	—
Subject also to the Duty of Excise.		
Rosin, of the Product of any of the Dominions or Plantations belonging to the Crown of Great Britain, the Hundred Weight	0 2 10	0 2 7
not of the Product of any of the Dominions or Plantations belonging	0 1 6	0 1 4

(169)

to the Crown of Great Britain, imported in a British built Ship, the Hundred Weight - - - - -	0	2	3	0	2	1
not of the Product of any of the Dominions or Plantations belonging to the Crown of Great Britain, imported in a Foreign Ship, the Hundred Weight - - - - -	0	2	4	0	2	1
Rubies, free of Duty. See the Note after Diamonds.						
Rugs, viz. Irish Rugs, the Piece - - -	0	3	0	0	2	8
Rum, of the Growth, Produce, or Manufacture of any British Colony or Plantation in America, the Gallon - - See the Note after Spirits.	0	0	5	0	0	5
Foreign Rum, the Gallon - - - Subject also to the Duty of Excise.	0	0	7	0	0	6
N. B. The Drawback on Rum of the British Sugar Plantations in America, shipped as Stores, allowed to the 5th July 1795, by the 28 Geo. III. Chap. 23. but not in Casks less than 100 Gallons, or in Ships less than 100 Tons Burthen.						
Saflower, the Pound - - - By the 8 Geo. I. Chap. 15. Sect. 10. Saflower may be legally imported free of Duty, if regularly entered and landed.	0	0	$1\frac{1}{2}$	0	0	0
Sago, the Pound - - -	0	0	3	0	0	2
imported by the East India Company, the Pound - -	0	0	3	0	0	2

TABLE A.

INWARDS.

Sago Powder.
By the 7 Geo. III. Chap. 30. and 21 Geo. III. Chap. 29. Sago Powder may be legally imported from any of his Majesty's Colonies in North America, free of Duty, until December 1, 1796.

Sail Cloth. See Linen.

Salt, viz.

	Duty. £. s. d.	Drawback. £. s. d.
to be used in curing of Fish, imported in a British built Ship, the Wey, containing 40 Bushels, each Bushel being 84 Pounds	0 5 11	0 5 3
to be used in curing of Fish, imported in a Foreign Ship, the Wey, containing 40 Bushels, each Bushel being 84 Pounds	0 6 3	0 5 3
not for curing of Fish, imported in a British built Ship, the Wey, containing 40 Bushels, each Bushel being 84 Pounds	0 11 5	0 10 9
not for curing of Fish, imported in a Foreign Ship, the Wey, containing 40 Bushels, each Bushel being 84 Pounds	0 11 9	0 10 9
imported from the Islands of Jersey, Guernsey, Sark, or Alderney, to be used in curing Fish, the Wey, containing 40 Bushels, each Bushel being 84 Pounds	0 5 11	0 5 3
imported from the Islands of Jersey, Guernsey, Sark, or Alderney, not		

for curing Fish, the Wey, containing 40 Bushels, each Bushel being 84 Pounds - - - 0 11 5 0 10 9

By the 26 Geo. III. Chap. 26. the Importer or Proprietor of any Foreign Salt may give Bond for the Payment of the whole Duties of Customs payable within the Space of twelve Calendar Months from the Date of the Bond, but without any Discount for prompt Payment; if such Salt shall be exported within the said Space of twelve Calendar Months, the Bond shall be cancelled and discharged, and if the full Duties shall have been paid at or before the Expiration of the said twelve Calendar Months, and such Salt shall be afterwards exported into Foreign Parts within the Time allowed by Law, a Drawback of all the said Duties shall be allowed; and such Salt shall be liable to all Rules, Regulations, Penalties, and Forfeitures, as formerly practised.

By the 3 Geo. II. Chap. 20. Foreign Salt may not be imported in Vessels less than 40 Tons Burthen, nor otherwise than in Bulk (except for the Ship's Provisions), under the Penalty of Forfeiture thereof and double the Value.

Salt is also subject to the Duties on Salt under the Management of the Commissioners of that Revenue, as follows.

TABLE A.

INWARDS.

	Duty. £. s. d.	Drawback. £. s. d.
Salt, made at any Salt Works, Rock Salt taken out of any Pits, or Salt refined from Rock Salt in England, Wales, or Berwick, the Bushel - - -	0 5 0	0 5 0
made in Scotland, if imported into England, the Bushel - -	0 1 6	0 1 6
All foul Salt made at any Salt Works to be liable to the same Duties as any English White Salt is now.	0 3 6	0 3 6

N.B. The Bushel of Rock Salt containing 65 Pounds Avoirdupois Weight, and the Bushel of other Salt containing 56 Pounds Avoirdupois Weight.

British Salt imported is forfeited and the Ship, if the Duties are not paid within ten Days after the Ship has reported, by the 2 and 3 Ann, Chap. 14.

By the 25 Geo. III. Chap. 63. and 26 Geo. III. Chap. 36. there is to be allowed for Waste on White and Rock Salt carried Coastwise not less than 20 Miles by Sea, after the Rate of one Bushel for every 40 Bushels of White Salt, and after the Rate of Half a Bushel for every 40 Bushels of Rock Salt; on White and Rock Salt exported to Ireland, after the Rate of two Bushels for every

40 Bushels of White Salt, and after the Rate of one Bushel for every 40 Bushels of Rock Salt; on White and Rock Salt exported to Jersey, Guernsey, Alderney, Sark, and the Isle of Man, after the Rate of one Bushel in 40 for every 40 Bushels of White Salt, and after the Rate of half a Bushel in 40 for every 40 Bushels of Rock Salt.

No Debenture is to be granted for Salt shipped to Ireland, Jersey, Guernsey, Alderney, Sark, or the Isle of Man, until a Certificate is produced from the Collector of the Customs at the respective Places, specifying the Quantity there landed, and not for more than the Quantity shipped, although the Quantity landed may by the Allowance for Waste exceed the Quantity shipped.

By the 25 Geo. III. Chap. 65. any Vessel employed in the White Herring Fishery to have the same Allowance upon Salt used in curing Cod, Ling, or Hake caught during their Continuance at Sea, as upon Salt used in curing Herrings, but no Bounty is to be allowed on the Exportation of such Fish. British Vessels and Boats may purchase and take from each other any unsalted Herrings, Cod, Ling, or Hake, which may be entered and landed in any Port of Great Britain upon Proof; and the Collector or Comptroller is to give a Certificate of the Particulars, which is to be admitted as Proof of the Consumption of the Salt. Masters of Ves-

TABLE A.

INWARDS.

	Duty. £. s. d.	Drawback. £. s. d.
Salt, viz. fels bound to the North Seas or Iceland, may take Salt for curing of Fish without paying Duty, under the Regulations of this Act; but no Bounty is to be allowed on the Exportation of any Fish imported into Great Britain from the North Seas or Iceland.		
By the 26 Geo. III. Chap. 81. Salt for the curing of Fish and Herrings caught in the Herring Fishery for Home Consumption or Exportation, may be taken from any Salt Works free of Duty, on the Terms specified in that Act.		
Glauber Salts, made in Great Britain, the Hundred Weight	1 0 0	0 10 0
Mineral Alkali, or Flux for Glass, made in Great Britain of Rock Salt, or Brine, or Sea Water, the Ton containing 20 Hundred Weight	1 0 0	0 0 0
By the 26 Geo. III. Chap. 90. so much of the 22 Geo. III. Chap. 39. as allows Rock Salt for making a Flux for Glass free of Duty, is repealed, and Glass Makers are allowed to take Rock Salt, Brine, or Sea Water, for making a Flux for Glass at their own Glass Works, free of Duty, upon the Terms specified in the 22 Geo. III. Chap. 39.		

(175)

Salt Petre, the Hundred Weight	-	0	2	3	0	1	9
imported by the East India Company, the Hundred Weight	-	0	7	9	0	7	3
By the 23 Geo. III. Chap. 77. continued by the 26 Geo. III. Chap. 53. and by the note in Schedule A, 27 Geo. III. Chap. 13. Page 438, the whole Duties of Customs on Salt Petre, used and consumed in making Oil of Vitriol, to be drawn back, under the Conditions expressed in the Note following Brimstone.						
Sark, Island of.						
See the Note following Alderney.						
Saulages, or Puddings, the Pound	-	0	0	3½		
Scarlet Powder, or Grain Powder, the Pound	-	0	0	9		
Sea Morse Teeth, or Sea Horse Teeth, the Pound	-	0	0	3		
Seeds, viz.						
Agnus, Castus Seeds, the Pound	-	0	0	3	0	0	2
Ameos Seeds, the Pound	-	0	0	2	0	0	1½
Amomi Seeds, the Pound	-	0	0	2	0	0	1½
Canary Seed, the Hundred Weight	-	0	16	6	0	14	7
Carraway Seeds, the Hundred Weight	-	0	5	0	0	3	4
Carthamus Seeds, the Pound	-	0	0	2	0	0	1½
Clover Seed, the Hundred Weight	-	0	2	9	0	2	6
Cole Seed, the Quarter, containing 8 Bushels	-	0	13	3	0	12	9
Coriander Seeds, the Hundred Weight	-	0	4	5	0	2	11

M 7

(176)

TABLE A.

INWARDS.

	Duty. £. s. d.	Drawback. £. s. d.
Seeds, viz.		
Cummin Seeds, the Hundred Weight	0 7 4	0 4 11
Fennel Seeds, the Pound	0 0 1½	0 0 1
Hemp Seed, the Quarter, containing 8 Bushels	0 9 3	0 9 2
Linseed.		
By the 3 Geo. I. Chap. 7. Linseed may be legally imported free of Duty.		
Lucerne Seed, the Hundred Weight	0 2 9	0 2 6
Maw Seed, the Hundred Weight	0 15 5	0 14 0
Miller Seed, the Hundred Weight	0 4 5	0 4 0
Mustard Seed, the Hundred Weight	0 2 3	0 2 0
Onion Seed, the Hundred Weight	0 17 8	0 15 8
Piony Seeds, the Pound	0 0 1½	0 0 1
Poppy Seeds, the Pound	0 0 1½	0 0 1
Rape Seed, the Quarter, containing 8 Bushels	0 13 3	0 12 9
Rape Seed, and all other Seeds commonly made use of for the Purpose of extracting Oil therefrom, being of the Growth of Ireland, and imported from thence, the Last containing 10 Quarters, each Quarter containing 8 Bushels	0 1 0	0 0 0

By the 15 Geo. III. Chap. 34. such Seeds may be imported on Payment of the Duty of one Shilling the Last, when Rape Seed shall be at or above the Price of seventeen Pounds ten Shillings the Last, according to the Regulations respecting the Importation or Exportation of Corn or Grain, which fee under the Title Corn or Grain; and also by the 30 Geo. III. Chap. 41. in British built Ships from his Majesty's Colonies, Plantations, and Provinces in North America; and by this last Act, from any of these Places, may be warehoused without Payment of any Duty, under the same Regulations as Corn, &c. for Home Consumption or Exportation, by the 13 Geo. III. Chap. 43.

Semen Cucumeris, Cucurb, Citrol, or Melons, the Pound	–	0	0	$1\frac{1}{2}$	0	0	1
Thlaspii Semen, the Pound	–	0	0	2	0	0	$1\frac{1}{2}$
Seeds for Gardens, the Pound	–	0	0	$1\frac{1}{2}$	0	0	1
Worm Seeds, the Pound	–	0	0	6	0	0	4
if not imported directly from the Place of its Growth, the Pound	–	0	1	6	0	1	0
imported by the East India Company, the Pound	–	0	0	6	0	0	4

Shaving for Hats. See Platting.
Sheep from Ireland.
By the 5 Geo. III. Chap. 10. and 16 Geo. III. Chap. 8. all Sorts

TABLE A.

INWARDS.

	Duty. £. s. d.	Drawback. £. s. d.
of Cattle allowed to be imported from Ireland into Great Britain free of Duty.		
Sheeps Guts, dried to make Whips, the Groce, containing 12 Dozen	0 0 6	0 0 5
Wool, Duty free.		
Shruff, or old Brass, fit only to be re-manufactured, the Hundred Weight	0 13 3	0 11 9
Shumac, the Hundred Weight	0 1 5	0 0 0
By the 8 Geo. I. Chap. 15. Sect. 10. Shumac may be legally imported free of Duty, if regularly entered and landed.		
Silk, viz.		
Organzine, and all Thrown Silk in the Gum, the Pound, containing 16 Ounces	0 7 4	* 0 0
By the 2 William and Mary, Sess. 1. Chap. 9. Thrown Silk can only be imported from Italy, Sicily, or the Kingdom of Naples.		
* Drawback, if exported to Ireland, the Pound, containing 16 Ounces	– – –	0 6 11
exported (except to Ireland), the Pound, containing 16 Ounces	– – –	0 6 5
Raw Silk, the Pound containing 16 Ounces	0 3 0	0 * 0

imported by the East India Company, the Pound, containing 16 Ounces - - - - - - - 0 3 0 * 0 0

By the 6 Geo. I. Chap. 14. Turkey Raw Silk can only be imported from Ports in the Dominions of the Grand Signior.

* Drawback,
if exported to Ireland, the Pound containing 16 Ounces - - - - - - 0 2 10
exported (except to Ireland), the Pound, containing 16 Ounces - - - - - - 0 2 0

By the 23 Geo. II. Chap. 20. Raw Silk of the Growth and Culture of any of his Majesty's Colonies or Plantations in America, may be imported directly from thence into the Port of London, in Ships legally qualified, without Payment of any Duty, provided the Master or other Person having Charge of the Ship importing the same, shall upon his arrival in the said Port deliver to the Collector, Comptroller, or other chief Officer of the Customs, a Certificate under the Hands and Seals of Office, of the Collector and Comptroller of the Customs, and Naval Officer in America, or any Two of them, expressing the Marks, Number, Tale, and Weight in each Package so loaded on board such Ship, with the Name and Place of Abode of the Exporter, and the Name and Place of Abode of the Person who shall have sworn the Silk to be of the

(180)

TABLE A.

INWARDS.

	Duty. £. s. d.	Drawback. £. s. d.
Silk, viz.		
Growth and Culture, and the Name of the Person to whom consigned; and the Master is to make Oath that the Package and Silk contained in such Certificate are the same as were taken on board in America; otherwise all such Raw Silk to be liable to the Duties on Raw Silk.		
Silk Knubs, or Husks of Silk, the Pound, containing 16 Ounces	0 0 4	0 0 3½
Thrown Silk dyed, the Pound, containing 16 Ounces	1 4 9	* 0 0
* Drawback,		
if exported to Ireland, the Pound, containing 16 Ounces	—	1 2 3
exported (except to Ireland), the Pound, containing 16 Ounces	—	1 1 9
Silk wrought, viz.		
Crapes or Tiffanies of the Manufacture of Italy, imported from thence in British built Ships, the Pound, containing 16 Ounces	1 13 5	0 0 0
otherwise imported, the Pound, containing 16 Ounces	1 15 9	0 0 0
By the 31 Geo. III. Chap. 37. Silk Crapes and Tiffanies of the Manufacture of Italy are not to be imported except directly from		

(181)

the Ports of Italy, upon Forfeiture thereof, and the Importer liable to the same Penalties as upon Importation of Foreign wrought Silks and Velvets, by the 6 Geo. III. Chap. 28. and no Drawback to be allowed on the Exportation of Silk Crapes or Tiffanies of the Manufacture of Italy imported after the 5th July 1791.

Silver. See Plate.
Sisters Thread, the Pound
Skins and Furs, viz.

Armin or Ermin Skins, undressed, the Timber containing 40 Skins	0	2	9	0	2	4½
Badger Skins, undressed, the Piece	0	11	0	0	10	6
Bear Skins, White, undressed, the Piece	0	0	7	0	0	0
Skins of any other Colour, undressed, the Piece	0	11	0	0	10	0
Beavers Skins, undressed, the Piece	0	5	6	0	5	0
Skins, from any of his Majesty's Dominions in America, the Skin	0	0	8¼	0	0	0
Beaver Wombs, the Piece	0	0	1	0	0	0
Buck or Deer Skins, undressed, the Skin	0	0	5½	0	0	0
Indian Half-dressed, the Skin	0	0	2	0	0	0
By the 28 Geo. III. Chap. 37. Sect. 7. no Buck or Deer Skins to be deemed Half dressed, but such as are usually imported under that Denomination, which have undergone no other Operation or Dressing but that of taking off the Hair.	0	0	2	0	0	0

TABLE A.

INWARDS.

	Duty. £ s. d.	Drawback. £ s. d.
Skins and Furs, viz.		
Calabar Skins, tawed, the Timber containing 40 Skins	0 2 3	0 2 0
Skins, untawed or undressed, the Timber containing 40 Skins	0 1 10	0 1 8
Calve Skins, of Ireland, undressed, the Dozen	0 1 10	0 1 8
Skins, of any other Country, undressed, the Dozen	0 2 9	0 2 6
By the 9 Geo. III. Chap. 39. raw or undressed Calve Skins may be imported from Ireland or any of the British Colonies or Plantations in America, free of Duty. Continued by 21 Geo. III. Chap. 29. and 27 Geo. III. Chap. 36. until the 1st June 1791, and to the End of the then next Session of Parliament.		
Calve Skins, tanned, the Pound	0 0 4½	0 0 0
Cat Skins undressed, the Hundred Skins	0 11 0	0 10 0
Coney Skins, the Dozen	0 0 3½	0 0 3
Cordivants dressed, viz.		
imported by the East India Company, the Dozen	1 3 6	0 14 9
of Turkey, the Dozen	0 16 2	0 7 6
of Spain, the Dozen	1 16 4	1 5 9
Deer Skins. See Buck Skins.		

Dog Skins undreffed, the Piece - - -	0	0	2½		0	0	2
Dog Fish Skins undreffed, the Dozen - -	0	2	0		0	1	9
Elk Skins undreffed, the Skin - -	0	0	4		0	0	0
Ermin. See Armin Skins.							
Fisher Skins undreffed, the Piece -	0	1	4¼		0	1	3
Fitches undreffed, the Timber containing 40 Skins -	0	3	8		0	3	4
Fox Skins, Black, undreffed, the Skin· -	2	15	0		2	10	0
Skins of all other Sorts, undreffed, the Skin -	0	0	0		0	0	4
Goat Skins of Ireland undreffed, the Dozen -	0	1	10		0	1	8
of any other Country undreffed, the Dozen -	0	5	6		0	5	0
By the 15 Geo. III. Chap. 35. raw or undreffed Goats Skins may be imported from any Port or Place whatfoever in Britifh built Ships legally navigated, free of Duty, if regularly entered and landed, otherwife subject to Duty. Continued by the 26 Geo. III. Chap: 53. until the 1ft June 1790. and to the End of the then next Seffion of Parliament, and by the 31ft Geo. III. Chap. 43. the 15 Geo. III. Chap. 35. made perpetual.							
Goat Skins tanned, the Dozen - -	1	15	0		0	15	0
Hare Skins undreffed, the 120 - -	0	0	11		0	0	10
Huffe Skins undreffed, the Skin - -	0	0	2		0	0	1 3/4
imported by the Eaft India Company, the Skin -	0	0	2		0	0	1 1/4
Kid Skins in the Hair, the 100 containing 5 Score -	0	19	3		0	6	3

TABLE A.

INWARDS.

	Duty.			Drawback.		
	£.	s.	d.	£.	s.	d.
Skins and Furs, viz.						
Kid Skins dressed, the 100 containing 5 Score	1	4	9	0	11	3
Lamb Skins undressed in the Wool, the 120	0	2	9	0	2	6
dressed in Alum, the 100 containing 5 Score	0	14	3	0	5	10
dressed in Oil, the 100 containing 5 Score	2	0	4	1	1	8
Slink Lamb Skins undressed in the Wool, the 120	0	1	4½	0	1	3
Leopard Skins undressed, the Piece	0	6	11	0	6	3
Lion Skins undressed, the Piece	0	2	9	0	2	6
Martins or Martrons undressed, the Timber containing 40 Skins	2	15	0	2	10	0
Tails undressed, the 120	0	11	0	0	10	0
Minks Skins tawed, the Timber containing 40 Skins	1	2	6	1	0	0
untawed or undressed, the Timber containing 40 Skins	0	16	6	0	15	0
Mole Skins undressed, the Dozen	0	0	2	0	0	1½
Moose Skins undressed, the Piece	0	2	9	0	2	6
Musquath Skins undressed, the 100 Skins	0	13	9	0	12	6
Otter Skins undressed, the Piece	0	1	5	0	1	3
Ounce Skins undressed, the Piece	0	3	6	0	3	1½
Panther Skins undressed, the Piece	0	5	6	0	5	0
Pelts of Goats dressed, the Dozen	0	2	9	0	2	6

undressed, the Dozen	—	—	0	1	4½	0	1	3
of all other Sorts undressed, the 100	—	—	0	8	3	0	7	6
Raccoon Skins undressed, the Hundred Skins	—	—	0	13	9	0	12	6
Sables undressed, the Timber containing 40 Skins	—	—	8	5	0	7	10	0
Tails or Tips of Sable undressed, the Piece	—	—	0	0	7	0	0	6
Seal Skins undressed, the Skin	—	—	0	0	6	0	0	5
caught and taken wholly by his Majesty's Subjects carrying on any Fishery from any of his Majesty's Colonies or Plantations in America, and usually residing in the said Colonies or Plantations, and imported in British built Ships, the Skin			0	0	2	0	0	1

By the 26 Geo. III. Chap. 26. Seals Skins caught and taken on the Banks and Shores of the Island of Newfoundland and Parts adjacent, wholly by his Majesty's Subjects carrying on the said Fishery from his Majesty's European Dominions, and usually residing in the said Dominions, Oath being made before the Collector or other chief Officer of the Customs, by the Master of the Ship importing the same, that the said Seals Skins were so caught or taken, or that they were purchased as aforesaid, in which Case of Purchase, a Certificate by the Naval Officer, or, if no Naval Officer, by the Commander of any of his Majesty's Ships on that Station, is to be produced by the Master of the Ship to the Collector or other chief Officer of the Customs, may be imported free of Duty.

TABLE A.

INWARDS.

	Duty. £. s. d.	Drawback. £. s. d.

Skins, viz.

The 26 Geo. III. Chap. 41. Sect. 14 and 15. allows to be imported into Great Britain free of Duty, until the 25th of December 1791, Blubber or Oil of Whales, Whale Fins, Seal Oil or Seal Skins, or any other Produce of Seals, or other Fish or Creatures taken or caught in the Greenland Seas or Davis's Streights, or in the Seas adjacent, by British Subjects usually residing in Great Britain, Ireland, Guernsey, Jersey, or Man, in British built Ships, owned by British Subjects usually residing in the Places beforementioned, Oath being made by the Master and Mate of the Ship importing the same, that the said Articles were caught and taken as aforesaid. The Greenland Seas and Davis's Streights to be deemed to extend to the Latitude of 59°. 30″. North, and no farther.

The 26 Geo. III. Chap. 50. Sect. 2, and 5. requires that the Ship fitted and cleared out from a Port of Great Britain, Ireland, Guernsey, Jersey, or Man, did appear by her Register to be British built, wholly owned by his Majesty's Subjects usually residing in some Part of the said Dominions, navigated by a Master and three fourths of the Mariners at the least, his Majesty's Subjects usually residing as aforesaid; or if the Ship shall clear from any Port of Great Britain, then such Ship may be navigated by Persons not being his Majesty's Subjects, but being Protestants, who have heretofore been employed in carrying on the Fishery to the Southward of the thirty-sixth Degree of South Latitude, who shall at the Time of the Ship clearing out, on board which they shall serve, make Oath or Affirmation, before Two of the principal Officers of the Customs of the Port in Great Britain from which the Ship shall clear out, if it be their first Voyage, that they have already established, or that it is their Intention to establish themselves and their Families in Great Britain as Inhabitants thereof, and Subjects of his Majesty, and if it shall be their Second or any subsequent Voyage, that they have actually established themselves and their Families as aforesaid, in Great Britain.

By Sect. 23. All Oil, Head Matter, or other Produce of Fish or Creatures living in the Seas, caught and taken as required by this Act, also all Whale Fins and Skins of Seals so caught and taken, and all Oil, Head Matter, or other Produce of Whales or other Creatures living in the Seas, Fins of Whales, and Skins of Seals, taken and caught in any Part of the Ocean, by the Crew of any Ship built in Great Britain, Guernsey, Jersey, or Man, wholly owned by his Majesty's Subjects usually residing therein respectively, and

TABLE A.

INWARDS.

	Duty. £. s. d.	Drawback. £. s. d.

Skins, viz. navigated in Manner aforesaid, shall upon Importation into Great Britain be admitted to Entry, and landed without Payment of any Duty whatever.

N. B. By the 28 Geo. III. Chap. 20. Sect. 3, and 10. Every Ship which shall sail or pass to the Eastward of the Cape of Good Hope, or to the Westward of Cape Horn, or through the Streights of Magellan, is obliged to have a Licence from the East India and South Sea Companies, and may pass to the Eastward of the Cape of Good Hope as far as the Equator Northward, and as far as fifty-one Degrees of Longitude East from London; to the Westward of Cape Horn, or through the Streights of Magellan, as far as the Equator Northward, and as far as one hundred and eighty Degrees of Longitude West from London, and no further. All Oil, Head Matter, or other Produce of Fish or other Creatures living in the Seas, taken by the Crew of any Ship fitted and cleared out under the Directions of this Act for the additional Premiums upon Importation into Great Britain to be admitted to Entry, and landed without Payment of any Duty.

By the 31 Geo. III. Chap. 26. Seals Skins caught as directed by the 26 Geo. III. Chap. 26. cured with Foreign Salt laden on board such Ships at Sea, from the Cape de Verd Islands, or other Islands or Places adjacent, may be imported without Payment of any Duty whatever, provided such Skins shall not be imported with more Salt or Brine than shall be necessary for the Preservation thereof; but all the Salt which shall fall off and not adhere to such Skins of Seals, and all the Brine and Liquor wherein the same shall be preserved, not necessary for the immediate Preservation thereof, shall be thrown away or otherwise destroyed, in the Presence of the proper Officers of the Customs. Oath to be made by the Master, that the Salt so used was taken on board the Vessel as aforesaid, and not made in or exported from Great Britain or Ireland, and no Drawback received.

Sheep Skins undressed in the Wool, the Dozen	-	0	0	10	0	0	9
dressed in Oil, the Dozen	-	0	4	9	0	2	6
otherwise dressed, the Dozen	-	0	2	6	0	1	8
Squirrel Skins undressed. See Calabar Skins.							
Swan Skins undressed, the Piece	-	0	0	11	0	0	10
Tiger Skins undressed, the Piece	-	0	2	9	0	2	6
Weasel Skins undressed, the 120	-	0	0	11	0	0	10
Wolf Skins tawed, the Piece	-	0	3	3	0	7	6

TABLE A.

INWARDS.

	Duty. £. s. d.	Drawback. £. s. d.
Skins and Furs, viz.		
Wolf Skins untawed or undressed, the Piece	0 6 4	0 5 9½
Wolverings undressed, the Skin	0 3 6	0 3 1½
N. B. The hereafter mentioned Furs being tawed, are by the 3 Edw. IV. Chap. 4. prohibited to be imported for Sale by any Persons except made and wrought in Ireland, viz.		
Armin, Badger, Bear, Beaver, Calabar, Cat, Fitch, Fox, Leopard, Martin or Martron, Mink, Mole, Otter, Ounce, Sable, Wolf, and Wolvering, or any other Kinds of Furs not hereinbefore specifically rated as Skins and Furs.		
Slates in Frames, the Dozen	0 0 11	0 0 10
Slick Stones, the Hundred, containing five Score	0 3 4	0 3 0
Slude, the Pound	0 0 6	0 0 5
Smalts, the Pound	0 0 4	0 0 3½
Snuff, imported by the East India Company, the Pound	0 1 3	0 0 0
from the British Plantations in America or the Spanish West Indies, the Pound	0 0 6	0 0 0
from any other Place, the Pound	0 0 10	0 0 0
Subject also to the Duty of Excise.		

cannot be imported into any other Ports of Great Britain than London, Bristol, Liverpool, Lancaster, Cowes, Falmouth, Whitehaven, Hull, Port Glasgow, Greenock, Leith, or Newcastle upon Tyne; and imported in any less Quantity than 450 lb. net, in any Package, or in any Ship less than 120 Tons Burthen, forfeited, and the Ship. For the Regulations respecting the Entry, &c. See the 29 Geo. III. Chap. 68.

Soap, viz.

Hard Soap, the Hundred Weight	-	2	4	0	0 0
Soft Soap, the Hundred Weight	-	1	17	5	0 0

Soap imported in any Package containing less than 224 lb. net, forfeited, and £. 50 by the Master of the Ship importing the same; must be stowed openly in the Hold of the Ship. 23 Geo. II. Chap. 21. Sect. 27.

Soapers Waste.

By the 18 Geo. II. Chap. 22. Soapers Waste may be legally imported free of Duty.

Spanish Wool, free of Duty.					
Spelter, the Hundred Weight	-	0	13	9	0 12 6
Spinal fine, to make Gauze, the Pound	-	0	2	9	0 2 6
Spinnel Short, or unwrought Incle, the Pound	-	0	0	3½	0 0 0

TABLE A.

INWARDS.

	Duty.			Drawback.		
	£.	s.	d.	£.	s.	d.
Spirits, or Strong Water, not otherwise enumerated and described, the Gallon	0	2	10	0	2	7
Subject also to the Duty of Excise. See Arrack, &c. under their respective Titles. By the 26 Geo. III. Chap. 73. Sect. 60. any Spirits imported (except Rum or Spirits from the British Sugar Plantations) stronger than 1 to 9 Hydrometer Proof, forfeited; in Casks from Europe or from the British Plantations in America, less than 60 Gallons, or in Ships less than 100 Tons, forfeited; but Spirits from the British Plantations in smaller Casks for private Use, may be admitted by Leave of the Commissioners of the Customs.						
Spunges, the Pound	0	0	9	0	0	6
if not imported directly from the Place of its Growth, the Pound	0	2	3	0	1	6
Starch, the Hundred Weight	5	5	8	0	0	0
Starch imported in any Package containing less than 224 lb. net, forfeited, and £. 50 by the Master of the Ship importing the same; must be stowed openly in the Hold of the Ship. 23 Geo. II. Chap. 21. Sect. 27.						
Steel, viz.						
Gad Steel, the Hundred Weight	2	5	2	2	0	8

Long Steel, the Hundred Weight - - - - -	0	12	8	0	11	11
Wisp Steel, the Hundred Weight - - - -	0	12	8	0	11	11½
Steel Wire, the Pound - - - - - -	0	0	10	0	0	9
Stock Fish, the 120 - - - - - - -	0	2	1	0	1	4
Stones, viz.						
Dog Stones, not exceeding four Feet in Diameter, above six Inches in Thickness, and under twelve Inches in Thickness, the Last containing three Pair - - - - -	8	11	8	7	12	2
Emery Stones, the Hundred Weight of Turkey, imported in a Foreign Ship, the Hundred Weight - - - - -	0	1	10	0	1	7
Grave Stones, of Marble unpolished, the Foot square superficial Measure	0	1	11	0	1	7
Grave Stones, of Marble polished, the Foot square superficial Measure	0	0	1¼	0	0	1
Grave Stones, of Marble polished or unpolished, the Foot square superficial Measure	0	0	2½	0	0	2
Marble Basons, Tables, Mortars, and other polished Marble (except Grave Stones, and Paving Stones polished), the Foot square superficial Measure	0	0	0½	0	0	0¼
Marble Blocks, the solid Foot - - - -	1	0	0	0	10	0
Marble Paving Stones rough, the Foot square superficial Measure	2	0	0	1	10	0
Marble Paving Stones polished, the Foot square superficial Measure	0	0	1¼	0	0	1
	0	0	2½	0	0	2

(194)

TABLE A.

INWARDS.

	Duty. £. s. d.	Drawback. £. s. d.
Stones, viz.		
Mill Stones, above four Feet in Diameter, or if twelve Inches in Thickness or upwards, the Piece	2 4 0	1 19 0
Paving Stones, not of Marble, the Foot square superficial Measure	0 0 0¼	0 0 0¼
Pebble Stones, the Ton	0 5 6	0 5 8
Pomice Stones, the Ton	0 3 0	0 2 8
Quern Stones large, three Feet in Diameter and not above four Feet in Diameter, and not exceeding six Inches in Thickness, the Last containing three Pair	0 19 10	0 17 6
Quern Stones small, under three Feet in Diameter, and not exceeding six Inches in Thickness, the Last containing three Pair	0 9 11	0 8 9
Slates in Frames, the Dozen	0 0 11	0 0 10
Slick Stones, the Hundred containing five Score	0 3 4	0 3 0
Tables of Slate without Frames, the Piece	0 0 6	0 0 5
Whetstones, the Hundred	0 3 8	0 3 3
Straw or Bass Hats or Bonnets, each Hat or Bonnet not exceeding 22 Inches in Diameter, the Dozen	0 2 9	0 2 6
exceeding 22 Inches in Diameter, the Dozen	0 5 6	0 5 0
By 10 Geo. III. Chap. 43. Sect. 6. to be imported into London only,		

in Bales or Tubs containing each 75 Dozen Hats or Bonnets, and in Ships exceeding 50 Tons Burthen, otherwise forfeited.						
Stuffs of all Sorts made of or mixed with Wool, the Yard	—	0	5	6	0	4	10
Sturgeon, the Keg	—	0	3	4	0	2	11
Succades Wet or Dry, the Pound	—	0	0	8	0	0	7
Succus Liquoritiæ, the Hundred Weight imported by the East India Company, the Pound	—	0	1	6	0	1	5
Sugar, viz.		0	1	8	0	0	0
refined, the Hundred Weight	—	4	18	8	4	10	2
Brown, and Muscovado, not of the British Plantations, the Hundred Weight	—	1	9	10	1	7	0
White, not of the British Plantations, the Hundred Weight	—	2	3	2	2	4	6
Brown, and Muscovado, of the British Plantations, the Hundred Weight	—	0	15	0	0	15	0
White, of the British Plantations, the Hundred Weight	—	1	11	8	1	11	8
From any of the British Colonies or Plantations on the Continent of America, upon Importation to be warehoused, the Hundred Weight To be subject to the same Regulations and Restrictions mentioned in the Note following Coffee. 6 Geo. III. Chap. 52.		0	0	3	0	0	0
When taken out of such Warehouse, in order to be used in the Kingdom, the Hundred Weight	—	1	6	11	0	0	0

TABLE A.

INWARDS.

	Duty. £. s. d.	Drawback. £. s. d.
Sugar, viz. N. B. See the Bounty upon the Exportation of Sugar refined from Sugar of the British Plantations in Table G.		
Sugar Candy, Brown, the Hundred Weight - -	2 15 0	2 10 0
imported by the East India Company, the Hundred Weight - - - - -	4 19 0	4 14 0
White, the Hundred Weight - -	4 2 6	3 15 0
imported by the East India Company, the Hundred Weight - - - - -	7 8 6	7 1 0
Swingles, the Groce, containing twelve Dozen -	0 16 6	0 15 0
Tables of Marble, Basons, Mortars, and other polished Marble, the Foot square, superficial Measure - -	0 1 6	0 0 10
Tables of Slate, without Frames, the Piece -	0 0 6	0 0 5
Tails of Cows, the Hundred containing five Score -	0 2 9	0 2 6
Tallow, the Hundred Weight - - -	0 9 2	0 0 0
By the 7 Geo. III. Chap. 12. Tallow may be legally imported from any Place free of Duty, if regularly entered and landed, otherwise subject to Duty. Continued by 26 Geo. III. Chap. 53. and		

29 Geo. III. Chap. 55. to 25th March 1791, and to the End of the then next Session of Parliament.

		£	s.	d.
Tamarinds, the Pound — — — — —		0	0	0
imported by the East India Company, the Pound		0	0	$1\frac{1}{2}$
Tar, not being the Product of any of the Dominions or Plantations of the Crown of Great Britain, viz.				
imported in a British built Ship, the Last containing 12 Barrels, each Barrel not exceeding 31 Gallons — — —		0	0	$1\frac{1}{2}$
imported in a Foreign Ship, the Last containing 12 Barrels, each Barrel not exceeding $31\frac{1}{2}$ Gallons — —	0 12 $4\frac{1}{2}$	0	11	$1\frac{1}{2}$
Tar, of the Product of any of the Dominions or Plantations of the Crown of Great Britain, the Last containing 12 Barrels, each Barrel not exceeding $31\frac{1}{2}$ Gallons — — —	0 13 1	0	11	$1\frac{1}{2}$
Tarras, the Bushel — — — — —	0 11 0	0	9	9
Tazels, the Thousand — — — — —	0 0 6	0	0	5
Thread, viz.	0 1 2	0	1	0
Bridges Thread, the Dozen Pounds — —	0 9 11	0	8	9
Crossbow Thread, the hundred Pounds —	0 14 8	0	13	0
Outnal Thread, the Dozen Pounds — —	0 17 8	0	16	2
Packthread, the hundred Pounds — —	0 13 3	0	11	9
Sifters Thread, the Pound — — —	0 2 9	0	2	$7\frac{1}{2}$
Whited brown Thread, the Dozen Pounds	0 17 8	0	15	8

TABLE A.

INWARDS.

	Duty. £. s. d.	Drawback. £. s. d.
By the 7 and 8 William III. Chap. 39. Thread and other Manufactures of Hemp or Flax, the Growth and Manufacture of Ireland, may be imported directly from thence free of Duty, subject to the Regulations and Restrictions in the Note following Flax. By the 16 Geo. II. the Oath of the Exporter from Ireland is dispensed with, provided the Requisites of the 7 and 8 William III. are performed.		
Thrums of Linen or Fustian, the Pound of Woollen, the Pound	0 0 1½ 0 0 3	0 0 1 0 0 2
Tiles, viz.		
Flanders Tiles to scour with, the Thousand	0 12 2	0 11 2
Galley Tiles, the Foot square	0 0 3	0 0 2½
By the 3 Edw. IV. Chap. 4. any painted Wares, which Galley Tiles are considered to be, cannot be imported for Sale except made in Ireland.		
Paving Tiles, not exceeding ten Inches square, the Thousand	1 9 9	1 8 3
exceeding ten Inches square, the Thousand	2 6 3	2 4 9
Pan Tiles, the Thousand	2 12 10	2 8 10
Tin, the Hundred Weight	2 13 0	0 0 0

		£. s. d.	£. s. d.
Tinglass, the Hundred Weight	—	0 13 3	0 11 9
Tobacco, viz.			
of the Growth, Production, or Manufacture of the Plantations or Dominions of Spain or Portugal, the Pound	—	0 1 6	0 0 0
of the Growth or Production of Ireland, or of the Growth or Production of his Majesty's Colonies, Plantations, Islands, or Territories in America, or of the Growth or Production of the United States of America, the Pound	—	0 0 6	0 0 0

By the 31 Geo. III. Chap. 47. damaged and mean Tobacco, upon which the Importer refuses to pay the Duty, which has been separated from the sound Tobacco, the Commissioners of the Customs and Excise shall cause such Tobacco to be burnt; and there is no Allowance for mean and damaged Tobacco upon which the Merchant refuses to pay the Duties.

| delivered out of the Warehouse for Exportation, the Pound | — | 0 0 1 | 0 0 0 |

If warehoused, the Duties of Importation only payable when delivered out for Home Trade or Exportation, at the Weight at the Time of Delivery, if there has arisen any Deficiency from Shrinkage.

Subject also to a Duty of Excise.

TABLE A.

INWARDS.

	Duty. £. s. d.	Drawback. £. s. d.
Tobacco, viz. If imported in any less Quantity than 450 lb. net, in any one Package, or in any Ship less than 120 Tons Burthen, forfeited, and the Ship; but not to extend to any Tobacco brought loose in the Ship for the Use of the Seamen, not exceeding five Pounds Weight for each Person. Tobacco cannot be imported into any other Port of Great Britain than London, Bristol, Liverpool, Lancaster, Cowes, Falmouth, Whitehaven, Hull, Newcastle upon Tyne, Port Glasgow, Greenock, or Leith, under Forfeiture of the Tobacco and Ship. See the 29 Geo. III. Chap. 68. and 30 Geo. III. Chap. 40. for the further Regulations and Restrictions respecting the Importation, entering, landing, and shipping of Tobacco. Drawbacks upon the Exportation of manufactured Tobacco to any Port or Place beyond the Seas, except the Islands of Faro and Ferro, viz.		
Short Cut, and Roll Tobacco, the Pound	- - -	0 0 6
Shag Tobacco, the Pound	- - -	0 0 6

(201)

	£	s.	d.	£	s.	d.
Carrot Tobacco, the Pound				0	0	9
N.B. Thumb Cut, Black Leaf, Lug, and Twist or Pig Tail Tobacco, is to be deemed Roll Tobacco. Entitled also to a Drawback of Part of the Duty of Excise.						
Tongues. See Neats Tongues.						
Tortoise Shell, the Pound	0	1	3	0	1	1½
Tow, the Hundred Weight	0	2	9	0	2	6
Tow of Muscovy or Russia, imported in a Foreign Ship, the Hundred Weight	0	2	11	0	0	6
Treacle Common, the Pound	0	0	4	0	0	2¼
of Venice, the Pound	0	1	6	0	1	0
Truffles, the Pound	0	2	3	0	2	0
Turbots.						
Turbots may be imported freely by any Persons whatever, in any Ships whatever, and without Payment of any Duty. By 1 Geo. I. Stat. 2. Chap. 18.						
Turpentine,						
Common, the Hundred Weight of Venice, Scio, or Cyprus, the Pound	0	2	3	0	1	6
of Germany or of any other Place, not otherwise enumerated, the Hundred Weight	0	0	4	0	0	2¾
	0	12	9	0	8	6
Oil of, the Pound	0	0	1¼	0	0	0¼

(202)

TABLE A.

INWARDS.	Duty. £. s. d.	Drawback. £. s. d.
Twine, the Hundred Weight - - -	0 11 0	0 9 9
Twist for Bandstrings, the Dozen Knots - -	0 2 3	0 2 0
N. B. Thirty-two Yards of Bandstring Twist is deemed a Knot.		
Valonia, the Hundred Weight - - -	0 1 2	0 0 0
By the 8 Geo. I. Chap. 15. Sect. 10. Valonia may be legally imported free of Duty, if regularly entered and landed.		
Varnish, the Hundred Weight - - -	0 8 9	0 5 10
Vellum, the Skin - - -	0 3 2	0 0 0
Verdigrease,		
Common, the Pound - - -	0 0 3	0 0 0
Crystallized, the Pound - - -	0 1 0	0 0 0
Vermicelli, the Pound - - -	0 0 2	0 0 1½
By the 7 Geo. III. Chap. 30. Vermicelli may be imported from any of his Majesty's Colonies in North America free of Duty. Continued by the 21 Geo. III. Chap. 29, until December 1, 1796.		
Vermillion, or Cinabrium, the Pound - -	0 0 7	0 0 4½
imported by the East India Company, the Pound	0 0 7	0 0 4½
Vinegar, the Tun, containing 252 Gallons - -	32 18 10	7 14 11

(203)

		£	s.	d.	£	s.	d.
Vinelloes, the Pound	—	0	8	3	0	7	6
Virginal Wire,							
of Brass, the Hundred Weight	—	6	11	6	12	11
of Iron, the Hundred Weight	—	7	8	0	6	4	0
Visney, the Gallon	—	7	2	10	0	2	7
Usquebaugh, the Gallon	—	0	2	10	0	2	7
Subject also to the Duty of Excise.							
Wafers, the Pound	—	0	0	6	0	0	5
Water, viz.							
Cordial water, Strong Water, or other Spirits, not otherwise described and enumerated, the Gallon	—	0	2	10	0	2	7
Subject also to the Duty of Excise.							
Spa Water, or Pyrmont Water, and all other Mineral or Natural Water, the Dozen Bottles or Flasks, each Bottle or Flask not exceeding three Pints	—	0	1	10	0	1	8
Wax, viz.							
Bees Wax White, or manufactured, the Hundred Weight	3	2	4	3	1	4
Bees Wax unmanufactured, the Hundred Weight	—	1	11	7	1	10	7
Hard Wax, the Pound	—	0	1	3	0	1	1
Bay or Myrtle Wax, the Pound	—	0	0	4	0	0	3½
Weld, the Hundred Weight	—	0	0	10	0	0	8½

TABLE A.

INWARDS.

	Duty. £. s. d.	Drawback. £. s. d.
Whale Fins, viz.		
of Foreign Fishing, the Ton containing 20 Hundred Weight	97 18 0	88 18 0
of British Fishing, imported in Shipping belonging to any of his Majesty's Colonies or Plantations, the Ton containing 20 Hundred Weight	2 15 0	1 10 0
of British Fishing, imported in Shipping belonging to Great Britain, the Ton containing 20 Hundred Weight	1 7 6	0 15 0
See under what Circumstances Whale Fins may be imported without Payment of Duty, by 26 Geo. III. Chap. 41. and 26 Geo. III. Chap. 50. fully explained in the Notes following Blubber.		
Wheat. See Corn.		
Wheat Flour. See Corn.		
Whetstones, the Hundred	0 3 8	0 3 3
Whipcord, the Pound	0 0 2	0 0 1½
Whisk or Flag Brooms, the Dozen	0 0 1¼	0 0 1
White Lead, the Hundred Weight	0 4 5	0 2 11
imported by the East India Company, the Hundred Weight	0 4 5	0 2 11
Wine, Rhenish, German, and Hungary Wine, viz.		

imported into any Port of Great Britain in a British built Ship, the Tun containing 252 Gallons	-	33	12	0	
in a Foreign Ship, the Tun containing 252 Gallons		37	16	0	33 12 0
exported to any British Colony or Plantation in America, the Tun containing 252 Gallons	-				
to any other Place, the Tun containing 252 Gallons	-				28 17 6
Portugal, Madeira, Spanish, and all other Wines not otherwise enumerated, viz.					
imported into the Port of London in a British built Ship, the Tun containing 252 Gallons	-	19	12	0	
in a Foreign Ship, the Tun containing 252 Gallons		22	8	0	
having been imported into the Port of London, and exported to any British Colony or Plantation in America, the Tun containing 252 Gallons	-				
exported to any other Place, the Tun containing 252 Gallons					19 12 0
imported into any Port of Great Britain, except the Port of London, in a British built Ship, the Tun containing 252 Gallons	-	16	16	0	16 9 0
in a Foreign Ship, the Tun containing 252 Gallons		19	12	0	
having been imported into any Port of Great Britain, except					

TABLE A.

INWARDS.

	Duty. £ s. d.	Drawback. £ s. d.
Wine, the Port of London, and exported to any British Colony or Plantation in America, the Tun containing 252 Gallons	—	16 16 0
exported to any other Place, the Tun containing 252 Gallons	—	13 13 0
By the 28 Geo. III. Chap. 33. All other Wines (except French European, Rhenish, German, Hungary, Portugal, Madeira, Spanish, or any of the Dominions of the King of Spain), imported into the Port of London, in a British built Ship, the Tun containing 252 Gallons	29 8 0	—
imported in a Foreign Ship, the Tun containing 252 Gallons	33 12 0	—
having been imported into the Port of London, and exported to any British Colony or Plantation in America, or to any British Settlement in the East Indies, the Tun containing 252 Gallons	—	29 8 0
exported to any other Place, the Tun containing 252 Gallons	—	24 13 6
imported into any Port of Great Britain (except the Port of London), in a British built Ship, the Tun containing 252 Gallons	25 4 0	—
in a Foreign Ship, the Tun containing 252 Gallons	29 8 0	—

having been imported into any Port of Great Britain (except the Port of London), and exported to any British Colony or Plantation in America, or to any British Settlement in the East Indies, the Tun containing 252 Gallons — — — 25 4 0
exported to any other Place, the Tun containing 252 Gallons — 20 9 6
N. B. Wine is also subject to the Duty of Excise.

Wine Lees are subject to the same Duty as Wine; but no Drawback is to be allowed for any Lees of Wine exported.

The Duties on French European Wines being imposed agreeable to the Commercial Treaty with France until 10th May 1800, and no longer, the same are inserted in Table C. See also the general Wine Tables at the End of the Work.

No Wines can be imported for Sale except in Casks containing 25 Gallons each, except Wines of the Growth of Tuscany in open Flasks, or Wines of Turkey or any other Parts of the Levant Seas, in the same Manner as they have usually been imported; and no French, Spanish, or Portugal Wines, can be imported for Sale in any Cask less than what is commonly called a Hogshead, except French Wine in Bottles or Flasks, which may be imported in Packages containing not less than three Dozen Bottles each, until the 10th May 1800; but the Commissioners of the Customs

T A B L E A.

INWARDS.

	Duty. £. s. d.	Drawback. £. s. d.

Wine, may admit to Entry any Wines imported in smaller Casks without Fraud or Concealment, for private Use, and not by way of Merchandise. No Wine can be imported in Ships unless more than 60 Tons Burthen, under Forfeiture of the Wine and Ship. See Article 4, in General Directions of Importation, preceding Table A.

Wines damaged, corrupt, or unmerchantable; if the Importer shall refuse to pay the Duties thereon, the Commissioners of the Customs may cause such Wines to be received into the Custody of the proper Officers, to be publicly sold in order to be distilled into Brandy, or made into Vinegar, and so much Salt or Vinegar to be put therein as they shall judge sufficient to prevent them from being used for any other Purpose; and shall cause the Produce of such Sale to be paid to the Importer, not exceeding the following Allowances, but no Allowance to be made for any Wines unless imported in Casks on board a Merchant's Ship directly from the Place of the Growth, or the usual Place of first Shipping (except as to Ships stranded). See the 6 Geo. I. Chap. 12.

8 Geo. I. Chap. 18. 12 Geo. I. Chap. 28. 5 Geo. III. Chap. 43. 26 Geo. III. Chap. 59.

	£	s.	d.
For every Tun of such Wine of the Growth of Germany, or which pays Duty as such - - - - - -	4	0	0
For every Tun of such Wine of the Growth of France - -	4	0	0
For every Tun of such Wine of the Growth of Spain, Portugal, or elsewhere - - - - - - -	8	0	0
Wine entered for Prisage, viz.			
Rhenish, German, or Hungary Wine, viz. imported into any Port of England, in a British built Ship, the Tun containing 252 Gallons -	24	6	9
in a Foreign Ship, the Tun containing 252 Gallons	27	1	9
exported to any British Colony or Plantation in America, the Tun containing 252 Gallons	24	6	0
to any other Place, the Tun containing 252 Gallons	20	13	0
Portugal, Madeira, Spanish, and all other Wines not otherwise enumerated, viz.			
imported into the Port of London in a British built Ship, the Tun containing 252 Gallons -	14	7	11
in a Foreign Ship, the Tun containing 252 Gallons -	16	4	6

P

(210)

TABLE A.

INWARDS.

	Duty. £. s. d.	Drawback. £. s. d.
Wine entered for Prisage, viz. Portugal, Madeira, Spanish, and all other Wines not otherwise enumerated, viz.		
having been imported into the Port of London, and exported to any British Colony or Plantation in America, the Tun containing 252 Gallons	—	14 7 11
exported to any other Place, the Tun containing 252 Gallons	—	11 18 1
imported into any Port of England, except the Port of London, in a British built Ship, the Tun containing 252 Gallons	12 11 2	
in a Foreign Ship, the Tun containing 252 Gallons	14 7 11	
having been imported into any Port of England, except the Port of London, and exported to any British Colony or Plantation in America, the Tun containing 252 Gallons	—	12 11 2
exported to any other Place, the Tun containing 252 Gallons	—	10 0 5
All other Wines (except French European, Rhenish, German, Hungary, Portugal, Madeira, Spanish, or of any of the Dominions		

of the King of Spain), imported into the Port of London in a British built Ship, the Tun containing 252 Gallons - 21 11 10

imported in a Foreign Ship, the Tun containing 252 Gallons - 24 6 9

having been imported into the Port of London, and exported to any British Colony or Plantation in America, or to any British Settlement in the East Indies, the Tun containing 252 Gallons - — — — 21 11 10

exported to any other Place, the Tun containing 252 Gallons - — — — 17 17 1

imported into any Port of England (except the Port of London), in a British built Ship, the Tun containing 252 Gallons - 18 16 10

in a Foreign Ship, the Tun containing 252 Gallons - 21 11 10

having been imported into any Port of England (except the Port of London), and exported to any British Colony or Plantation in America, or to any British Settlement in the East Indies, the Tun containing 252 Gallons - — — — 18 16 10

exported to any other Place, the Tun containing 252 Gallons - — — — 15 0 7

See the Wine Tables following Table I.

N.B. Wine imported into the Port of London by British Subjects is liable also to a Prisage Duty of two Shillings per Tun; but by the Charter granted to the City of London by Edward III. a complete resident Freeman of London is exempt from Prisage; and any Persons buying Wines in Foreign Parts and importing them for their own spending, are not subject to Prisage.

TABLE A.

INWARDS.

	Duty. £. s. d.	Drawback. £. s. d.

Wine imported by Aliens is subject to the Duty of Butlerage in the Port of London of two Shillings per Tun, in lieu of Prisage; also the further Duty of Scavage to the City of London, of two Shillings per Tun on all Wines except Rhenish, upon which the Scavage is Sixpence per Aum; and Wines imported by any Persons in Foreign Ships, are subject to this Duty. There is likewise a Duty of 4s. per Tun, payable to the Orphans' Fund, upon all Wines imported into the Port of London, until the Orphans' Debt is wholly paid. Levant, Sacks, Canaries, Malagas, Madeiras, Romneys, Hollocks, Bastards, Tents, and Alicant Wines, imported into any Port by Strangers, are subject to a Duty of ten Shillings per Butt or Pipe, which is payable to the Town of Southampton.

Wines imported into any Port of this Kingdom except London, pay Prisage ten Shillings per Tun; also the Town or Port Duties in every Port which they were liable to pay prior to the Consolidation Act, 27 Geo. III. Chap. 13.

The Prisage Duties recited in Table A, do not concern the Importer, but are paid to the Prisage Master out of the Duties received by the Collector of the Customs; being one Tun of Wine in every Ship importing ten Tuns of Wine, and two Tuns of Wine in every Ship importing twenty Tuns of Wine and upwards, which have been compounded for thus:

	Rhenish.	French.	Other Wines.
	£. s. d.	£. s. d.	£. s. d.
A Ship bringing 10 Tuns and under 20 Tuns of Wine	9 5 3	7 16 2	5 4 1
A Ship bringing 20 Tons and upwards	18 10 6	15 12 4	10 8 2

The Prisage Duties enumerated in Table A, are the reserved Duties received by the Collector of the Customs after paying the Prisage beforementioned, and are the Amount of the Duties of Customs retained by him to be paid into the Exchequer on account of Customs upon Prisage Wines.

Wire, viz.

Brass or Copper Wire not otherwise enumerated, the Hundred Weight	2 12 3	2 9 0
Iron Wire, the Hundred Weight	2 17 9	2 14 0
Latten Wire, the Hundred Weight	2 13 0	2 9 8
Steel Wire, the Pound	0 0 10	0 0 9
Virginal Wire of Brass, the Hundred Weight	7 6 11	6 12 11
of Iron, the Hundred Weight	7 8 0	6 14 0

(214)

TABLE A.

INWARDS.

	Duty. £ s. d.	Drawback. £ s. d.
Woad, viz.		
Green Woad, the Ton containing 20 Hundred Weight	1 13 0	1 5 6
Thouloufe Woad, the Hundred Weight	0 3 8	0 2 10
Wood, viz.		
Anchor Stocks,		
imported in a British built Ship, the Piece	0 2 3	0 2 1
in a Foreign Ship, the Piece	0 2 4	0 2 1
See the Notes inferted at the End of Wood.		
Balks, five Inches Square and under eight Inches Square, or if 24 Feet in Length or upwards,		
imported in a British built Ship, the 120	2 13 0	2 10 6
in a Foreign Ship, the 120	2 14 5	2 10 6
under five Inches Square, and under 24 Feet in Length,		
imported in a British built Ship, the 120	1 1 3	1 0 3
in a Foreign Ship, the 120	1 1 9	1 0 3
See the Notes inferted at the End of Wood.		
Barrel Staves. See Staves.		
Battens, 8 Feet in Length and not exceeding 20 Feet in Length, not		

(215)

	l. s. d.	l. s. d.
above 7 Inches in Width, and not exceeding 2¾ Inches in Thickness,		
imported in a British built Ship, the 120	1 6 6	1 5 3
in a Foreign Ship, the 120	1 7 3	1 5 3
exceeding 20 Feet in Length, not above 7 Inches in Width, or if exceeding 2¾ Inches in Thickness,		
imported in a British built Ship, the 120	2 13 0	2 10 6
in a Foreign Ship, the 120	2 14 5	2 10 6
See the Notes inferted at the End of Wood.		
Batten Ends, under 8 Feet in Length, not above 7 Inches in Width, and not exceeding 2¼ Inches in Thickness,		
imported in a British built Ship, the 120	0 8 10	0 8 5
in a Foreign Ship, the 120	0 9 1	0 8 5
under 8 Feet in Length, not above 7 Inches in Width, and exceeding 2½ Inches in Thickness,		
imported in a British built Ship, the 120	0 17 8	0 16 10
in a Foreign Ship, the 120	0 18 2	0 16 10
See the Notes inferted at the End of Wood.		
Beech Boards. See Boards.		
Beech Plank, 2 Inches in Thickness or upwards, imported in a British built Ship, the Load containing 50 Cubic Feet	0 13 3	0 12 3

TABLE A.

INWARDS.

	Duty. £. s. d.	Drawback. £. s. d.
Wood, viz.		
Beech Plank, 2 Inches in Thickness or upwards, imported in a Foreign Ship, the Load containing 50 Cubic Feet	0 13 9	0 12 3
See the Notes inserted at the End of Wood.		
Beech Quarters, 5 Inches Square, and under 8 Inches Square, or if 24 Feet in Length or upwards,		
imported in a British built Ship, the 120	2 13 0	2 10 6
in a Foreign Ship, the 120	2 14 5	2 10 6
under 5 Inches Square, and under 24 Feet in Length,		
imported in a British built Ship, the 120	1 1 3	1 0 3
in a Foreign Ship, the 120	1 1 9	1 0 3
See the Notes inserted at the End of Wood.		
Boards, viz.		
Beech Boards, under 2 Inches in Thickness, and under 15 Feet in Length,		
imported in a British built Ship, the 120	1 6 5	1 4 5
in a Foreign Ship, the 120	1 7 6	1 4 5

(217)

under 2 Inches in Thickness, and if 15 Feet in Length or upwards,							
imported in a British built Ship, the 120	2	12	10		2	8	10
in a Foreign Ship, the 120	2	13	11		2	8	10
Clap Boards, not exceeding 5 Feet 3 Inches in Length, and under 8 Inches Square,							
imported in a British built Ship, the 120	1	0	0		0	19	6
in a Foreign Ship, the 120	1	0	2		0	19	6
Linn Boards or White Boards for Shoemakers, under 4 Feet in Length, and under 6 Inches in Thickness,							
imported in a British built Ship, the 120	1	19	8		1	16	8
in a Foreign Ship, the 120	2	1	3		1	16	8
for Shoemakers, 4 Feet in Length, or 6 Inches in Thickness,							
imported in a British built Ship, the 120	3	19	4		3	13	4
in a Foreign Ship, the 120	4	0	11		3	13	4
Millboards. See Pasteboards.							
Oak Boards, under 2 Inches in Thickness, and under 15 Feet in Length,							
imported in a British built Ship, the 120	2	12	10		2	8	10
in a Foreign Ship, the 120	2	15	0		2	8	10

TABLE A.

INWARDS.

	Duty. £. s. d.	Drawback. £. s. d.
Wood, viz. Boards, viz.		
Oak Boards, under 2 Inches in Thickness, and if 15 Feet in Length or upwards,		
imported in a British built Ship, the 120	5 5 8	4 17 8
in a Foreign Ship, the 120	5 7 10	4 17 8
Paling Boards hewed on one Side, and not exceeding 7 Feet in Length,		
imported in a British built Ship, the 120	0 5 0	0 4 10
in a Foreign Ship, the 120	0 5 1	0 4 10
hewed on one Side, and exceeding 7 Feet in Length,		
imported in a British built Ship, the 120	0 10 0	0 9 8
in a Foreign Ship, the 120	0 10 1	0 9 8
Paste Boards, or Mill Boards,		
imported in a British built Ship, the Hundred Weight	0 10 0	0 9 8
in a Foreign Ship, the Hundred Weight	0 10 2	0 9 8

				£	s.	d.
Pipe Boards, above 5 Feet 3 Inches in Length, and not exceeding 8 Feet in Length, and under 8 Inches Square,						
imported in a British built Ship, the 120	-	1	10	0	1	9	6
in a Foreign Ship, the 120	-	1	10	3	1	9	6
exceeding 8 Feet in Length, and under 8 Inches Square,						
imported in a British built Ship, the 120	-	3	0	0	2	19	0
in a Foreign Ship, the 120	-	3	0	3	2	19	0
Scale Boards,						
imported in a British built Ship, the Hundred Weight	-	0	11	0	0	10	11
in a Foreign Ship, the Hundred Weight	-	0	11	1	0	10	11
Wainscot Boards, the Inch or Foot, containing 12 Feet in Length, and 1 Inch in Thickness, and so in Proportion for any greater or lesser Length or Thickness,						
imported in a British built Ship	-	0	0	9½	0	0	8
in a Foreign Ship	-	0	0	9½	0	0	8

White Boards. See Linn Boards for Shoemakers.
See the Notes inserted at the End of Wood.

TABLE A.

INWARDS.

	Duty. £. s. d.	Drawback. £. s. d.
Wood, viz.		
Boom Spars. See Spars.		
Boxwood,		
imported in a British built Ship, the Ton containing 20 Hundred Weight	2 13 0	2 9 0
in a Foreign Ship, the Ton containing 20 Hundred Weight	2 15 0	2 9 0
See the Notes inserted at the End of Wood.		
Brazil or Fernambuck Wood for Dyers' Use, the Hundred Weight	0 5 10	0 0 0
By the 8 Geo. I. Chap. 15. Sect. 10. Brazil Wood may be legally imported free of Duty, if regularly entered and landed.		
See also the Notes inserted at the End of Wood.		
Brazilletto or Jamaica Wood for Dyers' Use, the Hundred Weight	0 3 7	0 0 0
By the 8 Geo. I. Chap. 15. Sect. 10. Brazilletto Wood may be legally imported free of Duty, if regularly entered and landed. The N. B. in Schedule A, annexed to the 27 Geo. III. Chap. 13. following the Duty on this Article, says, Brazilletto or Jamaica Wood.		
See also the Notes inserted at the End of Wood.		

(221)

		£ s. d.	£ s. d.
Cant Spars. See Spars.			
Capravens. See Spars.			
Clapholt. See Clap Boards.			
Deals, above 7 Inches in Width, exceeding 20 Feet in Length, and not exceeding 4 Inches in Thickness,			
imported in a British built Ship, the 120	-	5 19 0	5 11 6
in a Foreign Ship, the 120	-	6 3 2	5 11 6
above 7 Inches in Width, exceeding 20 Feet in Length, and exceeding 4 Inches in Thickness,			
imported in a British built Ship, the 120	-	11 18 0	11 3 0
in a Foreign Ship, the 120	-	12 2 2	11 3 0
above 7 Inches in Width, being 8 Feet in Length and not above 20 Feet in Length, and not exceeding 3¼ Inches in Thickness,			
imported in a British built Ship, the 120	-	2 13 0	2 10 6
in a Foreign Ship, the 120	-	2 14 5	2 10 6
above 7 Inches in Width, being 8 Feet in Length and not above 20 Feet in Length, and exceeding 3¼ Inches in Thickness,			
imported in a British Ship, the 120	-	5 6 0	5 1 0
in a Foreign built Ship, the 120	-	5 7 5	5 1 0
See the Notes inserted at the End of Wood.			

TABLE A.

INWARDS.

	Duty. £. s. d.	Drawback. £. s. d.
Wood, viz.		
Deal Ends, above 7 Inches in Width, being under 8 Feet in Length, and not exceeding 3¼ Inches in Thickness,		
imported in a British built Ship, the 120	0 17 8	0 16 10
in a Foreign Ship, the 120	0 18 2	0 16 10
above 7 Inches in Width, being under 8 Feet in Length, and exceeding 3¼ Inches in Thickness,		
imported in a British built Ship, the 120	1 15 4	1 13 8
in a Foreign Ship, the 120	1 16 3	1 13 8
See the Notes inserted at the End of Wood.		
Ebony,		
imported in a British built Ship, the Hundred Weight	0 13 3	0 12 3
in a Foreign Ship, the Hundred Weight	0 13 9	0 12 3
By the 27 Geo. III. Chap. 32. Sect. 25. Ebony unmanufactured, the Growth and Product of Africa, may be imported into this Kingdom directly from any Part of Africa in British built Ships, navigated according to Law, without Paying any Duty whatever.		
See the Notes inserted at the End of Wood.		
Firkin Staves. See Staves.		

(223)

Firewood, the Fathom 6 Feet wide and 6 Feet high, imported in a British built Ship	—	0 2 8	0 2 6
in a Foreign Ship	—	0 2 9	0 2 6
See the Notes inserted at the End of Wood.			
Fir Quarters, 5 Inches Square, and under 8 Inches Square, or if 24 Feet in Length or upwards, imported in a British built Ship, the 120	—	2 13 0	2 10 6
in a Foreign Ship, the 120	—	2 14 5	2 10 6
under 5 Inches Square, and under 24 Feet in Length, imported in a British built Ship, the 120	—	1 1 3	1 0 3
in a Foreign Ship, the 120	—	1 1 9	1 0 3
See the Notes inserted at the End of Wood.			
Fir Timber, 8 Inches Square or upwards, imported in a British built Ship, the Load containing 50 Cubic Feet	—	0 6 8	0 6 4
in a Foreign Ship, the Load containing 50 Cubic Feet	—	0 6 10	0 6 4
See the Notes inserted at the End of Wood.			
Fustick for Dyers' Use, the Hundred Weight	—	0 0 10	0 0 0

By the 8 Geo. I. Chap. 15. Sect. 10. Fustick may be legally imported free of Duty, if regularly entered and landed.
See also the Notes inserted at the End of Wood.

(224)

TABLE A.

INWARDS.

	Duty. £. s. d.	Drawback. £. s. d.
Wood, viz.		
Handfcoops, the Dozen —	0 0 11	0 0 10
Handfpikes, under 7 Feet in Length,		
imported in a British built Ship, the 120 —	0 6 8	0 6 2
in a Foreign Ship, the 120 —	0 6 11	0 6 2
7 Feet in Length or upwards,		
imported in a British built Ship, the 120 —	0 13 4	0 12 4
in a Foreign Ship, the 120 —	0 13 7	0 12 4
See the Notes inferted at the End of Wood.		
Heading Staves. See Staves.		
Kilderkin Staves. See Staves.		
Knees of Oak, under 5 Inches Square,		
imported in a British built Ship, the 120 —	0 3 4	0 3 1
in a Foreign Ship, the 120 —	0 3 6	0 3 1
5 Inches Square, and under 8 Inches Square,		
imported in a British built Ship, the 120 —	1 13 0	1 10 6
in a Foreign Ship, the 120 —	1 14 5	1 10 6
8 Inches Square or upwards,		

imported in a British built Ship, the Load containing 50 Cubic Feet	–	0	9	11	0	9	2
in a Foreign Ship, the Load containing 50 Cubic Feet	–	0	10	4	0	9	2
See the Notes inserted at the End of Wood.							
Lathwood, in Pieces under 5 Feet in Length, the Fathom 6 Feet wide and 6 Feet high,							
imported in a British built Ship	–	0	13	3	0	12	3
in a Foreign Ship	–	0	13	9	0	12	3
in Pieces 5 Feet in Length or upwards, the Fathom 6 Feet wide and 6 Feet high,							
imported in a British built Ship	–	0	19	10	0	18	4
in a Foreign Ship	–	1	0	4	0	18	4
See the Notes inserted at the end of Wood.							
Lignum Vitæ, the Hundred Weight	–	0	2	3	0	2	0
See the Notes inserted at the End of Wood.							
Logwood for Dyers' Use, the Ton containing 20 Hundred Weight	11	0	0	0	0	0
By the 8 Geo. I. Chap. 15. Sect. 10. Logwood may be legally imported free of Duty, if regularly entered and landed.							
See also the Notes inserted at the End of Wood.							
Mahogany, the Ton containing 20 Hundred Weight	–	2	4	0	2	0	0
See the Notes inserted at the End of Wood.							

TABLE A.

INWARDS.

	Duty. £. s. d.	Drawback. £. s. d.
Wood, viz.		
Masts under 6 Inches in Diameter. See Spars.		
Masts, 6 Inches in Diameter, and under 8 Inches,		
imported in a British built Ship, the Mast	0 1 1½	0 1 0
in a Foreign Ship, the Mast	0 1 2	0 1 0
8 Inches in Diameter, and under 12 Inches,		
imported in a British built Ship, the Mast	0 3 4	0 3 1
in a Foreign Ship, the Mast	0 3 6	0 3 1
12 Inches in Diameter or upwards,		
imported in a British built Ship, the Mast	0 6 8	0 6 2
in a Foreign Ship, the Mast	0 6 11	0 6 2
Nicaragua Wood for Dyers' Use, the Hundred Weight	0 1 4	0 0 0
By the 8 Geo. I. Chap. 15. Sect. 10. Nicaragua Wood may be legally imported free of Duty, if regularly entered and landed. See also the Notes inserted at the End of Wood.		
Oak Boards. See Boards.		
Oak Plank, 2 Inches in Thickness or upwards, imported in a British built Ship, the Load containing 50 Cubic Feet	0 19 10	0 18 4

in a Foreign Ship, the Load containing 50 Cubic Feet — 1 0 8 | 0 18 4

See the Notes inserted at the End of Wood.

Oak Timber, 8 Inches Square or upwards, imported in a British built Ship, the Load containing 50 Cubic Feet — 0 9 11 | 0 9 2

in a Foreign Ship, the Load containing 50 Cubic Feet — 0 10 4 | 0 9 2

See the Notes inserted at the End of Wood.

Oars, imported in a British built Ship, the 120 — 1 19 8 | 1 16 8

in a Foreign Ship, the 120 — 2 1 3 | 1 16 8

See the Notes inserted at the end of Wood.

Olive Wood, imported in a British built Ship, the Ton containing 20 Hundred Weight — 3 6 0 | 3 1 0

in a Foreign Ship, the Ton containing 20 Hundred Weight — 3 8 9 | 3 1 0

See the Notes inserted at the End of Wood.

Paling Boards. See Boards.
Pipe or Hogshead Staves. See Staves.
Planks of Ireland, the 100 Feet — 0 2 9 | 0 2 6
Plasters of Wood, the Shock containing 60 — 0 2 9 | 0 2 6

TABLE A.

INWARDS.

	Duty. £. s. d.	Drawback. £. s. d.
Wood, viz.		
Red or Guinea Wood for Dyers' Use, the Ton containing 20 Hundred Weight	3 6 0	0 0 0
By the 8 Geo. I. Chap. 15. Sect. 10. Red Wood may be legally imported free of Duty, if regularly entered and landed. The N. B. in Schedule A, annexed to the 27 Geo. III. Chap. 13. following the Duty on this Article, says, Red or Guinea Wood.		
Round Wood, under 8 Inches Square, and under 6 Feet in Length, imported in a British built Ship, the 120	0 13 3	0 12 3
in a Foreign Ship, the 120	0 13 9	0 12 3
under 8 Inches Square, and if 6 Feet in Length or upwards,		
imported in a British built Ship, the 120	1 6 6	1 4 6
in a Foreign Ship, the 120	1 7 0	1 4 6
See the Notes inserted at the End of Wood.		
Scale Boards. See Boards.		
Scoops of Wood, the Dozen	0 0 11	0 0 10
Shovels of Wood unshod, the Dozen	0 2 9	0 2 6
Skeets for Whitsters, the Skeet	0 0 3	0 0 2½

Spars, under 22 Feet in Length, and under 4 Inches in Diameter exclusive of the Bark,						
imported in a British built Ship, the 120	–	0	6	8	0	6	2
in a Foreign Ship, the 120	–	0	6	11	0	6	2
22 Feet in Length, or upwards, and under 4 Inches in Diameter exclusive of the Bark,						
imported in a British built Ship, the 120	–	0	11	0	0	10	2
in a Foreign Ship, the 120	–	0	11	6	0	10	2
4 Inches in Diameter, and under 6 Inches exclusive of the Bark,						
imported in a British built Ship, the 120	–	1	4	3	1	2	5
in a Foreign Ship, the 120	–	1	5	3	1	2	5
6 Inches in Diameter or upwards. See Masts.						
Speckled Wood, the Hundred Weight						
See the Notes inserted at the End of Wood.	–	0	4	5	0	4	1
Spokes for Wheels, not exceeding 2 Feet in Length,						
imported in a British built Ship, the 1000	–	0	19	10	0	18	4
in a Foreign Ship, the 1000	–	1	0	8	0	18	4
exceeding 2 Feet in Length,						
imported in a British built Ship, the 1000	–	1	19	8	1	16	8

(230)

TABLE A.

INWARDS.

	Duty. £. s. d.	Drawback. L. s. d.
Wood, viz.		
Spokes for Wheels, exceeding 2 Feet in Length, imported in a Foreign Ship, the 1000.	2 1 3	1 16 8
See the Notes inserted at the End of Wood.		
Staves, not exceeding 36 Inches in Length, not above 3 Inches in Thickness, and not exceeding 7 Inches in Breadth, imported in a British built Ship, the 120	0 4 0	0 3 10
in a Foreign Ship, the 120	0 4 1	0 3 10
above 36 Inches in Length and not exceeding 50 Inches in Length, not above 3 Inches in Thickness, and not exceeding 7 Inches in Breadth, imported in a British built Ship, the 120	0 7 6	0 7 3
in a Foreign Ship, the 120	0 7 7	0 7 3
above 50 Inches in Length and not exceeding 60 Inches in Length, not above 3 Inches in Thickness, and not exceeding 7 Inches in Breadth, imported in a British built Ship, the 120	0 10 0	0 9 8
in a Foreign Ship, the 120	0 10 1	0 9 8
above 60 Inches in Length and not exceeding 72 Inches in		

Length, not above 3 Inches in Thickness, and not exceeding 7 Inches in Breadth,		
imported in a British built Ship, the 120	0 15 0	0 14 6
in a Foreign Ship, the 120	0 15 1	0 14 6
above 72 Inches in Length, not above 3 Inches in Thickness, and not exceeding 7 Inches in Breadth,		
imported in a British built Ship, the 120	0 17 6	0 16 8
in a Foreign Ship, the 120	0 17 7	0 16 8
Staves, above 3 Inches in Thickness, or above 7 Inches in Breadth, and not exceeding 5 Feet 3 Inches in Length, shall be deemed Clapboards and pay Duty accordingly.		
above 3 Inches in Thickness, or above 7 Inches in Breadth, and exceeding 5 Feet 3 Inches in Length, shall be deemed Pipeboards and pay Duty accordingly.		
See the Notes inserted at the End of Wood.		
Sweet Wood, the Hundred Weight	0 5 6	0 4 10
See the Notes inserted at the End of Wood.		
Timber of Ireland, the Ton or Load	0 3 0	0 2 3
Timber of all Sorts not otherwise particularly enumerated and described, being 8 Inches Square or upwards, imported in a British built Ship, the Load containing 50 Cubic Feet	0 6 8	0 6 4

TABLE A.

INWARDS.

	Duty. £. s. d.	Drawback. £. s. d.
Wood, viz.		
Timber of all Sorts not otherwise particularly enumerated and described, being 8 Inches Square or upwards, imported in a Foreign Ship, the Load containing 50 Cubic Feet —	0 6 10	0 6 4
See the Notes inserted at the End of Wood.		
Trays of Wood, the Shock containing sixty —	0 4 5	0 3 11
Trenchers of Wood, the Groce containing 12 Dozen —	0 0 11	0 0 10
Trunnels or Treenails, the Thousand —	0 2 3	0 2 0
Tubs of Wood, the Dozen —	0 0 5	0 0 4
Ufers, under 5 Inches Square, and under 24 Feet in Length, imported in a British built Ship, the 120 —	1 1 3	1 0 3
in a Foreign Ship, the 120 —	1 1 9	1 0 3
5 Inches Square and under 8 Inches Square, or if 24 Feet in Length or upwards, imported in a British built Ship, the 120 —	2 13 0	2 10 6
in a Foreign Ship, the 120 —	2 14 5	2 10 6
See the Notes inserted at the End of Wood.		
Wainscot Boards. See Boards.		

Wainscot Logs, being 8 Inches Square or upwards, imported in a British built Ship, the Load containing 50 Cubic Feet - - - - 0 9 11 | 0 9 2

in a Foreign Ship, the Load containing 50 Cubic Feet - - - - 0 10 4 | 0 9 2

See the Notes inserted at the End of Wood.

Wood for Dyers' Use not otherwise enumerated, the Hundred Weight 0 1 8 | 0 0 0

See the Notes inserted at the End of Wood.

Wood Scoops. See Scoops of Wood.

By the 11 Geo. III. Chap. 41. any Sort of unmanufactured Wood (except Masts, Yards, and Bowsprits), may be imported into this Kingdom by any Person from any Part of America, being the Growth and Product of America, in British Vessels legally navigated, free of Duty, if regularly entered and landed, otherwise liable to Duty.

By the 8 Geo. I. Chap. 12. any Sort of Wood, Plank, or Timber whatsoever, wrought or unwrought, or any of the Goods called Lumber, that is Deals of several Sorts, Timber Balks of several Sizes, Barrel Boards, Clap Boards, Pipe Boards or Pipe Holt, White Boards for Shoemakers, Broom and Cant Spars, Bow Staves, Capravens, Clap Holt, Ebony Wood, Headings for Pipes, and for Hogsheads and Barrels, Hoops for Coopers,

TABLE A.

INWARDS.	Duty. £. s. d.	Drawback. £. s. d.
Oars, Pipe and Hogshead Staves, Barrel Staves, Firkin Staves, Trunnels, Speckled Wood, Sweet Wood, Small Spars, Oak, Plank, and Wainscot, may be imported by every Person directly from any of his Majesty's British Colonies or Plantations in America, in any Ship which may lawfully trade to or from his Majesty's said Colonies or Plantations in America, legally navigated, being the Growth and Product of the said Colonies or Plantations (except Masts, Yards, and Bowsprits), free of Duty. Continued by the 26 Geo. III. Chap. 53. until the 29th September 1792, and to the End of the then next Session of Parliament.		
Woollen Cloths, all manner of, the Yard	1 17 5	1 13 1
See Woollen Manufactures of the European Dominions of the French King in Table C.		
Stuffs of all Sorts, made or mixed with Wool, the Yard	0 5 6	0 4 10
Yarn, viz.		
Cable Yarn, the Hundred Weight	0 8 6	0 0 6
Camel or Mohair Yarn, the Pound	0 0 7	0 0 6

Cotton Yarn, the Pound - - - 0 0 0 0 0 3
    imported by the East India Company, the Pound - 0 0 0 0 3
By the 18 Geo. III. Chap. 56. Cotton Yarn of the Manufacture of Ireland may be imported directly from thence into Great Britain free of Duty, if the Master of the Vessel brings with him a Certificate as directed, and makes Oath before the Collector or other principal Officer at the Port of Importation, that the Packages and Goods are those taken on board by virtue of the Certificate.

Grogram Yarn, the Pound - - - 0 0 0 0 0 8
Irish Yarn, the Pack containing four Hundred Weight, at six Score Pounds to the Hundred Weight - 1 2 0 0 19 6
By the 7 and 8 William III. Chap. 39. and 16 Geo. II. Chap. 26. Yarn of the Manufacture of Ireland may be imported directly from thence free of Duty. For the Regulations and Restrictions, see the Note following Flax.

Raw Linen Yarn, the Pound - - - 0 0 $1\frac{1}{4}$ 0 0 0
By the 29 Geo. II. Chap. 15. any Raw or Brown Linen Yarn made of Flax may be imported in British or Irish built Ships, legally navigated, free of Duty, if regularly entered and landed, otherwise liable to Duty; but must be legally imported whether subject to Duty or not. Continued by the 19 Geo. III. Chap. 27. and 28 Geo. III. Chap. 24.

TABLE A.

INWARDS.

	Duty. £. s. d.	Drawback. £. s. d.
Yarn, viz.		
Wick Yarn, the Hundred Weight		
Woollen or Bay Yarn, the Hundred Weight	1 12 8	1 8 0
By the 12 Geo. II. Chap. 21. Woollen or Bay Yarn may be imported from Ireland in British or Irish built Ships, wholly owned by British or Irish, free of Duty, but not to extend to Worsted Yarn made of two or more Threads, twisted or thrown, or Crewel; and all Wool and Woollen Manufactures therein specified, to be exported from the Ports of Ireland into the Ports of Great Britain only as therein named, and in Ships as before described; and by the 26 Geo. II. Chap. 11. any Wool, Woollen or Bay Yarn, Wool Fells, Shortlings or Mortlings, Wool Flocks, or Worsted Yarn, may be exported from any Port in Ireland to any Port in Great Britain.	0 14 8	0 13 0
Worsted Yarn, being of two or more Threads, twisted or thrown, the Pound	0 0 10	0 0 9

(237)

TABLE A.
OUTWARDS.

See Table K, for the several Goods, Wares, and Merchandise, either circumstantially or absolutely prohibited to be exported as there mentioned.

	Duty.
	£. s. d.
Agarick, trimmed or pared, Foreign, the Pound	0 0 3
rough or untrimmed, Foreign, the Pound	0 0 1
Alum, British, the Hundred Weight	0 1 2
Annotto, Foreign, the Pound	0 0 1
Antimonium Crudum, Foreign, the Hundred Weight	0 0 3
Aqua Fortis, Foreign, the Gallon	0 0 4
Argol, Foreign, the Hundred Weight	0 0 8
Arsnick, Foreign, the Pound	0 0 0¼
Bay Berries, Foreign, the Hundred Weight	0 0 2
Brazil or Fernambuco Wood, Foreign, the Hundred Weight	0 1 0
Brazilletto or Jamaica Wood, Foreign, the Hundred Weight	0 0 8
Cambricks, Foreign, and French Lawns, having been secured in Warehouses under the Regulations directed by the 32 Geo. II. Chap. 32. and 7 Geo. III. Chap. 43. on Exportation to his Majesty's Colonies in America, the Piece containing 13 Ells	0 3 4

See the Note after Cambricks in Linen, Table A inwards.

TABLE A.

OUTWARDS.

	Duty.		
	£.	s.	d.
Cards, viz.			
New Wool Cards, British, the Dozen	0	0	7
Old Wool Cards, British, the Dozen	0	0	4
Cloth, viz.			
White Woollen Cloth, commonly called Broad Cloth, the Piece	0	5	6
By the 28 Geo. III. Chap. 33. this Duty is not to extend to White Woollen Cloth which shall have been dyed or dressed in this Kingdom, but the precise Quantity of Woollen Cloth exported is to be indorsed.			
Coals, usually sold by Measure, viz.			
exported to Ireland or the Isle of Man, the Chalder containing 36 Bushels, Winchester Measure	0	1	2
to any British Colony or Plantation in America, the Chalder containing 36 Bushels Winchester Measure	0	2	3
exported to any other Place, viz.			
in British built Ships, the Chalder Newcastle Measure	0	15	5
in Foreign Ships, the Chalder Newcastle Measure	1	7	6
exported in certain Quantities from the Ports of Newcastle and Swansea, to the Islands of Jersey, Guernsey, and Alderney, provided the Conditions, Regula-			

tions, Restrictions, and Limitations, directed by the 6 Geo. III. Chap. 40. are duly complied with, the Chalder Newcastle Measure - - - 0 11 0

usually sold by Weight, viz.

    exported to Ireland or the Isle of Man, the Ton containing 20 Hundred Weight - - - 0 0 9

    to any British Colony or Plantation in America, the Ton containing 20 Hundred Weight - - - 0 1 6

    exported to any other Place, viz.

        in British built Ships, the Ton containing 20 Hundred Weight - - - 0 5 2

        in Foreign Ships, the Ton containing 20 Hundred Weight - - - 0 9 2

Cochineal, Foreign, the Pound - - - 0 0 3

Cream of Tartar, Foreign, the Hundred Weight - - - 0 0 2

Culm exported to Lisbon, provided the Conditions, Regulations, and Restrictions, directed by the 31 Geo. II. Chap. 15. and the 13 Geo. III. Chap. 70. are duly complied with.

    in a British built Ship, the Chalder Newcastle Measure - - - 0 1 2

    in a Foreign Ship, the Chalder Newcastle Measure - - - 0 1 8

The 31 Geo. II. Chap. 15. permits Culm to be exported to Lisbon upon the specified Duty, Security being given for the due Exportation. If the Ship goes out of Port before such Security is given, the Ship and Culm forfeited. The 13 Geo. III. Chap. 70. permits the Exportation of Culm to Lisbon in any Foreign Ship at the specified Duty, subject to the beforementioned Regulations.

Fustick, Foreign, the Hundred Weight - - - 0 0 2

TABLE A.

OUTWARDS.	Duty.		
	£.	s.	d.
Galls, Foreign, the Hundred Weight	0	1	2
Glue, British, the Hundred Weight	0	0	11
Gum Arabic, Foreign, the Hundred Weight	1	13	4
Gum Senega, Foreign, the Hundred Weight	0	5	10
By the 6 Geo. III. Chap. 46. Gum Senega or Gum Arabic may be exported free of Duty from Great Britain to Ireland, by the Natives of either Place, being British Subjects, by Licence from the Lords of the Treasury, so that the Quantity of both Gums exported in one Year does not exceed thirty Tons Weight Avoirdupois.			
Hair, viz.			
Hart's Hair, the Hundred Weight	0	1	10
Horse Hair, the Hundred Weight	0	6	8
Cow or Ox Hair, the Hundred Weight	0	2	3
Horses, Mares, or Geldings, each	0	5	6
Indico of all Sorts, Foreign, the Pound	0	0	1¼
Isinglass, Foreign, the Hundred Weight	0	0	11
Lawns, See Cambricks.			
Lead, cast or uncast, the Fodder or Ton containing 20 Hundred Weight	2	5	2
Leather of all Sorts, Tanned, Tawed, or Dressed, the Hundred Weight	0	1	2

(241)

		£	s.	d.
Litharge of Lead, the Hundred Weight	-	0	0	3
Litmus, Foreign, the Hundred Weight	-	0	0	7
Logwood, Foreign, the Hundred Weight	-	0	1	2
By the 7 Geo. III. Chap. 47. Logwood may be exported free of Duty in British built Ships, being regularly entered and shipped, otherwise subject to Duty.				
Madder, Foreign, the Hundred Weight	-	0	0	10
Madder Roots, Foreign, the Pound	-	0	0	0¼
Nicaragua Wood, Foreign, the Ton containing 20 Hundred Weight	-	0	4	5
Orchal, Foreign, the Hundred Weight	-	0	1	2
Orchelia, Foreign, the Hundred Weight	-	0	0	7
Pomegranate Peels, Foreign, the Hundred Weight	-	0	0	5
Red or Guinea Wood, Foreign, the Hundred Weight	-	0	0	10
Saflower, Foreign, the Pound	-	0	0	1
Sal Armoniac, Foreign, the Pound	-	0	0	0¼
Sal Gem, Foreign, the Pound	-	0	0	0¼
Sapan Wood, Foreign, the Hundred Weight	-	0	0	4
Saunders Red, Foreign, the Hundred Weight	-	0	0	9
Shumac, Foreign, the Hundred Weight	-	0	0	5
Skins, viz.				
Badger Skins, the Piece	-	0	0	1
Beaver Skins, the Skin or Piece of Skin	-	0	0	3
Beaver Wool or Wombs, the Pound	-	0	1	8

R

(242)

TABLE A.

OUTWARDS.

	Duty.
	£. s. d.

Skins, viz.

	£	s	d
Calve Skins, tanned, tawed, or dressed, the Hundred Weight	0	1	2
Cat Skins, the 100	0	1	6
Coney Skins, dressed or tawed, the 120	0	1	2
Black, with Silver Hairs or without, dressed or tawed, the 120	0	3	0
Dog Skins, the Dozen	0	0	2
Elk Skins raw, the Piece	0	1	2
Fitches, the Timber containing 40 Skins	0	1	10
Fox Skins, the Piece	0	0	1
Kid Skins in the Hair, the 100	0	0	7
dressed, the 100	0	0	9
Otter Skins raw, the Piece	0	0	0¼
tawed, the Piece	0	0	1
Sheep and Lamb Skins dressed, without Wool, the 120	0	2	9
Sheep Skins tanned, tawed, or dressed, the Hundred Weight	0	1	2
Squirrel Skins, the 1000	0	2	9
Swan Skins, the Piece	0	0	2
Wolf Skins tawed, the Piece	0	0	4
Sticklack, Foreign, the Pound	0	0	0¼

(243)

Tin unwrought, the Hundred Weight	-	0	3	4
By the 30 Geo. III. Chap. 4. no Duty is to be paid on Tin unwrought exported to any of the Countries beyond the Cape of Good Hope, provided Bond be given to land it beyond the Cape of Good Hope.			
Turnefole, Foreign, the Pound	-	0	0	0½
Valonia, Foreign, the Ton containing 20 Hundred Weight	-	0	3	11
Verdigrise, Foreign, the Pound	-	0	0	1
Wool, viz. Beaver Wool, the Pound	-	0	1	8

COASTWISE.

TABLE A.

COASTWISE.

	Duty. £. s. d.	Drawback. £. s. d.
Coals (except Charcoal made of Wood), brought Coastwise from Port to Port in Great Britain (except into the Port of London); viz. in cafe they are fuch as are moſt uſually ſold by Weight, the Ton containing 20 Hundred Weight	0 3 8	0 3 8
in cafe they are fuch as are moſt uſually ſold by the Chalder, or by any other Meaſure reducible thereto, the Chalder containing 36 Buſhels Winchefter Meaſure	0 5 6	0 5 6
The 12 Ann, Stat. 2. Chap. 17. fixes the Dimenſions and Contents of the Coal Buſhel at nineteen Inches and one Half Inch, from Outſide to Outſide, to contain one Winchefter Buſhel and one Quart of Water, according to the Standard of the 13 William III.; to be made round, with a plain and even Bottom.		
By the 13 and 14 William III. Chap. 5. Sect. 28. the Winchefter Buſhel is to be made round, with a plain and even Bottom. Eighteen Inches and one Half Inch wide throughout, and eight Inches deep.		
Culm, brought Coaſtwiſe from Port to Port in Great Britain (except into the Port of London), the Chalder containing 36 Buſhels Winchefter Meaſure	0 1 2	0 1 2

Cynders, made of Pit Coal, brought Coastwife from Port to Port in Great Britain, for every Chalder containing 36 Bushels Winchester Measure	—	0	5	6	0	0	0
Coals, Culm, and Cynders, carried from the Bridge of Sterling which is on the Firth of Forth to the Town of Dunbar, or to Redhead, or to any Part betwixt them, or from Ellen Foot to Bank End in the County of Cumberland, or from any Creek or Place to any other Creek or Place between Ellen Foot and Bank End aforesaid, are not by reason of such Carriage liable to any Duty of Customs.				
Coals, except Charcoal made of Wood, brought Coastwife into the Port of London, viz.				
in case they are such as are most usually sold by Weight, the Ton containing 20 Hundred Weight	—	0	7	0	0	4	0
in case they are such as are most usually sold by the Chalder, or by any other Measure whatever, reducible thereto, the Chalder containing 36 Bushels Winchester Measure	—	0	8	10	0	5	10
Culm, brought Coastwife into the Port of London, the Chalder containing 36 Bushels Winchester Measure	—	0	4	5	0	1	5
Coals, brought Coastwife into the Port of London for the only Use and Service of the Royal Hospital at Chelsea, not exceeding 100 Chalder by the Year, the Chalder containing 36 Bushels Winchester Measure	—	0	5	6	0	0	0

TABLE A.

COASTWISE

		Drawback.
	£. s. d.	£. s. d.

Coals, For all Coals that shall be used for melting Copper and Tin Ores within the Counties of Cornwall and Devon, or in Fire Engines for the draining Water out of the Mines of Tin and Copper within the County of Cornwall, there shall be repaid a Drawback of all the Duties paid thereon.

The 9 Ann, Chap. 6. Sect. 54. allows a Drawback of all the Duties on Coals that shall be used for melting Copper and Tin Ores within the Counties of Cornwall and Devon; Proof being made on Oath before the Collector or Customer, of the Duties having been paid, and the Coals having been so used: and the 14 Geo. II. Chap. 4. Sect. 3. allows a Drawback of all the Duties on Coals which shall be used in Fire Engines for draining Water out of Mines of Tin and Copper within the County of Cornwall, upon the Proofs beforementioned.

For all Coals that shall be used in calcining or smelting Copper and Lead Ores within the Isle of Anglesey, or in Fire Engines for draining Water out of the Mines of Copper and Lead within the said Isle, there shall be repaid a Drawback of all the Duties paid thereon, provided the Amount of such Drawbacks shall not exceed the Sum of £. 1500 in any one Year.

The 26 Geo. III. Chap. 104. allows the Drawback of all the Duties before paid on all Coals used in calcining or smelting Copper and Lead Ores within the Isle of Anglesey; Proof upon Oath being made before the Customer or Collector, that the Coals have been so used: the Drawbacks not to exceed £. 1500 in one Year.

N.B. British Corn brought into the River Thames Eastward of London Bridge, sold and delivered, to pay 1d. per Last of 10 Quarters, and Foreign Corn delivered out of any Vessel in the Port of London, to pay 2d. per Last to the Corn Inspector.

Culm, to be used for the burning of Lime, viz. sent Coastwise in any Ships, Vessels, or Boats, not exceeding 30 Tons Burthen, from any Place within the Limits of the Port of Milford, in the County of Pembroke, to any other Place within the Counties of Pembroke, Carmarthen, Cardigan, or Merioneth, the Chalder containing 36 Bushels Winchester Measure — 0 1 2 0

By the 33 Geo. II. Chap. 15. upon Sufferance by the Collector or his Deputy, at the Port of Milford, which he is required to grant the Master of the Vessel for the Quantity to be laden, and the Officer to whom the Sufferance is directed attending the

TABLE A.

COASTWISE.

	Duty. £. s. d.	Drawback. £. s. d.
Culm, shipping, and certifying on the Sufferance the Quantity shipped, after which, the Duty being paid, the Collector is to grant a Certificate thereof under the Seal of his Office, which is to be a sufficient Let Pass, or Clearance; and the Master of the Vessel, upon his Return to Milford, is to make Oath before the Collector of the landing of the Culm, without which he is not to be permitted to load any more Culm. Proof being made of the Loss of Culm, a like Quantity is to be allowed to be shipped free of Duty.		
Wine, in Bottles exceeding three Dozen, or in a Cask or Casks exceeding ten Gallons in Quantity, sent Coastwise or by Land Carriage into the Port of London or the Members thereof, or to any Place whatever within the Distance of twenty Miles from the Royal Exchange of London, to be paid to the proper Officers of the Customs nearest to the Place from whence such Wine is intended to be removed, viz.		
of the Produce of the European Dominions of the French King, the Tun containing 252 Gallons	4 4 0	

of any other Sort, except Rhenish, German, and Hungary Wines, the Tun containing 252 Gallons — 2 16 0

The 27 Geo. III. Chap. 13. Sect. 13. directs, that no Wine of any Sort, exceeding the Quantity of ten Gallons, which shall have been imported from Foreign Parts into any Out Port of this Kingdom, shall be brought from such Out Port or any Place whatsoever, by Land or by Water, into the Port of London or Members thereof, or to any Place whatsoever within the Distance of twenty Miles from the Royal Exchange of London, before the Proprietor shall have paid to the Collector or other proper Officer of the Customs nearest to the Place from whence such Wine is intended to be removed, the Difference of the respective Duties payable at the Out Ports and in the Port of London, in Addition to the Duties which shall have been paid on the Importation into the Out Port, agreeable to what is set forth in Table A, Coastwise; and if any Quantity of Wine in Bottles exceeding three Dozen, or in a Cask or Casks exceeding ten Gallons, shall at one and the same Time, and in one and the same Carriage, be brought either by Land or Water into the Port of London or the Members thereof, or to any Place whatever within twenty Miles of the said Royal Exchange, without a Certificate from the Collector or other proper Officer of the Cus-

TABLE A.

COASTWISE.

	Duty. £. s. d.	Drawback. £. s. d.
Wine,		

toms, expressing the Quality and Quantity of the Wine, and that the Difference between the Duties payable at the Port of London on Importation, and those which are due in the Port of London on Importation, have been duly paid, or that the Wine was sold for Salvage, or that it was compounded for or condemned, such Wine shall be forfeited, together with the Casks and Vessels containing the same. Section 14, provides, that if after the Removal of any such Wine, and after Payment of the Duties payable thereon in the Out Port, and also of the Difference of the respective Duties payable at the Out Ports and the Port of London on Importation, and before the same shall be brought into the Port of London or the Members thereof, or to any Place whatever within the Distance of twenty Miles from the Royal Exchange of London, such Wine shall happen to be staved or spilt, or perish, the Commissioners of his Majesty's Customs (Proof having been made upon Oath, to their Satisfaction, that the Wine has been staved, lost, or has perished), shall cause Repayment to be made to the Proprietor of so much Money as the Difference of the

Duties payable for such Wine in any Out Port and in the Port of London shall amount to.

Wine being also subject to the Duties of Excise, a Permit must be obtained from the Officer of Excise before it is removed; and the Regulations adopted by the Commissioners of Excise respecting the Removal of Wines in the Possession of Persons not being Dealers must also be conformed to.

TABLE B.

A Table of the Duties of Customs payable on the Importation into this Kingdom, and of the Drawbacks to be allowed on the Exportation from thence, of Goods, Wares, and Merchandise, being imported by the United Company of Merchants of England trading to the East Indies and not being particularly charged with Duty when so imported.

TABLE B.

	Duty. £. s. d.	Drawback. £. s. d.
Arangoes, For every £.100 of the true and real Value thereof according to the Grofs Price at which fuch Goods fhall have been fold at the Public Sales of the United Company of Merchants of England trading to the Eaft Indies	31 13 4	29 16 0
China Ware, For every £.100 of the true and real Value thereof according to the Grofs Price at which fuch Goods fhall have been fold at the Public Sales of the United Company of Merchants of England trading to the Eaft Indies	47 10 0	45 5 0
Cotton Manufactures, not otherwife particularly enumerated or defcribed, for every £.100 of the true and real Value thereof according to the Grofs Price at which fuch Goods fhall have been fold at the Public Sales of the United Company of Merchants of England trading to the Eaft Indies	50 0 0	48 10 0
Cowries, For every £.100 of the true and real Value thereof according to the Grofs Price at which fuch Goods fhall have been fold at the Public Sales of the United Company of Merchants of England trading to the Eaft Indies	31 13 4	29 16 0

TABLE B.

	Duty. £. s. d.	Drawback. £. s. d.
Drugs, manufactured, not otherwise particularly enumerated or described, for every £.100 of the true and real Value thereof according to the Gross Price at which such Goods shall have been sold at the Public Sales of the United Company of Merchants of England trading to the East Indies	40 0 0	38 6 3
unmanufactured, not otherwise particularly enumerated or described, for every £.100 of the true and real Value thereof, according to the Gross Price at which such Goods shall have been sold at the Public Sales of the United Company of Merchants of England trading to the East Indies	31 0 0	29 2 6
Japanned or Lacquered Wares, for every £.100 of the true and real Value thereof according to the Gross Price at which such Goods shall have been sold at the Public Sales of the United Company of Merchants of England trading to the East Indies	49 10 0	47 0 0
Muslins Plain, Nanquin Cloth, Muslins or White Callicos flowered or stitched, for every £.100 of the true and real Value thereof according to the Gross Price at which such Goods shall have been sold at the Public Sales of the United Company of Merchants of England trading to the East Indies	18 0 0	10 0 0

Tea, For every £. 100 of the true and real Value thereof according to the Grofs Price at which it shall have been sold at the Public Sales of the United Company of Merchants of England trading to the East Indies — — — — 5 0 0

exported to Ireland or any of the British Colonies or Plantations in America, for every £. 100 of the true and real Value thereof as abovementioned — — — — — — 5 0 0

By the 25 Geo. III. Chap. 74. referring to the 21 Geo. II. Chap. 14. Tea is allowed to be exported to Ireland and any of his Majesty's Plantations in America, in the Package it was originally imported, and in the entire Lot sold at the Sale of the East India Company, upon Bond being given for the due Exportation; the Certificate of landing in Ireland to be produced in six Months, and of landing in America in eighteen Months. Certificates being produced to the Warehousekeeper that the Entry has been made, and the Security given, the Tea is to be delivered out of the Warehouses with a Permit or Certificate to accompany it till shipped for Exportation; which Permit is to be delivered to the Searchers, and the outside Package is to be marked in four different Places by the Searchers; but by the 12 Geo. III. Chap. 60. no Tea is to be exported to Ireland in Ships of less Burthen than eighty Tons.

N. B. Tea is also subject to the Duty of Excise.

TABLE B.

Goods, Wares, and Merchandise prohibited to be worn or used in Great Britain, imported for Exportation only, for every £. 100 of the true and real Value thereof according to the Gross Price at which such Goods shall have been sold at the Public Sales of the United Company of Merchants of England trading to the East Indies -

On Exportation to Africa (except to the Islands of Madeira, the Canary Islands, the Azores or Western Isles), the following Drawbacks are to be allowed, viz.

	Duty. £ s. d.	Drawback. £ s. d.
	6 15 0	0 0 0
Allejars, the Piece	- - -	0 0 7
Bejuapauts, the Piece	- - -	0 1 0
Byrampauts, the Piece	- - -	0 0 9
Blue Long Cloths, the Piece	- - -	0 2 0
Brawls, the Piece	- - -	0 0 2
Callawapores, the Piece	- - -	0 0 9
Cushtaes, the Piece	- - -	0 0 7
Coopees, the Piece	- - -	0 0 7
Chintz, the Piece	- - -	0 0 9
Chelloes, the Piece	- - -	0 0 9
Cotton Romals, the Piece	- - -	0 0 6

(257)

Guinea Stuffs, the Piece	—	—	0 0 2
Niccanees, Small, the Piece	—	—	0 0 7
Niccanees, Large, the Piece	—	—	0 0 9
Neganepauts, the Piece	—	—	0 1 0
Photaes, the Piece	—	—	0 0 9
Saftracundies, the Piece	—	—	0 1 0
Tapseils, the Piece	—	—	0 0 9
Manufactured Goods, Wares, and Merchandise, not otherwise particularly enumerated or described, for every £. 100 of the true and real Value thereof according to the Grofs Price at which such Goods shall have been sold at the Public Sales of the United Company of Merchants of England trading to the East Indies	37 16 3		36 3 3
Unmanufactured Goods, Wares, and Merchandise, not otherwise particularly enumerated or described, for every £. 100 of the true and real Value thereof according to the Grofs Price at which such Goods shall have been sold at the Public Sales of the United Company of Merchants of England trading to the East Indies	28 5 0		26 5 0

S

TABLE C.

A Table of the Duties of Customs to be paid on the Importation into Great Britain, and of the Drawbacks thereof to be allowed on the Exportation from thence, of certain Goods, Wares, and Merchandise, being of the Growth, Produce, or Manufacture of the European Dominions of the French King, until the 10th May 1800.

TABLE C.

INWARDS.

	Duty. £ s. d.	Drawback. £ s. d.
Wine of the Produce of the European Dominions of the French King, viz. imported into the Port of London in a British built Ship, the Tun containing 252 Gallons	29 8 0	
in a Foreign Ship, the Tun containing 252 Gallons	33 12 0	
having been imported into the Port of London, and exported to any British Colony or Plantation in America, or to any British Settlement in the East Indies, the Tun containing 252 Gallons	— —	29 8 0
exported to any other Place, the Tun containing 252 Gallons	— —	24 13 6
imported into any Port of Great Britain (except the Port of London), in a British built Ship, the Tun containing 252 Gallons	25 4 0	
in a Foreign Ship, the Tun containing 252 Gallons	29 8 0	
having been imported into any Port of Great Britain (except the Port of London), and exported to any British Colony or Plantation in America, or to any British Settlement in the East Indies, the Tun containing 252 Gallons	— —	25 4 0
exported to any other Place, the Tun containing 252 Gallons	— —	20 9 6

N. B. Subject also to the Duty of Excise.

TABLE C.

INWARDS.

Wine of the Produce of the European Dominions of the French King entered for Prisage, viz.

	Duty. £. s. d.	Drawback. £. s. d.
imported into the Port of London in a British built Ship, the Tun containing 252 Gallons	21 11 10	
imported into the Port of London in a Foreign Ship, the Tun containing 252 Gallons	24 6 9	
having been imported into the Port of London, and exported to any British Colony or Plantation in America, or to any British Settlement in the East Indies, the Tun containing 252 Gallons	—	21 11 10
exported to any other Place, the Tun containing 252 Gallons	—	17 17 1
imported into any Port of England except the Port of London, in a British built Ship, the Tun containing 252 Gallons	18 16 10	
imported into any Port of England except the Port of London, in a Foreign Ship, the Tun containing 252 Gallons	21 11 10	
having been imported into any Port of England except the Port of London, and exported to any British Colony or Plantation in America, or to any British Settlement in the East Indies, the Tun containing 252 Gallons	—	18 16 10
exported to any other Place, the Tun containing 252 Gallons	—	15 0 7

N. B. Subject also to the Duty of Excise.

Vinegar of the Produce or Manufacture of the European Dominions of the French King, the Tun containing 252 Gallons	-	32	18	10	7	14	11
Sallad Oil, viz.							
Sallad Oil of the Manufacture of the European Dominions of the French King, imported in a British built Ship, the Gallon	-	0	1	1	0	1	0
imported in a Foreign Ship, the Gallon	-	0	1	2	0	1	0
Ordinary Oil of Olives of the Manufacture of the European Dominions of the French King, imported in a British built Ship, the Tun containing 252 Gallons	-	7	0	9	6	4	9
imported in a Foreign Ship, the Tun containing 252 Gallons	-	7	9	8	6	4	9
Brandy of the Produce or Manufacture of the European Dominions of the French King, the Gallon	-	0	0	9	0	0	8
N. B. Subject also to the Duty of Excise.							
Beer of the Produce or Manufacture of the European Dominions of the French King, imported directly from thence into Great Britain, in Ships of the Built of either Country, owned and navigated according to Law, for every £. 100 of the Value thereof	-	30	0	0	0	0	0
N. B. Subject also to the Duty of Excise.							
Cabinet Ware, Turnery, and Musical Instruments, of the Manufacture of the European Dominions of the French King, imported directly from thence into Great Britain, in Ships of the Built of either Country owned and navigated according to Law, for every £. 100 of the Value thereof	10	0	0	0	0	0

S 3

TABLE C.

INWARDS.

	Duty. £. s. d.	Drawback. £. s. d.
Coaches, Chariots, Landaus, Berlins, Chaises, or any other Carriages whatever, of the Manufacture of the European Dominions of the French King imported directly from thence, in Ships of the Built of either Country, owned and navigated according to Law, for every £.100 of the Value thereof	— — —	0 0 0
Articles composed of Iron or Steel, separately or mixed, or worked or mounted with other Substances, such Articles not exceeding in their Value fifty Shillings by the Hundred Weight, being of the Manufacture of the European Dominions of the French King, and imported directly from thence into Great Britain, in Ships of the Built of either Country, owned and navigated according to Law, for every £.100 of the Value thereof	15 0 0	0 0 0
Articles composed of Iron or Steel, separately or mixed, or worked or mounted with other Substances, and exceeding in their Value fifty Shillings by the Hundred Weight, and all Buckles, Buttons, Knives, or Scissars, and all other Articles of Hardware or Cutlery, and all Articles composed of Copper or Brass, separately or mixed, or worked or mounted with other Substances, all such Articles being of the Manufacture of the European Dominions of the French King, and imported directly from thence into Great Britain, in Ships of the Built of either Coun-	5 0 0	0 0 0

try, owned and navigated according to Law, for every £.100 of the Value thereof - - - - - 10 0 0

Manufactures of Cottons, and also Woollens, whether knit or wove, including Hosiery, being of the Produce or Manufacture of the European Dominions of the French King, and imported directly from thence into Great Britain, in Ships of the Built of either Country, owned and navigated according to Law, for every £.100 of the Value thereof 12 0 0

N. B. Cottons, if stained or printed, are subject also to Duties of Excise.

Cambricks of the Manufacture of the European Dominions of the French King, imported directly from thence into Great Britain, in Ships of the Built of either Country, owned and navigated according to Law, viz.

The Demi-piece, not exceeding 7¾ Yards in Length, and not exceeding 7/8 of a Yard in Breadth, or exceeding 7/8 of a Yard in Breadth, but not being above the Value of fifty Shillings, and so in Proportion for the like Sorts imported in any Pieces of any greater Length - - - - 0 5 0

exported to any British Colony or Plantation in America, and so in Proportion for the like Sorts exported in any Pieces of any greater Length - - - - - - 0 2 10

exceeding ½ of a Yard in Breadth, and being above the Value of

TABLE C.

INWARDS.

	Duty. £. s. d.	Drawback. £. s. d.
Cambricks, fifty Shillings the Demi-piece of 7¾ Yards in Length, for every £.100 of the Value thereof	- 10 0 0	5 13 4
Lawns of the Manufacture of the European Dominions of the French King, imported directly from thence into Great Britain, in Ships of the Built of either Country, owned and navigated according to Law, viz.		
The Demi-piece, not exceeding 7¾ Yards in Length, and not exceeding 1¼ Yard in Breadth, or exceeding 1¼ Yard in Breadth, but not being above the Value of fifty Shillings, and so in Proportion for the like Sorts imported in Pieces of any greater Length	0 5 0	
exported to any British Colony or Plantation in America, and so in Proportion for the like Sorts exported in Pieces of any greater Length	-	0 2 10
exceeding 1¼ Yard in Breadth, and being above the Value of fifty Shillings the Demi-piece of 7¾ Yards in Length, for every £.100 of the Value thereof	- 10 0 0	

	£	s	d
exported to any British Colony or Plantation in America	5	13	4
By the 27 Geo. III. Chap. 13. Sect. 24. Cambricks and French Lawns are forfeited if imported in Ships less than 60 Tons Burthen, or otherwise than in Bales, Cases, or Boxes, covered with Sackcloth or Canvas, and each Bale, Case, or Box, containing less than one Hundred Whole Pieces, or two Hundred Demi or Half Pieces of Cambricks or French Lawns.	—	—	—
Linen of the Manufacture of the European Dominions of the French King, viz.			
Damask Tabling, not exceeding 1 Ell ⅛ in Breadth, the Yard	0	5	4
exceeding 1 Ell ⅛, and under 2 Ells in Breadth, the Yard	0	6	2
of the Breadth of 2 Ells or upwards, and under 3 Ells, the Yard	0	7	0
of the Breadth of 3 Ells or upwards, the Yard	0	10	4
Damask Towelling and Napkining, the Yard	0	1	11
Diaper Tabling, not exceeding 1 Ell ⅛ in Breadth, the Yard	0	2	5
exceeding 1 Ell ⅛, and under 2 Ells in Breadth, the Yard	0	2	10
of the Breadth of 2 Ells or upwards, and under 3 Ells, the Yard	0	3	2
of the Breadth of 3 Ells or upwards, the Yard	0	4	8

	£	s	d
	0	4	10
	0	5	8
	0	6	6
	0	9	10
	0	1	8
	0	2	2
	0	2	6
	0	2	10
	0	4	4

(266)

TABLE C.

INWARDS.

	Duty. £. s. d.	Drawback. £. s. d.
Linen of the Manufacture of the European Dominions of the French King, viz.		
Diaper Towelling and Napkining, the Yard	0 0 10	0 0 8
Sail Cloth, not exceeding 36 Inches in Breadth, the 120 Ells	2 3 1	0 0 0
Sail Cloth, exceeding 36 Inches in Breadth, the 120 Ells	3 16 1	0 0 0
Sails ready made, for every £.100 of the Value thereof	45 0 0	0 0 0
Linen of the Manufacture of the European Dominions of the French King, not otherwise enumerated or described, viz.		
not exceeding 1 Ell 1/8 in Breadth, the Ell	0 1 4	0 1 2
exceeding 1 Ell 1/2, and under 2 Ells in Breadth, the Ell	0 1 1	0 1 5
of the Breadth of 2 Ells or upwards, and under 3 Ells, the Ell	0 1 9	0 1 7
of the Breadth of 3 Ells or upwards, the Ell	0 2 7	0 2 5
N. B. Linen printed or stained, is also subject to Duties of Excise.		
Sadlery of the Manufacture of the European Dominions of the French King, imported directly from thence into Great Britain, in Ships of the Built of either Country, owned and navigated according to Law, for every £.100 of the Value thereof	15 0 0	0 0 0
Gauzes of all Sorts of the Manufacture of the European Dominions of the French King, imported directly from thence into Great Britain, in		

(267)

	£	s	d
Ships of the Built of either Country, owned and navigated according to Law, for every £. 100 of the Value thereof	10	0	0
Millinery made up of Muslin, Lawn, Cambrick, or Gauze of any Kind, of the Manufacture of the European Dominions of the French King, imported directly from thence into Great Britain, in Ships of the Built of either Country, owned and navigated according to Law, for every £. 100 of the Value thereof	12	0	0
If any other Article which may be legally imported into this Kingdom shall be used in such Millinery, such Articles shall pay Duty as if separately imported.			
Porcelain, Earthen Ware, and Pottery, of the Manufacture of the European Dominions of the French King, imported directly from thence into Great Britain, in Ships of the Built of either Country, owned and navigated according to Law, for every £. 100 of the Value thereof	12	0	0
Plate Glass, and Glass Ware, of the Manufacture of the European Dominions of the French King, imported directly from thence into Great Britain, in Ships of the Built of either Country, owned and navigated according to Law, for every £. 100 of the Value thereof	12	0	0

N. B. Subject also to the Duty of Excise.

For the Additional Duty of Customs on European French green Glass Bottles, imposed by the 28 Geo. III. Chap. 33. in lieu of the Duty of Excise, see Bottles in Table A.

TABLE C.

INWARDS.

N. B. It has been determined by the Commissioners of the Customs, that Clocks and Watches of the Manufacture of the European Dominions of the French King, imported directly from thence, shall pay for every £. 100 of the Value £. 27 : 10 : 0.

	Duty. £. s. d.	Drawback. £. s. d.

TABLE D.

A Table of the Duties of Cuſtoms payable on the Importation into this Kingdom, and of the Drawbacks thereof to be allowed on the Exportation from thence, of all Goods, Wares, and Merchandiſe whatever ſubject to Duty, not being particularly enumerated or deſcribed, or otherwiſe charged with Duty in the preceding Tables.

TABLE D.

INWARDS.

	Duty. £. s. d.	Drawback. £. s. d.
Cotton, viz.		
Manufactures of Cotton not otherwise particularly enumerated or described, for every £.100 of the Value thereof	44 0 0	41 10 0
Earthen Ware not otherwise particularly enumerated or described, for every £.100 of the Value thereof	41 16 0	36 11 0
Glass, viz.		
Plate Glass and all other Glass Manufactures not otherwise particularly enumerated or described, for every £.100 of the Value thereof	60 0 0	43 0 0
Hides and Skins and Pieces of Hides and Skins tanned, tawed, or dressed, not otherwise particularly enumerated or described, for every £.100 of the Value thereof	77 0 0	25 0 0
Leather, viz.		
Manufactures of Leather or any Manufacture whereof Leather is the most valuable Part, for every £.100 of the Value thereof	77 0 0	25 0 0
Linen, viz.		
Linen not being chequered, or striped, or printed, painted, stained, or dyed after the Manufacture, or in the Thread or Yarn before the Manufacture, and not being otherwise particularly enume-		

rated or described, for every £.100 of the Value thereof	-	33	6	8	30 16 8
Linen of the Manufacture of Ireland chequered or striped, painted, stained, or dyed after the Manufacture, or in the Thread or Yarn before the Manufacture, if imported under the Conditions, Regulations, and Restrictions directed by the 7 and 8 Will. III. Chap. 39. and 16 Geo. II. Chap. 26. for every £.100 of the Value thereof	-	49	10	0	49 10 0
See the Conditions and Restrictions in the Note following Flax in Table A.					
Linen chequered or striped, or printed, painted, stained, or dyed after the Manufacture, or in the Thread or Yarn before the Manufacture, not prohibited to be imported, worn, or used in Great Britain, and not otherwise particularly enumerated or described, for every £.100 of the Value thereof	-	80	4	2	77 14 2
Paper, viz.					
Painted Paper or Paper Hangings for Rooms, for every £.100 of the Value thereof	-	75	0	0	0 0 0
Paper not otherwise particularly enumerated or described, for every £.100 of the Value thereof	-	55	0	0	0 0 0
Sails, for every £.100 of the Value thereof	-	45	0	0	0 0 0
Ships with their Tackle, Apparel, and Furniture (except Sails), for every £.100 of the Value thereof	-	5	10	0	0 0 0

(272)

TABLE D.

INWARDS.	Duty. £. s. d.	Drawback. £. s. d.
Toys, for every £.100 of the Value thereof	33 0 0	29 13 4
Wood unmanufactured not otherwise enumerated or described, imported into Great Britain from any Part of Europe, for every £.100 of the Value thereof	33 0 0	30 10 0
Goods, Wares, and Merchandise prohibited to be used in this Kingdom, but allowed to be brought in and secured in Warehouses for Exportation, not otherwise enumerated or described, for every £.100 of the Value thereof	7 10 0	0 0 0
Goods, Wares, and Merchandise not otherwise particularly enumerated or described, not prohibited to be used in Great Britain, but allowed by Law to be imported and secured in Warehouses for Exportation, for every £.100 of the Value thereof	2 10 0	0 0 0
All other Goods, Wares, and Merchandise whatever, not being particularly enumerated or described, or otherwise charged with Duty, not prohibited to be imported or used in Great Britain and not being exempt from Duty, for every £.100 of the Value thereof	27 10 0	25 0 0

FORM of the Declaration for Goods subject to Duty upon Importation according to the Value thereof, by the 27 Geo. III. Chap. 13. Sect. 17. which is to be subscribed by the Importer or Proprietor thereof, or his known Agent or Factor, in the Presence of two of the principal Officers of the Customs at the Port of Importation.

I A. B. do hereby declare, that the Goods mentioned in this Entry, and contained in two Cases marked F. I. Number 1 and 2, are of the *Growth*, *Production*, or *Manufacture* of Germany, and that I am the Importer or Proprietor thereof; or that C. D. is the Proprietor or Importer thereof, and that I am duly authorized by him, and I do enter the same at the Value of one Hundred and twenty Pounds. Witness my Hand the seventh Day of September, One Thousand Seven Hundred and Ninety One.

A. B.

The above Declaration signed the
7th Day of September 1791, in
the Presence of
    E. F. Collector.
    G. H. Comptroller, or other principal Officer.

If upon Examination by the proper Officers of the Customs it shall appear that the Goods are undervalued they may detain them; but they must be

TABLE D.

INWARDS.

taken in London or Leith within eight Days from the landing, in other Ports within fifteen Days from the landing, and the Importer or Proprietor is to be paid the Value of the Goods so declared, ten per Cent. thereon, and the Duties paid on Importation, without any further Allowance for Freight, or any other Charge or Expence whatever, which is to be paid within fifteen Days after the Goods are taken, if exceeding twenty Pounds, and not exceeding twenty Pounds without Delay.

TABLE E.

A Table of the Duties payable on the Exportation from Great Britain, of Goods, Wares, and Merchandife, not being particularly enumerated or defcribed, or otherwife charged with Duty on the Exportation.

TABLE E.

OUTWARDS.

	Duty.
	£. s. d.
Copperas, British, for every £.100 of the Value thereof	5 10 0
Hair not particularly enumerated, and not prohibited to be exported, for every £.100 of the Value thereof	5 10 0
Lapis Caliminaris, for every £.100 of the Value thereof	5 10 0
Lead Ore, for every £.100 of the Value thereof	5 10 0
Skins not particularly enumerated, and not prohibited to be exported, for every £.100 of the Value thereof	5 10 0
Cotton Wool of the Growth or Produce of the British Plantations in America, for every £.100 of the Value thereof	5 10 0
By the 19 Geo. III. Chap. 53. Cotton Wool, the Growth or Produce of the British Colonies or Plantations in America, having been duly entered outwards and regularly shipped, may be exported in British built Ships free of Duty.	
All other Goods, Wares, and Merchandise, of the Growth, Production, or Manufacture of Great Britain, the Exportation of which is not prohibited by Law, may be exported without Payment of Duty, provided the same are regularly entered and shipped; but on Failure thereof, such Goods, Wares, and Merchandise, shall be subject and liable to Duty, viz. for every £.100 of the Value thereof	5 10 0

See Table K, for the several Goods, Wares, and Merchandise, either circumstantially or absolutely prohibited to be exported as there mentioned.

FORM of the Declaration of the Exporter of Goods subject to Duty on Exportation according to the Value thereof, by the 27 Geo. III. Chap. 13. Sect. 19. which is to be subscribed by the Exporter, or his known Agent or Factor, in presence of two of the principal officers of the Customs at the Port of Exportation.

I   of   do hereby declare that I am the Exporter or Proprietor of the Goods mentioned in this Entry, and I do enter the same at the Value of   witness my Hand the   Day of

A. B.

The above Declaration signed the   Day of   in the Presence of
C. D. Collector.
E. F. Comptroller, or other principal Officer.

If upon Examination by the proper Officers of the Customs it shall appear that the Goods are undervalued, they may detain them; and the Exporter or Proprietor is to be paid within fifteen Days after the Goods are detained the Value so declared, ten per Cent. thereon, and the Customs paid on the Entry of the Goods for Exportation, without any further Allowance whatever.

TABLE E.

OUTWARDS.

N. B. This last mentioned Duty upon British Goods otherwise free of any Duty if regularly entered and shipped, having changed the former Situation of such Goods with respect to the Regulations of Exportation according to the Rates of the 12 Charles II. Chap. 4. and the 8 Geo. I. Chap. 15. it appeared only necessary to class the several Articles formerly rated Alphabetically, by the Hundred Weight, Pound Weight, Ton Weight, or otherwise, viz.

Goods, Wares, and Merchandise of the Growth, Production, or Manufacture of Great Britain, not being subject to Duty upon Exportation if regularly entered and shipped, which must be entered outwards by the Hundred Weight.

Alum.
Anvils.
Apothecary.
Bell Metal.
Bird Lime.
Books, bound or unbound.
Brass, wrought or unwrought.
Playing Cards.
Cheese.
Confectionary.

Fennel Seed.
Flax.
Gun Powder.
Haberdashery Ware.
Hartshorn.
Hops.
Iron Ordnance.
Iron, wrought.
Maps and Sea Cards.
Mustard Seed.

Russetting for Painters.
Salt Petre.
Soap, Hard.
Starch.
Steel, called Gad Steel.
Tallow.
Tin, unwrought.
Ditto wrought, called Pewter.
Wax.
Weld.

(279)

Copper, wrought or unwrought.
Cordage, tarred or untarred.
Emery Stones.
Nails.
Oker, Yellow or Red.
Pictures, painted or printed.

Gambray Wood.
Red Wood.

N.B. Haberdashery Ware includes all Sorts of Threads, Packthread, Hooks and Eyes, and all Sorts of Wares sold by Haberdashers. Iron wrought, includes all Ironmongers' Wares, all Tools, Fowling Pieces, Knives, Scissars, Jack Work, and Clock Work.

Goods, Wares, and Merchandise of the Growth, Production, or Manufacture of Great Britain, not being subject to Duty upon Exportation if regularly entered and shipped, which must be entered outwards by the Pound Weight.

Agarick.
Boots.
Cambodium.
Candles, the Dozen Pounds.
Coney Hair or Wool.
Lace of Gold or Silver.

Leather Manufactures, not being particularly mentioned.
Saffron.
Sea Morse Teeth.
Shoes and Slippers.
Shreds and Pieces of Broad Cloth.

Silk, thrown or manufactured.
Stuffs.
Tapestry or Dornix.
Hangings of any Sort.
Thrums, the hundred Pounds.
Wax, Hard.
Yarn, called Grogram Yarn.

T 4

TABLE E.

OUTWARDS.

Goods, Wares, and Merchandise of the Growth, Production, or Manufacture of Great Britain, not being subject to Duty upon Exportation if regularly entered and shipped, which must be entered outwards by the Ton Weight or the Tun Liquid.

Beer, or Beer Eager, the Tun.
Cyder, the Tun.
Iron, New or Old, the Ton.
Melasses or Rameales, the Ton.
Mum, the Tun.
Train Oil made in Great Britain, the Tun.
Vinegar of Wine, the Tun.
Woad, the Ton.
Box Wood, the Ton.

Goods, Wares, and Merchandise of the Growth, Production, or Manufacture of Great Britain, not being subject to Duty upon Exportation if regularly entered and shipped, which must be entered outwards as hereafter mentioned.

Alabaster, the Load.
Apples, the Bushel.
Aqua Vitæ, the Hogshead.
Ashes of British Wood, the Last containing 12 Barrels.
Bacon, the Flitch.
Bags, the Dozen.
Bandaliers, the hundred Collars.
Bays, called Barnstaple, coarse, of 20 Pounds Weight and under, the Bay.

Manchester, or Barnstaple, fine, and all other single Bays, not exceeding 34 Pounds Weight, the Piece.
Double Bays, the Piece, in Weight from 34 Pounds Weight to 60 Pounds Weight.
Minikin Bays, containing in Weight from 60 Pounds Weight to 90 Pounds Weight, as three single Bays.
And if they do contain above 90 Pounds in Weight, and not above 112 Pounds, as for four single Bays, and no more.

Beef, the Barrel.
Bellows, the Dozen.
Billets, the Thousand.
Bones, called Ox Bones, the Thousand.
Bridles, the Dozen.
Brushes, of Heath, the Dozen.
Butter, the Barrel.
Caps, called Monmouth Caps, plain or trimmed, the Dozen.
 of Wool, Black, buttoned, the Dozen.
Cards, called Stock Cards, Tow Cards, Wool Cards, the Dozen.
Card Boards, the small Groce containing 12 Dozen.
Carpets, Northern, the Piece.
Catlings, or British Hat Makers Strings, the Groce containing 12 Dozen.
Chairs, called Sedan Chairs, the Piece,

TABLE E.
OUTWARDS.

Cloak Bags, the Dozen.

Cloths, the Short Cloth, containing in Length not above 28 Yards, and in Weight not above 64 Pounds, white or coloured, and so after that Rate for all other Sorts of Cloths of greater Length and Weight, allowing not above 28 Yards and 64 Pounds to a Short Cloth.

What and how many Sorts of the lesser Woollen Cloths hereafter specified, shall be allowed to a Short Cloth.

Seven	Cardinals, Dorset and Somerset Dozen Rudge washed, Pin Whites, Statutes, Stockbridges, Straits, Taverstocks.	To be accounted for a Short Cloth after the Rate of the Short Cloth as beforementioned.
Five	Tauntons, Bridgewaters, and Dunsters, the Five not exceeding 64 Pounds in Weight.	
Four	Devon Dozen, containing 12 or 13 Yards, in Weight 13 Pounds.	
	Ordinary Penistones, or Forest Whites, containing between 12 and 13 Yards, and in Weight 28 Pounds.	
	Sorting Penistones, containing 13 or 14 Yards, and in Weight 35 Pounds unfrized.	
Three	Narrow Yorkshire Kerseys, White and Red, containing not above 17 or 18 Yards, and in Weight 22 Pounds.	
	Hampshire ordinary Kerseys.	
	Newbury Whites, and other Kerseys of like making, containing 24 Yards, and in Weight 28 Pounds.	

Sorting Hampshire Kerseys, containing 28 Yards, and in Weight 32 Pounds.

Two {
Northern Dozen, single Sorting Penistones, containing between 14 and 15 Yards, and in Weight 35 Pounds frized.
One Northern Dozen Double.
The new Sort of Cloth, called Spanish Cloth, otherwise Narrow List; Western Broad Cloth, not exceeding 25 Yards in Length, and 43 Pounds in Weight, to be accounted two Thirds of the Short Cloth beforementioned.
Cloth Rashes, alias Cloth Serges, containing 30 Yards, weighing 40 Pounds, to be accounted two Thirds of the Short Cloth beforementioned.
}

White Woollen Broad Cloth, the Piece.
Coaches and Chariots of all Sorts, the Piece.
Coin of Gold or Silver, or Bullion, Foreign, upon Entry, free.
Cobweb Lawns, the Yard.
Corn, all Sorts, the Quarter, containing eight Bushels.
Corn exported contrary to the Directions and Regulations of the 31 Geo. III. Chap. 30. is subject to Forfeiture, as also the Ship, Furniture, Tackle, and Apparel, in which the same shall be exported, and may be seized by any Officer of the Customs. Every Person concerned in the Exportation is subject to a Penalty of twenty Shillings per Bushel: but the Export is not restrained of so much as is necessary for the Sustenance, Diet, and Support of the Ship's Crew and Passengers; or for the Use of Cattle, Live Stock, or other Animals on board; or for victualling or providing any of his Majesty's Forces, Forts, or Garrisons; nor to prohibit at

TABLE E.
OUTWARDS.

Corn, any Time the Export of Beans to the British Forts, Castles, or Factories in Africa, or for the Use of British Ships trading on that Coast, which have been usually supplied from Great Britain; nor to the carrying Corn Coastwise, upon the Security being given required by Law; nor to the Export from certain Ports of this Kingdom to certain Places out of this Kingdom, nor from Guernsey, Jersey, or Alderney, of the different Sorts now allowed.to be imported there, it being for the Fisheries at Newfoundland or the British American Fisheries, as permitted by the 9 Geo. III. Chap. 28. of the several Sorts and Quantities specified in Table L.

Cottons, Northern, Manchester, Taunton, Welsh Plains, and Welsh Cottons, the hundred Goads.
N. B. The Goad is considered to be one Yard in Quantity.

Coverlets of Caddas, Wool, and Hair, the Piece.

Cushions of Yorkshire, the Dozen.

Cows or Heifers, each.

Darnix, the Yard.

Coverlets, the Piece.

Dimity, the Yard.

Dust of Cloves, of Ginger, of Lignum Vitæ, of Mace, of Nutmegs, of Pepper, of all Spices, and the like, to be exported Custom free, having paid at the Importation.

Earthen Ware, called Bricks and Tiles of all Sorts, the Thousand.

Figurettoes, narrow or broad, the Piece.

Flannel, the Yard.
Freezes, the Yard.
Fustians of all Sorts to go out free, the Piece.
Garments, or Wearing Apparel, of all Sorts, ready made, the Garment.
Garterings of Cruel, the Groce containing 12 Dozen.
Garters of Worsted, the Groce containing 12 Dozen.
Girdles of Leather, for Men or for Children, the Groce containing 12 Dozen.
 of Norwich, the Dozen.
Glass, Broken, the Barrel.
 for Windows, the Chest.
Glasses to drink in, Bottles, and all other Sorts of Glasses, the Hundred.
Gloves, of Buck Leather, the Dozen.
 plain, of Sheep, Kid, or Lamb's Leather, fringed and stitched with Silk, or furred with Coney Wool, the Dozen Pair.
Glovers Clippings, the Fat or Maund, being eight Hundred Weight.
Goose Quills, the Thousand.
Grindle Stones, the Chalder.
Guts, called Ox Guts, the Barrel.
Hair Cloth, the Piece.
Hake Fish, the Hundred containing six Score.
Harness, called Coach Harness, the Pair, with Bridles.
Hatbands of Cruel, the Groce containing 12 Dozen.

(236)

TABLE E.

OUTWARDS.

Hats, called Bevers and Demicasters, Felts, and all other Hats, the Dozen.

By the 24 Geo. III. Chap. 51. Sect. 24. Hats not less in Quantity than two Dozen in any one Package may be exported without the Stamp affixed thereto, by a Certificate from the Distributor of Stamps nearest to whom the Exporter of the Hats resides, which is to be given without Fee or Reward.

Hawks Hoods, the Dozen.
Hemp Seed, the Quarter containing eight Bushels.
Herrings, called Winter Herrings, white, full or shotten, packed, the Last containing 12 Barrels. unpacked, or Sea Sticks, the Last containing 18 Barrels.
red, full or shotten, the Last containing 20 Cades, each Cade 500.
called Summer Herrings, shotten, white, packed, the Last containing 12 Barrels. unpacked, or Sea Sticks, the Last containing 18 Barrels.
shotten, red, the Last containing 20 Cades, each Cade 500.

All other Sea Fish taken by the Subjects of this Realm, as the same are denominated.
Holsters, the Dozen Pair.
Hoops for Barrels, the Thousand.
Horns, called Blowing Horns, small, Powder Horns, and Shoeing Horns, the Dozen.
of Bucks or Stags, the Hundred.

(287)

for Lanthorns, the thousand Leaves.
Horse Litters, the Piece.
called Ox Horns, of Rams, of Sheep, or Tips of Horns, the Thousand.
Collars, the Hundred containing five Score.
Tails with Hair, the Hundred containing five Score.
Jewels, Pearls, and precious Stones, Foreign or British, free of Entry.
Irish Mantles, the Mantle.
Statute Lace, the Groce containing 12 Dozen.
Lamperns, the Thousand.
Lime, the Chalder.
Linen, viz. all Sorts of Cloth made of Hemp or Flax, fine or coarse, the Piece not exceeding 40 Ells.
Shreds, the Maund or Fat.
Linseed, the Quarter containing eight Bushels.
Lifts of Cloth, the thousand Yards.
Loom Work, the Yard.
Nuts, small, the Barrel containing three Bushels.
Oat Meal, the Barrel containing three Bushels.
Oysters, the small Barrel, in Pickle.
Oxen, the Ox.
Parchment, the Roll.
Pasteboards, the Groce containing 12 Dozen.
Pilchards, the Ton by Strangers.

TABLE E.
OUTWARDS.

Points of Leather, the small Groce containing 12 Dozen.
Pork, the Barrel.
Purls of Broad Cloth, the Piece.
Rape Cakes, the Thousand.
Seed, the Quarter containing eight Bushels.
Rugs, called Irish Rug, the Yard.
 Irish Rugs for Beds, the Rug.
Saddles of all Sorts, the Piece.
Saddle Trees, the Dozen.
Scabbards for Swords, the Dozen.
Shoes, Old, the hundred Dozen Pair.
Shovels, shod or unshod, the Dozen.
Soap, the Barrel.
Sprats, the Cade containing a Thousand.
Stockings, Irish, Woollen or Worsted, for Men or Children, the Dozen.
 Kersey long, the Pair.
 Kersey short, the Dozen Pair.
Stones, called Hilling Stones, the Thousand.
 Slate, the Thousand.
Swine or Hogs, each.

Ticking, the Piece.
Tobacco Pipes, the small Groce containing 12 Dozen.
Velures, the single Piece containing 7 Yards.
 the double Piece containing 15 Yards.
Virginals, the Pair.
Wadmoll, the Yard.
Watches of all Sorts, the Piece
Whalefins, the Groce containing 12 Dozen.
Wine Lees, the Butt.
Woadnets, the Hundred containing five Score.
Worsteds, narrow or broad, the Piece.

All other Goods not beforementioned, being of the Growth, Production, or Manufacture of Great Britain, are entered outwards by their Value; such as Cabinet Wares, Crooked Lane Wares, Millinery, Perfumery, Pope's Head Alley Toys, Stationary Wares, Upholstery, &c. but Cards, called Playing Cards, and Dice, must be entered out as such, and not as Stationary.

As a Comparison between Foreign Measures and Weights and British Measures and Weights, may be useful to ascertain the Quantities of Merchandise imported, the following Tables, with very little Addition, have been taken from Mr. Crouch's Practice of the Officers of the Customs at the Waterside in the Port of London, printed in the Year 1746.

Comparison of Measures.

		Ell British.
The Ell at Amsterdam	makes	,5900
Antwerp	—	,6000
Arras	—	,6060
Bruges	—	,6097
Cologne	—	,4807
Dantzick	—	,7228
Embden	—	,4850
Francfort	—	,4792
Hamburg	—	,4850
Lisle	—	,6024
Lubec	—	,5000
Maestricht	—	,6369
Nurenburg	—	,5747
Vienna	—	,6869

(291)

The Aune at	Calais	,6369
	Lyons	,9836
	Paris	1,0526
	Rouen	,9708
	Rochelle	,9778
	Touloufe	,9334
The Brace at	Florence	,4901
	Leghorn	,5000
	Lucca	,5000
	Madeira	,9681
	Milan { Silk	,4347
	{ Linen	,5000
	Venice { Silk	,5102
	{ Linen	,5555
The Vare at	Andalusia	,7339
	Castile	,7407
	Granada in Spain	,7339
	Lisbon	1,0000
	Seville	,7407
The Palm at Genoa		,2079
The Afhin at Moscow		,6200

(292)

Comparison of Measures.

		Ell British.
The Cane at	Barcelona	1,4035
	Marseilles	1,7000
	Rome	1,7875
	Saragossa	1,8181
	Valencia	,8247

The foregoing Table is collected from several Authors who have treated of the Proportion between Foreign and British Measures: but in the present Practice of the Customs and Trade, there is some Variation; for in the Measures of the following Places the Proportion is generally held to be, viz.

Flanders and Holland	The Aune or Ell Flemish With an Allowance of 2 per Cent for shortness of Measure.	,6 British Ell.
France	The Aune, by the Standard of Paris	47 British Inches.
Germany and East Country	The Aune or Ell With an Allowance of 2 per Cent for shortness of Measure.	,25 British Ell.
Moscovy or Russia	The Ashin	,57 British Ell. ,7125 Yard.
The Ashin or Archeen, now computed for the Duties, at		,60 of a British Ell.
Turkey	The Pyke	,4333 British Ell.

Comparison of Weights.

	British Pound Avoirdupois.
The Pound of Abbeville is equal to	1,0989
Ancona	,7800
Amsterdam	1,1111
Antwerp	1,0460
Aquila	,7125
Avignon	,8928
Bologna	,8000
Bourdeaux	1,0989
Bruges	1,0204
Burgoyn	1,0989
Calabria	,7300
Calais	,9345
Dantzick	,8620
A Lipound, 16 Dantzick Pounds.	
A Shipound, 20 Lispounds.	
Dieppe is equal to	1,0989
Ferrara	,7500
Flanders in general	,9433
Florence	,7800
Francfort	1,1313

U 3

Comparison of Weights.

	British Pounds Avoirdupois.
The Pound of Geneva is equal to	
Genoa { Suttle	1,0700
Genoa { Grofs	,7125
Hamburg	,7000
Holland	1,0865
Leghorn	1,0526
Leipfic	,7500
Lifbon	1,1061
Lubec	1,1350
Lucca	1,1516
Lyons { Common Weight	,7088
Lyons { Silk Weight	,9345
Lyons { Cuftom Weight	1,0204
Marfeilles	1,1111
Milan	,8928
Mirandola	,7000
Naples	,7500
Nuremburg	,7100
Paris	1,1363
	1,1225

Rouen	{ By Vicount	—	1,1428
	Common Weight	—	1,1089
Rochelle	—	—	,8928
Rome	—	—	,7874
Ruffia	{ A Pood 35½ Pounds or } Avoirdupois.		,9259
	{ 63 Poods 1 Ton }		,8928
Seville	—	—	,8200
Touloufe	—	—	16,0000
Turin	—	—	2,4375
Turkey	{ the Batman qt. 2400 Drams	—	,6666
	the Oak qt. 43 Ounces	—	,6400
	the Rotula qt. 100 Drams	—	
Venice	{ Suttle	—	1,0600
	Grofs	—	1,2300
Vienna	—	—	

Comparison of Weights.

The foregoing Table is collected from several Authors who have treated of the Proportions between Foreign and British Weights: but in the present Practice of the Customs and Trade, there is some Variation; for in the Weights of the following Places, the Proportion is generally held to be, viz.

		British Pound Avoirdupois.
Dantzick, the Pound	-	,9600
Germany { the 106 Pounds	-	112,0000
{ the Pound	-	1,0566
Holland { the 104 Pounds	-	112,0000
{ the Pound	-	1,0769
Italy, the Pound	-	,7500

The Cattie of China is accounted to be 20½ Ounces Avoirdupois British.
The Pickle of China is accounted to be 100 Catties.

With an Addition of 3 per Cent.

Upon each Weight of Goods taken for the Duties of Customs to be charged (except Tobacco and Snuff, for which there is a special Allowance of two Pounds, given by the 29 Geo. III. Chap. 68. Sect. 54. upon the Weight of each Package), the following Draughts are deducted, but no Allowance is given under ¼ of a Hundred Weight.

Allowance for Draught.

	lb.
under 1 Cwt.	1.
from 1 to 2	2.
2 to 3	3.
3 to 10	4.
10 to 18	7.
18 and upwards	9.

In weighing Tobacco and Snuff the Turn of the Scale is given in favour of the Revenue; in all other Goods the Turn of the Scale is given in favour of the Merchant.

TABLE F.

Duties, Allowances, Bounties, and Drawbacks, of Excise.

TABLE F.

EXCISE DUTIES.

AUCTION.

	£.	s.	d.
FOR every twenty Shillings of the Purchase Money arising or payable by virtue of any Sale at Auction in Great Britain of any Interest in Possession or Reversion, in any Freehold, Copyhold, or Leasehold Lands, Tenements, Houses, or Hereditaments, and of any Annuities or Sums of Money charged thereon; and of any Utensils in Husbandry and Farming Stock, Ships and Vessels; and of any reversionary Interest in the Public Funds; and of any Plate or Jewels; and so in Proportion for any greater or lesser Sum of such Purchase Money; to be paid by the Auctioneer, Agent, Factor, or Seller by Commission, Threepence Halfpenny.	0	0	3½
For every twenty Shillings of the Purchase Money arising or payable by virtue of any Sale at Auction in Great Britain of Furniture, Fixtures, Pictures, Books, Horses, and Carriages, and all other Goods and Chattels whatsoever; to be paid by the Auctioneer, Agent, Factor, or Seller by Commission, of such Purchase Money; or lesser Sum Sevenpence	0	0	7

TABLE F.

AUCTION.

£. s. d.

The Exemptions from the above Duties on Sales at Auction are as follow, by the 17 Geo. III. Chap. 50.

Sales by Order of the Court of Chancery or Exchequer before the Masters in Chancery, or Deputy Remembrancer of the Exchequer, by the East India Company, Hudson's Bay Company, Commissioners of Customs or Excise, Board of Ordnance, Commissioners of the Navy or Victualling, by the Sheriff in Execution of Judgments, Goods distrained for Rent or Non Payment of Tithes, Goods and Effects of Bankrupts by Order of Assignees.

Goods imported as Merchandise from any British Colony or Plantation in America, on the first Sale by or for the Account of the original Importer, to whom consigned, and by whom entered at the Custom House at the Port of Importation, if sold within twelve Months after imported.

Ships, or their Tackle, Apparel, and Furniture, or the Cargoes taken and condemned as Prize, sold for the Benefit of the Captors; Ships or Goods wrecked or stranded, sold for the Benefit of the Insurers or Proprietors, or sold free of Duty to pay Salvage.

Sales for the Benefit of Creditors by Direction of any Deed, and Sales by Trustees chosen pursuant to an Act of the 12 Geo. III. Chap. 23.

Effects bought in by the Owner or Agent, previous Notice having been given to the Auctioneer in writing, signed by the Owner and Person authorized to bid.

Sales of Estates to be held by Lease or Copy of Court Roll, for Life or Years; and of Woods, Coppices, the Produce of Mines or Quarries, and for cutting or working the same, and Sales of Materials used in working the same; and of Cattle, live or dead Stock, and unmanufactured Produce of Lands, sold by the Proprietors or their Agents.

Sales by Lords of Manors for granting of Copyhold or Customary Estates, for Life or Years, and by the Owners for Life or Years; and of Woods, Coppices, the Produce of Mines or Quarries, or concerning the same, or the cutting or working thereof, and of Cattle, alive or dead.

If the Sale of the Estate is void through Defect of Title, the Commissioners of Excise or Justices of the Peace in the Country, may relieve, on Oath, for the Duties paid; but by the 28 Geo. III. Chap. 37. Sect. 19. Claim must be made within twelve Months after the Sale, if rendered void within that Time, or if not rendered void within that Time, within three Months after the Discovery.

Skins from East and West Florida, being the Produce thereof, within twelve Months from the Time of Importation; by the 28 Geo. III. Chap. 37.

Piece Goods by the Manufacturer or first Purchaser, the same having been wove or fabricated in this Kingdom, being sold in a Place entered with the proper Officer of Excise, also openly shewn and exposed at the Time and Place of Sale; by the 29 Geo. III. Chap. 63.

Goods imported as Merchandise from Yucatan in South America, on the first Sale by or for the Account of the original Importer, to whom consigned, if sold

TABLE F.

within twelve Months from the Time of Importation; by the 30 Geo. III. Chap. 26.

	l.	s.	d.

BEER.

For every Barrel of Beer or Ale above six Shillings the Barrel (exclusive of the Duty hereby imposed on such Beer or Ale, and not being Twopenny Ale mentioned and described in the seventh Article of the Treaty of Union, nor being Beer or Ale commonly called *Table Beer*, which shall be brewed and made in that Part of Great Britain called England by the Common Brewer, under, subject, and according to the Rules, Regulations, Restrictions, and Provisions contained and provided in and by an Act of Parliament, made in the twenty-second Year of the Reign of his present Majesty, concerning Beer or Ale commonly called *Table Beer*), which shall be brewed in Great Britain by the Common Brewer or any other Person or Persons who shall sell or tap out Beer or Ale publicly or privately; to be paid by such Common Brewer or other Person or Persons respectively, and so in Proportion for any greater or lesser Quantity, eight Shillings - 0 8 0

For every Barrel of Beer or Ale of six Shillings the Barrel or under (exclusive of the Duty hereby imposed thereon), which shall be brewed in Great Britain by the Common Brewer or any other Person or Persons who shall sell or tap out such Beer or Ale publicly or privately; to be paid by such Common Brewer or by such other Person or Persons respectively, and so in Proportion for any greater or lesser Quantity, one Shilling and Fourpence. - - - - - - 0 1 4

For every Barrel of Beer or Ale above six Shillings the Barrel (exclusive of the Duty hereby imposed thereon), and not exceeding eleven Shillings, exclusive of such Duty, commonly called *Table Beer*, which shall be brewed and made in that Part of Great Britain called England by the Common Brewer, under, subject, and according to the Rules, Regulations, Restrictions, and Provisions contained and provided in and by the said Act, made in the twenty-second Year of the Reign of his present Majesty, and so in Proportion for any greater or lesser Quantity; to be paid by such Common Brewer, three Shillings - - - - - - - 0 3 0

For every Barrel of Two-penny Ale mentioned and described in the seventh Article of the Treaty of Union; to be paid by the Common Brewer or Victualler, three Shillings and Fourpence Farthing and thirteen nineteenth Parts of a Farthing - - 0 3 4 4/19 1/13

For every Barrel of French Beer, Ale, or Mum, which shall be imported into Great Britain directly from any of the European Dominions of the French King, and so in Proportion for any greater or lesser Quantity; to be paid by the Importer thereof before the landing thereof, eight Shillings - - - - - 0 8 0

For every Barrel of Beer, Ale, or Mum (other than French Beer, Ale, or Mum imported as aforesaid), which shall be imported from beyond the Seas into Great Britain, and so in Proportion for any greater or lesser Quantity; to be paid by the Importer thereof before the landing thereof, seventeen Shillings and Threepence - - 0 17 3

TABLE F.

	£.	s.	d.

By the 12 Char. II. Chap. 23. the Barrel of Beer is to contain 36 Gallons, and the Barrel of Ale 32 Gallons; and by the 1 William and Mary, Seff. 1. Chap. 24. this Meafure is limited within the Bills of Mortality.

By the 1 of William and Mary, Seff. 1. Chap. 24. the Barrel of Beer and Ale brewed in any Part of England, Wales, or Town of Berwick upon Tweed, other than within the Cities of London and Weftminfter, and within the weekly Bills of Mortality, is to contain 34 Gallons.

By the 27 Geo. III. Chap. 31. the Barrel of French Beer, Ale, or Mum, is to contain 36 Gallons.

By the 31 Geo. III. Chap. 82. the Duty continued of two Pennies Scots, or one fixth Part of a Penny Sterling, upon every Scots Pint of Ale and Beer which fhall be brewed for Sale, brought into, tapped, or fold, within the Town of Kirkaldy and Liberties thereof.

BRICKS AND TILES.

For every Thoufand of Bricks which fhall be made in Great Britain, and fo in Proportion for any greater or leffer Quantity, two Shillings and Sixpence - - - 0 2 6

For every Thoufand of Plain Tiles which fhall be made in Great Britain, and fo in Proportion for any greater or leffer Quantity, three Shillings - - - 0 3 0

For every Thoufand of Pan Tiles, or Ridge Tiles, which fhall be made in Great Britain, and fo in Proportion for any greater or leffer Quantity, eight Shillings - - - 0 8 0

For every Hundred of Paving Tiles which fhall be made in Great Britain not exceeding ten Inches fquare, and fo in Proportion for any greater or leffer Quantity, one Shilling and Sixpence - - - - - 0 1 6

For every Hundred of Paving Tiles which fhall be made in Great Britain exceeding ten Inches fquare, and fo in Proportion for any greater or leffer Quantity, three Shillings 0 3 0

For every Thoufand of Tiles which fhall be made in Great Britain other than fuch as are hereinbefore enumerated or defcribed, by whatfoever Name or Names fuch Tiles are or may be called or known, and fo in Proportion for any greater or leffer Quantity, three Shillings - - - - - 0 3 0

The faid Duties upon Bricks and Tiles refpectively to be paid by the Maker thereof.

C A N D L E S.

For every Pound Weight Avoirdupois of Candles of Tallow and other Candles whatfoever (except Wax and Spermaceti Candles), which fhall be made in Great Britain, and fo in Proportion for any greater or leffer Quantity, one Penny Halfpenny - - - 0 0 1½

For every Pound Weight Avoirdupois of Candles which fhall be made in Great Britain of Wax or of Spermaceti, or which are ufually called or fold either for Wax or Spermaceti Candles (notwithftanding the Mixture of any other Ingredients therewith), and fo in Proportion for any greater or leffer Quantity, three Pence Halfpenny - - - 0 0 3½

The faid Duties upon Candles to be paid by the Maker thereof.

X

TABLE F.

COACHES.

	£.	s.	d.
For every Coach, Berlin, Landau, Chariot, Calash with four Wheels, Chaife Marine, Chaife with four Wheels, or Caravan, or by whatfoever Name fuch Carriages are or may be called, which fhall be built or conftructed in Great Britain for Sale; to be paid by the Maker thereof, one Pound - - - -	1	0	0
For every Calash, Chaife, and Chair, with two Wheels, or by whatfoever Name fuch Carriages are or may be called or known, which fhall be built or conftructed in Great Britain for Sale; to be paid by the Maker thereof, ten Shillings - -	0	10	0

COCOA NUTS AND COFFEE.

For every Pound Weight Avoirdupois of Cocoa Nuts, of the Growth or Produce of any Britifh Colony or Plantation in America, imported into Great Britain, and which fhall be delivered out of the Warehoufe in which the fame fhall have been lodged under the Care and Cuftody of the proper Officers for fecuring the Duties payable thereon for Home Confumption, and fo in Proportion for any greater or leffer Quantity, Sixpence Half-penny - - - -	0	0	6½
For every Pound Weight Avoirdupois of Cocoa Nuts, of the Growth or Produce of any other Place, imported into Great Britain, and which fhall be delivered out of the Ware-			

house in which the same shall have been lodged under the Care and Custody of the proper Officers for securing the Duties payable thereon for Home Consumption, and so in Proportion for any greater or lesser Quantity, one Shilling and Eightpence - - - 0 1 8

For every Pound Weight Avoirdupois of Coffee, of the Growth or Produce of any British Colony or Plantation in America, imported into Great Britain, and which shall be delivered out of the Warehouse in which the same shall have been lodged under the Care and Custody of the proper Officer for securing the Duties payable thereon for Home Consumption, and so in Proportion for any greater or lesser Quantity, Sixpence Halfpenny - - - 0 0 $6\frac{1}{2}$

For every Pound Weight Avoirdupois of Coffee, of the Growth or Produce of any other Place, imported into Great Britain, and which shall be delivered out of the Warehouse in which the same shall have been lodged under the Care and Custody of the proper Officers for securing the Duties payable thereon for Home Consumption, and so in Proportion for any greater or lesser Quantity, one Shilling and Eightpence - - - 0 1 8

CYDER AND PERRY.

For every Hogshead of Cyder or Perry which shall be made and sold by Retail in Great Britain; to be paid by the Retailer thereof, and so in Proportion for any greater or lesser Quantity, fourteen Shillings and Sevenpence - - - 0 14 7

For every Hogshead of Cyder or Perry which shall be made and sold in Great Britain in Quantities of twenty Gallons or upwards, by any Dealer in or Retailer of Cyder or Perry,

TABLE F.

CYDER AND PERRY.

	£.	s.	d.
from Fruit of the Growth of such Dealer or Retailer; to be paid by such Dealer or Retailer, and so in Proportion for any greater or lesser Quantity, six Shillings and Elevenpence	0	6	11
For every Hogshead of such last-mentioned Cyder or Perry, which shall be received into the Custody or Possession of any Person or Persons to be by such Person or Persons sold or disposed of; to be paid by such Person or Persons, and so in Proportion for any greater or lesser Quantity, seven Shillings and Eightpence	0	7	8
For every Hogshead of Cyder or Perry which shall be made in Great Britain, and which shall be sent or consigned to any Factor or Agent who shall receive the same to sell or dispose of; to be paid by such Factor or Agent, and so in Proportion for any greater or lesser Quantity, nineteen Shillings and Twopence	0	19	2
For every Tun of Cyder or Perry which shall be imported from beyond the Seas into Great Britain, and so in Proportion for any greater or lesser Quantity; to be paid by the Importer thereof before the landing thereof, seventeen Pounds sixteen Shillings and Sixpence	17	16	6

GLASS.

For every Hundred Weight of Materials or Metal, or other Preparations whatsoever, by what Name soever the same are or may be called or known, that shall be made Use of in

Great Britain in the making of Plate or Flint Glaſs, or Enamel, Stained or Paſte Glaſs, or Phial Glaſs, and ſo in Proportion for any greater or leſſer Quantity, one Pound one Shilling and Fivepence Halfpenny - - - - - - - - 1 1 5½

By the 27 Geo. III. Chap. 28. Sect. 5. in lieu of the Duty of Exciſe now payable for any Materials or Metal, or other Preparations made Uſe of in Great Britain in the making of Caſt Plate Glaſs, there ſhall be paid at and after the Rate of per Hundred Weight for all Caſt Plate Glaſs which ſhall be made in Great Britain, and which ſhall be ſquared into Plates of a Superficies not leſs than one Thouſand four Hundred and eighty-five Inches, and of a Thickneſs according to their Superficies, as afterementioned and deſcribed - - - - - 1 1 5½

Viz. That all ſuch Caſt Plates of Glaſs ſhall be ten twentieth Parts of an Inch at the leaſt in Thickneſs, if the ſuperficial Content of ſuch Plate ſhall be ſix Thouſand one Hundred and Forty-ſeven Square Inches, and upwards; nine twentieth Parts of an Inch at the leaſt in Thickneſs, if the ſuperficial Content of ſuch Plate ſhall be under ſix Thouſand one Hundred and Forty-ſeven, and not leſs than five Thouſand two Hundred and Fifteen Square Inches; eight twentieth Parts of an Inch at the leaſt in Thickneſs, if the ſuperficial Content of ſuch Plate ſhall be under five Thouſand two Hundred and Fifteen, and not leſs than four Thouſand two Hundred and Eighty-two Square Inches; ſeven twentieth Parts of an Inch at the leaſt in Thickneſs, if the ſuperficial Content of ſuch Plate ſhall be under four Thouſand two Hundred and Eighty-two, and not leſs than three Thouſand

TABLE F.

GLASS.

	l.	s.	d.
three Hundred and Fifty Square Inches; six twentieth Parts of an Inch at the least in Thickness, if the superficial Content of such Place shall be under three Thousand three Hundred and Fifty, and not less than two Thousand four Hundred and Seventeen Square Inches; and five twentieth Parts of an Inch at the least in Thickness, if the superficial Content shall be under two Thousand four Hundred and Seventeen, and not less than one Thousand four Hundred and Eighty-five Square Inches.			
For every Hundred Weight of Materials or Metal, or other Preparations whatsoever, by what Name soever the same are or may be called or known, that shall be made Use of in Great Britain in the making of Spread Window Glass, commonly called or known by the Name of *Broad Glass*, and so in Proportion for any greater or lesser Quantity, eight Shillings and one Halfpenny	0	8	0½
For every Hundred Weight of Materials or Metal, or other Preparations whatsoever, by what Name soever the same are or may be called or known, that shall be made Use of in Great Britain in the making of all other Window Glass (not being Spread Glass), whether flashed or otherwise manufactured, and commonly called or known either by the Name of *Crown Glass*, or of *German Sheet Glass*, and so in Proportion for any greater or lesser Quantity, sixteen Shillings and one Penny Farthing	0	16	1¼
For every Hundred Weight of Materials or Metal, or other Preparations whatsoever, by what Name soever the same are or may be called or known, that shall be made Use of			

(311)

in Great Britain in the making of common Bottles (the same not being Phials), and of Vessels made Use of in Chemical Laboratories, and of Garden Glasses, and of all other Vessels or Utensils made of common Bottle Metal, and so in Proportion for any greater or lesser Quantity, four Shillings and one Farthing - - - - 0 4 0¼

The said several Rates and Duties upon the Materials or Metal, or other Preparations for making Glass, to be paid by the Maker or Makers thereof respectively.

By the 27 Geo. III. Chap. 28. the following Duties of Excise were imposed upon all Glass imported into Great Britain directly from any of the European Dominions of the French King, or from any other Place whatsoever.

	Duty.
For every Square Foot superficial Measure, of French Plate Glass - -	0 1 5½
For every Hundred Weight of French Flint Glass, or French Enamel, stained, or Paste Glass, or French Phial Glass - -	1 9 0
For every Hundred Weight of French Spread Window Glass, commonly called Broad Glass - -	0 8 1
For every Hundred Weight of other French Window Glass (not being Spread Glass), whether flashed or otherwise manufactured, and commonly called or known either by the Name of Crown Glass, or of German Sheet Glass - -	0 19 10
For every Hundred Weight of French Bottles (not being Phials), which shall contain more or less than a Quart - -	0 4 0½

N. B. By the 28 Geo. III. Chap. 33. Sect. 9. the Duties of Excise on Foreign green Glass Bottles imported into Great Britain, are to cease and determine.

TABLE F.

GLASS.

	£.	s.	d.
For every Hundred Weight of Plate Glass, and all other Glass Manufactures not otherwise particularly enumerated or described - - - - -	1	8	0

HIDES AND SKINS.

	£.	s.	d.
For every Pound Weight Avoirdupois of Hides of what Kind soever, and of Calve Skins, Kips, Hogs Skins, Dog Skins, and Seal Skins, which shall be tanned in Great Britain, and Sheep Skins and Lamb Skins, which shall be tanned in Great Britain for Gloves and Bazils, and so in Proportion for any greater or lesser Quantity, one Penny Halfpenny	0	0	1½
For every Dozen of Goat Skins which shall be tanned with Shumack, or otherwise, in Great Britain, to resemble Spanish Leather, and so in Proportion for any greater or lesser Quantity, four Shillings - - -	0	4	0
For every Dozen of Sheep Skins which shall be tanned for Roans (being after the Nature of Spanish Leather), in Great Britain, and so in Proportion for any greater or lesser Quantity, two Shillings and Threepence - - -	0	2	3
For every one Hundred Pounds of the true and real Value of all other Skins, and Parts and Pieces of Hides and Skins, which shall be tanned in Great Britain, not hereinbefore particularly charged, and so in Proportion for any greater or lesser Number or Quantities, thirty Pounds - -	30	0	0

The said several Rates and Duties for and upon all such Hides and Skins, and Parts

(313)

and Pieces of Hides and Skins, which shall be so tanned in Great Britain, to be paid by the Tanners thereof respectively.

For all Hides of Horses, Mares, and Geldings, which shall be dressed in Alum and Salt or Meal, or otherwise tawed in Great Britain, for every such Hide, and so in Proportion for a greater or lesser Quantity or Number of such Hides, one Shilling and Sixpence - - - - - - - 0 1 6

For and upon all Hides of Steers, Cows, or any other Hides of what Kind soever (those of Horses, Mares, and Geldings excepted), which shall be so dressed in Alum and Salt, or Meal, or otherwise tawed in Great Britain, for every such Hide, and so in Proportion for any greater or lesser Number or Quantity, three Shillings - - - 0 3 0

For every Pound Weight Avoirdupois of all Calve Skins, Kips, and Seal Skins, which shall be so dressed in Alum and Salt, or Meal, or otherwise tawed in Great Britain, and so in Proportion for any greater or lesser Quantity, one Penny Halfpenny - 0 0 1½

For every Dozen of Slink Calve Skins which shall be so dressed in Alum and Salt, or Meal, or otherwise tawed in Great Britain with the Hair on, and so in Proportion for any greater or lesser Number or Quantity, three Shillings - - - 0 3 0

For every Dozen of Slink Calve Skins which shall be so dressed or tawed without Hair, and every Dozen of Dogs Skins which shall be tawed as aforesaid in Great Britain, and for every Dozen of Kid Skins which shall be tawed in Great Britain (except such Kid Skins as paid the full Duty on the Importation thereof), and so in Proportion for any greater or lesser Number or Quantity, one Shilling - - - - - 0 1 0

TABLE F.

HIDES AND SKINS.

	£.	s.	d.
For every Pound Weight Avoirdupois of Buck and Doe Skins (except such as paid the full Duty on the Importation thereof), which shall be dressed in Alum and Salt, or Meal, or be otherwise tawed as aforesaid in Great Britain, and so in Proportion for any greater or lesser Quantity, Sixpence	0	0	6
For every Dozen of Goat Skins, and of Beaver Skins, which shall be so dressed in Alum and Salt, or Meal, or be otherwise tawed in Great Britain, and so in Proportion for any greater or lesser Number or Quantity, two Shillings	0	2	0
For every Pound Weight Avoirdupois of Sheep Skins and Lamb Skins, which shall be dressed in Alum and Salt, or Meal, or otherwise tawed in Great Britain, and so in Proportion for any greater or lesser Quantity, one Penny Farthing	0	0	$1\frac{1}{4}$
For every one Hundred Pounds of the true and real Value of all other Skins, and Parts and Pieces of Hides and Skins, which shall be tawed in Great Britain (not hereinbefore particularly charged), and so in Proportion for greater or lesser Numbers or Quantities, thirty Pounds	30	0	0

The said several Rates and Duties for and upon all Hides and Skins, and Parts and Pieces of Hides and Skins, which shall be dressed in Alum and Salt, or Meal, or otherwise tawed in Great Britain, to be paid by such Persons who shall be the Tawers or Makers thereof into Leather respectively.

N. B. So charged by 28 Geo. III. Chap. 37.

For every Pound Weight Avoirdupois of all Buck, Deer, and Elk Skins, which shall be dressed in Oil in Great Britain, and so in Proportion for any greater or less Quantity	0	1	0
For every Pound Weight Avoirdupois of all Sheep and Lamb Skins, which shall be dressed in Oil in Great Britain, and so in Proportion for any greater or less Quantity	0	0	3
For every Pound Weight Avoirdupois of all other Hides and Skins, and Parts and Pieces of Hides and Skins, which shall be dressed in Oil in Great Britain, and so in Proportion for any greater or less Quantity	0	0	6
The said several Duties for and upon all Hides and Skins, and Parts and Pieces of Hides and Skins, which shall be so dressed in Oil in Great Britain, to be paid by the Oil Leather Dressers thereof respectively.			
For every Dozen of Vellum which shall be made in Great Britain, and so in Proportion for any greater or lesser Quantity; to be paid by the Maker thereof, three Shillings and Five-pence Halfpenny	0	3	$5\frac{1}{2}$
For every Dozen of Parchment which shall be made in Great Britain, and so in Proportion for any greater or lesser Quantity; to be paid by the Maker thereof, one Shilling and Eightpence three Farthings	0	1	$8\frac{1}{4}$

HOPS.

For every Pound Weight Avoirdupois of Hops growing or to grow in Great Britain, which shall be cured and made fit for Use, and so in Proportion for a greater or lesser Quantity, to be paid by the respective Owners or Possessors thereof, one Penny and twelve twentieth Parts of a Farthing	0	0	$1\frac{12}{20}$

TABLE F.

By the 26 Geo. III. Chap. 5. Hops may be exported to Ireland before the Duties are paid, proper Notice being given to the Officers of Excise, and the several Regulations of the Commissioners of Excise being conformed to; and fee the Table of Excise Drawbacks upon the Exportation thereof to Ireland after the Duties have been paid.

	£.	s.	d.
MALT.			
For every Bushel of Malt which shall be made of Barley or any other Corn or Grain within that Part of Great Britain called England, and so in Proportion for any greater or lesser Quantity; to be paid by the Maker thereof, Ninepence three Farthings	- 0	0	9¾
And by the 31 Geo. III. Chap. 7. in Addition for every Bushel of Malt made as aforesaid in England	-	0	3
For every Bushel of Malt which shall be made of Barley or any other Corn or Grain within that Part of Great Britain called Scotland, and so in Proportion for any greater or lesser Quantity; to be paid by the Maker thereof, Fourpence three Farthings and ten twentieth Parts of a Farthing	- 0	0	4 $\frac{110}{4}$
And by the 31 Geo. III. Chap. 7. in Addition for every Bushel of Malt made as aforesaid in Scotland	-	0	1½
For every Bushel of Malt which shall be brought from Scotland into that Part of Great Bri-			

tain called England, accompanied with a Certificate from the proper Officer that it hath paid the Duty of Fourpence three Farthings and ten twentieth Parts of a Farthing hereby imposed for every Bushel thereof, and entered with the proper Officer and in such Manner as in and by an Act made in the thirty-third Year of the Reign of his late Majesty King George the Second is mentioned, directed and appointed with respect to Malt brought from Scotland into England, Wales, or Berwick upon Tweed, between the twenty-third Day of June one Thousand seven Hundred and Sixty and the twenty-fourth Day of June one Thousand seven Hundred and Sixty-one; to be paid down in ready Money to such Officers respectively, in Manner as the Duties are directed to be paid by the said last mentioned Act of Parliament, Fourpence three Farthings and ten twentieth Parts of a Farthing - - - - - - 0 0 4$\frac{3}{4}\frac{10}{20}$

For and upon every Bushel of Malt which shall be brought from Scotland into that Part of Great Britain called England without such Certificate as aforesaid; to be paid in Manner as the Duties by the said last mentioned Act are payable with respect to Malt brought from Scotland into England, Wales, or the Town of Berwick upon Tweed, Ninepence three Farthings - - - - - - - - 0 0 9$\frac{3}{4}$

METHEGLIN, - OR MEAD.

For every Gallon of Metheglin or Mead which shall be made in Great Britain for Sale, and so in Proportion for any greater or lesser Quantity; to be paid by the Maker thereof, one Shilling and a Halfpenny - - - - - - - - 0 1 0$\frac{1}{2}$

TABLE F.

PAPER.

First Table.

	£.	s.	d.
For every Ream of Paper which shall be made in Great Britain, called Imperial, of the Value of two Pounds eleven Shillings per Ream and upwards, and not exceeding the Dimensions of twenty-two Inches by thirty Inches and a Quarter, thirteen Shillings and Ninepence Halfpenny	0	13	9½
For every Ream of Paper which shall be made in Great Britain, called Super Royal, of the Value of one Pound eighteen Shillings per Ream and upwards, and not exceeding the Dimensions of nineteen Inches and a Quarter by twenty-seven Inches and an Half, ten Shillings and Fourpence Farthing	0	10	4¼
For every Ream of Paper which shall be made in Great Britain, called Royal, of the Value of one Pound nine Shillings per Ream and upwards, and not exceeding the Dimensions of nineteen Inches and a Quarter by twenty-four Inches, seven Shillings and Ninepence Farthing	0	7	9¼
For every Ream of Paper which shall be made in Great Britain, called Medium, of the Value of one Pound two Shillings and Sixpence per Ream and upwards, and not exceeding the Dimensions of seventeen Inches and an Half by twenty-two Inches and an Half, six Shillings and Fourpence	0	6	4
For every Ream of Paper which shall be made in Great Britain, called Demy, of the Value			

(319)

of fixteen Shillings per Ream and upwards, and not exceeding the Dimenfions of fifteen Inches and an Half by twenty Inches, four Shillings and Threepence three Farthings - 0 4 3¾

For every Ream of Paper which shall be made in Great Britain, called Thick Poft, of the Value of thirteen Shillings per Ream and upwards, and not exceeding the Dimenfions of fifteen Inches and a Quarter by nineteen Inches and an Half, three Shillings and Fivepence Halfpenny - 0 3 5½

For every Ream of Paper which shall be made in Great Britain, called Thin Poft, of the Value of ten Shillings per Ream and upwards, and not exceeding the Dimenfions of fifteen Inches and a Quarter by nineteen Inches and an Half, two Shillings and Eightpence Farthing - 0 2 8¼

For every Ream of Paper which shall be made in Great Britain, called Small Poft, of the Dimenfions of thirteen Inches and an Half by fixteen Inches and an Half, two Shillings and one Farthing - 0 2 0¼

For every Ream of Paper which shall be made in Great Britain, called Fools Cap, of the Value of ten Shillings per Ream and upwards, and not exceeding the Dimenfions of thirteen Inches and an Half by fixteen Inches and three Quarters, two Shillings and Threepence Halfpenny - 0 2 3½

For every Ream of Paper which shall be made in Great Britain, called Pott, of the Value of fix Shillings and Ninepence per Ream and upwards, and not exceeding the Dimenfions of twelve Inches and an Half by fifteen Inches and an Half, one Shilling and Sixpence Halfpenny - 0 1 6½

TABLE F.

PAPER.

	£.	s.	d.
For every Ream of Paper which shall be made in Great Britain, called Large Thick Post, of the Value of fifteen Shillings per Ream and upwards, and not exceeding the Dimensions of sixteen Inches and an Half by twenty-one Inches, three Shillings and Tenpence	0	3	10
For every Ream of Paper which shall be made in Great Britain, called Large Thin Post, of the Value of twelve Shillings per Ream and upwards, and not exceeding the Dimensions of sixteen Inches and an Half by twenty-one Inches, three Shillings and three Farthings	0	3	0¾

Second Table.

	£.	s.	d.
For every Ream of Paper which shall be made in Great Britain, called Double Atlas, of the Value of fifteen Pounds and not exceeding the Value of twenty-one Pounds per Ream, and not exceeding the Dimensions of fifty-five Inches by thirty-one Inches and an Half, two Pounds six Shillings	2	6	0
For every Ream of Paper which shall be made in Great Britain, called Demy, of the Value of twelve Shillings and under the Value of sixteen Shillings per Ream, and not exceeding the Dimensions of fifteen Inches and an Half by twenty Inches, two Shillings and Eightpence Farthing	0	2	8¼
For every Ream of Paper which shall be made in Great Britain, called Copy, of the Value of seven Shillings and Sixpence, and not exceeding the Value of eleven Shillings per			

Ream, and not exceeding the Dimensions of sixteen Inches by twenty Inches and a Quarter, one Shilling and Sixpence Halfpenny - 0 1 6½

For every Ream of Paper which shall be made in Great Britain, called Fools Cap, of the Value of Six Shillings and under the Value of ten Shillings per Ream, and not exceeding the Dimensions of thirteen Inches and an Half by sixteen Inches and three Quarters, one Shilling and Threepence - 0 1 3

For every Ream of Paper which shall be made in Great Britain, called Littris Fools Cap, of the Value of six Shillings and not exceeding the Value of ten Shillings per Ream, and not exceeding the Dimensions of thirteen Inches and an Half by seventeen Inches and an Half, one Shilling and Threepence - 0 1 3

For every Ream of Paper which shall be made in Great Britain, called Port, of the Value of four Shillings and under the Value of six Shillings and Ninepence per Ream, and not exceeding the Dimensions of twelve Inches and an Half by fifteen Inches and an Half, Elevenpence Halfpenny - 0 0 11½

For every Ream of Paper which shall be made in Great Britain, called Grand Eagle or Double Elephant, of the Value of four Pounds and not exceeding the Value of five Pounds and five Shillings per Ream, and not exceeding the Dimensions of twenty-six Inches and three Quarters by forty Inches, seventeen Shillings and Threepence - 0 17 3

For every Ream of Paper which shall be made in Great Britain, called Colombier, of the Value of two Pounds and ten Shillings and not exceeding the Value of three Pounds and ten Shillings per Ream, and not exceeding the Dimensions of twenty-three Inches and an Half by thirty-four Inches and an Half, twelve Shillings and one Penny - 0 12 1

TABLE F.

PAPER.

	£.	s.	d.
For every Ream of Paper which shall be made in Great Britain, called Atlas, of the Value of three Pounds and not exceeding the Value of four Pounds and five Shillings per Ream, and not exceeding the Dimensions of twenty-six Inches and a Quarter by thirty-four Inches, seventeen Shillings and Threepence	0	17	3
For every Ream of Atlas Inferior Paper which shall be made in Great Britain, of the Value of two Pounds and under the Value of three Pounds per Ream, and not exceeding the Dimensions of twenty-six Inches and a Quarter by thirty-four Inches, ten Shillings and Fourpence Farthing	0	10	4¼
For every Ream of Paper which shall be made in Great Britain, called Small Atlas, of the Value of one Pound and ten Shillings and not exceeding the Value of two Pounds and ten Shillings per Ream, and not exceeding the Dimensions of twenty-five Inches by thirty-one Inches, eight Shillings and Sevenpence Halfpenny	0	8	7½
For every Ream of Paper which shall be made in Great Britain, called Imperial, of the Value of one Pound and ten Shillings and under the Value of two Pounds and eleven Shillings per Ream, and not exceeding the Dimensions of twenty-two Inches by thirty Inches and a Quarter, seven Shillings and Fivepence three Farthings	0	7	5¼
For every Ream of Paper which shall be made in Great Britain, called Super Royal, of the Value of one Pound and five Shillings and under the Value of one Pound and eighteen Shillings per Ream, and not exceeding the Dimensions of nineteen Inches and a Quarter by twenty-seven Inches and an Half, five Shillings and Ninepence	0	5	9

For every Ream of Paper which shall be made in Great Britain, called Long Royal, of the Value of one Pound and not exceeding the Value of one Pound and ten Shillings per Ream, and not exceeding the Dimensions of twenty-seven Inches and an Half by eighteen Inches, four Shillings and Sevenpence Farthing	0	4	7¼
For every Ream of Paper which shall be made in Great Britain, called Royal, of the Value of eighteen Shillings and under the Value of one Pound and nine Shillings per Ream, and not exceeding the Dimensions of nineteen Inches and a Quarter by twenty-four Inches, four Shillings and one Farthing	0	4	0¼
For every Ream of Paper which shall be made in Great Britain, called Demy, of the Value of thirteen Shillings and not exceeding the Value of one Pound and one Shilling per Ream, and not exceeding the Dimensions of seventeen Inches and an Half by twenty-two Inches, two Shillings and Eightpence Farthing	0	2	8¼
For every Ream of Paper which shall be made in Great Britain, called Short Demy or Crowns, of the Value of nine Shillings and not exceeding the Value of fourteen Shillings per Ream, and not exceeding the Dimensions of fourteen Inches by twenty Inches and a Quarter, or of fifteen Inches by twenty Inches, one Shilling and Elevenpence	0	1	11
For every Ream of Paper which shall be made in Great Britain, called Large Fan, of the Value of fourteen Shillings and not exceeding the Value of one Pound and one Shilling per Ream, and not exceeding the Dimensions of twenty-three Inches and an Half by twenty Inches and an Half, three Shillings and Fivepence Halfpenny	0	3	5½
For every Ream of Paper which shall be made in Great Britain, called Small Fan, of the Value of eleven Shillings and not exceeding the Value of eighteen Shillings per Ream,			

TABLE F.

PAPER.

	£.	s.	d.
and not exceeding the Dimensions of twenty-two Inches and a Quarter by thirteen Inches and a Quarter, two Shillings and Sevenpence	0	2	7
For every Ream of Paper which shall be made in Great Britain, called Elephant, of the Value of fifteen Shillings and not exceeding the Value of one Pound and seven Shillings per Ream, and not exceeding the Dimensions of twenty-three Inches by twenty-eight Inches, three Shillings and Fivepence Halfpenny	0	3	5½
For every Ream of Paper which shall be made in Great Britain for Bank or Bankers Bills or Notes, allowing two Bills or Notes in each Sheet, and so in Proportion for a greater or less Number of Bills or Notes in each Sheet, three Shillings and Fivepence Halfpenny	0	3	5½

Third Table.

	£.	s.	d.
For every Bundle of Paper which shall be made in Great Britain, called Double Demy, of the Value of one Pound and eighteen Shillings and not exceeding the Value of three Pounds per Bundle, and not exceeding the Dimensions of twenty-six Inches by thirty-eight Inches and an Half, eight Shillings and Fourpence	0	8	4
For every Bundle of Paper which shall be made in Great Britain, called Royal, of the Value of one Pound and four Shillings and under the Value of one Pound and sixteen Shillings per Bundle, and not exceeding the Dimensions of nineteen Inches and a Quarter, by twenty-four Inches, or of twenty Inches by twenty-six Inches, five Shillings and Fourpence Halfpenny	0	5	4½

For every Bundle of Paper which shall be made in Great Britain, called Royal Inferior, of the Value of fourteen Shillings and under the Value of one Pound and four Shillings per Bundle, and not exceeding the Dimensions of nineteen Inches and a Quarter by twenty-four Inches, three Shillings and three Farthings	0	3	$0\frac{3}{4}$
For every Bundle of Paper which shall be made in Great Britain, called Medium, of the Value of one Pound and not exceeding the Value of one Pound and eight Shillings per Bundle, and not exceeding the Dimensions of eighteen Inches by twenty-three Inches, Four Shillings and Twopence Halfpenny	0	4	$2\frac{1}{2}$
For every Bundle of Paper which shall be made in Great Britain, called Demy Single, of the Value of seventeen Shillings and under the Value of one Pound and six Shillings per Bundle, and not exceeding the Dimensions of seventeen Inches and an Half by twenty-two Inches, or of nineteen Inches and a Quarter by twenty-one Inches and a Quarter, three Shillings and Tenpence	0	3	10
For every Bundle of Paper which shall be made in Great Britain, called Demy Inferior, of the Value of ten Shillings and under the Value of seventeen Shillings per Bundle, and not exceeding the Dimensions of seventeen Inches and an Half by twenty-two Inches, two Shillings and Threepence Halfpenny	0	2	$3\frac{1}{2}$
For every Bundle of Paper which shall be made in Great Britain, called Double Crown, of the Value of seventeen Shillings and not exceeding the Value of one Pound three Shillings and Sixpence per Bundle, and not exceeding the Dimensions of twenty Inches by thirty Inches, three Shillings and Fivepence Halfpenny	0	3	$5\frac{1}{2}$

TABLE F.

PAPER.

	£.	s.	d.
For every Bundle of Paper which shall be made in Great Britain, called Double Crown Inferior, of the Value of twelve Shillings and under the Value of seventeen Shillings per Bundle, and not exceeding the Dimensions of twenty Inches by thirty Inches, two Shillings and Eightpence Farthing	0	2	8¼
For every Bundle of Paper which shall be made in Great Britain, called Single Crown, of the Value of thirteen Shillings and not exceeding the Value of one Pound per Bundle, and not exceeding the Dimensions of fifteen Inches by twenty Inches, three Shillings and three Farthings	0	3	0¾
For every Bundle of Paper which shall be made in Great Britain, called Single Crown Inferior, of the Value of eight Shillings and under the Value of thirteen Shillings per Bundle, and not exceeding the Dimensions of fifteen Inches by twenty Inches, one Shilling and Elevenpence	0	1	11
For every Bundle of Paper which shall be made in Great Britain, called Demy Tissue, of the Value of eight Shillings and not exceeding the Value of twelve Shillings per Bundle, and not exceeding the Dimensions of seventeen Inches and an Half by twenty-two Inches, one Shilling and Elevenpence	0	1	11
For every Bundle of Paper which shall be made in Great Britain, called Crown Tissue, of the Value of five Shillings and not exceeding the Value of nine Shillings per Bundle, and not exceeding the Dimensions of fifteen Inches by twenty Inches, one Shilling and Threepence	0	1	3

(327)

For every Bundle of Paper which shall be made in Great Britain, called Double Pott, of the Value of nine Shillings and not exceeding the Value of sixteen Shillings per Bundle, and not exceeding the Dimensions of seventeen Inches by twenty-five Inches and an Half, two Shillings and Threepence Halfpenny -	0	2	$3\frac{1}{2}$

Fourth Table.

For every Ream of Paper which shall be made in Great Britain, called Cartridge, not exceeding the Dimensions of twenty-one Inches by twenty-six Inches, two Shillings and Eightpence Farthing -	0	2	$8\frac{1}{4}$
For every Ream of Paper which shall be made in Great Britain, called Square Cartridge, not exceeding the Dimensions of twenty-four Inches and an Half by twenty-five Inches and an Half, three Shillings and three Farthings	0	3	$0\frac{3}{4}$
For every Ream of Paper which shall be made in Great Britain, called Small Cartridge, not exceeding the Dimensions of nineteen Inches and a Quarter by twenty-four Inches, two Shillings and Threepence Halfpenny -	0	2	$3\frac{1}{2}$
For every Ream of Paper which shall be made in Great Britain, called Elephant Common, not exceeding the Dimensions of twenty-three Inches by twenty-eight Inches, one Shilling and Elevenpence -	0	1	11
For every Ream of Paper which shall be made in Great Britain, called Sugar Blue, not exceeding the Dimensions of twenty-one Inches and an Half by thirty-three Inches, three Shillings and three Farthings	0	3	$0\frac{3}{4}$

Y 4

TABLE F.
PAPER.

	£.	s.	d.
For every Ream of Paper which shall be made in Great Britain, called Sugar Blue Smaller Size, not exceeding the Dimensions of eighteen Inches and three Quarters by twenty-seven Inches, two Shillings and Threepence Halfpenny -	0	2	3½
For every Ream of Paper which shall be made in Great Britain, called Sugar Blue Demy Size, not exceeding the Dimensions of seventeen Inches and an Half by twenty-two Inches, one Shilling and Elevenpence -	0	1	11
For every Ream of Paper which shall be made in Great Britain, called Sugar Blue Crown Size, not exceeding the Dimensions of fifteen Inches by twenty Inches, one Shilling and Elevenpence -	0	1	11
For every Ream of Paper which shall be made in Great Britain, called Purple Royal, not exceeding the Dimensions of nineteen Inches and an Half by twenty-four Inches and a Quarter, one Shilling and Sixpence Halfpenny -	0	1	6½
For every Ream of Paper which shall be made in Great Britain, called Blue Elephant, not exceeding the Dimensions of twenty-three Inches by twenty-eight Inches, two Shillings and Threepence Halfpenny -	0	2	3½
For every Bundle of Paper which shall be made in Great Britain, called Blue Royal, not exceeding the Dimensions of nineteen Inches and an Half by twenty-four Inches and a Quarter, three Shillings and three Farthings -	0	3	0¼
For every Bundle of Paper which shall be made in Great Britain, called Blue Demy and			

(329)

Blossom, not exceeding the Dimensions of seventeen Inches by twenty-two Inches, two Shillings and one Farthing — — — 0 2 0¼

For every Bundle of Paper which shall be made in Great Britain, called Blue Crown Single, not exceeding the Dimensions of fifteen Inches by twenty Inches, one Shilling and one Penny three Farthings — — — 0 1 1¼

Fifth Table.

For every Ream of Whited Brown Paper which shall be made in Great Britain, called Royal Hand Thick, not exceeding the Dimensions of twenty-four Inches by nineteen Inches and a Quarter, one Shilling and Fourpence — 0 1 4

For every Bundle of Whited Brown Paper which shall be made in Great Britain, called Royal Hand, not exceeding the Dimensions of twenty-four Inches by nineteen Inches and a Quarter, one Shilling and Sixpence Halfpenny 0 1 6½

For every Bundle of Whited Brown Paper which shall be made in Great Britain, called Lumber Hand, not exceeding the Dimensions of twenty-three Inches by eighteen Inches, one Shilling and Sixpence Halfpenny — 0 1 6½

For every Bundle of Whited Brown Paper which shall be made in Great Britain, called Double Two Pound, not exceeding the Dimensions of twenty-four Inches by sixteen Inches, one Shilling and one Penny three Farthings — — — 0 1 1¾

For every Bundle of Whited Brown Paper which shall be made in Great Britain, called Single Two Pound, not exceeding the Dimensions of sixteen Inches by eleven Inches, Fivepence three Farthings — — — 0 0 5¾

TABLE F.

PAPER.

	L.	s.	d.
For every Bundle of Whited Brown Paper which shall be made in Great Britain, called Middle Hand Double, not exceeding the Dimensions of thirty-three Inches by twenty-one Inches, two Shillings and Threepence Halfpenny	0	2	3½
For every Bundle of Whited Brown Paper which shall be made in Great Britain, called Middle Hand, not exceeding the Dimensions of twenty-two Inches by fixteen Inches, one Shilling and one Penny three Farthings	0	1	1¼
For every Bundle of Whited Brown Paper which shall be made in Great Britain, called Small Hard Double, not exceeding the Dimensions of thirty-two Inches by twenty Inches, one Shilling and Sixpence Halfpenny	0	1	6½
For every Bundle of Whited Brown Paper which shall be made in Great Britain, called Small Hand, not exceeding the Dimensions of nineteen Inches and three Quarters by sixteen Inches, Ninepence Farthing	0	0	9¼
For every Bundle of Whited Brown Paper which shall be made in Great Britain, called Couples Pound and Half Pound, not exceeding the Dimensions of twelve Inches by ten Inches, and of nine Inches by seven Inches and an Half, Fivepence three Farthings	0	0	5¾
For every Ream of Brown Paper which shall be made in Great Britain, called Imperial Cap, not exceeding the Dimensions of twenty-nine Inches by twenty-two Inches, one Shilling and Sixpence Halfpenny	0	1	6½
For every Ream of Brown Paper which shall be made in Great Britain, called Haven Cap,			

not exceeding the Dimensions of twenty-four Inches by twenty Inches, one Shilling and one Penny three Farthings -	0	1 1¼
For every Ream of Brown Paper which shall be made in Great Britain, called Bag Cap, not exceeding the Dimensions of twenty-three Inches and an Half by nineteen Inches, Elevenpence Halfpenny -	0	0 11½
For every Ream of Brown Paper which shall be made in Great Britain, called Kentish Cap, not exceeding the Dimensions of twenty-one Inches by eighteen Inches, Ninepence Farthing -	0	0 9¼
For every Ream of Brown Paper which shall be made in Great Britain, called Four Pounds, not exceeding the Dimensions of twenty Inches by sixteen Inches, Ninepence Farthing	0	0 9¼
For every Ream of Brown Paper which shall be made in Great Britain, called Small Cap, not exceeding the Dimensions of twenty Inches by fifteen Inches, Fivepence three Farthings -	0	0 5¼
For every Ream of Brown Paper which shall be made in Great Britain, called Double Four Pounds, not exceeding the Dimensions of thirty-three Inches by twenty Inches, one Shilling and Sixpence Halfpenny -	0	1 6½
For every Bundle of Brown Paper which shall be made in Great Britain, called Single Two Pounds, not exceeding the Dimensions of sixteen Inches by eleven Inches, Ninepence Farthing -	0	0 9¼
For every Bundle of Brown Paper which shall be made in Great Britain, called Couples Pound and Half Pound, not exceeding the Dimensions of twelve Inches by ten Inches, and of nine Inches by seven Inches and an Half, Fivepence three Farthings -	0	0 5¼

TABLE F.

PAPER.

	L.	*s.*	*d.*
For every Hundred Weight of Pasteboard, Millboard, Scaleboard, and Glazed Paper, which shall be made in Great Britain, six Shillings and Tenpence three Farthings	0	6	10¾
And after those Rates for any greater or less Quantity of such Papers, Pasteboards, Millboards, Scaleboards, and Glazed Paper, respectively.			
The said several Rates and Duties upon the said several sorts of Paper, Pasteboard, Millboard, Scaleboard, and Glazed Paper, to be paid by the Makers thereof respectively.			
For every Sort or Kind of Paper not hereinbefore enumerated and described which shall be made in Great Britain, a Duty after the Rate of twenty Pounds and fourteen Shillings for every one Hundred Pounds of the true and real Value of the same including the Duties hereby charged thereon	20	14	0
The said Duties for such Sorts or Kinds of Paper respectively to be paid by the Makers thereof respectively.			

PRINTED GOODS.

For every Yard Square of Paper which shall be printed, painted, or stained in Great Britain, to serve for Hangings or other Uses (over and above the Duties payable for such Paper before the printing, painting, or staining thereof), and so in Proportion for any greater Quantity; to be paid by the Printer, Painter, or Stainer thereof, one Penny three Farthings - - - - 0 0 1¾

For every Yard in Length, reckoning Yard wide, of Foreign Muslin, which shall be printed, stained, painted, or dyed in Great Britain (except such as shall be dyed throughout of one Colour only), and so in Proportion for any greater or lesser Quantity, Sevenpence - - - - 0 0 7

For every Yard in Length, reckoning Yard wide, of all Linens and of all Stuffs made either of Cotton or Linen mixed with other Materials, Fustians, Velvets, Velverets, Dimities, and other Figured Stuffs made of Cotton and other Materials mixed or wholly made of Cotton Wool, wove in Great Britain, which shall be printed, stained, painted, or dyed in Great Britain (except such as shall be dyed throughout of one Colour only, and Stuffs made of Woollen or whereof the greatest Part in Value shall be Woollen), and so in Proportion for any greater or lesser Quantity, Threepence Halfpenny - - - - 0 0 3½

For every Yard in Length, reckoning Yard wide, of Stuffs wholly made of Cotton Wool, wove in Great Britain, commonly called British Manufactory, and of British Muslins, which shall be printed, stained, painted, or dyed, in Great Britain (except such as shall be dyed throughout of one Colour only), and so in Proportion for any greater or lesser Quantity, Threepence Halfpenny - - - -

For every Yard in Length, reckoning Yard wide, of all Stuffs, other than such Stuffs as are before enumerated (and except such thereof as shall be dyed throughout of one Colour only, and Stuffs made of Woollen, or whereof the greatest Part in Value shall be 0 0 3½

TABLE F.

PRINTED GOODS.

Woollen), which shall be printed, stained, painted, or dyed in Great Britain, and so in Proportion for any greater or lesser Quantity - - - 0 0 3¼

N. B. This last mentioned Duty charged by 28 Geo.III. Chap. 37.

For every Yard in Length, reckoning Half Yard wide, of all Silks which shall be printed, stained, or painted in Great Britain (Silk Handkerchiefs excepted), over and above the Duties payable upon the Importation of them or any of them, and so in Proportion for any greater or lesser Quantity, one Shilling and one Penny three Farthings - 0 1 1¼

For every Yard Square of Silk Handkerchiefs, which shall be printed, stained, painted, or dyed in Great Britain, and so in Proportion for wider or narrower Silk Handkerchiefs, over and above the Duties payable upon the Importation of them or any of them, and so in Proportion for any greater or lesser Quantity, Fourpence Halfpenny - 0 0 4½

The said Duties on printed, stained, painted, or dyed Goods, which shall be printed, stained, painted, or dyed in Great Britain, to be paid by the Printer, Stainer, Painter, or Dyer thereof.

For every Yard in Length, reckoning Yard wide, of French printed, stained, painted, or dyed Calicos and Muslins (except such as shall be dyed throughout of one Colour only), which shall be imported into Great Britain directly from any of the European Dominions of the French King, and so in Proportion for any greater or lesser Quantity; to be paid by the Importer thereof before the landing thereof, Sevenpence - - 0 0 7

For every Yard in Length, reckoning Yard wide, of all French printed, stained, painted, or dyed Linens and Stuffs, made either of Cotton or Linen mixed with other Materials, Fustians, Velvets, Velverets, Dimities, and other Figured Stuffs made of Cotton and other Materials mixed or wholly made of Cotton Wool (except such as shall be dyed throughout of one Colour only), which shall be imported into Great Britain directly from any of the European Dominions of the French King, and so in Proportion for any greater or lesser Quantity; to be paid by the Importer thereof before the landing thereof, Three-pence Halfpenny - - - - - - 0 0 $3\frac{1}{2}$

S N U F F.

By the 29 Geo. III. Chap. 68.

For every Pound Weight of Snuff which shall be imported or brought into Great Britain by the United Company of Merchants of England trading to the East Indies - - 0 2 0
For every Pound Weight of Snuff which shall be imported or brought into Great Britain from any British Plantation in America, or from the Spanish West Indies - - 0 1 0
For every Pound Weight of Snuff which shall be imported or brought into Great Britain from any other Place - - - - - 0 1 4

N. B. If warehoused, the Duties of Importation only payable when delivered out of the Warehouse.

S O A P.

For every Pound Weight Avoirdupois of Hard Cake Soap, or Ball Soap, which shall be

TABLE F.

SOAP.

	£.	s.	d.
made in Great Britain, and so in Proportion for a greater or a lesser Quantity; to be paid by the Maker thereof, Twopence Farthing	0	0	2¼
For every Pound Weight Avoirdupois of Soft Soap which shall be made in Great Britain, and so in Proportion for a greater or lesser Quantity; to be paid by the Maker thereof, one Penny three Farthings	0	0	1¾

SPIRITS.

	£.	s.	d.
For every Gallon of Fermented Wort or Wash which shall be brewed or made in that Part of Great Britain called England on or before the fifth Day of July One Thousand Seven Hundred and Eighty-eight, for extracting Spirits for Home Consumption from any Malt, Corn, Grain, or Tilts, or any Mixture with the same; to be paid by the Makers or Distillers thereof, Sixpence	0	0	6
And by the 31 Geo. III. Chap. 1. for every Gallon described as above, the Additional Duty of	0	0	1
For every Gallon of Cyder or Perry, or any other Wash or Liquor, which shall be brewed or made as aforesaid from any Sort or Kind of British Materials (except such as are beforementioned), or from any Mixture therewith, for extracting Spirits for Home Consumption; to be paid by the Makers or Distillers thereof, Fivepence	0	0	5

(337)

And by the 31 Geo. III. Chap. 1. for every Gallon described as above, the Additional Duty of one Penny - - - - - - 0 0 1

For every Gallon of Fermented Wort or Wash which shall be brewed or made as aforesaid from Melasses or Sugar, or any Mixture therewith, for extracting Spirits for Home Consumption; to be paid by the Makers or Distillers thereof, Eightpence three Farthings 0 0 8¾

And by the 31 Geo. III. Chap. 1. for every Gallon described as above, the Additional Duty of one Penny Halfpenny - - - - - 0 0 1½

For every Gallon of Wash which shall be brewed or made as aforesaid from Foreign refused Wine or Foreign Cyder, or Wash prepared from Foreign Materials (except Melasses and Sugar), or any Mixture therewith, for extracting Spirits for Home Consumption; to be paid by the Makers or Distillers thereof, one Shilling - - 0 1 0

And by the 31 Geo. III. Chap. 1. for every Gallon described as above, the Additional Duty of Twopence - - - - - - 0 0 2

For every seventy-two Gallons of Wash, which George Bishop of Maidstone shall produce on or before the fifth Day of July One Thousand Seven Hundred and Eighty-eight from a Weight of Malt, or other Corn, including the Bran thereof, and not exceeding one Hundred and twelve Pounds Avoirdupois; to be paid by the said George Bishop, and so in Proportion for any greater or lesser Quantity of such Wash, eighteen Shillings 0 18 0

And by the 31 Geo. III. Chap. 1. for every 96 Gallons as before described, the Additional Duty of two Shillings and Eightpence three Farthings - - 0 2 8¾

For every Gallon of Wash from which twenty-four Gallons shall be taken and distilled by the Officer of Excise, according to the Directions and under the Authority of an Act

Z

TABLE F.
SPIRITS.

	£.	s.	d.
made in the twenty-sixth Year of the Reign of his present Majesty, among other Things, to discontinue for a limited Time the Payment of Duties on Low Wines and Spirits for Home Consumption, and for granting and securing the due Payment of other Duties in lieu thereof, and such twenty-four Gallons of Wash so distilled shall be found to produce more than two Gallons and three-fourth Parts of a Gallon of Spirits, at the Strength of One in Seven under Hydrometer Proof; to be paid by the said George Bishop, one Shilling	0	1	0
For every Gallon of British Spirits of a Strength not exceeding that of One to Ten over Hydrometer Proof, which shall be manufactured in Scotland and brought from thence into any other Part of the United Kingdom on or before the fifth Day of July One Thousand Seven Hundred and Eighty-eight; to be paid by the Importer thereof, two Shillings	0	2	0
And by the 31 Geo. III. Chap. 1. for every Gallon as beforementioned, the Additional Duty of	0	0	5½
And for every Gallon of all such Spirits as last aforesaid of a greater Strength than One to Ten over Hydrometer Proof, and not exceeding Three per Centum over and above One to Ten over Hydrometer Proof, two Shillings	0	2	0
And also a farther Duty proportioned to the Degree of Strength in which such Spirits shall exceed the said Strength of One to Ten over Hydrometer Proof; to be paid by the Importer thereof, or the Person bringing the same.			

For every Gallon of Single Brandy which shall be imported into Great Britain; to be paid by the Importer before the landing thereof, four Shillings and Threepence -	0	4	3
And by the 31 Geo. III. Chap. I. for every Gallon as beforementioned, the Additional Duty of Tenpence -	0	0	10
For every Gallon of Brandy above Proof which shall be imported into Great Britain; to be paid by the Importer before the landing thereof, eight Shillings and one Penny -	0	8	1
And by the 31 Geo. III. Chap. I. for every Gallon as beforementioned, the Additional Duty of one Shilling and Eightpence -	0	1	8
For every Gallon of Rum, Spirits, or Aqua Vitæ, of the Produce of the British Colonies or Plantations, which shall be imported from beyond the Seas into Great Britain; to be paid by the Importer before the landing thereof, three Shillings and Sevenpence -	0	3	7
And by the 31 Geo. III. Chap. I. for every Gallon as beforementioned, the Additional Duty of Eightpence -	0	0	8
For every Gallon of Rum, Spirits, or Aqua Vitæ above Proof, of the Produce of the British Colonies or Plantations, which shall be imported from beyond the Seas into Great Britain; to be paid by the Importer before the landing thereof, six Shillings and Eightpence -	0	6	8
And by the 31 Geo. III. Chap. I. for every Gallon as beforementioned, the Additional Duty of one Shilling and Fourpence -	0	1	4
For every Gallon of Single Spirits, or Aqua Vitæ (other than such Brandy, Rum, Spirits, or Aqua Vitæ as aforesaid), which shall be imported from beyond the Seas into Great Britain; to be paid by the Importer before the landing thereof, four Shillings and Threepence -	0	4	3

TABLE F.

SPIRITS.

	L.	*s.*	*d.*
And by the 31 Geo. III. Chap. 1. for every Gallon as beforementioned, the Additional Duty of Tenpence	0	0	10
For every Gallon of Spirits, or Aqua Vitæ (other than such Brandy, Rum, Spirits, or Aqua Vitæ as aforesaid), above Proof, which shall be imported from beyond the Seas into Great Britain; to be paid by the Importer before the landing thereof, eight Shillings and one Penny	0	8	1
And by the 31 Geo. III. Chap. 1. for every Gallon as beforementioned, the Additional Duty of one Shilling and Eightpence	0	1	8

N.B. By the 31 Geo. III. Chap. 1. the Additional Duty on Rum, Spirits, or Aqua Vitæ, of the Produce of the British Colonies or Plantations in America, is permitted to be bonded, and is to be allowed on the shipping thereof as Stores to be consumed in any Voyage to Parts beyond the Seas, in like Manner as Rum of the British Sugar Plantations in America was permitted to be warehoused for 12 Months without Payment of Duty, and to be taken out for Exportation; or upon paying the Duties for Home Consumption. The Drawback on Rum shipped as Stores, is by the 28 Geo. III. Chap. 23. allowed until the 5th July 1795; but no Rum can be exported for the Drawback in Casks containing less than 100 Gallons each, or in Ships less than 100 Tons Burthen.

STARCH.

	l.	s.	d.
For every Pound Weight Avoirdupois of Starch of what Kind soever which shall be made in Great Britain, and so in Proportion for any greater or lesser Quantity; to be paid by the Maker thereof, Threepence Farthing -	0	0	3¼

SWEETS.

For every Barrel of Liquor which shall be made in Great Britain for Sale, by Infusion, Fermentation, or otherwise, from Fruit or Sugar, or from Fruit or Sugar mixt with any other Ingredients or Materials whatsoever, commonly called Sweets, or called or distinguished by the Name of Made Wines, and so in Proportion for a greater or lesser Quantity; to be paid by the Maker thereof, eighteen Shillings and Fourpence three Farthings - - - - - - 0 18 4¾

By the 1 Richard III. Chap. 13. the Barrel of Wine is to contain 31½ Gallons; therefore all Made Wines and other Liquors rated by the Barrel, are chargeable by that Measure, except Beer, Ale, Vinegar, and French Mum.

TEA.

For and upon all Tea which shall be sold in Great Britain by the United Company of Merchants of England trading to the East Indies, seven Pounds ten Shillings per Centum, to

TABLE F.

TEA.

	£.	s.	d.
be computed upon the Gross Prices at which such Tea shall be sold; to be paid by the Purchaser or Purchasers of such Tea to the said United Company, and to be paid by the said United Company to the Commissioners of Excise for the Time being - - -	7	10	0

TOBACCO.

By the 29 Geo. III. Chap. 68.

	£.	s.	d.
For every Pound Weight of Tobacco of the Growth, Production, or Manufacture of the Plantations or Dominions of Spain or Portugal, imported or brought into Great Britain, two Shillings - - - - -	0	2	0
If warehoused according to the Directions of this Act, the Duties on Importation only payable when delivered out of the Warehouse for Home Trade, or Exportation.			
For every Pound Weight of the like Tobacco which shall be delivered for Exportation out of the Warehouse in which the same shall be secured according to the Directions of the 29 Geo. III. Chap. 68. Twopence - - - -	0	0	2
For every Pound Weight of Tobacco of the Growth or Production of Ireland, or of the Growth or Production of his Majesty's Colonies, Plantations, Islands, or Territories in America, or of the United States of America, imported into Great Britain, Ninepence	0	0	9
If warehoused according to the Directions of this Act, the Duties on Importation not to be payable until delivered for Home Trade, Consumption, or Manufacture.			

VERJUICE.

	£.	s.	d.
For every Hogshead of Verjuice which shall be made in Great Britain for Sale; to be paid by the Maker thereof, and so in Proportion for a greater or lesser Quantity, seven Shillings and Eightpence -	0	7	8

By the 7 and 8 Will. III. Chap. 30. Sect. 28. Verjuice having been first chargeable with the same Duty as Cyder and Perry, the Hogshead is to contain 63 Wine Gallons.

VINEGAR.

For every Barrel of Vinegar, Vinegar Beer, or Liquors preparing for Vinegar, which shall be brewed or made in Great Britain for Sale; to be paid by the Maker thereof, and so in Proportion for a greater or less Quantity, ten Shillings and three Farthings -	0	10	0¼

WINE.

For every Tun of French, Rhenish, German, or Hungary Wine which shall be imported into Great Britain, and so in Proportion for any greater or lesser Quantity; to be paid by the Importer thereof before the landing thereof, seventeen Pounds seventeen Shillings -	17	17	0
For every Tun of all other Wines which shall be imported into Great Britain, and so in Proportion for any greater or lesser Quantity; to be paid by the Importer thereof before the landing thereof, eleven Pounds eighteen Shillings -	11	18	0

TABLE F.

WINE.

By the 28 Geo. III. Chap. 33.

This last mentioned Duty of Excise is payable upon Portugal and Madeira Wine, and Wine of the Produce of Spain, or any of the Dominions of the King of Spain only. See the following Duty of Excise payable upon all other Wine.

	£.	s.	d.
For every Tun of Wine which shall be imported into Great Britain (except Wine of the Produce of the European Dominions of the French King, Rhenish, German, and Hungary Wine, Portugal and Madeira Wine, and Wine of the Produce of Spain, or of any of the Dominions of the King of Spain), to be paid by the Importer thereof before the landing thereof, seventeen Pounds seventeen Shillings - - - -	17	17	0

WIRE.

	£.	s.	d.
For every ounce Troy of Gilt Wire which shall be made in Great Britain, and so in Proportion for any greater or lesser Quantity; to be paid by the Maker thereof, Ninepence Farthing - - - -	0	0	9¼
For every Ounce Troy of Silver Wire which shall be made in Great Britain, and so in Proportion for any greater or lesser Quantity; to be paid by the Maker thereof, Sevenpence	0	0	7

ALLOWANCES.

BREWERS.

Upon every Barrel of Beer or Ale above six Shillings the Barrel (exclusive of the Duty hereby imposed on such Beer or Ale, and not being Beer or Ale commonly called Table Beer, which shall be brewed and made as aforesaid), which shall be brewed by the Common Brewer or by any other Person or Persons who doth or shall sell or tap out Beer or Ale, publicly or privately, within the Cities of London and Westminster or within the Limits of the weekly Bills of Mortality, and returned by the Gauger, and so in Proportion for any greater or lesser Quantity, one Shilling and Fourpence - - - - 0 1 4

And by the 31 Geo. III. Chap. 1. a further Allowance upon every Barrel as aforesaid of Eightpence - - - - - - - 0 0 8

Upon every Barrel of Beer or Ale above six Shillings the Barrel (exclusive of the Duty hereby imposed on such Beer or Ale, not being Two-penny Ale mentioned and described in the seventh Article of the Treaty of Union, or such Table Beer), which shall be brewed by the Common Brewer or by any other Person or Persons who doth or shall sell or tap out Beer or Ale, publicly or privately, in that Part of Great Britain called England not within the said Cities of London and Westminster, nor within the weekly Bills of Mortality, and returned by the Gauger, and so in Proportion for any greater or lesser Quantity, one Shilling and Eightpence - - - - - 0 1 8

And by the 31 Geo. III. Chap. 1. a further Allowance upon every Barrel as aforesaid of Tenpence - - - - - - - 0 0 10

TABLE F.

BREWERS.

	l.	*s.*	*d.*
Upon every Barrel of Beer or Ale of six Shillings the Barrel or under (exclusive of the Duty hereby imposed on such Beer or Ale), which shall be brewed in that Part of Great Britain called England by the Common Brewer, or by any other Person or Persons who doth or shall sell or tap out Beer or Ale, publicly or privately, in that Part of Great Britain called England, and returned by the Gauger, and so in Proportion for any greater or lesser Quantity, Fourpence	0	0	4
And by the 31 Geo. III. Chap. 1. a further Allowance upon every Barrel as aforesaid of Twopence	0	0	2
Upon every Barrel of Beer or Ale above six Shillings the Barrel (exclusive of the Duty hereby imposed thereon), which shall be brewed by the Common Brewer or by any other Person or Persons who doth or shall sell or tap out Beer or Ale, publicly or privately, in that Part of Great Britain called Scotland, and returned by the Gauger, and so in Proportion for any greater or lesser Quantity, Tenpence	0	0	10
And by the 31 Geo. III. Chap. 1. a further Allowance upon every Barrel as aforesaid of Fivepence	0	0	5
Upon every Barrel of six Shillings Beer or Ale or under, which shall be brewed by the Common Brewer or any other Person or Persons who doth or shall sell or tap out Beer or Ale, publicly or privately, in that Part of Great Britain called Scotland, and returned by the Gauger, and so in Proportion for any greater or lesser Quantity, Threepence	0	0	3

And by the 31 Geo. III. Chap. 1. a further Allowance upon every Barrel as aforesaid of one Penny - - - - - 0 0 1

Upon every Barrel of Twopenny Ale mentioned and described in the seventh Article of the Treaty of Union, which shall be brewed within that Part of Great Britain called Scotland, and returned by the Gauger, and so in Proportion for any greater or lesser Quantity, Sixpence - - - - - - 0 0 6

And by the 31 Geo. III. Chap. 1. a further Allowance upon every Barrel as aforesaid, of Twopence - - - - - - - 0 0 2

MALT.

For every Quarter of Malt which shall be made and locked up for Exportation, and exported according to the Directions of an Act made in the twelfth Year of the Reign of King George the First, concerning Malt made for Exportation, Threepence - 0 0 3

PAPER.

For any Quantities of Paper which shall be used in printing any Books in the Latin, Greek, Oriental, or Northern Languages, within the two Universities of Oxford and Cambridge, or either of them, by Permission of the Vice Chancellors of the same respectively, the Duties of Excise by 27 Geo. III. Chap. 13. imposed thereon.

TABLE F.

PAPER.

	l.	*s.*	*d.*
For any Quantities of Paper which shall be used in printing any Books in the Latin, Greek, Oriental, or Northern Languages, within the Universities of Scotland, or any of them, by Permission of the Principals of the same respectively, the Duties of Excise by the 27 Geo. III. Chap. 13. imposed thereon.			

SOAP.

	l.	*s.*	*d.*
For every Pound Weight Avoirdupois of Hard Cake Soap, or Ball Soap, which shall be employed, spent, or consumed in Great Britain, in the making any Cloths, Serges, Kerseys, Bays, Stockings, or other Manufactures of Sheep or Lambs Wool only, or Manufactures whereof the greatest Part of the Value of the Materials shall be Wool, or in the finishing the said Manufactures or preparing the Wool for the same, one Penny Halfpenny	0	0	1½
For every Pound Weight Avoirdupois of Soft Soap, which shall be employed, spent, or consumed in Great Britain, in the making of any Cloths, Serges, Kerseys, Bayze, Stockings, or other Manufactures of Sheep or Lambs Wool only, or Manufactures whereof the greatest Part of the Value of the Materials shall be Wool, or in the finishing the said Manufactures or preparing the Wool for the same, one Penny and one twelfth Part of a Penny	0	0	1 1/12
For every Pound Weight Avoirdupois of Hard Cake Soap, or Ball Soap, which shall be			

employed, spent, or consumed in Great Britain, in the whitening of new Linen in the Piece in order to the Sale of such Linen, one Penny Farthing - - - 0 0 1¼

For every Pound Weight Avoirdupois of Soft Soap which shall be employed, spent, or consumed in Great Britain, in the whitening of new Linen in the Piece in order to the Sale of such Linen, three Farthings - - - - 0 0 0¾

For every Pound Weight Avoirdupois of Soap which shall be made in Great Britain, and be used and consumed in Great Britain on or before the twenty-fifth Day of March One Thousand Seven Hundred and Ninety-three in preparing and finishing any Manufactures from Flax or Cotton for Sale (except such as shall be used in whitening new Linen in the Piece in order to the Sale thereof), three Farthings - - - 0 0 0¾

STARCH.

For every Pound Weight Avoirdupois of Starch which shall be made in Great Britain, and be used and consumed in Great Britain on or before the twenty-fifth day of March One Thousand Seven Hundred and Ninety-three in preparing and finishing any Manufactures from Flax or Cotton for Sale (except such Starch as shall be used and consumed in finishing new Linen in the Piece for Sale as hereinaftermentioned), one Penny Halfpenny - 0 0 1½

For every Pound Weight Avoirdupois of Starch which shall be made in Great Britain, and be used and consumed in Great Britain in finishing new Linen in the Piece for Sale, Three-pence - - - - - - - - - 0 0 3

TABLE F.

BOUNTIES.

	£.	s.	d.
For every Barrel of Beer or Ale above six Shillings the Barrel, exclusive of the Duty hereby imposed on such Beer or Ale, which shall be proved to have been brewed in Great Britain from malted Corn, and whereupon the Duties for Strong Beer or Ale shall be proved to have been charged or paid, and which shall be exported to Foreign Parts as Merchandise, when Barley is at twenty-four Shillings per Quarter or under, one Shilling	0	1	0
For every Tun of Spirits drawn or made in Great Britain from Corn, under, subject, and according to the Rules, Regulations, Restrictions and Provisions, contained and provided in and by an Act of Parliament, made in the second Year of the Reign of his present Majesty, for the better regulating and encouraging the Exportation of British made Spirits and for securing the Payment of the Duties upon Spirituous Liquors, or any other Act or Acts of Parliament now in Force concerning British Spirits made or drawn from Corn for Exportation, which shall be exported to Foreign Parts as Merchandise, three Pounds twelve Shillings	3	12	0

By the 30 Geo. III. Chap. 36. the like Drawback of the Duties of Excise to be paid or allowed to the Exporters of Goods to the Settlement of Yucatan in South America as is now allowed on the Exportation of such Goods to the British Colonies or Plantations in America.

DRAWBACKS.

BEER OR ALE.

For every Barrel of Beer or Ale above six Shillings the Barrel (exclusive of the Duty hereby imposed in respect of such Beer or Ale, and not being Twopenny Ale mentioned and described in the seventh Article of the Treaty of Union, nor being Beer or Ale commonly called Table Beer, which shall be brewed and made as aforesaid), for which the Duty by the 27 Geo. III, Chap. 13. imposed in respect thereof shall have been paid, and exported as Merchandise to Foreign Parts, and so in Proportion for any greater or lesser Quantity, deducting Threepence per Tun for the Charges of the Officers, eight Shillings 0 8 0

BRICKS AND TILES.

For all Bricks and Tiles respectively which shall be made in Great Britain (for which the Duties by the 27 Geo. III. Chap. 13. imposed in respect thereof shall have been paid), and exported as Merchandise to Foreign Parts, the several and respective Duties by this Act imposed in respect of such Bricks or Tiles.

CANDLES.

For every Pound Weight Avoirdupois of Candles of Tallow and other Candles whatsoever, which shall be made in Great Britain (except Wax and Spermaceti Candles, for which

TABLE F.

CANDLES.

	£.	s.	d.
the Duties by the 27 Geo. III. Chap. 13. imposed in respect thereof shall have been paid, and exported as Merchandise to Foreign Parts, one Penny Halfpenny	0	0	1½
For every Pound Weight Avoirdupois of Candles which shall be made in Great Britain of Wax, or of Spermaceti, or which are usually called or sold for Wax or Spermaceti Candles (for which the Duties by the 27 Geo. III. Chap. 13. imposed in respect thereof shall have been paid), and exported as Merchandise to Foreign Parts, Threepence Halfpenny	0	0	3½

CHOCOLATE.

For every Pound Weight Avoirdupois of Chocolate which shall be made in Great Britain of Cocoa Nuts of the Growth or Produce of any British Colony or Plantation in America, imported into Great Britain (for which the Duties by the 27 Geo. III. Chap. 13. imposed in respect thereof shall have been paid), and exported as Merchandise to Foreign Parts, Fivepence	0	0	5
For every Pound Weight Avoirdupois of Chocolate which shall be made in Great Britain of Cocoa Nuts of the Growth or Produce of any other Place imported into Great Britain (for which the Duties by the 27 Geo. III. Chap. 13. imposed in respect thereof shall have been paid), and exported as Merchandise to Foreign Parts, one Shilling and Fourpence	0	1	4

CYDER AND PERRY.

For every Hogshead of Cyder or Perry which shall be made in Great Britain (for which the Duties by the 27 Geo. III. Chap. 13. imposed in respect thereof shall have been paid), and exported as Merchandise to Foreign Parts, and so in Proportion for any greater or lesser Quantity, the several and respective Duties by this Act imposed in respect of such Cyder and Perry, deducting Threepence per Tun for the Charges of the Officers. — 0 1 5½

GLASS.

By the 27 Geo. III. Chap. 28.

For every Square Foot superficial Measure, of Plate Glass which shall be made in Great Britain, from Materials or Metal, or other Preparations (for which the Duties by the 27 Geo. III. Chap. 13. imposed in respect thereof shall have been paid), and exported as Merchandise to Foreign Parts, one Shilling and Fivepence Halfpenny —

For every Hundred Weight of Flint Glass, or enamelled, stained, or Paste Glass, or Phial Glass, which shall be made in Great Britain from Materials or Metal, or other Preparations (for which the Duties by the 27 Geo. III. Chap. 13. imposed in respect thereof shall have been paid), and exported as Merchandise to Foreign Parts, one Pound and nine Shillings — 1 9 0

For every Hundred Weight of Spread Window Glass, commonly called or known by the Name of Broad Glass, which shall be made in Great Britain from Materials or Metal, or other Preparations (for which the Duties by the 27 Geo. III. Chap. 13. imposed in re-

TABLE F.

GLASS.

spect thereof shall have been paid), and exported as Merchandise to Foreign Parts, eight Shillings and one Penny - - - - - £0 8 1

For every Hundred Weight of all other Window Glass, not being Spread Glass, whether flashed or otherwise manufactured, and commonly called or known either by the Name of Crown Glass, or of German Sheet Glass, which shall be made in Great Britain from Materials or Metal, or other Preparations (for which the Duties by the 27 Geo. III. Chap. 13. impoſed in reſpect thereof ſhall have been paid), and exported as Merchandise to Foreign Parts, nineteen Shillings and Tenpence - - - £0 19 10

For every Hundred Weight of common Bottles, the ſame not being Phials, and of Veſſels made Uſe of in Chymical Laboratories, and of Garden Glaſſes, and of all other Veſſels or Utenſils made of common Bottle Metal, which ſhall be made in Great Britain from Materials or Metal, or other Preparations (for which the Duties by the 27 Geo. III. Chap. 13. impoſed in reſpect thereof ſhall have been paid), and exported as Merchandise to Foreign Parts, four Shillings and one Halfpenny - - - £0 4 0½

HIDES.

For all Hides and Calve Skins reſpectively which ſhall be tanned, tawed, or dreſſed in Great Britain and duly marked (for which the Duties by this Act impoſed in reſpect thereof ſhall have been paid), and exported as Merchandise to Foreign Parts, two Thirds of the Duties of Excise by the 27 Geo. III. Chap. 13. imposed in respect thereof respectively.

For all Sheep Skins and Lambs Skins respectively which shall be tanned, tawed, or dressed in Great Britain (for which the Duties by the 27 Geo. III. Chap. 13. imposed in respect thereof shall have been paid), and exported as Merchandise to Foreign Parts, two Thirds of the Duties of Excise by this Act imposed in respect thereof respectively.

For every Pound Weight Avoirdupois of Hides and Calve Skins respectively which shall be dressed or curried in Great Britain (for which the Duties by the 27 Geo. III. Chap. 13. imposed in respect thereof shall have been paid), and exported as Merchandise to Foreign Parts, one Penny — — — — — — 0 0 1

For every Pound Weight Avoirdupois of Seal Skins which shall be tanned or tawed in Great Britain (for which the Duties by the 27 Geo. III. Chap. 13. imposed in respect thereof shall have been paid), and exported as Merchandise to Foreign Parts, one Penny — 0 0 1

For every Pound Weight Avoirdupois of Leather tanned in Great Britain, chargeable by the 27 Geo. III. Chap. 13. to pay a Duty by Weight (for which the Duties thereby imposed in respect thereof shall have been paid), which shall be manufactured and actually made into Goods or Wares, and exported as Merchandise to Foreign Parts, one Penny Halfpenny — — — — — — 0 0 $1\frac{1}{2}$

For every Pound Weight Avoirdupois of Boots, Shoes, Gloves, or other Manufactures, made of any Kind of tawed or dressed Leather, chargeable by the 27 Geo. III. Chap. 13. to pay a Duty by Weight (for which the Duties thereby imposed in respect thereof shall

(356)

TABLE F.

HIDES.

have been paid), exported as Merchandise to Foreign Parts, two Thirds of the Duties of Excise by this Act imposed in respect thereof respectively.

By the 28 Geo. III. Chap. 37.

	L.	s.	d.
For every Pound Weight Avoirdupois of all Buck, Deer, and Elk Skins, which shall be dressed in Oil in Great Britain (and for which the Duties imposed by this Act shall have been paid), whether manufactured and actually made into Goods, Wares, or not, and exported as Merchandise to Foreign Parts, one Shilling	0	1	0
For every Pound Weight Avoirdupois of all Sheep and Lamb Skins, which shall be dressed in Oil in Great Britain (and for which the Duties imposed by this Act shall have been paid), which shall be manufactured and actually made into Goods or Wares, and exported as Merchandise to Foreign Parts, Threepence	0	0	3
For every Pound Weight Avoirdupois of all other Hides and Skins, which shall be dressed in Oil in Great Britain (and for which the Duties imposed by this Act shall have been paid), which shall be manufactured and actually made into Goods or Wares, and exported as Merchandise to Foreign Parts, Sixpence	0	0	6

For every Pound Weight Avoirdupois of all Sheep Skins, which shall have been dressed in Oil in Great Britain, and duly marked (and for which the Duties imposed by this Act shall have been paid), and exported as Merchandise to Foreign Parts, two Thirds of the Duties by this Act imposed in respect thereof respectively.

For every Pound Weight Avoirdupois of all other Hides and Skins (except Lamb Skins), which shall have been dressed in Oil in Great Britain, and duly marked (and for which the Duties imposed by this Act shall have been paid), and exported as Merchandise to Foreign Parts, two Thirds of the Duties imposed by this Act imposed in respect thereof respectively.

N. B. No Excise Drawback whatsoever is to be paid or payable on the Exportation of any Hides or Skins, or Parts or Pieces of Hides or Skins, dressed in Oil, whether manufactured or made into Goods or Wares or not, except the Drawbacks above specified to be granted by the 28 Geo. III. Chap. 37.

H O P S.

For every Pound Weight Avoirdupois of Hops growing or to grow in Great Britain, and which shall be cured or made fit for Use, and on which the Duties of Excise by the 27 Geo. III. Chap. 13. imposed in respect thereof shall have been duly charged, exported as Merchandise to Ireland, one Penny and twelve twentieth Parts of a Farthing 0 0 $1\tfrac{12}{20}$

P A P E R.

For all Paper which shall be made in Great Britain (for which the Duties by the 27 Geo. III. Chap. 13. imposed in respect thereof shall have been paid), and exported as Merchandise to Foreign Parts, the Whole of the Duties by this Act imposed in respect thereof.

TABLE F.

PRINTED GOODS.

	£	s.	d.
For every Yard square of Paper which shall be printed, painted, or stained in Great Britain, for Hangings or other Uses for which the Duties by the 27 Geo. III. Chap. 13. imposed in respect thereof shall have been paid), and shall be exported as Merchandise to Foreign Parts, one Penny three Farthings	0	0	1¾
For all Linens, Stuffs, Fustians, Velvets, Velverets, Dimities, Figured Stuffs, Stuffs wholly made of Cotton Wool wove in Great Britain, commonly called British Manufactory Calicos and Muslins, which shall be printed, painted, or dyed in Great Britain (for which the Duties by the 27 Geo. III. Chap. 13. imposed in respect thereof shall have been paid), and exported as Merchandise to Foreign Parts, the Whole of the Duties of Excise by this Act imposed in respect thereof.	—	—	—
For all Silks and Silk Handkerchiefs which shall be printed, stained, painted, or dyed in Great Britain (for which the Duties by the 27 Geo. III. Chap. 13. imposed in respect thereof shall have been paid), and exported as Merchandise to Foreign Parts, the Whole of the Duties of Excise by this Act imposed in respect thereof.	—	—	—

SOAP.

For every Pound Weight Avoirdupois of Hard Cake Soap, or Ball Soap, which shall be made in Great Britain (for which the Duties by the 27 Geo. III. Chap. 13. imposed in respect thereof shall have been paid), and exported as Merchandise to Foreign Parts, Twopence Farthing - - - - - - 0 0 2¼

For every Pound Weight Avoirdupois of Soft Soap which shall be made in Great Britain for which the Duties by the 27 Geo. III. Chap. 13. imposed in respect thereof shall have been paid), and exported as Merchandise to Foreign Parts, one Penny three Farthings 0 0 1¾

S T A R C H.

For every Pound Weight Avoirdupois of Starch which shall be made in Great Britain (for which the Duties by the 27 Geo. III. Chap. 13. imposed in respect thereof shall have been paid), and exported as Merchandise to Foreign Parts, Threepence Farthing - 0 0 3¼

By the 31 Geo. III. Chap. 30. Starch may be exported when by the high Price of Corn, Corn and Grain cannot.

T E A.

For all Tea (for which the Duties by the 27 Geo. III. Chap. 13. imposed in respect thereof shall have been paid), which shall be exported to Ireland or his Majesty's Plantations in America, the Whole of the Duties of Excise by this Act imposed in respect thereof.

TABLE F.

TOBACCO.

By the 29 Geo. III. Chap. 68.

Upon the Exportation of any Short Cut Tobacco, Shag Tobacco, Roll Tobacco, and Carrot Tobacco, respectively manufactured at either of the enumerated Ports, or within two Miles thereof, from Tobacco delivered for Home Trade, Consumption, or Manufacture, out of the Warehouses appointed under the Directions of this Act, by the licensed Manufacturer, who manufactured the same, from any of the enumerated Ports to any Port or Place beyond the Seas, except the Islands of Faro or Ferro, subject to all the Regulations and Restrictions respecting the Exportation of Tobacco, there shall be paid the following Drawbacks of Excise, viz.

	£.	s.	d.
For every Pound Weight of such Short Cut Tobacco so exported, Ninepence	0	0	9
For every Pound Weight of such Shag Tobacco so exported Eightpence Farthing	0	0	8¼
For every Pound Weight of such Roll Tobacco so exported, Ninepence	0	0	9
For every Pound Weight of such Carrot Tobacco so exported, Eightpence	0	0	8

N. B. No Tobacco manufactured or unmanufactured, to be entered or shipped for Exportation to any Parts beyond the Seas (Ireland excepted), in any Ship or Vessel less than seventy Tons Burthen; and if the Master or Person in Command shall enter or clear out any Ship or Vessel having Tobacco on Board for Exportation (Ireland excepted), to Foreign Parts, as of the Burthen of seventy Tons or

WINE.

For every Tun of French Wine which shall be imported into Great Britain directly from any of the European Dominions of the French King (for which all the Duties by the 27 Geo. III. Chap. 13. imposed in respect thereof shall have been paid), and which shall be exported from Great Britain as Merchandise to any British Colony or Plantation in America, or to any British Settlement in the East Indies, and so in Proportion for any greater or lesser Quantity, fourteen Pounds seven Shillings - - - 14 7 0

For every Tun of French Wine which shall be imported as aforesaid (for which all the Duties by the 27 Geo. III. Chap. 13. imposed in respect thereof shall have been paid), and which shall be exported from Great Britain as Merchandise to any other Part or Place beyond the Seas, and so in proportion for any greater or lesser Quantity, five Pounds thirteen Shillings - - - - 5 13 0

For every Tun of Rhenish, German, or Hungary Wine (for which all the Duties by the 27 Geo. III. Chap. 13. imposed in respect thereof shall have been paid), which shall be exported from Great Britain as Merchandise to any British Colony or Plantation in America, and so in Proportion for any greater or lesser Quantity, fourteen Pounds seven Shillings - - - - 14 7 0

TABLE F.
WINE.

	£.	s.	d.
For every Tun of Rhenish, German, or Hungary Wine (for which all the Duties by the 27 Geo. III. Chap. 13. imposed in respect thereof shall have been paid), which shall be exported from Great Britain as Merchandise to any British Settlement in the East Indies, and so in Proportion for any greater or lesser Quantity, nine Pounds seventeen Shillings	9	17	0
For every Tun of Rhenish, German, or Hungary Wine (for which all the Duties by the 27 Geo. III. Chap. 13. imposed in respect thereof shall have been paid), which shall be exported from Great Britain as Merchandise to any other Part or Place beyond the Seas, and so in Proportion for any greater or lesser Quantity, five Pounds thirteen Shillings	5	13	0
For every Tun of all other Wines which shall be imported into Great Britain (for which all the Duties by the 27 Geo. III. Chap. 13. imposed in respect thereof shall have paid), and which shall be exported from Great Britain as Merchandise to any British Colony or Plantation in America, and so in Proportion for any greater or lesser Quantity, nine Pounds eleven Shillings and Fourpence	9	11	4
For every Tun of all other Wines which shall be imported into Great Britain (for which all the Duties by the 27 Geo. III. Chap. 13. imposed in respect thereof shall have been paid), and which shall be exported from Great Britain as Merchandise to any British Settlement in the East Indies, and so in Proportion for any greater or lesser Quantity, six Pounds eleven Shillings and Fourpence	6	11	4

For every Tun of all other Wines which shall be imported into Great Britain (for which all the Duties by the 27 Geo. III. Chap. 13. imposed in respect thereof shall have been paid), and which shall be exported from Great Britain as Merchandise to any other Part or Place beyond the Seas, and so in Proportion for any greater or lesser Quantity, three Pounds fifteen Shillings and Fourpence - - - - 3 15 4

By the 28 Geo. III. Chap. 33.

For every Tun, containing two Hundred and fifty two Gallons of Wine, except Wine of the Produce of the European Dominions of the French King, Rhenish, German, and Hungary Wine, Portugal and Madeira Wine, and Wine of the Produce of Spain, or of any of the Dominions of the King of Spain, for which all the Duties by this Act imposed in respect thereof shall have been paid, and which shall be exported from Great Britain as Merchandise to any British Colony or Plantation in America, or to any British Settlement in the East Indies, and so in Proportion for any greater or lesser Quantity, fourteen Pounds seven Shillings - - - - - 14 7 0

For every Tun, containing two Hundred and fifty-two Gallons of Wine (except the Wine above before excepted), which shall be imported into Great Britain, for which all the Duties by this Act imposed in respect thereof shall have been paid, and which shall be exported from Great Britain as Merchandise to any other Part or Place beyond the Seas, and so in Proportion for any greater or lesser Quantity, five Pounds thirteen Shillings 5 13 0

TABLE F.

GOLD THREAD.

	£.	s.	d.
For every Pound Weight Avoirdupois of Gold Thread, Gold Lace, or Gold Fringe, made of Plate Wire spun upon Silk, such Plate Wire being made of Gilt Wire, which shall be made in Great Britain (for which the duties by the 27 Geo. III. Chap. 13. imposed in respect thereof shall have been paid), and exported as Merchandise to Foreign Parts, and so in Proportion for any greater or lesser Quantity, seven Shillings and Eightpence	0	7	8

SILVER THREAD.

	£.	s.	d.
For every Pound Weight Avoirdupois of Silver Thread, Silver Lace, or Silver Fringe, made of Plate Wire spun upon Silk, such Plate Wire being made of Silver Wire, which shall be made in Great Britain (for which the Duties by the 27 Geo. III. Chap. 13. imposed in respect thereof shall have been paid), and exported as Merchandise to Foreign Parts, and so in Proportion for any greater or lesser Quantity, five Shillings and Ninepence	0	5	9

TABLE G.

PREMIUMS AND ALLOWANCES.

	£.	s.	d.

The Bounties payable upon the Exportation of Goods, which not having been liable to the Duties of Excise are not inferred in Table F; also the Drawbacks allowed upon the Exportation of Goods which have paid the Duties under the Management of the Commissioners of Salt and Stamp Duties.

Cordage, wrought up and manufactured in Great Britain from Foreign rough Hemp, or Hemp of the Growth of Great Britain (except Hemp of the British Colonies or Plantations in America, or of the United States of America, or in less Quantity than three Tons Weight), exported under the Regulations required by 6 Geo. III. Chap. 45. 12 Geo. III. Chap. 60. 13 Geo. III. Chap. 74. 26 Geo. III. Chap. 85. to any Part of Europe (except the Isle of Man, the Islands of Faro or Ferro, Madeira, the Canaries, or the Azores or Western Islands), the Hundred Weight, two Shillings and Fourpence three Farthings — — — — 0 2 4¾

By the 31st Geo. III. Chap. 43. continued until the 1st July 1794, and to the End of the then next Session of Parliament.

N.B. No Cordage to be exported unless a Certificate shall be produced under the Hands of three of the Commissioners of his Majesty's Navy, signifying that such Cordage hath been tendered to them for the Use of his Majesty's Dock Yards,

TABLE G.

at the fair and then Market Price of such Cordage in London, and that the same hath been refused by that Board.

CORN, viz.	Price.			Bounty.		
	£.	s.	d.	£.	s.	d.
Barley, Beer, or Bigg, if under, the Quarter	1	2	0	0	2	6
Malt made therefrom	—	—	—	0	2	6
Barley Meal, Beer Meal, and Big Meal, the Hundred Weight	—	—	—	0	0	10
Oats, the Quarter	—	—	—	0	2	0
Oat Meal, the Hundred Weight	0	14	0	0	1	0
Rye, the Quarter	1	8	0	0	3	0
Rye Meal, and Flour, the Hundred Weight	—	—	—	0	0	9
Wheat, the Quarter	2	4	0	0	5	0
Wheat Meal, the Hundred Weight	—	—	—	0	1	3
Wheat Flour, and Biscuit made of Wheat, the Hundred Weight	—	—	—	0	1	6

By the 31 Geo. III. Chap. 30. from the 15th November 1791, the beforementioned Bounties are allowed upon the Exportation in British built Ships, of the several Sorts of ground or unground Corn above recited, being of the Growth or Product of this Kingdom, when the Prices of middling British Corn or Grain shall respectively appear to be under the beforementioned Prices per Quarter, within the Districts allotted by this Act to regulate the Exportation of the several

Sorts of Corn or Grain from the different Ports of this Kingdom, under the Reftrictions therein provided, which fee in Page 89 to 93; but when the Parliament is not fitting, if the Average of the Returns of the whole Kingdom of any Sort of Corn beforementioned, appears to be above the Price at which that Sort of Foreign Corn may be imported at the lowest Duty, his Majefty, with the Advice of his Privy Council, may by Order of Council prohibit the Exportation of that Sort of Corn. Wheat Meal, or Wheat Flour, to be adjudged by Trial to pass it through a Sieve or Cloth called a fourteen Shilling Cloth; and if it does not pass through the Sieve or Cloth, it is not to be confidered as Wheat Flour. — 0 4 6

Gunpowder, of the Manufacture of Great Britain, exported to Parts beyond the Seas by Way of Merchandife, under the Regulations required by the 4 Geo. II. Chap. 39. 18 Geo. III. Chap. 45. and 26 Geo. III. Chap. 53. until the 29th September 1792, for every Barrel containing one Hundred Pounds net Weight, and fo in Proportion for any greater or lesser Quantities, four Shillings and Sixpence -

Hemp, Water rotted, bright and clean, of the Growth of Ireland, imported directly from thence under the Regulations required by the 19 Geo. III. Chap. 37. from June 24, 1786, to June 24, 1793, for every Ton, fix Pounds - 6 0 0
Ditto, from June 24, 1793, to June 24, 1800, for every Ton, four Pounds - 4 0 0
Water rotted, bright and clean, or Flax rough and undreffed, imported directly from the British Colonies or Plantations in America, under the Regulations required by the 4 Geo. III. Chap. 26. and the 26 Geo. III. Chap. 53. until June 24, 1806, for every Ton, four Pounds - 4 0 0

TABLE G.

N. B. Upon landing any such Hemp for the Bounty, the Commissioners of the Navy are to have the Pre-emption or Refusal; and if within twenty Days after such Tender the Commissioners shall not bargain for the same, the Importer may otherwise dispose of it.

	£.	s.	d.
Linen, made of Hemp or Flax in Great Britain, Ireland, or the Isle of Man, exported under the Regulations required by the 29 Geo. II. Chap. 15. 5 Geo. III. Chap. 43. 10 Geo. III. Chap. 36. 19 Geo. III. Chap. 27. 28 Geo. III. Chap. 24. and 31 Geo. III. Chap. 43. to Africa, America, Spain, Portugal, Gibraltar, the Island of Minorca, or the East Indies, until the 24th June 1792, and from thence to the End of the then next Session of Parliament.	-	-	-
For every Yard of the Breadth of 25 Inches or more, under the Value of 5d. the Yard, one Halfpenny	0	0	0½
For every Yard of the Breadth of 25 Inches or more, Value 5d. and under the Value of 6d. the Yard, one Penny	0	0	1
For every Yard of the Breadth of 25 Inches or more, Value 6d. and not exceeding the Value of 1s. 6d. the Yard, one Penny Halfpenny	0	0	1½
For every Yard of British checked or striped Linen, of the Breadth of 25 Inches or more, and not exceeding 1s. 6d. and not under 7d. in Value, per Yard, one Halfpenny	0	0	0½

For every square Yard of Diaper, Huckabacks, Sheeting, and other Species of Linen, upwards of one Yard English in Breadth, and not exceeding 1s. 6d. the square Yard in Value, one Penny Halfpenny	0	0	1½
By the 21 Geo. III. Chap. 40. ⎫ the following Bounties to be paid during the 23 Geo. III. Chap. 21. ⎬ Continuance of an Act passed in Ireland 24 Geo. III. Chap. 14. ⎭ in the 20th Year of his present Majesty's Reign, by which certain Bounties were granted on the Exportation of Linens, Buckrams, and Tillettings of the Manufacture of that Kingdom.			
For every Yard of British and Irish Buckrams or Tillettings, one Halfpenny	0	0	0½
For every Yard of British and Irish Linens, and of British Calicos and Cottons, or Cotton mixed with Linens printed, painted, or stained in Great Britain, of the Breadth of 25 Inches or more, which before the printing, painting, or staining thereof, shall be under the Value of 5d. per Yard, one Halfpenny	0	0	0½
For every Yard of the Value of 5d. and under the Value of 6d. per Yard, one Penny	0	0	1
For every Yard of the Value of 6d. and not exceeding 8d. per Yard, one Penny Halfpenny	0	0	1½
Sail Cloth, British made, exported under the Regulations required by Law, for every Ell, Twopence	0	0	2
N. B. By the 29 Geo. III. Chap. 55. the Bounty is not to be paid for Sails exported unless they are stamped before shipping.			
Plate, Silver wrought or manufactured in Great Britain, the Ounce Troy, Sixpence	0	0	6
Gold wrought or manufactured in Great Britain, the Ounce Troy, eight Shillings	0	8	0

TABLE G.

N.B. This is a Drawback (upon Exportation) of the Duties imposed by the 24 Geo. III. Chap. 53. and all wrought Silver and Gold Plate intended to be exported must be taken to the Assay Office, and there be stamped or marked with the Figure of a Britannia; but no Boxes, Cases, or Dial Plates of Silver or Gold for Clocks or Watches, may be exported without the Movements made up fit for Use, with the Maker's Name engraved thereon.

	£.	s.	d.
Salted Beef and Pork, exported for Sale, salted with Salt which has paid the Duty, for every Barrel, five Shillings — Granted by 5 Ann, Chap. 29. 5 Geo. II. Chap. 6. 18 Geo. II. Chap. 5. and 26 Geo. II. Chap. 3. by which last Act this Allowance is granted without any Limitation of Time.	0	5	0
White Herrings, the Barrel of 32 Gallons, two Shillings and Eightpence —	0	2	8
full Red Herrings, the Barrel of 32 Gallons, one Shilling and Ninepence — By the 5 Geo. I. Chap. 18; and the same Bounty is allowed on Herrings exported from the Isle of Man by 26 Geo. III. Chap. 81; all subject to the Regulations of the 5 Geo. I. Chap. 18. and those from the Isle of Man, to the Regulations of the 26 Geo. III. Chap. 81.	0	1	9
Red, clean, shotten Herrings, the Barrel of 32 Gallons, one Shilling — By the 5 Geo. I. Chap. 18.	0	1	0

dried Ling, Cod, and Hake, being 14 Inches long and upwards, from the Bone in the Fin to the third Joint in the Tail, the Hundred Weight, three Shillings — 0 3 0

By the 5 Geo. I. Chap. 18. and the 26 Geo. III. Chap. 81.

wet Ling, Cod and Hake, the Barrel of 32 Gallons, two Shillings — 0 2 0

By the 5 Geo. I. Chap. 18.

Pilchards or Scads, for every Cask or Vessel containing 50 Gallons, seven Shillings 0 7 0

By the 5 Geo. I. Chap. 18.

This additional Bounty of 2s. expired and not continued. {And by the 25 Geo. III. Chap. 58. and 26 Geo. III. Chap. 45. additional for five Years from 24th June 1786, on no more than twenty Thousand Hogsheads in one Year, or in that Proportion for a less Quantity two Shillings} 0 2 0

And by the 31 Geo. III. Chap. 45. from the 24th June 1791, to 24th June 1798, additional, one Shilling and Sixpence — 0 1 6

Salmon, the Barrel of 42 Gallons, four Shillings and Sixpence — 0 4 6

dried Red Sprats, the Last, one Shilling — 0 1 0

By the 5 Geo. I. Chap. 18.

On British Manufactures of Silk hereafter mentioned, exported under the Regulations required by Law, the following Bounties are to be allowed to June 24, 1795.

By the 8 Geo. I. Chap. 15. 14 Geo. III. Chap. 86. 24 Geo. III. Chap. 49. 25 Geo. III. Chap. 69. and 29 Geo. III. Chap. 55.

TABLE G.

	£.	s.	d.
Ribbons and Stuffs of Silk only, the Pound Avoirdupois Weight,			
Silk Gauzes, ⅓ of the Weight of which is allowed for Gum, five Shillings	0	5	0
Silk Crapes, ¼ of the Weight of which is allowed for Dress, the Pound Avoirdupois Weight, six Shillings and Eightpence	0	6	8
Silk and Ribbons of Silk mixed with Gold or Silver, the Pound Avoirdupois Weight, three Shillings	0	3	0
Silk Stockings, Silk Gloves, Silk Fringes, Silk Laces, stitching or sewing Silk, the Pound Avoirdupois Weight, one Shilling and Two-pence	0	1	2
Stuffs of Silk and Grogram Yarn, the Pound Avoirdupois Weight, one Shilling and Eightpence	0	1	8
Stuffs of Silk, mixed with Incle or Cotton, the Pound Avoirdupois Weight, Tenpence	0	0	10
Stuffs of Silk and Worsted, the Pound Avoirdupois Weight, Tenpence			
Slaves, carried in British built Ships (which have cleared out from Ports in Great Britain for the Slave Trade), from the Coast of Africa to the British West India Islands, provided there have not died more than 2 in 100 of the Number taken on board from the first Arrival upon the Coast of Africa, until the Arrival at the Port of Delivery in the West Indies,			
To the Master, one Hundred Pounds	100	0	0
To the Surgeon, fifty Pounds	50	0	0

(373)

Provided there shall not have died more than 3 in 100,
To the Master, fifty Pounds - - - - 50 0 0
To the Surgeon, twenty-five Pounds - - - 25 0 0
Subject to the Regulations of the 28 Geo. III. Chap. 54. the 29 Geo. III. Chap. 66.
30 Geo. III. Chap. 33. and 31 Geo. III. Chap. 54.
Continued to August 1, 1792.
Sugar refined, from Sugar of the Produce of the British Plantations, exported agreeable to
the Regulations of the 5 Geo. III. Chap. 45. 21 Geo. III. Chap. 16. and
31 Geo. III. Chap. 15. by which Acts the Bounties are allowed,
in Loaves complete and whole, and in Lumps duly refined, for every Hundred Weight, one Pound six Shillings - - - 1 6 0
called Bastards, ground or powdered Sugar, Loaf Sugar broken in Pieces,
and all Sugar called Candy, properly refined, the Hundred Weight, fifteen
Shillings - - - - - 0 15 0

WHALE FISHERY.

In the Greenland Seas, Davis's Streights, or the adjacent Seas, which are deemed to extend
to 59 Degrees 30 Minutes North, and no farther.
For every British built Ship from Great Britain, Guernsey, Jersey, or Man, the Owners
being British residing in Great Britain, Guernsey, Jersey, or Man, which shall proceed
on the said Fishery (the several Provisions and Directions relating thereto in the hereafter
mentioned Acts being complied with), for every Ton, one Pound ten Shillings - 1 10 0

B b 3

TABLE G.

l. s. d.

11 Geo. III. Chap. 38. continued by 15 Geo. III. Chap. 31. and 18 Geo. III. Chap. 55; further Regulations adopted by 26 Geo. III. Chap. 41, and the Bounty continued for five Years from 25th December 1786, and by the 31 Geo. III. Chap. 43. continued until the 25th December 1792.

By the 26 Geo. III. Chap. 41. the Ships employed in this Fishery are to sail from the Place where they are fitted out before the 10th of April in every Year, and are to continue in the Seas beforementioned, until the 10th of August following, unless entitled to quit those Seas under the Provisions of this Act. Ships of 150 Tons Burthen entitled to the Bounty; but no Ship is to receive for more than 400 Tons, and if not employed in this Fishery before the 25th December 1786, for no more than 300 Tons; and Ships fitted out from Ireland agreeable to the Regulations of this Act are entitled to the Bounty. By the 29 Geo. III. Chap. 53. Ships are to be entitled to the Bounty although they leave the beforementioned Seas before the 10th of August, and although they are not laden according to the Regulations of the 26 Geo. III. Chap. 41. in case it shall appear by the Log Book that they continued in those Seas diligently endeavouring to catch Whales, and did not depart from thence until sixteen Weeks after the Time of sailing from the Port from whence they cleared out, and did not touch at any other Port.

In the Gulf of Saint Lawrence, on the Coast of Labrador, Newfoundland, or in any Seas to the Southward of the Greenland Seas, and Davis's Streights, but not to extend to any Whales caught to the Southward of the said Greenland Seas or Davis's Streights exceeding 44 Degrees of North Latitude. The several Bounties hereaftermentioned are by the 15 Geo. III. Chap. 31. 16 Geo. III. Chap. 47. 18 Geo. III. Chap. 55. and 20 Geo. III. Chap. 60. allowed annually for eleven years for five Ships employed in this Fishery, provided the several Regulations and Restrictions of the beforementioned Acts are complied with, viz. Such British built Ships (owned by his Majesty's Subjects residing in Great Britain, Ireland, Guernsey, Jersey, or Man, and being the entire Property of such Subjects residing in that Part of his Majesty's Dominions from whence the Ship is fitted and cleared out, except as to such Owners residing in Great Britain or Ireland respectively, although the said Owners do not reside in that Part of his Majesty's Dominions beforementioned), fitted and cleared out after the 1st of January 1776, and after that Day in each succeeding Year, which shall take and kill one Whale at least in the Seas beforementioned, and shall return within one Year to some Port in England with the Oil of such Whale or Whales so taken as aforesaid

For the Ship which shall so arrive in each Year with the greatest Quantity of Oil so taken as beforementioned, five Hundred Pounds - - - 500 0 0

For the Ship which shall in like Manner arrive in the same Year with the next greatest Quantity of Oil so taken as aforesaid, four Hundred Pounds - - - 400 0 0

For the Ship which shall in like Manner arrive in the same Year with the next greatest Quantity of Oil so taken as aforesaid, three Hundred Pounds - - - 300 0 0

TABLE G.

	£.	s.	d.
For the Ship which shall in like Manner arrive in the same Year with the next greatest Quantity of Oil so taken as aforesaid, two Hundred Pounds	200	0	0
For the Ship which shall in like Manner arrive in the same Year with the next greatest Quantity of Oil so taken as aforesaid, one Hundred Pounds	100	0	0

In the Seas to the Southward of the seventh Degree of North Latitude.

The several Bounties hereaftermentioned are by the 26 Geo. III. Chap. 50. and 28 Geo. III. Chap. 20. allowed annually for ten Years for fifteen Ships employed in this Fishery, provided the several Regulations and Restrictions of the beforementioned Acts are complied with; viz. Such British built Ships owned by his Majesty's Subjects in Great Britain, Ireland, Guernsey, Jersey, or Man, and being the entire Property of such Subjects usually residing in any of the Dominions beforementioned, as shall fit and clear out after the 15th of April and before the 1st of November 1788, and between the 1st of January and the 1st of November in every succeeding Year which shall take and kill one Whale at least in the Seas beforementioned, and shall return to some Port of Great Britain before the 31st day of December in the Year subsequent to that in which they cleared out.

For the 3 Ships which shall so sail and first arrive in each Year with the greatest Quantity of Oil taken as beforementioned, being not less than 20 Tons, and being the Produce of one or more Whale or Whales, or other Creatures living in the Seas, taken by the Crews of every Ship respectively, each five Hundred Pounds - - - 500 0 0

For the 3 Ships as beforementioned, with the next greatest Quantity taken as aforesaid, and being not less than 20 Tons, each four Hundred Pounds - - - 400 0 0

For the 3 Ships as beforementioned, with the next greatest Quantity taken as aforesaid, and being not less than 20 Tons, each three Hundred Pounds - - - 300 0 0

For the 3 Ships as beforementioned, with the next greatest Quantity taken as aforesaid, and being not less than 20 Tons, each two Hundred Pounds - - - 200 0 0

For the 3 Ships as beforementioned, with the next greatest Quantity taken as aforesaid, and being not less than 20 Tons, each one Hundred Pounds - - - 100 0 0

In the Seas to the Southward of the thirty-sixth Degree of South Latitude.

The several Bounties hereaftermentioned are by the 26 Geo. III. Chap. 50, and 28 Geo. III. Chap. 20. allowed annually for ten Years for five other of such Ships employed in this Fishery, provided the several Regulations and Restrictions of the beforementioned Acts are complied with; viz. Such British built Ships owned by his Majesty's Subjects in Great Britain, Ireland, Guernsey, Jersey, or Man, and being the entire Property of such Subjects usually residing in any of the Dominions beforementioned, as shall fit and clear out after the 15th of April and before the 1st of November in every succeeding Year, which shall proceed of January and the 1st of November in every succeeding Year, which shall proceed to the Southward of the 36th Degree of South Latitude, shall there carry on the said

TABLE G.

	L.	s.	d.
Fishery and return to some Port of Great Britain on or before the 31st of December in the Year subsequent to that of their clearing out, but not in less Time than fourteen Months from the clearing out of such Ship, nor remain longer than twenty-eight Months from the 1st of May in the Year which such Ship cleared out.			
For the 1st Ship which shall so fail and first arrive with the greatest Quantity of Oil or Head Matter taken in those Seas by the Crews of every Ship respectively, being the Produce of one or more Whale or Whales or other Creatures living in the Seas, and not being less than 20 Tons, seven Hundred Pounds	700	0	0
For the 2d Ship as beforementioned, with the next greatest Quantity, not being less than 20 Tons, six Hundred Pounds	600	0	0
For the 3d Ship as beforementioned, with the next greatest Quantity, not being less than 20 Tons, five Hundred Pounds	500	0	0
For the 4th Ship as beforementioned, with the next greatest Quantity, not being less than 20 Tons, four Hundred Pounds	400	0	0
For the 5th Ship as beforementioned, with the next greatest Quantity, not being less than 20 Tons, three Hundred Pounds	300	0	0

South Whale Fishery.

By the 28 Geo. III. Chap. 20. and 29 Geo. III. Chap. 53. the following additional

Bounties are granted to three of the 20 Ships to which Bounties are given by the 26 Geo. III. Chap. 50. which shall be fitted and cleared out from some Port of Great Britain or Ireland, or the Islands of Guernsey, Jersey, or Man, between the 1st January and 1st November, and which shall double Cape Horn, or pass through the Streights of Magellan into the South Seas and carry on the said Fishery during the Space of four Months to the Westward of Cape Horn in those Seas, viz;

To the Owners of such Ship so fitted and cleared out carrying on such Fishery, that shall return to some Port in Great Britain on or before the 1st Day of December in the second Year after that in which such Ship shall have so fitted and cleared out, but not in less time than fifteen Months from the clearing out of such Ship, and which shall so return with the greatest Quantity of Oil or Head Matter (being not less in the whole than 30 Tons, caught during the said Voyage either outward or homeward) there shall be paid the Premium of eight Hundred Pounds - - - - 800 0 0

To the Owners of such Ship so fitted out which shall return as aforesaid with the next greatest Quantity of Oil or Head Matter (being not less in the whole than 30 Tons, caught during the said Voyage either outward or homeward), there shall be paid seven Hundred Pounds - - - 700 0 0

To the Owners of such Ship so fitted out which shall return as aforesaid with the next greatest Quantity of Oil or Head Matter (being not less in the whole than 30 Tons, caught during the said Voyage either outward or homeward), there shall be paid six Hundred Pounds - - - 600 0 0

TABLE G.

No Ship to be entitled within or during the Periods of Time respectively limited for such Ship to fail on and to return from the Voyage to more than one additional Premium, although such Ship shall make two Voyages within any one of the Periods.

BRITISH WHITE HERRING FISHERY.

By the 26 Geo. III. Chap. 81.

The Bounties hereafter mentioned are allowed annually for seven Years, from the 1st of June 1787.

	£.	s.	d.
To the Owner of every British built decked Vessel, of 15 Tons or upwards, properly equipped, viz. 12 Bushels of Salt in new Barrels, for every Last of Fifth such Vessel is capable of containing, and as many more new Barrels as such Ship can carry; also 250 square Yards of Netting, with other Materials for mounting the same; also 5 Men for the first 15 Tons, and one additional Man for every 5 Tons such Ship shall measure; and to clear from a British Port where such Vessel belongs, between the 1st of June and the 1st of October, and to proceed directly upon the Fishery from that Part of the United Kingdom to which such Vessel belongs; to continue fishing for three Months from the Day the Nets are first shot, and to return to a Port with a full Complement of Men and with a full Cargo, taken wholly by the Crew of such Vessel, shall receive a Bounty per Ton, of one Pound	1	0	0

For every Barrel of Pickled Herrings, twice packed and completely cured (and not exceeding in Quantity the Proportion of 2½ Barrels per Ton, which the Veſſel in which ſuch Herrings are imported ſhall meaſure), a Bounty of per Barrel, four Shillings - 0 4 0
Exceeding the Proportion of 2½ Barrels per Ton, one Shilling - 0 1 0
N.B. The Quantity to be computed while in the Sea Stocks, 4 Barrels of which to be deemed equal to 3 Barrels of cured Herrings.
Every Veſſel not being entitled to a Bounty on her Tonnage, a Bounty is allowed on her Cargo; viz. for all Herrings which ſhall be landed from any Boat or Veſſel not entitled as aforeſaid, per Barrel, one Shilling - 0 1 0

To the Owners of Veſſels employed in the Deep Sea Fiſhery the following Premiums are given:

For the greateſt Quantity of Herrings imported in one Veſſel between the 1ſt of June and the 1ſt of November, eighty-four Pounds - 84 0 0
The next greateſt Quantity, ſixty-three Pounds - 63 0 0
The next ditto, forty-two Pounds - 42 0 0
The next ditto, twenty-one Pounds - 21 0 0
The Owners of Herrings taken and cured, as the Act of 26 Geo. III. Chap. 81. directs for Exportation, are entitled to a Bounty of per Barrel, three Shillings - 0 3 0
And are allowed the Drawback of the whole Duty on Salt with which ſuch Herrings are cured.

TABLE G.

	£.	s.	d.

Vessels returning with less than their proper Number of Men, unless the Default was occasioned by Death, Sickness, or Desertion, and without a full Cargo of Herrings, are not entitled to a Bounty. By a subsequent Act, 27 Geo. III. a full Cargo of Herrings is deemed to be in Proportion as 4 Barrels once packed, to 3 Barrels twice packed, for every Ton Burthen.

By the above subsequent Act all decked Vessels of not less than 15 Tons, are entitled to all the Bounties mentioned in the Act 26 Geo. III. before recited, provided they take in one Year the Proportion of 6 Barrels of Herrings, when cured, for every Ton Burthen; although they may not have fitted out with the Quantity of Salt and Barrels required by the said Act.

If after October 1, 1786, any Fish (except fresh Fish) are packed in Casks not branded with the Name of the Curer, such Casks with the Fish are forfeited.

Staves of Barrels (in which Herrings are packed for Exportation), not being 1½ Inch thick, and full bound, are together with the Fish forfeited.

Masters of Vessels not making a true Entry of the Quantity of Fish, and where taken, at the Port where they intend to land them, such Ships and Cargos are forfeited.

Salt carried Coastwise for the Purpose of the Fishery, unless Bond and other Securities have been given, as the Act recites, such Salt to be forfeited, with double its Value, besides the Duties.

Officers taking Fees of any Kind, to forfeit treble the Value and be discharged.

The Inhabitants of the Isle of Man who comply with the Terms of these Acts (26 and 27 Geo. III.) for all the Herrings that are caught or taken by them, are entitled for each Barrel to a Bounty of one Shilling - - - - - 0 1 0
White Herrings exported beyond the Seas, by 5 Geo. I. Chap. 18. the Barrel, two Shillings and Eightpence - - - - - 0 2 8
Red Herrings exported beyond the Seas, the Barrel, one Shilling and Ninepence - 0 1 9
N.B. The Duties formerly payable on Herrings imported into Great Britain from the Isle of Man are by the above Acts to cease.

IRISH WHITE HERRING FISHERY.

By the Acts of the Irish Legislature now in Force, the Owners of every Vessel, being Irish Property, who resort to the Fishery of that Kingdom, are entitled to a Bounty per Ton, of one Pound ten Shillings - - - - - 1 10 0
Viz. 10s. per Ton on the Vessel, and 20s. per Ton on the Cargo, and in Proportion for any Quantity of Herrings they cure; whether the same are caught by the Ship's Crew, or purchased of the Native Fishermen.

All such Red Herrings, White Herrings, Salmon, Cod, Ling, Tusk, or other white Fish, conveyed Coastwise from one Port or Place in Great Britain to another, upon Exportation to be entitled to the Bounties granted by the 5 Geo. I. Chap. 18. By the 27 Geo. III. Chap. 10. the Restriction to decked Vessels repealed, and the

TABLE G.

L. s. d.

Bounty granted by 26 Geo. III. Chap. 81. extended to all Busses and Vessels whatever built in Great Britain, subject to all the Directions of that Act.
No Vessel to be deemed to have a full Cargo if under the Proportion of 4 Barrels of Herrings once packed, or three twice packed, for every Ton Burthen.
From June 1, 1787, decked Vessels, of not less than 15 Tons, shall be entitled to the Bounties granted by the recited Act, if they take in one Year in the Deep Sea Fishery, the Proportion of 6 Barrels of Herrings when cured, for every Ton Burthen, and also one Shilling per Barrel for Red or White Herrings, notwithstanding the Vessel may not have been fitted out with the Quantity of Nets, Salt, and Barrels, required by the said Act; but no more than 50 Vessels fitted out in one Year from any one Port, to be entitled to the Bounty of twenty Shillings per Ton, which shall not have been furnished with the Quantity of Nets, Salt, and Barrels required by the 26 Geo. III. Chap. 81. and if more than 50 such Vessels so fitted out from any one Port shall have taken within the Time the Quantity of Herrings, the Bounty is to be paid to those 50 Vessels that shall have taken the greatest Quantity.

NEWFOUNDLAND FISHERY.

By the 26 Geo. III. Chap. 26. the Bounties hereaftermentioned are allowed annually for ten Years from the 1st January 1787, to Vessels employed in this Fishery, manned as directed by the 10 and 11 Will. III. Chap. 25. under the Regulations and Restrictions of the 26 Geo. III. Chap. 26. viz. such British built Vessels wholly owned by his Majesty's Subjects residing in Great Britain, Ireland, Guernsey, Jersey, or Man, which shall fit and clear out from Great Britain, Guernsey, Jersey, or Alderney, after the 1st of January 1787, and after that Day in each succeeding Year, which shall proceed to the Banks of Newfoundland, and having caught a Cargo of Fish upon those Banks, consisting of not less than 10,000 by Tale, shall land the same at any one of the Ports between Cape Saint John and Cape Ray, on or before the 15th of July in each Year, and shall make one more Trip at the least to the said Banks, and return with another Cargo of Fish caught there to the same Port, in which Case

The 100 Vessels first arriving at the said Island of Newfoundland from the Banks thereof, with a Cargo of Fish caught there, consisting of 10,000 Fish by Tale at the least, and which, after landing the same at one of the Ports within the Limits beforementioned in Newfoundland, shall proceed again to the said Banks and return to the said Island with another Cargo of Fish, if navigated with not less than 12 Men, shall be entitled to, each Vessel, forty Pounds - - - - - - 40 0 0

if less than 12, and not less than 7, each Vessel, twenty-five Pounds - - 25 0 0

But provided any of the 100 Vessels so first arriving shall be navigated by not less than 12 Men who go out on Shares of the Profits in lieu of Wages, shall be entitled to, each Vessel, fifty Pounds - - - - - - - 50 0 0

TABLE G.

	£.	s.	d.
The 100 Vessels which shall so next arrive under the same Regulations and Restrictions, navigated with not less than 12 Men, shall be entitled to, each Vessel, twenty-five Pounds	25	0	0
if less than 12, and not less than 7 Men, each Vessel, eighteen Pounds	18	0	0
But provided any of the 100 Vessels so arriving shall be navigated by not less than 12 Men who go out on Shares in lieu of Wages, shall be entitled to, each Vessel, thirty-five Pounds	35	0	0
if less than 12, and not less than 7 Men, each Vessel, twenty-one Pounds	21	0	0

The 100 Vessels if less than 12, and not less than 7 Men, each Vessel, thirty-five Pounds — 35 0 0

TABLE H.

The following Extracts of the Charter granted to the City of London, which was confirmed by the Act of 2 William and Mary, Chap. 8. relating to the several Duties of Scavage, Package, Balliage, and Portage payable to the City of London by Aliens, or by Denizens born within the Allegiance of the British Crown, being the Sons of Aliens born under Foreign Allegiance, and of the several Clauses in subsequent Acts of Parliament confirming the same, are recited to shew the Merchants liable to pay those Duties the Authorities by which they are collected.

EXTRACT of the 12 Charles II. Chap. 18. Sect. 9.

Be it hereby enacted by the Authority aforesaid, that for the Prevention of the great Frauds daily used in colouring and concealing of Aliens' Goods, all Wines of the Growth of France or Germany, which from and after the twentieth Day of October, One Thousand Six Hundred and Sixty, shall be imported into any the Ports or Places aforesaid, in any other Ship or Vessel than which doth truly and without Fraud belong to England, Ireland, Wales, or Town of Berwick upon Tweed, and navigated with the Mariners thereof, as aforesaid, shall be deemed Aliens' Goods, and pay all Strangers' Customs and Duties to his Majesty, his Heirs and Successors, as also to the Town or Port into which they shall be imported; and that all Sorts of Masts, Timber, or Boards, as also all Foreign Salt, Pitch, Tar, Rosin, Hemp, Flax, Raisins, Figs, Prunes, Olive Oils, all Sorts of Corn or Grain, Sugar, Pot Ashes, Spirits, commonly called Brandy Wine, or Aqua Vitæ, Wines of the Growth of

C c 2

Spain, the Islands of the Canaries, or Portugal, Madeira, or Western Islands; and all the Goods of the Growth, Production, or Manufacture of Muscovy or Russia, which from and after the first Day of April, which shall be in the Year of our Lord One Thousand Six Hundred and Sixty-one, shall be imported into any the aforesaid Places in any other than such Shipping, and so navigated, and all Currants and Turkey Commodities which from and after the first Day of September, One Thousand Six Hundred and Sixty-one, shall be imported into any of the Places aforesaid, in any other than English built Shipping, and navigated as aforesaid, shall be deemed Aliens Goods, and pay accordingly to his Majesty, his Heirs and Successors, and to the Town or Port into which they shall be imported.

EXTRACT from the CHARTER granted to the CITY of LONDON by Charles II.

That from henceforth, for ever hereafter, there shall be within the said Port of London, and the Limits and Bounds thereof, within the Liberties and Franchises of the said City and Suburbs thereof, an Office and Offices, Employment and Employments of Package of all Woollen Cloths, Wool Fells, Calve Skins, Goat Skins, Bales of Tin, and of all other Merchandises whatsoever, to be packed, casked, piped, barrelled, or any Ways vesselled, with a Survey of the Measure, Number and Weight of the said Merchandises, and also the Survey of all Customable Merchandises to the said Port, within the Liberties and Franchises of the said City and Suburbs thereof coming, *and out of the same Port going, as well by Land as by Water, within the Liberties and Franchises of the City aforesaid, and Suburbs thereof, as well of the Goods of any Denizen, whose Father is or shall be an Alien, as of the Goods of Aliens wheresoever the same shall be customed:* as also an Office or Employment of Carriage and Portage of all Wools, Wool Fells, Bales of Tin, and of all other Merchandiſes whatſoever, as well of any Denizen, whoſe Father is or ſhall be an Alien, born without the Allegiance of us, our Heirs or Succeſſors, as of Aliens born without the Allegiance of us, our Heirs or Succeſſors, and under any Foreign Allegiance in any the Parts beyond the Seas, which ſhall be carried into London, from the River of Thames, to the Houſe or Warehouſe of ſuch Alien, and from thence to the ſaid River: together with the Fees, Sums of Money, Profits, and Emoluments of the ſaid Office or Employments, and other the Premiſes, in two Tables or Schedules hereunto annexed, mentioned, and reſpectively limited and appointed. All and ſingular which Fees, Sums of Money, Profits and Emoluments in the ſaid Tables or Schedules, expreſſed as due and lawful Fees to the ſaid ſeveral Offices of Package and Portage annexed and belonging, and in the Execution of the ſame Offices, and either of them reſpectively, to be had and taken, we do for us, our Heirs and Succeſſors, ratify, eſtabliſh, and confirm, by theſe Preſents, and the ſame Fees, Sums of Money, Profits and Emoluments in the ſaid Tables or Schedules beforementioned, We do for us, our Heirs and Succeſſors, grant unto the ſaid Mayor, Commonalty and Citizens of the City aforeſaid, and their Succeſſors for ever by theſe Preſents. And furthermore, of our ſpecial Grace, certain Knowledge, and mere Motion, for the Conſideration aforeſaid, We do for us, our Heirs and Succeſſors, give and grant to the ſaid Mayor, Commonalty and Citizens of the City aforeſaid, and their Succeſſors, the ſaid Office or Employment of Package of all and all Manner of Woollen Cloths, Wool Fells, Calves Skins, Goat Skins, Bales of Tin, and all other Merchandiſes whatſoever, to be packed, caſked, piped, barrelled, or any ways veſſelled; with the Survey of the Meaſure, Number and Weight of the ſaid Merchandiſes, together with the Fees, Sums of Money, Profits and Emoluments aforeſaid; and alſo the Office or Employment of Carriage and Portage of all Wools, Wool Fells, Bales of Tin, and all other Merchandifes whatfoever, as well of any Denizen, whofe Father is or fhall be an Alien born, without the Allegiance of us, our Predeceffors, Heirs or Succeffors, as of any Alien born without the Allegiance of us, our Predeceffors, Heirs or Succeffors, and under any Foreign Allegiance, in Parts beyond the Seas, *which fhall be carried into London, from the River of Thames to the Houfe of fuch Alien, and from thence to the faid River, together with the Fees, Sums of Money, Profits and Emoluments aforefaid,* to hold and exercife the Offices and Employments aforefaid, and either of them, with their Appurtenances, and the Difpofitions, Orderings, Surveyings and Corrections thereof, and of either of them; together with all Fees, Sums of Money, Profits and Emoluments whatfoever, to the faid Offices or Employments, or either of them, in the faid two Tables or Schedules to thefe Prefents annexed, mentioned and refpectively appointed to the faid Mayor and Commonalty and Citizens of the faid City, and their Succeffors, for ever: and alfo to exercife and occupy the faid Offices or Employments, and every and either of them, by themfelves, or by their fufficient Minifter or Minifters, Deputy or Deputies, without any Account or other Thing, to be therefore rendered or made to us, our Heirs and Succeffors (befides the Rent hereafter in thefe Prefents mentioned to be referved and paid to us, our Heirs and Succeffors), and without incurring any Penalty or Forfeiture of the Offices aforefaid, or either of them, or of any Parcel thereof, although they or their Deputies, Officers or Servants, do not pack the faid Goods or Merchandifes, when they are ready, and upon reafonable Requeft and Notice thereof given for the performing the faid Services. And that no other Porter or Carrier, or any other Perfon or Perfons whatfoever, fhall prefume to intermit or intrude him or themfelves to carry or lade any of the faid Goods or Merchandifes from any Wharf or Shore within the Limits aforefaid, into any Ship or Veffel, or to unlade any Goods or Merchandifes from any Ship or Veffel, upon any Wharf, Shore, or Lane within the Limits aforefaid, without the fpecial Appointment or

Licence of the said Mayor, Commonalty and Citizens of the City aforesaid, or of their Officers or Deputies for that Purpose, first had or obtained. And that the Porter or Carrier appointed, and from Time to Time to be appointed, by the said Mayor and Commonalty and Citizens, and their Successors, or by their sufficient Officers or Deputies for the Time being, shall have, take or receive of or from the said Merchants, as well Aliens born without the Allegiance of us, our Predecessors, Heirs or Successors, and under any Foreign Allegiance in Parts beyond the Seas, as of the said Denizens born, or to be born within the Power or Allegiance of us, our Predecessors, Heirs or Successors, whose Father is, or shall be an Alien born without the Allegiance of us, our Predecessors, Heirs or Successors, for the Carriage or Portage of the said Goods and Merchandises, such Sums of Money for their Labour aforesaid, as in a certain Schedule to these Presents annexed, are mentioned and appointed, without any Account or other Thing to be therefore rendered or made to us, our Heirs or Successors (besides the Rents hereafter in these Presents mentioned, to be paid to us, our Heirs or Successors). And further, of our more abundant Grace, certain Knowledge, and mere Motion, and for the Consideration aforesaid, we do for us, our Heirs and Successors, give and grant to the said Mayor, and Commonalty, and Citizens of the City aforesaid, and their Successors, the Office or Employment of the Scavage and Surveying, and also the Scavage of all the Goods and Wares customable whatsoever, of any Merchants, as well Aliens as Denizens, whose Father is or shall be an Alien born or to be born without the Allegiance of us, our Predecessors, Heirs or Successors, and to be brought from any Parts beyond the Seas, within the Liberties and Franchises of the said City and Suburbs thereof, on account of Merchandising, and also the Surveying, Delivering, or Balliage of all the Goods and Wares of any of the said Merchants, within the Liberties and Franchises of the said City, which shall be carried out into Parts beyond the Seas by Way of Merchandise, through and upon the River Thames, within the Limits aforesaid, in any Ship, Boat, Barge, or Vessel whatsoever, floating, laden, remaining or being off of any Shore of the said River of Thames, and which upon any Bank, Wharf, or Shore of the said River, shall happen to remain and be delivered or unladen within the Liberties and Franchises of the said City and Suburbs thereof; together with the Fees, Sums of Money, Profits and Emoluments in a certain Table or Schedule to these Presents annexed, mentioned, and respectively limited and appointed, according to the Form of the Statute made and published in the two and twentieth Year of Henry the Eighth, late King of England. All and singular which said Fees, Sums of Money, Profits and Emoluments, in the said Table or Schedule last mentioned and expressed, as due and lawful Fees to the said several Offices of Scavage and Ballage aforesaid, annexed and belonging, and in the Execution of the same Offices and either of them respectively hereafter to be had and taken, we do for us, our Heirs and Successors, ratify, establish, and confirm, by these Presents; and the same Fees, Sums of Money, Profits and Emoluments in the said last mentioned Table or Schedule, we do for us, our Heirs and Successors, grant to the said Mayor, and Commonalty, and Citizens of the City aforesaid, and their Successors for ever, by these Presents. To have and exercise the said Offices and Employments last mentioned, and either of them, with the Appurtenances, and the disposings, orderings, supervisings, and Corrections of the same, and either of them, together with all the Fees, Sums of Money, Profits and Emoluments to the said Offices or Employments, and either of them, in the said Table or Schedule to these Presents annexed, mentioned and respectively appointed, unto the said Mayor, and Commonalty, and Citizens of the said City, and their Successors for ever; and also to exercise and occupy the said Offices or Employments, by themselves, or by their sufficient Minister or Ministers, Deputy or Deputies, without any Account or other Matter to be rendered or made to us, our Heirs or Successors, for the same (befides the Rents hereafter in thefe Prefents mentioned to be referved and paid to us, our Heirs and Succeffors), and without incurring any Penalty of the faid Offices or Employments, or either of them, or any Parcel thereof, although they or their Deputies, Officers or Servants, fhall not furvey or deliver the Goods and Merchandifes aforefaid, when they fhall be ready, upon reafonable Requeft or Notice thereof given, for the performing the faid Works or Services. Willing, and by thefe Prefents, for us, our Heirs and Succeffors, enjoining and commanding all and fingular fuch Aliens and Denizens aforefaid, that they, from Time to Time, do make and deliver, or caufe to be made and delivered, unto the faid Mayor, and Commonalty, and Citizens, and their Succeffors, or their Servants, Deputies or Collectors of the Scavage aforefaid for the Time being, true and perfect Bills of Entry of all and every their Goods, Merchandifes and Wares, which fhall be, from Time to Time, brought within the Liberties and Franchifes of the faid City and Suburbs thereof, under Pain of our Royal Indignation, and of being further punifhed for their Contempt of our Command in this Behalf. And whereas we are informed, that with Intent to defraud and deceive the faid Mayor, and Commonalty, and Citizens of the City aforefaid, of the Fees and Profits to the faid feveral Offices belonging and appertaining, feveral Goods and Merchandifes have been fraudulently laden and unladen, by divers Perfons, at certain Wharfs or Places commonly called *St. Katharine's, Tower Wharf, Southwark, Dick Shore, Wapping, Rotherhithe, Deptford, Greenwich,* and *Blackwall,* and other Places between Blackwall and London Bridge, on both Sides of the River Thames aforefaid, fuppofing the fame Places to be without the Port of London aforefaid, and the Liberties, Franchifes, and Suburbs thereof; we will, and by thefe Prefents for us, our Heirs and Succeffors, do ordain and declare, That for ever hereafter, all and fingular Merchant Strangers born without our Allegiance, in Parts beyond the Seas, and under Foreign Obedience, and alfo the Sons of fuch Merchant Strangers who henceforth fhall lade or unlade any Goods or Merchandifes cuftomable in the Port of the City of London aforefaid, or in any of the faid Places or Wharfs abovementioned, fhall, from Time to Time, render and pay, or make and caufe to be rendered and paid, unto the faid Mayor, Commonalty, and Citizens of the City aforefaid, and their Succeffors, or their Officers, Deputies and Servants, fuch Wages and Fees as are in the faid Tables or Schedules mentioned and expreffed. And farther, becaufe we are given to underftand that divers Goods and Merchandifes of Merchants, as well Aliens born without our Allegiance, under Foreign Obedience, in Parts beyond the Seas, as alfo fuch Denizen, whofe Father is or fhall be an Alien, and born under Foreign Allegiance in Parts beyond the Seas, which are carried out of the Port of the faid City, and brought into the faid Port from Foreign Parts and beyond the Seas, are very often fubtilly concealed and coloured under the Names of other Perfons, to defraud us of our Cuftoms and other Things to us belonging, for fuch Goods and Merchandifes, to the Prejudice and Lofs of us, our Heirs and Succeffors, and alfo of the faid Mayor and Commonalty, and Citizens of the faid City, of the Fees and Sums of Money, fo as aforefaid refpectively limited, appointed, and ordained, by reafon of the Exercife of the Offices aforefaid or any of them: We therefore being willing to look after our Indemnity in this Behalf, and alfo to the Intent that the faid Mayor, and Commonalty, and Citizens, may the better detect the Frauds, Covins, and Deceits of all Perfons concealing and withdrawing the faid Goods and Merchandifes, and the Fees aforefaid, we do for us, our Heirs and Succeffors, give, and by thefe Prefents grant, to the faid Mayor and Commonalty, and Citizens, and their Succeffors, that the Mayor of the City aforefaid, for the Time being, and the fufficient Deputies, Servants or Officers of the faid Mayor, Commonalty, and Citizens of the City aforefaid, in that Behalf, from Time to Time, duly affigned, fhall and may have full Power and Authority to give and adminifter the Oath upon the Holy Evangelifts, from Time to Time, to all fuch

Persons suspected, or to be suspected of the said Withdrawings, Concealments, Colourings, Frauds, or Covins. And that it shall and may be lawful to the said Mayor, his Minister and Deputy, or Officer for the Time being, by all lawful Ways and Means to compel all such Persons suspected, or to be suspected, as shall refuse and deny to take the said Oath, to take the same Oath. Although express Mention of the true Yearly Value, or of the Certainty of the Premisses, or any of them, or of any other Gifts or Grants by us, or by any of our Progenitors or Predecessors, to the said Mayor and Commonalty, and Citizens of the City aforesaid, or any of them heretofore made, is not made in these Presents; or any Statute, Act, Ordinance, Provision, Proclamation, or Restraint to the contrary thereof, heretofore had, made, published, ordained or provided, or any other Thing, Cause, or Matter whatsoever, in any wise notwithstanding. In Witness whereof, we have caused these our Letters to be made Patents: Witness our Self, at Westminster, the fifth Day of September, in the sixteenth Year of our Reign.

The Duties of SCAVAGE, PACKAGE, BAILIAGE, and PORTAGE, payable to the City of London for all the Goods and Merchandises of Aliens, or Denizens born within the Allegiance of the British Crown, being the Sons of Aliens, born under Foreign Allegiance, imported into or exported out of the said City: granted to the Mayor and Commonalty, and Citizens, by their Charter dated the 5th Day of September, in the 16th Year of the Reign of King Charles the Second, confirmed by the 20th Rule of the Book of Rates, and by 2 William and Mary, Chap. 8.

Which said Duty of Scavage is by the Act of Navigation passed 12 Char. II. Chap. 18. Sect. 9. and the Acts of Frauds passed 13 and 14 Char. II. Chap. 11. Sect. 6. also payable for several Commodities, though of British Property, when imported in any other than Ships belonging to the People of Great Britain or Ireland, and whereof the Master and at least three Fourths of the Mariners, are British, or in Foreign built Ships, although owned and manned by British, unless such as are taken as Prize; and for Currants and Turkey Commodities, as well as all Goods, the Growth, Manufacture, or Production of Muscovy or Russia, imported in any other than British built Shipping, and navigated as aforesaid; the particular Species whereof are thus marked * in the following Table. Scavage (Sceavage or Shewage), is an antient Toll or Custom, exacted by Mayors, Sheriffs, &c. from Merchant Strangers, for Wares shewed or offered to Sale within their Precincts: but by the 19 Henry VII. Chap. 8. was prohibited to be levied, except by the Mayor and Commonalty of London.

By the 22 Henry VIII. Chap. 8. Sect. 2, 4. it is directed, that Tables thereof be set up in the City of London, approved and subscribed by the Chancellor and Treasurer of England, the President of the King's Council, Lord Privy Seal, Lord Steward of the Houshold, and the two Chief Justices of the King's Bench and Common Pleas, or four of them at the least.

EXTRACT of an Act 24 Geo. III. Chap. 16. to discontinue the Petty Customs on Aliens' Goods imported into Great Britain, &c. so far as it concerns the Duties of Package and Scavage, or any other Duties granted to the Mayor and Commonalty of the City of London.

Sect. 2. Provided always, and it is hereby farther enacted, that this Act shall not extend, or be construed to extend, to repeal or anywise alter the Duties, due and payable by any Act of Parliament, upon Goods imported into, or exported from this Kingdom, in any Foreign Ship or Vessel; nor to the Duties of Package and Scavage, or any Duties granted by Charter to the Mayor, and Commonalty, and Citizens, of the City of London.

Sect. 3. And the better to prevent the said Mayor, and Commonalty, and Citizens, from being fraudulently injured, be it enacted by the Authority aforesaid, that every Merchant or other, passing any Goods, Wares, or Merchandises, inwards or outwards, shall by himself or his known Servant, Factor, or Agent, subscribe one or more Bill or Bills of Entry, whether such Goods are on Alien or British Account, and if required, make Oath of the same before the Officer appointed to receive the said Duties (who is authorized, by the Charter granted to the said Mayor, and Commonalty, and Citizens, to administer the same); and no Entry on Alien Account shall be permitted by the Officer of the Customs to pass, or the Goods to be delivered, unless the Signature or Mark of the City's Collector, or his Deputy, appears on the Face of such Warrant; and if any Goods be entered on British Account, which are (*bona fide*) Aliens Property, the Merchant, or others entering the same, shall forfeit and pay the Sum of fifty Pounds, to be recovered by Action of Debt, Bill, Plaint, or Information, in any of his Majesty's Courts of Record at Westminster, in the Name of the Officer or Collector appointed to receive the said Dues, in Behalf of the said Mayor, and Commonalty, and Citizens; and the Damages so to be recovered shall be paid into the Chamber of London, for the Use of the said Mayor, and Commonalty, and Citizens.

These Duties further enforced by the 27 Geo. III. Chap. 13. as referred to by the Abstract of that Act, Page 16.

(398)

TABLE H.

The Scavage Rates Inwards, for all Goods and Merchandise imported from Parts beyond the Seas.

SCAVAGE.

	£.	s.	d.
Alum, the Hundred Weight containing 112 Pounds	0	0	2
Andirons, see Brass.			
Annotto, the Hundred Weight containing five Score	0	0	4
Apples and Pears, the little Barrel	0	0	1¼
*Aqua Vitæ, the Hogshead	0	0	6
Argol, white or red, the Hundred Weight containing 112 Pounds	0	0	1½
*Ashes, called Potashes, for every 20s. of the Rate	0	0	1
Babies Heads, the Dozen	0	0	0½
Bacon, the Hundred Weight containing 112 Pounds	0	0	3
Band-strings, the Dozen Knots	0	0	0¼
*Balks, viz.			
Great, the Hundred containing six Score	0	1	6
Middle, the Hundred containing six Score	0	0	9
Small, the Hundred containing six Score	0	0	4
*Barlings, the Hundred containing six Score	0	0	4

*Barley, the Quarter containing 8 Bushels	-	0	0 0½
Barilla, or Saphora, the Barrel containing two Hundred Weight	-	0	0 4
Basket Rods, the Dozen Bundles	-	0	0 4
Baft Ropes, the Hundred Weight containing 112 Pounds	-	0	0 0½
Battery, Bashrones, or Kettles, the Hundred Weight containing 112 Pounds	-	0	0 6
*Beans, the Quarter	-	0	0 0½
Beef, the Barrel	-	0	0 1
Bell Metal, the Hundred Weight containing 112 Pounds	-	0	0 2
Bermillians, see Fustians	-	0	0 2
Blackung, or Lamp-black, the Hundred Weight containing 112 Pounds	-	0	0 3
Bottles of all Sorts, the Dozen	-	0	0 0½
*Boards, viz.			
Barrel Boards, the Thousand	-	0	0 4
Clap Boards, the Hundred containing six Score	-	0	0 1
Pipe Boards, the Hundred containing six Score	-	0	0 1
Boratoes, or Bombasines, viz.			
Narrow, the single Piece not above 15 Yards	-	0	0 2
Broad, the single Piece not above 15 Yards	-	0	0 3
Books unbound, the Basket or Maund	-	0	0 8
*Bow Staves, the Hundred containing six Score	-	0	0 2

N.B. Those Goods marked * are liable to Scavage when imported by British Subjects in Foreign built or Foreign owned Ships.

(400)

TABLE H.
SCAVAGE.

	£	s.	d.
Brass Andirons, Laver Cocks, Chafing Dishes, and all other Brass or Latten wrought, the Hundred Pound containing five Score	0	0	3
Brimstone, the Hundred Weight containing 112 Pounds	0	0	0½
Bristles, the Dozen Pounds	0	0	0½
Buckrams viz.			
of Germany, the Dozen Pieces	0	0	3
of France, the Dozen Pieces	0	0	2
Buffins, Liles, or Mocadoes, viz.			
Narrow, the single Piece not above 15 Yards	0	0	1
Broad, the single Piece not above 15 Yards	0	0	2
Bullrushes, the Load	0	0	1
Burs for Millstones, the Hundred containing five Score	0	0	3
Butter, the Hundred Weight containing 112 Pounds	0	0	1
Cable Ropes for Cordage, the Hundred Weight containing 112 Pounds	0	0	1
Cabinets, viz.			
Great, the Piece	0	0	2
Small, the Piece	0	0	1
Caddas, or Cruel Ribbon, the Dozen Pieces, each Piece 36 Yards	0	0	1

Candlewick, the Hundred Weight containing 112 Pounds	-	1 0	1
Candles of Tallow, the Dozen Pounds	-	1 0	0¼
Capers, the Hundred Pounds containing five Score	-	1 0	2
*Capravens, the Hundred containing six Score	-	1 0	3
Cards, viz.			
Playing Cards, the small Groce containing 12 Dozen Pair	-	1 0	2
Wool Cards, the Dozen Pair	-	1 0	0¼
Carpets, viz.			
Turkey, Persia, East India and Venice, long, the Piece	-	1 0	6
of the same, or like Sort, short, the Piece	-	1 0	4
Carpets of all other Sorts, the Piece	-	1 0	0½
Cases, viz.			
for Looking Glasses, gilt, from No. 3. to No. 10. the Dozen	-	1 0	1½
for Looking Glasses, ungilt, the Dozen	-	1 0	0½
Catlings, see Lutestrings			
Chamlets, Mohairs, and Turkey Grograms, each 15 Yards	-	1 0	1½
Cheese, the Hundred Weight containing 112 Pounds	-	1 0	1
Cherries, the Hundred Weight containing 112 Pounds	-	1 0	1½
Cloth, viz.			
French Walloon, each 20 Yards	-	1 0	8
Scarlet, the Yard	-	1 0	1

(402)

TABLE H.
SCAVAGE.

	l.	*s.*	*d.*
Cochineal, viz.			
Silvester, or Campechea, the Pound - - -	0	0	0½
of all other Sorts, the Pound - - - -	0	0	1
Combs of Box or Light Wood, the Groce containing 12 Dozen -	0	0	0½
Copper Bricks, or Plates, round or square, the Hundred Weight containing 112 Pounds	0	0	4
Copperas, the Hundred Weight containing 112 Pounds - -	0	0	1
Coral, rough or polished, the Mast containing two Pounds and an Half	0	0	2
Cordage, see Cable Ropes.			
Cork, viz.			
The Hundred Weight containing 112 Pounds - -	0	0	1
The Dozen Pieces, for Shoemakers - - -	0	0	0¼
Corn, viz.			
Barley, fee in B.			
Beans, fee in B.			
Malt, fee in M.			
Oats, fee in O.			
Pease, fee in P.			
Rye, fee in R.			
Wheat, fee in W.			

(403)

Item	£	s	d
*Deal Boards of all Sorts, the Hundred containing six Score	—	0	1	0
Dogs of Earth, the small Groce containing 12 Dozen	—	0	0	1½
Durance or Duretties, viz.			
With Thread, each 15 Yards	—	0	0	1½
With Silk, each 15 Yards	—	0	0	2
Drugs, viz.			
Ambergris, the Ounce	—	0	0	1½
Aloes Succotrina, the Pound	—	0	0	0½
Barley hull'd, the Hundred Weight containing 112 Pounds	—	0	0	1
Carraway and Cummin Seeds, the Hundred Weight	—	0	0	1½
China Roots, the Hundred Pounds containing five Score	—	0	1	6
Civet, the Ounce	—	0	0	1
Coral, see in C.			
Frankincense, see in F.			
Gum Arabick, see in G.			
Gum Armoniack, the Hundred containing five Score	—	0	0	6
Musk, the Ounce	—	0	0	1
Cods, the Dozen	—	0	0	1
Quicksilver, see in Q.			
Saunders, white or red, the Hundred containing five Score	—	0	0	6
Treacle, common, the Hundred containing five Score	—	0	0	2
Turpentine, common, the Hundred Weight containing 112 Pounds	—	0	0	1

(404)

TABLE H.
SCAVAGE.

	l.	s.	d.
Earthern Ware, called Tiles, fee in T.			
Feathers for Beds, the Hundred Weight containing 112 Pounds	0	0	2
Fish, viz.			
Cod fish, the Hundred containing fix Score	0	0	4
Cole fish, the Hundred containing fix Score	0	0	1
Eels, the Barrel	0	0	1
Quick, the Ship's Lading	0	10	0
Herrings, white or red, the Laft	0	0	6
Lings, the Hundred containing fix Score	0	0	6
Lub Fish, the Hundred containing fix Score	0	0	2
Croplings, the Hundred containing fix Score	0	0	1
Titling, the Hundred containing fix Score	0	0	0½
Sturgeon, the Firkin	0	0	1
the Keg	0	0	0½
Salmon, the Barrel	0	0	1½
* Flax, viz.			
Undreffed, the Hundred Weight containing 112 Pounds	0	0	1½
Dreffed or wrought, the Hundred Weight containing 112 Pounds	0	0	4
Flox, the Hundred Weight containing 112 Pounds	0	0	2

(405)

Frankincense, the Hundred Weight containing 112 Pounds	—	0	1 1/2
Fustian, viz.			
Bernillians, the Piece, or two Half Pieces containing 15 Yards each Half Piece	—	0	2
Naples Fustian, Tripe, or Velure, the Piece containing 15 Yards	—	0	2
Furs, viz.			
Beaver Skins, the Piece	—	0	0 1/2
Beaver Bellies, or Wombs, the Dozen	—	0	4
Budge, tawed or untawed, the Hundred containing five Score	—	0	2
Fox Skins, the Hundred containing five Score	—	0	4
Foyns, without Tails, the Dozen	—	0	1 1/2
Galley Dishes, each 12 Dozen	—	0	1
Galls, the Hundred containing 112 Pounds	—	0	2
Glass, viz.			
for Windows, the Chest or Case	—	0	3
Venice Drinking Glasses, the Dozen	—	0	0 1/2
Looking Glasses, viz.			
Halfpenny Ware, the Groce containing 12 Dozen	—	0	0 1/4
Penny Ware, the Groce containing 12 Dozen	—	0	0 1/2
of Steel, small, the Dozen	—	0	0 1/2
large, the Dozen	—	0	1
of Crystal, small, the Dozen under No. 6	—	0	1

(406)

TABLE H.
SCAVAGE.

	l.	s.	d.
Looking Glasses, viz.			
of Crystal, the Dozen, No. 7, 8, 9, 10 -	0	0	4
middle Sort, the Dozen, No. 6 -	0	0	2
the Dozen, No. 11 and 12 -	0	1	6
Glass Stone Plates for Spectacles, the Dozen -	0	0	0½
Glass Plates, or Sights for Looking Glasses unfoiled, viz.			
of Crystal, small, under No. 6, the Dozen -	0	0	0½
No. 6, the Dozen -	0	0	1
No. 7, 8, 9, 10 -	0	0	2
No. 11, 12, the Dozen -	0	1	0
Gloves of Spanish Leather, the Dozen Pair -	0	0	0½
Goats Hair, the Hundred Pounds, containing five Score -	0	0	6
Grain for Dyers, viz.			
of Scarlet Powder, the Pound -	0	0	0½
of Sevil in Berries, and Grains of Portugal or Rotta, the Pound -	0	0	0¼
Grocery, viz.			
Almonds, the Hundred Weight containing 112 Pounds -	0	0	3
Annifeeds, the Hundred Weight containing 112 Pounds -	0	0	2
Cinnamon, the Hundred containing five Score -	0	1	0
Cloves, the Hundred containing five Score -	0	1	6

† *Currants, the Hundred Weight containing 112 Pounds — 0 0 2
† N. B. Not only Currants, but all Turkey Commodities, are chargeable according to the Act of 12 Charles II. in the Preface.
Dates, the Hundred Weight containing 112 Pounds — 0 0 4
* Figs, the Hundred Weight containing 112 Pounds — 0 0 1
Fuffes of Cloves, the Hundred Pounds containing five Score — 0 0 8
Ginger, the Hundred Pounds containing five Score — 0 1 0
Liquorice, the Hundred containing 112 Pounds — 0 0 1½
Mace, the Hundred containing five Score — 0 0 6
Nutmegs, the Hundred containing five Score — 0 2 6
Pepper, the Hundred containing five Score — 0 1 6
* Prunes, the Hundred containing 112 Pounds — 0 0 1
* Raisins, great or Malaga, the Hundred containing 112 Pounds — 0 0 1
  of the Sun, the Hundred Weight containing 112 Pounds — 0 0 2
* Sugar, Refined, the Hundred containing 112 Pounds — 0 0 10
  Candy brown, or white, the Hundred Weight — 0 0 8
  Muscovadoes, and white, the Hundred Weight — 0 0 4
  St. Thome and Pannelles, the Hundred Weight — 0 0 2

Grogram, fee Chamlets.
Gunpowder, the Barrel containing 112 Pounds — 0 0 3
Gum Arabick, the Hundred Weight containing 112 Pounds — 0 0 2
Hair, called Goats Hair, fee in G.

TABLE H.

SCAVAGE.

	l.	*s.*	*d.*
Hawks of all Sorts, the Hawk Hats, viz.	0	0	2
Baſt or Straw Hats knotted, the Dozen	0	0	0¼
Baſt or Straw Hats plain, the Groce containing 12 Dozen	0	0	1½
Wool Felts, the Dozen	0	0	1
Demi Caſtors, the Piece	0	0	0½
Beaver Hats, the Piece	0	0	2
* Headings for Pipes, Hogſheads, or Barrels, the Thouſand	0	0	2
Heath for Bruſhes, the Hundred Weight containing 112 Pounds	0	0	1
*Hemp, viz.			
undreſſed, the Hundred Weight containing 112 Pounds	0	0	1
dreſſed, the Hundred Weight containing 112 Pounds	0	0	2
Hides, viz.			
Buff Hides, the Piece	0	0	0½
Cow Hides, or Horſe Hides, the Dozen Hides	0	0	3
Honey, the Barrel	0	0	1½
Horſes and Mares, each Horſe or Mare	0	0	6
Hops, the Hundred Weight	0	0	2
Indico, the Hundred Pounds containing five Score	0	2	6

Indico Dust, the Hundred Pounds containing five Score	1	0	8
Incle, viz.			
wrought, the Dozen Pounds	0	0	$1\tfrac{1}{2}$
Rolls, the Dozen Pieces, containing 36 Yards, each Piece	0	0	1
unwrought, the Hundred Pounds containing five Score	0	0	4
Iron wrought, the Hundred containing 112 Pounds	0	0	1
Iron unwrought, the Ton	0	0	6
Iron Pots, the Dozen	0	0	$1\tfrac{1}{2}$
Juice of Lemons, fee Lemons.			
Lampblack, fee Blacking.			
Latten, viz.			
fhaven Latten, the Hundred Weight containing 112 Pounds	0	0	6
black Latten, the Hundred Weight containing 112 Pounds	0	0	3
Lace, viz.			
Bone Lace of Thread, the Dozen Yards	0	0	$0\tfrac{1}{2}$
Silk Bone Lace, the Pound containing 16 Ounces	0	0	2
Silk Lace of all other Sorts, the Pound containing 16 Ounces	0	0	1
Lemons, viz.			
the Thousand	0	0	1
Juice of Lemons, the Pipe	0	0	6
Pickled Lemons, the Pipe	0	0	3

(410)

TABLE H.

SCAVAGE.

	l.	s.	d.
Linseed, the Quarter	0	0	1
Leaves of Gold, the Hundred Leaves containing five Score	0	0	0½
Lines for Hawks, the Dozen	0	0	0½
Leather, viz.			
Bazil Leather, the Dozen Skins	0	0	0¼
Hangings, gilt, the Piece	0	0	3
Leather for Masks, the Dozen Pounds	0	0	2
Lutes, the Dozen	0	0	4
Lutestrings, viz.			
Catlings, great Groce containing 12 small Groce of Knots	0	0	1
Minikins, the Groce containing 12 Dozen Knots	0	0	0½
Linen, Brabant, Flemish, Embden, viz.			
British Cloth, the Hundred Ells containing five Score	0	0	2
Frieze Cloth, Ghentish Holland, Isinghams, Overissels Cloth, Rows, Cowfield, or Plats Cloth, each 30 Ells	0	0	2
Calicos, or Dutties, the Piece	0	0	0½
Cambricks, the whole Piece containing 13 Ells	0	0	2
Damask for Tabling, viz.			
of Holland making, the Dozen Yards	0	0	4
of Silesia making, the Dozen Yards	0	0	2

Damask for Towelling and Napkining, viz.			
of Holland making, the Dozen Yards	—	0 0	2
of Silesia making, the Dozen	—	0 0	1
Diaper for Tabling, viz.			
of Holland making, the Dozen Yards	—	0 0	2
of Silesia making, the Dozen Yards	—	0 0	1
Diaper for Towelling and Napkining, viz.			
of Holland making, the Dozen Yards	—	0 0	1
of Silesia making, the Dozen Yards	—	0 0	0½
French or Normandy Canvas, and Line Narrow, Vandales, or Vitry Canvas, Dutch Barras, and Heffens Canvas, the Hundred Ells containing six Score	—	0	2
Gutting and Spruce Canvas, Drillings, Pack Duck, Hinderlings, Middle good, Headlake, Muscovia, Line Narrow, Hamburg Cloth, Narrow Irish Cloth, the Hundred Ells containing six Score	—	0 0	1
Hamburg and Silesia Cloth, Broad, the Hundred Ells containing six Score	—	0 0	3
Poledavies, the Bolt	—	0 0	1
French Canvas and Line, Ell and ½ Quarter broad, or upwards, the six Score Ells	—	0 0	3
Lawns, the whole Piece containing 13 Ells	—	0 0	2
Calico Lawns, the Piece	—	0 0	0½
French Lawns, the Piece	—	0 0	1½
Lockrams, the Piece, of all Sorts, containing 106 Ells	—	0 0	1½
Soultwich, the Hundred Ells containing six Score	—	0 0	1½

TABLE H.
SCAVAGE.

	l.	s.	d.
Linen, Strasburg Linen, each 30 Ells	0	0	1
Striped or tufted Canvas with Thread, the Piece containing 15 Yards	0	0	1
Striped, tufted, or quilted Canvas with Silk, the Piece containing 15 Yards	0	0	1
Litmus, the Hundred Weight containing 112 Pounds	0	0	1
*Malt, the Quarter	0	0	0½
Magnus, the Hundred Weight containing 112 Pounds	0	0	1
Masks of Velvet or Satin, the Dozen	0	0	1
*Masts, viz.			
great, the Mast	0	0	2
middle, the Mast	0	0	1
small, the Mast	0	0	0½
Maps, printed, the Ream	0	0	1
Madder, viz.			
Crop Madder, and all other Bale Madder, the Hundred Weight containing 112 Pounds	0	0	2
Fat Madder, the Hundred Weight containing 112 Pounds	0	0	1½
Mull Madder, the Hundred Weight containing 112 Pounds	0	0	0½
*Meal, the Last containing 12 Barrels	0	0	4

(413)

Minikins, see Lutestrings.					
Mocado Ends, the Dozen Pounds	-	-	-	0	1½
Mohairs, see Chamlets.					
*Oars, the Hundred containing six Score	-	-	-	0	4
*Oats, the Quarter	-	-	-	0	0½
Oils, viz.					
*Sevil Oil, Majorca Oil, Minorca Oil, Provence, Portugal Oil, and Sallad Oil, the Tun	-	-	-	2	8
Rape and Linseed Oil, the Tun	-	-	-	2	6
Train Oil of Greenland or Newfoundland, the Tun	-	-	-	1	4
Olives, the Hogshead	-	-	-	0	4
Onions, viz.					
the Hundred Bunches	-	-	-	0	1
Seed, the Hundred Weight containing 112 Pounds	-	-	-	0	3
Oranges, the Thousand	-	-	-	0	1
Orchal, the Hundred Weight containing 112 Pounds	-	-	-	0	1½
Packthread, the Hundred Pounds containing five Score	-	-	-	0	1½
Pans, viz.					
Dripping or Frying Pans, the Hundred containing 112 Pounds	-	-	-	0	1½
Warming Pans, the Dozen	-	-	-	0	1½

(414)

TABLE H.
SCAVAGE.

	£.	s.	d.
Paper, viz.			
Brown, the Hundred Bundles	0	0	6
of all other Sorts, each five Score Reams	0	1	8
Pears, see Apples.			
*Peafe the Quarter	0	0	0½
*Pitch or Tar, the Laſt	0	0	3
Plates, viz.			
ſingle, white or black, the Hundred Plates	0	0	1
double, white or black, the Hundred Plates	0	0	2
Pomegranates, the Thouſand	0	0	2
Pork, the Barrel	0	0	1½
Pots, viz.			
of Earth or Stone, covered, the Hundred containing five Score	0	0	1
of Earth or Stone, uncovered, the Hundred Caſt, containing a Gallon to every Caſt, whether in one Pot or no	0	0	2
Quails, the Dozen	0	0	0¼
Quickſilver, the Hundred containing five Score	0	0	10
Quinces, the Hundred containing five Score	0	0	0½

(415)

Item	£	s	d
Rape Seed, the Quarter	0	0	1
* Rosin, the Ton	0	0	8
Rice, the Hundred Weight containing 112 Pounds	0	0	1
* Rye, the Quarter	0	0	0½
Rims for Sieves, the Groce containing 12 Dozen	0	0	0½
* N.B. All Goods of the Growth, Production, or Manufacture of Muscovy or Russia, for every 20s. of their Rates, or Values, on Oath	0	0	1
Saffron, the Pound	0	0	0½
Safflower, the Hundred Pounds containing five Score	0	0	4
* Salt, the Wey	0	0	2
Salt-petre the Hundred containing 112 Pounds	0	0	1½
Says, viz.			
Double Says, or Flanders Serges, the Piece	0	0	3
Haunscot, and mild Says, the Piece	0	0	2
Shumac, the Hundred containing 112 Pounds	0	0	1½
Silk, viz.			
Bridges, Granados, Naples, Organzine, Pole, and Spanish Satin Silk, Sleeve Silk, fine and thrown Silk, the Pound containing 16 Ounces	0	0	1
Raw China Silk, the Pound containing 24 Ounces	0	0	1
Ferret or Floret Silk, Fillozel, Sleeve Silk coarse, the Pound containing 16 Ounces	0	0	0¼
Raw long Silk, the Pound containing 24 Ounces	0	0	0½

TABLE H.

SCAVAGE.

	£	s.	d.
Silk, Raw short Silk, and Raw Morea Silk, the Pound containing 24 Ounces	0	0	0½
Silk Stockings, the Pair	0	0	1½
Silks wrought, viz.			
Boratos of Silk, Catalophers, China, Damask, Silk Chamlet, China, Grograms, Tabby Grograms, Philofellos, narrow Tabbies of Silk, Towers Taffaty, the Dozen Yards	0	0	2
Silk Grograms narrow, Silk Say, Calamancos and Philofellos broad, the Dozen Yards	0	0	3
Grograms broad, Caffa or Damask, the Dozen Yards	0	0	4
Satins, of Bolonia, Lukes, Jeans, others of like making, the Dozen Yards	0	0	6
Bridges, China, and Turkey Satin, the Dozen Yards	0	0	1
Sarsenets, of Bolonia or Florence, the Dozen Ells	0	0	1¼
of China, the Dozen Ells	0	0	1
Sypers, of Silk, broad, the Dozen Yards	0	0	0½
of Silk, narrow, each 24 Yards	0	0	0¼
Taffaty, Fill broad, each Dozen Yards	0	0	2
China and Levant, each Dozen Yards	0	0	0½
Velvets, China Velvets, each Dozen Yards	0	0	1
All other Velvets or Plushes, each Dozen Yards	0	0	6
Skins, viz.			
Cordivant Skins, the Dozen	0	0	2

(417)

	l	s	d
Goat Skins, in the Hair, the Dozen	—	0	0	5
Kid Skins of all Sorts, the Hundred containing five Score	—	0	0	2
Smalts, the Hundred containing five Score	—	0	0	4
*Spars, viz.				
Boomspars, the Hundred containing six Score	—	0	0	3
Cantspars, the Hundred containing six Score	—	0	0	2
Small Spars, the Hundred containing six Score	—	0	0	1
*Spirits, as Brandy, &c. for every 20s. of their Rates, or Values on Oath	—	0	0	1
Stocking of Silk, see Silk				
Stones, viz.				
Dog Stones, the Last	—	0	0	6
Marble Stones, the Ton	—	0	0	8
Mill Stones, the Piece	—	0	0	6
Quern Stones, the Last	—	0	0	3
Sword Blades, the Dozen	—	0	0	1
*Staves, viz.				
Pipe or Hogshead Staves, the Thousand	—	0	0	6
Barrel Staves, the Thousand	—	0	0	3
Firkin Staves, the Thousand	—	0	0	1½
Steel, viz.				
Long Steel, Whisp Steel, and such like, the Hundred Weight containing 112 Pounds	—	0	0	2
Gad Steel, the Half Barrel	—	0	0	4

E e

(418)

TABLE H.
SCAVAGE.

	l.	s.	d.
Sturgeon, fee in Fish.	—	—	—
Succades, wet or dry, the Hundred containing five Score	0	0	10
*Syder, the Tun	0	0	4
Tallow, the Hundred Weight, containing 112 Pounds	0	0	1
Tapestry, viz.			
with Hair, the Hundred Flemish Ells containing five Score	0	0	4
with Wool, the Hundred Flemish Ells containing five Score	0	0	6
with Caddas, the Hundred Flemish Ells containing five Score	0	1	0
with Silk, the Dozen Flemish Ells	0	0	2
Tarras, the Barrel	0	0	0¼
Teazels, the Thousand	0	0	0¼
Tykes of all Sorts, the Tyke	0	0	1½
Thread, viz.			
Bridges Thread, the Dozen Pounds	0	0	1
Outnal Thread, the Dozen Pounds	0	0	1
Whited Brown, or piecing Thread, the Dozen Pounds	0	0	1½
Sifters Thread, the Pound	0	0	0½
Lyons or Paris Thread, the Bale containing an Hundred Bolts	0	0	8

Tobacco, viz.

Spanish, Varinas, Brasil Tobacco, the Hundred containing five Score	—	0	2	0
St. Christopher's Tobacco, or the like, the Hundred Pound containing five Score	—	0	0	6
Tiles, called Pan Tiles, or Flanders Tiles, the Thousand	—	0	0	2
*Timbers, for every 20s. of their Rates, or Values on Oath	—	0	0	1
Tow, the Hundred containing 112 Pounds	—	0	0	0½
Tripe, see Fustians.				
*Turkey Goods, for every 20s. of their Rates or Values on Oath	—	0	0	1

Vellure, see Fustians.
Vinegar, see Wine Eager.

Wax, the Hundred containing 112 Pounds	—	0	0	4
*Wainscots, the Hundred containing five Score	—	0	0	6
Whale Fins, the Dozen Fins	—	0	0	4
*Wheat, the Quarter containing eight Bushels	—	0	0	1
*Wine, viz.				
Eager, the Tun	—	0	0	6
Gascoign, French Wines, all other Wines of the Growth of the French King's Dominions, the Tun	—	0	2	0
Rhenish Wine, the Awm	—	0	0	6
Muscadel, all other Wines of the Growth of the Levant, the Butt	—	0	1	0

(420)

TABLE H.
SCAVAGE.

	£	s.	d.
Wine, viz.			
Sacks, Canaries, Malagas, Madeiras, Romneys, Bastards, Tents, and Alicants, the Butt or Pipe -	0	1	0
Wire, called Latten Wire, and all other Wire, the Hundred Weight containing 112 Pounds	0	0	4
Woad, viz.			
Island Woad, the Ton -	0	1	0
Tholose Woad, the Hundred Weight containing 112 Pounds -	0	0	1
Wood, viz.			
*Boxwood, the Thousand Pieces -	0	0	2
Brasil, or Fernambuco Wood, the Hundred Weight containing 112 Pounds -	0	0	3
Braziletto, or Jamaica Wood, the Hundred Weight containing 112 Pounds -	0	0	1
Fustick, the Hundred containing 112 Pounds -	0	0	$0\frac{1}{2}$
Red, or Guinea Wood, the Hundred Weight containing 112 Pounds -	0	0	2
Sweet Wood of West India, the Hundred Weight containing 112 Pounds -	0	0	1
All other Sorts, for every 20s. of the Rates, or Value on Oath -	0	0	1
Wool, viz.			
Beaver Wool, the Pound -	0	0	$1\frac{1}{2}$
Cotton Wool, the Hundred Pounds containing five Score -	0	0	3
Irish, combed, the Hundred containing five Score -	0	0	4
uncombed, the Hundred Weight containing 112 Pounds -	0	0	2

(421)

Estridge Wool, the Hundred Weight containing 112 Pounds — — 0 0 2
Polonia Wool, the Hundred Weight containing 112 Pounds — — 0 0 3
French Wool, the Hundred Weight containing 112 Pounds — — 0 0 2
Lambs Wool, the Hundred Weight containing 112 Pounds — — 0 0 3
Spanish Wool, the Hundred Weight containing 112 Pounds — — 0 0 4
Red Wool, the Pound — — — — 0 0 0¼

Yarn, viz.
Cable Yarn, the Hundred Weight containing 112 Pounds — 0 0 1
Camel, Grogram, or Mohair Yarn, the Hundred containing five Score — 0 1 6
Cotton Yarn, the Hundred containing five Score — — 0 0 4
Irish Yarn, the Pack containing four Hundred Weight at six Score Pounds to the Hundred — — — 0 0 6
Raw Linen Yarn, Dutch or French, the Hundred containing five Score — 0 0 4
Spruce or Muscovia Yarn, the Hundred Weight containing 112 Pounds — 0 0 2

All other Goods not mentioned in this Table, shall pay for Scavage Duties Inwards, after the Rate of one Penny in the Pound, according as they are expressed or valued in His Majesty's late Book of Rates; and all other not expressed therein shall pay the same Rates, according to the true Value.

All Merchants, Aliens and Denizens, are to make and deliver to the proper Collector of this Duty, true and perfect Bills of Entry of all the Goods and Merchandise by them imported.

TABLE I.

The PACKAGE RATES OUTWARDS, for all Goods and Merchandife, to be packed, cafked, piped, barrelled, or any ways veffelled, in order to be tranfported to Parts beyond the Seas; although the Mayor and Commonalty, or their Officers, do not pack the faid Goods when they are ready, and upon reafonable Requeft and Notice given.

PACKAGE.	£.	s.	d.
Annotto, the Hundred containing five Score Pounds	0	0	3
Aqua Vitæ, the Hogfhead	0	0	4
Argol, white or red, the Hundred Weight containing 112 Pounds	0	0	$1\frac{1}{2}$
Afhes, viz.			
Pot Afhes, the Barrel containing two Hundred Weight	0	0	2
Soap Afhes, the Laft	0	1	0
Awl Blades for Shoemakers, the Thoufand	0	0	$0\frac{1}{2}$
Barilla or Saphora, the Barrel containing two Hundred Weight	0	0	4
Beer, the Tun	0	0	6
Birding Shot Lead, the Hundred Weight containing 112 Pounds	0	0	2
Books, the Maund	0	1	0
Bottles of Glafs covered with Leather, the Dozen	0	0	1

(423)

Brimstone, the Hundred Weight containing 112 Pounds	—	—	0	1
Brushes, the Dozen	—	—	0	0½
Broken Glass, the Barrel	—	—	0	0¼
Buttons, called Brass, Steel, Copper, or Latten Buttons, the great Groce containing 12 small Groce	—	—	0	1
Hair Buttons, the great Groce	—	—	0	1
Silk Buttons, the great Groce	—	—	0	1½
Thread Buttons, the great Groce	—	—	0	1¼
Buckweed, the Quarter	—	—	0	1
Buckrams of all Sorts, the Dozen Pieces	—	—	0	2
Caps for Sailors, Monmouth, and others, the Dozen	—	—	0	1
Canary Seed, the Bushel	—	—	0	0½
Cloaks, old, the Piece	—	—	0	0½
Cloths, see Woollen Drapery.				
Coals, see Sea Coals in S.				·
Cobweb Lawns, each 12 Yards	—	—	0	1
Cochineal, viz.				
Silvester, or Campechia, the Pound	—	—	0	0½
of all other Sorts, the Pound	—	—	0	1
Combs Ivory, see Ivory.				
Copperas, the Hundred Weight containing 112 Pounds	—	—	0	1

(424)

TABLE I.

PACKAGE.	*L. s. d.*
Drugs, called Affafoetida, Gum Armoniack, Gum Lack, Olibanum, and Saffafras Wood, the Hundred containing five Score Pounds	1 0 0 6
Caffia Fiftula, the Hundred containing five Score	1 0 0 8
Lignea, the Hundred containing five Score	1 0 0 8
Cubebs, the Hundred containing five Score	1 0 0 6
Frankincenfe, fee in F.	
Quickfilver, fee in S.	
Red Lead, fee in R.	1 0 0 1
Rhubarb, the Pound	1 0 0 1
Scamony, the Pound	
Wormfeeds, fee in W.	
Elephants Teeth, the Hundred containing five Score Pounds	1 0 0 4
Eftridge Feathers, undreffed, the Pound	1 0 0 0½
Feathers, called Eftridge Feathers, fee in E.	
Filing of Iron, called Swarf, the Barrel	1 0 0 2
Fifh, *viz*	
Herrings full or fhotten, the Laft	1 0 0 6

Stockfish of all Sorts, the Last	—	0	0	6
Flasks of Horn, the Dozen	—	0	0	1
Flax, viz.				
dressed, the Hundred Weight containing 112 Pounds	—	0	0	4
undressed, the Hundred Weight containing 112 Pounds	—	0	0	2
Frankincense, the Hundred Weight containing 112 Pounds	—	0	0	1½
Furs, fee Skins.				
Fustians, viz.				
English Millain, the Piece containing 2 Half Pieces of 15 Yards the Piece	—	0	0	1
Venetian, English make, each 15 Yards	—	0	0	1
Galls, the Hundred Weight containing 112 Pounds	—	0	0	2
Garble, viz.				
of Almonds, the Hundred Weight containing 112 Pounds	—	0	0	1
of Cloves, the Hundred Pounds containing five Score	—	0	0	4
of Ginger, the Hundred Pounds containing five Score	—	0	0	1
of Mace, the Hundred Pounds containing five Score	—	0	0	9
of Pepper, the Hundred Pounds containing five Score	—	0	0	3
Glass, broken, fee in B.				
Glew, the Hundred Weight containing 112 Pounds	—	0	0	1
Glovers Clippings, the Maund or Basket	—	0	0	1½

TABLE I.

PACKAGE.	L.	s.	d.
Gloves, viz.			
Bucks Leather, the Dozen Pair - - -	0	0	1
Gloves with Silk Fringe, faced with Taffaty, the Dozen Pair	0	0	1
Gloves lined with Coney or Lamb Skin, or plain, the Dozen Pair	0	0	0½
Grains, viz.			
Scarlet Powder, and of Sevil in Berries, and Grain of Portugal, or Rotta, the Hundred Pounds - - - -	0	2	6
Grain, French or Guinea, the Hundred Pounds -	0	0	4
Grocery, called Almonds, the Hundred Weight containing 112 Pounds	0	0	2
Almonds, Garble; fee Garble.			
Anniseeds, the Hundred Weight containing 112 Pounds -	0	0	2
Cinnamon, the Hundred Pounds containing five Score	0	1	0
Cloves, the Hundred Weight containing 112 Pounds -	0	1	0
Cloves, Garble; fee Garble			
Currants, the Hundred Weight containing 112 Pounds	0	0	3
Dates, the Hundred Weight containing 112 Pounds -	0	0	4
Figs, the Hundred Weight containing 112 Pounds	0	0	0½
Ginger, the Hundred Pounds containing five Score	0	0	9
Ginger, Garble; fee Garble.			

Liquorice, the Hundred Weight containing 112 Pounds	—	0	0	1 1/2
Mace, the Hundred Pounds containing five Score	—	0	1	6
Mace, Garble; fee Garble.				
Nutmegs, the Hundred containing five Score	—	0	1	0
Pepper, the Hundred containing five Score	—	0	0	6
Pepper, Garble; fee Garble.				
Prunes, the Hundred Weight containing 112 Pounds	—	0	0	0 1/2
Raisins Great, and Malaga, the Hundred Weight containing 112 Pounds	—	0	0	1
Raisins of the Sun, the Hundred Weight containing 112 Pounds	—	0	0	2
Sugar Candy, the Hundred Weight containing 112 Pounds	—	0	0	8
Sugar of St. Thome and Panelles, the Hundred Weight containing 112 Pounds	—	0	0	3
Sugar of all Sorts, the Hundred Weight containing 112 Pounds	—	0	0	6

Hats, viz.

Beaver Hats, the Piece	—	0	0	2
Demy Castors, the Piece	—	0	0	1
Felt Hats, plain, the Dozen	—	0	0	1 1/2
Felt Hats, lined or faced, the Dozen	—	0	0	2

Hair, viz.

Coney Hair, the Hundred Pounds containing five Score	—	0	0	4
of Goats or Kids, the Hundred containing five Score	—	0	0	4

TABLE I.

PACKAGE.

	£	s.	d.
Hair, viz.			
Ox or Cow Tail Hair, the Hundred Weight containing 112 Pounds	0	0	0½
Hemp, the Hundred Weight containing 112 Pounds	0	0	1½
Hides, India; see India.			
Horns, viz.			
Ink Horns, the small Groce containing 12 Dozen	0	0	0½
Horns of Lanthorns, the Thousand Leaves	0	0	2
Tips of Horns, the Thousand	0	0	1
Hops, the Hundred Weight containing 112 Pounds	0	0	2
Indico of all Sorts, the Hundred Pounds containing five Score	0	1	0
Indico Dust, the Hundred Pounds containing five Score	0	0	6
India Hides, the Hundred containing five Score	0	1	6
Irish Rugs, the Piece	0	0	1
Iron, viz.			
the Ton, unwrought			
wrought, the Hundred Weight containing 112 Pounds	0	0	6
Spurs, the Dozen Pair	0	0	1
Ivory Combs, the Dozen Pounds	0	0	2

Knives, called London Knives, ordinary, the small Groce	—	0	0	3
Sheffield Knives, the small Groce	—	0	0	$1\frac{1}{2}$
Shoemakers paring Knives, the small Groce	—	0	0	$0\frac{1}{2}$
Lace, viz.			
Bone Lace of Thread, the Dozen Yards	—	0	0	$0\frac{1}{2}$
Silk Lace, the Pound containing 16 Ounces	—	0	0	$1\frac{1}{2}$
Lamperns, the Thousand	—	0	0	$1\frac{1}{2}$
Lead, the Fother	—	0	0	8
Lead, fee Birding Shot.			
Lemons, pickled the Pipe	—	0	0	3
Lemon Juice, the Pipe	—	0	0	6
Linseed, the Quarter	—	0	0	1
Linen, called Calico, the Piece	—	0	0	$0\frac{1}{2}$
Cambricks, two Half Pieces containing 13 Ells	—	0	0	$1\frac{1}{2}$
Damask, for Tabling, of all Sorts, the Dozen Yards	—	0	0	2
Damask, for Towelling and Napkining, of all Sorts, the Dozen Yards	—	0	0	1
Diaper for Tabling of all Sorts, the Dozen Yards	—	0	0	$0\frac{1}{2}$
Diaper for Towelling and Napkining, of all Sorts, the Dozen Yards	—	0	0	$1\frac{1}{2}$
Lawns, the Piece containing 13 Ells			
Linen Cloth, called Brabant, Embden, Flemish, Freeze, Ghentish, Holland, Isinghams, Overissels, and Rouse Cloth, each 30 Ells	—	0	0	2

TABLE I.

PACKAGE.	£	s.	d.
Linen, viz.			
French and Normandy Canvas, the 100 Ells containing fix Score	0	0	3
Dutch Barras, Heffens, Vitry Canvas, the Hundred Ells containing fix Score	0	0	3
Canvas tufted, or quilted with Copper, Silk or Thread, or such like, the Piece containing 15 Yards	0	0	1
Linen Shreds, the Maund	0	0	2
Madder, all but Mull Madder, the Hundred Weight containing 112 Pounds	0	0	2
Melaſſes, the Hogſhead	0	0	4
Muſtard Seed, the Hundred Weight containing 112 Pounds	0	0	0½
Nails, viz.			
Chair Nails, Braſs or Copper, the Thouſand	0	0	0½
Copper Nails, Roſe Nails, and Sadlers Nails, the Sum containing 10000	0	0	0½
Oaker, red or yellow, the Hundred Weight containing 112 Pounds	0	0	1
Onion Seed, the Hundred Weight containing 112 Pounds	0	0	4
Orchal, the Hundred Weight containing 112 Pounds	0	0	1
Ox Bones, the Thouſand	0	0	1
Ox Guts, the Barrel	0	0	2

(431)

Item	£	s	d
Oil, viz.			
Sevil, Majorca, Minorca Oil, Provence, Portugal, Linseed, or Rape Oil, the Tun	0	1	4
Train or Whale Oil, the Tun	0	0	8
Paper, Printing and Copy Paper, the Hundred Reams containing five Score	—	—	—
Pewter, the Hundred Weight containing 112 Pounds	0	1	6
Points of Thread, see in T.	0	0	4
Rape Seed, the Quarter	0	0	1
Rape Cakes, the Thousand	0	0	0½
Red Lead, the Hundred Weight containing 112 Pounds	0	0	1
Red Earth, the Hundred Weight containing 112 Pounds	0	0	0¼
Rice, the Hundred Weight containing 112 Pounds	0	0	1
Rosin, the Ton	0	0	6
Rugs, Irish; see Irish.			
Saffron, the Pound	0	0	1
Salt, the Wey	0	0	2
Salt Petre, the Hundred Weight containing 112 Pounds	0	0	2
Sea Horse Teeth, the Hundred Pounds containing five Score	0	0	10
Sea Coals, the Chalder	0	0	4
Shot, see Birding Shot Lead.			

(432)

TABLE I.

PACKAGE.	£.	s.	d.
Shumac, the Hundred Weight containing 112 Pounds	0	0	2
Silk, viz.			
Raw of all Sorts, the Pound containing 16 Ounces	0	0	1
Nubs or Husks of Silk, the Hundred containing 21 Ounces the Pound	0	0	4
British Thrown, the Pound containing 16 Ounces	0	0	1
Silver, called Quicksilver, the Hundred containing five Score	0	0	8
Skins and Furs, viz.			
Badger Skins, the Hundred containing five Score	0	0	6
Beaver Skins, the Hundred containing five Score	0	2	6
Cat Skins, the Hundred containing five Score	0	0	4
Calve Skins, the Hundred containing five Score	0	0	8
Coney Skins grey, tawed, seasoned, or stag, the Hundred containing six Score	0	0	2
Coney Skins, black, the Hundred containing six Score	0	0	$2\frac{1}{2}$
Elk Skins, the Piece	0	0	$0\frac{1}{2}$
Fitches, the Timber	0	0	1
Fox Skins, the Hundred containing five Score	0	0	8
Jennet Skins, black, seasoned or raw, the Skin	0	0	$0\frac{1}{2}$
Kid Skins, the Hundred containing five Score	0	0	2
Lamb Skins, tawed, or in Oil, the Hundred containing six Score	0	0	6

(433)

Morkins, tawed or raw, the Hundred containing six Score	-	0	0 4
Otter Skins, the Hundred containing five Score	-	0	0 8
Rabbit Skins, the Hundred containing five Score	-	0	0 1
Sheep Skins, the Hundred containing six Score	-	0	0 6
Sheep Pelts, the Hundred containing five Score	-	0	0 3
Squirrel Skins, the Thousand	-	0	0 3
Slip, the Barrel	-	0	0 1
Soap, viz.			
Hard Castle, the Hundred Weight containing 112 Pounds	-	0	0 2
the Barrel	-	0	0 3
Spectacles without Cases, the 12 Dozen	-	0	0 0½
Stockings, viz.			
Children's Stockings, the Dozen Pair	-	0	0 0½
Kersey or Leather, the Dozen Pair	-	0	0 1
Silk Stockings, the Pair	-	0	0 0½
Worsted Stockings, the Dozen Pair	-	0	0 2
Woollen knit Stockings, the Dozen Pair	-	0	0 1½
Stuffs, called Buffins, the Piece, broad, containing 14 Yards	-	0	0 2
the Piece, narrow, containing 14 Yards	-	0	0 1
Bridgewaters, the Piece	-	0	0 2
Carrels, the Piece	-	0	0 1
Camelians, the Piece containing 25 Yards	-	0	0 2

F f

TABLE I.

PACKAGE.	£	s.	d.
Stuffs called Chamlets or Grograms, the Piece containing 14 or 15 Yards	0	0	2
Dammofellos, or Damafins, the Piece	0	0	2
Durants, the Piece	0	0	1
Dimity, each thirty Yards	0	0	1
Floramedos, the Piece	0	0	1
Figurettos	0	0	2
Hangings of Briftol, or ftriped Stuff, the Piece	0	0	4
Linfey Woolfey, the Piece	0	0	1½
Liles, the Piece, broad or narrow, not above 15 Yards	0	0	2
Mocados, fingle or tufted, the Piece containing 14 Yards	0	0	1
Mocados, double, the Piece containing 28 Yards	0	0	2
Mohairs, the Piece not above 15 Yards	0	0	1½
Mifcellauny, the Piece containing 30 Yards	0	0	1
Perpetuanas, Yard broad, the Piece	0	0	2
Perpetuanas, the Piece Ell broad	0	0	2½
Paragon, or Parapus, the Piece	0	0	2
Pyramides or Marinuff, the narrow Piece	0	0	1
the broad Piece	0	0	2
Rafhes of all Sorts, the Piece about 24 Yards	0	0	4
Says, called Hounfcot Says, or milled, the Piece	0	0	3

Says of all other Sorts, the Piece	—	0	2½
Serges, single Piece, Yard broad containing 12 Yards	—	0	2
Serges, double Piece, Yard broad containing 24 Yards	—	0	3
See also Woollen Drapery.			
Succades, wet or dry, the Hundred Pounds containing five Score	—	0	8
Swarf, see Filings of Iron.			
Tallow, the Hundred Weight containing 112 Pounds	—	0	1
Tapestry, viz.			
with Hair, Hundred Flemish Ells containing five Score	—	0	4
with Wool, Hundred Flemish Ells containing five Score	—	0	6
with Caddas, Hundred Flemish Ells containing five Score	—	0 1	0
with Silk, the Dozen Flemish Ells	—	0	2
Taffaty, viz.			
Ell broad, the Dozen Yards	—	0	2
Silk Tuff Taffaty, broad, the Dozen Yards	—	0	4
Silk Tuff Taffaty, narrow, the Dozen Yards	—	0	2
Thread, whited brown, or coloured, the Dozen Pounds	—	0	1
Tiffany, each Dozen Yards	—	0	1
Tobacco, viz.			
Spanish, the Hundred containing five Score	—	0 2	0
of all other Sorts, the Hundred containing five Score	—	0	6

(436)

TABLE I.
PACKAGE.

	£	s.	d.
Tin, viz.			
wrought, the Hundred containing 112 Pounds	0	0	4
unwrought, the Hundred Weight containing 112 Pounds	0	0	3½
Thread Points, the great Groce	0	0	0½
Vellures, British, viz.			
the single Piece	0	0	1
the Double Piece	0	0	2
Vinegar of Wine, the Ton	0	0	2½
Waistcoats, viz.			
of Kersey or Flannel, the Dozen	0	0	2
of Woollen, knit, the Dozen	0	0	4
of Worsted knit, the Piece	0	0	0½
wrought with Cruel, the Piece	0	0	0¼
wrought with Silk, the Piece	0	0	1
Wax, viz.			
British Wax, the Hundred Weight containing 112 Pounds	0	0	4
British hard Wax, the Hundred containing five Score	0	0	8

		l.	s.	d.
Wine, viz.				
French Wines of all Sorts, the Tun	—	0	0	8
Muscadel, and Wines of the Levant, the Butt	—	0	0	6
Sacks, Canaries, Madeiras, Romney and Hullocks, the Butt or Pipe	—	0	0	6
Wood, viz.				
Box Wood, the Hundred Weight containing 112 Pounds	—	0	0	0½
Brasil Wood, the Hundred Weight containing 112 Pounds	—	0	0	3
Ebony Wood, the Hundred Weight containing 112 Pounds	—	0	0	1½
Fustick Wood, the Hundred Weight containing 112 Pounds	—	0	0	0½
Red Wood, the Hundred Weight containing 112 Pounds	—	0	0	1½
Wool, viz.				
Cotton Wool, the Hundred Pounds containing five Score	—	0	0	3
Estridge Wool, the Hundred Weight containing 112 Pounds	—	0	0	2
French Wool, the Hundred Weight containing 112 Pounds	—	0	0	2
Spanish Wool, the Hundred Weight containing 112 Pounds	—	0	0	4
Woollen Drapery, called Bayze, the single Piece	—	0	0	2
the Double Piece	—	0	0	4
Minikins Bayze, the Piece	—	0	0	6
Broad Cloth, the short Piece containing 24 Yards	—	0	0	6
Broad Cloth, the long Piece containing 32 Yards	—	0	0	8
Cottons of all Sorts, the Hundred Goads	—	0	0	6
Devonshire Dozens, the Piece	—	0	0	1

TABLE I.

PACKAGE.	l.	s.	d.
Woollen Drapery, called Frizados, the Piece	0	0	3
Kerseys of all Sorts, the Piece	0	0	2
Lifts of Cloth, the Thousand Yards	0	0	6
Northern Dozens, single, the Piece	0	0	3
double, the Piece	0	0	6
Spanish Cloth, British making, each 20 Yards	0	0	6
Penistones, the Piece	0	0	2
Worm Seed, the Hundred Pounds containing five Score	0	0	6
Yarn, called Cotton Yarn, the Hundred containing five Score	0	0	4
Grogram, or Mohair Yarn, the Hundred containing five Score	0	1	6
Raw Linen Yarn of all Sorts, the Hundred Pounds	0	0	4

All other Goods not mentioned in this Table, shall pay for Package Duties, after the Rate of one Penny in the Pound, according as they are expressed or valued in his Majesty's late Book of Rates; and all other not expressed therein shall pay the same Rate according to their true Value.

For every Entry in the Packer's Book for writing Bills to each Entry Outward, as usually they have done, 12d.

(439)

The Strangers shall pay the labouring Porters for making up their Goods, at their own Charge, as always they have done.

The Strangers shall pay the Water Side Porters belonging to the Package Office, for landing and shipping their Goods, as they have usually such Fees and Duties, paid within these ten Years last past.

The BALLIAGE DUTIES OUTWARDS, for the surveying or delivering of all Goods and Merchandise, in order to be exported into Parts beyond the Seas, or otherwise.

	l.	s.	d.
Beer, the Tun	-	0	4
Canvas, the Hundred Ells containing six Score	-	0	2
Cloths, see Drapery.			
Coals, the Chalder	-	0	1
Cochineal, see Dying Commodities.			
Drapery of Woollen or Worsted, viz.			
Broad Cloth, the Piece	-	0	1½
Kerseys of all Sorts the Piece	-	0	0½
Perpetuanas, the Piece	-	0	0½
Stuffs, Woollen or Worsted, the single Piece	-	0	0½
Stuffs, Woollen or Worsted, the double Piece	-	0	1

(440)

TABLE I.
BALLIAGE.

	L.	*s.*	*d.*
Dying Commodities, viz.			
Cochineal, the Hundred containing five Score Pounds	0	1	0
Indico, the Hundred containing five Score	0	0	4
Wood of all Sorts, for Dyers, the Hundred Weight containing 112 Pounds	0	0	1
Fur, see Skins.			
Fustians, British making, each fifteen Yards	0	0	0½
Flax or Hemp, the Hundred Weight containing 112 Pounds	0	0	1
Grocery, viz.			
Cloves, Mace, Nutmegs, or Cinnamon, the Hundred containing five Score	0	0	6
Pepper or Ginger, the Hundred containing five Score	0	0	2
Raisins, the Piece or Frail	0	0	0½
Raisins Solis, the Hundred Weight containing 112 Pounds	0	0	1
Hemp, see Flax.			
Indico, see Dying Commodities.			
Iron, viz.			
the Ton, unwrought	0	0	6
wrought, the Hundred Weight containing 112 Pounds	0	0	1
Lamperns, the Thousand	0	0	0½

(441)

Item	£	s	d
Lead, the Fother	1	0	0 6
Linen, see Canvas.			
Pewter, see Tin.			
Saffron, the Pound	0	0	0½
Salt, the Wey	0	0	2
Salt Petre, the Hundred Weight containing 112 Pounds	0	0	1
Silk Raw, or thrown Silk, the Pound containing 16 Ounces	0	0	0¼
Skins and Furs, viz.			
Beaver Skins, the Hundred containing five Score	0	1	6
Badger Skins, the Hundred containing five Score	0	0	6
Coney Skins black, the Hundred containing six Score	0	0	2
Cat Skins, the Hundred containing five Score	0	0	2
Calve Skins, the Hundred containing five Score	0	0	2
Fox Skins, the Hundred containing five Score	0	0	6
Fitches, the Timber	0	0	1
Morkins, the Hundred containing six Score	0	0	2
Otter Skins, the Hundred containing five Score	0	0	6
Sheep or Lamb Skins, the Hundred containing six Score	0	0	2
Squirrel Skins, the Thousand	0	0	1
Stuffs, see Drapery.			
Tin or Pewter, the Hundred Weight containing 112 Pounds	0	0	2
Wax, the Hundred Weight containing 112 Pounds	0	0	2

TABLE I.

BALLIAGE.

	£	s.	d.
Wood for Dyers, &c Dying Commodities	—	0	0	2
Wool of all Sorts, the Hundred Weight containing 112 Pounds			
Other Merchandise, Liquid or Dry, that are not particularly rated in this Table, shall pay Balliage Duties Outwards, by their Bulk, as followeth, viz.			
A great Pacquet or Fardle, containing between 15 or 20 Cloths, or other Goods to that Proportion	0	1	6
An ordinary Pack, Truss, or Fardle, containing in bigness about ten or twelve Cloths, 12 or 14 Bayze, or to the like Proportion in Friezes, Cottons, or other Goods	0	1	0
A Bale containing three or four Cloths, four or five Bayze, or the like Proportion in other Goods	0	0	6
For a great Maund, or great Basket	0	0	8
For a small Maund, or Basket, weighing 300 Weight or under	0	0	4
For a Hamper or Coffer, weighing 200 Weight or under	0	0	3
For a Butt or Pipe	0	0	8
For a Hogshead or Puncheon	0	0	4
For a Barrel	0	0	2
For a Firkin	0	0	1

For a Dry Fat	—	0	8
For a Drum Fat	—	0	4
For a Bale	—	0	6
For a great Cheſt, or great Caſe	—	0	8
For a ſmall Cheſt or Caſe containing 300 Weight, or under	—	0	4
For a ſmall Box	—	0	2
For a great Trunk	—	0	6
For a ſmall Trunk, not above two Hundred Weight	—	0	3
For a Bag or Sack	—	0	4
For a Seron	—	0	3

The Packers Water Side Porters Table of Duties, or landing Strangers Goods, and of the like Duties or Rates to be paid unto them for Shipping out their Goods, called PORTAGE.

For a Butt of Currants	—	1	4
For a Carateel of Currants	—	0	8
For a Quarterole of Currants	—	0	4
For a Bag of Currants	—	0	4
For Pieces of Raiſins, the Ton	—	1	8
For a Barrel of Raiſins	—	0	4

TABLE I.
PORTAGE.

	£	s.	d.
For all Sorts of Puncheons	0	0	6
For a Barrel of Figs	0	0	2
For Tapnets and Frails of Figs, per Ton	0	1	8
For Brasil, or other Wood for Dying, per Ton	0	1	8
For Iron, the Ton	0	1	2
For Copperas, the Ton	0	1	2
For Oil, Wine, or Vinegar, per Tun	0	1	2
For Hemp and Flax, the Last	0	1	8
For loose Flax and Tow, the Hundred Weight	0	0	2
For a great Bag of Tow	0	0	8
For a small Bag of Tow	0	0	4
For a great Bag of Hops	0	0	8
For a Packet or little Bag of Hops	0	0	4
For Packs, Trusses, Fats, or Maunds, per Piece	0	0	8
For a great Chest	0	0	8
For a small Chest	0	0	4
For all Cases, Barrels, or Bales, per Piece	0	0	4
For a Bale of Madder	0	0	8
For a Bale of Ginger or Shumac containing 400 Weight	0	0	8

(445)

For a Faggot of Steel	—	0	0 1
For any Serons, the Piece	—	0	0 4
For a Fat of Pot Ashes	—	0	0 8
For a Laſt of Sope Aſhes	—	0	1 0
For a Laſt of Pitch or Tar	—	0	1 0
For a Laſt of Fiſh	—	0	1 0
For Wainſcots, the Hundred containing ſix Score	—	0	5 6
For Clap Boards, the Hundred containing ſix Score	—	0	0 6
For Deal Boards, the Hundred containing ſix Score	—	0	1 4
For a great Maſt	—	0	5 0
For a middle Maſt	—	0	2 6
For a ſmall Maſt	—	0	1 3
For great Balks, the Hundred containing ſix Score	—	0	5 0
For middle Balks, the Hundred containing ſix Score	—	0	2 6
For ſmall Balks, the Hundred containing ſix Score	—	0	1 3
For a Mill Stone	—	0	5 0
For a Dog Stone	—	0	2 6
For a Wolf Stone	—	0	2 0
For a Yard Stone	—	0	0 3
For a Grindle Stone	—	0	1 0
For a Step Stone, or Grave Stone	—	0	0 8
For Quern Stones, the Laſt	—	0	1 0

TABLE I.
PORTAGE.

	l.	s.	d.
For Emery Stones, the Ton	0	1	2
For ten Hundred Weight of Holland Cheese	0	1	0
For Rosin, the Ton	0	1	2
For Woad, the Ton	0	1	2
For a Chest of Sugar	0	0	6
For Half Wainscots, the Hundred containing six Score	0	2	6
For Raw Hides, the Hundred containing five Score	0	5	0
For Boomspars, the Hundred containing six Score	0	0	6
For small Spars, the Hundred containing six Score	0	0	4
For Ends of Boomspars, the Hundred containing six Score	0	0	9
For a Horse, Gelding, or Mare	0	2	6
For Alum, the Ton	0	1	8
For Heath for Brushes, the Hundred Weight containing 112 Pounds	0	0	1
For Iron Pots, the Dozen	0	0	3
For Rings of Wire, loose, the Ring	0	0	0½
For Pipe Staves, the Thousand	0	2	6
For Rhenish Wine, the Awm	0	0	6
For Burstones, the Hundred containing five Score	0	2	6
For half Packs of Teazels, the Piece	0	0	4

For Wicker Bottles, the Dozen	—	0	0	0½
For Stone Pots, the Hundred containing five Score	—	0	0	1
For loose Fith, the Hundred, landing	—	0	0	3
For a Barrel of Salmon	—	0	0	2
For a Barrel of Stub Eels	—	0	0	0½
For a Bundle of Basket Rods	—	0	0	8
For a Ton of Cork	—	0	1	0
For a Thousand of Ox Bones	—	0	1	6
For a Thousand Tips of Horns	—	0	0	0
For a Thousand Shank Bones	—	0	1	3
For Brimstone, the Ton, loose	—	0	1	2
For a Fodder of Lead	—	0	1	0
For Rims of Sieves, the Load	—	0	0	0
For a Load of Fans	—	0	1	8
For a Load of Bullrushes	—	0	0	0
For a Hundred Reams of Paper, loose	—	0	1	2
For a Barrel of Tarras	—	0	0	2
For a Barrel of Lings	—	0	0	0½
For a Keg of Sturgeon	—	0	0	1
For Iron Backs for Chimneys, the Piece	—	0	0	1
For one Hundred Weight of Elephants Teeth	—	0	0	0½
For Copper and Iron Plates, per Piece	—			

TABLE I.
PORTAGE.

	l.	s.	d.
For a Hundred small Barrels of Blacking	0	1	0
For a Dozen of Scales	0	0	1
For a Hundred of Oars	0	2	6
For every twenty Sugar Flags	0	0	4
For a Barrel of Shot	0	0	4
For a Bundle of Canes	0	0	1
For a Cage of Quails	0	0	4
For a Cage of Pheasants	0	0	4
For a Cage of Hawks	0	0	4
For a Winch of Cable Yarn	0	0	4
For a Firkin of Shot	0	0	2

All other Goods, not mentioned in this Table, shall pay Portage Duties, as other Goods do of like Bulk, or like Condition, herein expressed.

For the more certain and better levying and collecting the aforesaid Duties of Package, Scavage, &c. the Mayor and Commonalty, or their proper Officers, or Deputies, may, by all lawful Ways and Means, compel Person: suspected of any Concealments, Colourings or Frauds, to take their Oaths upon the Holy Evangelists,

Note, the City of London is likewise entitled to the Survey of the Measures, Numbers, and Weights of all Merchandises of Aliens or Denizens, coming into, or going out of the said City, as well by Land, as by Water: And also the Portage and Carriage of all Goods of Denizens, whole Fathers are Aliens, born under foreign Allegiance, or of Aliens born under foreign Allegiance in Parts beyond the Seas, carried in London from the River of Thames, to the Houses or Warehouses of such Merchants, and from thence to the said River.

TABLE K.

A LIST of GOODS prohibited to be imported into or exported from Great Britain, 1791.

Goods prohibited to be imported.

Artificial Flowers, made of Silk, except for private Use with the Permission of the Commissioners of the Customs.
Bandstrings.
Barley, ground.
Beans, ground.
Beer or Bigg, ground.
Books, English, reprinted abroad.
Buttons, of all Sorts.
Calicos, Muslins, or Stuffs made of Linen Yarn, or Cotton Wool, or of Linen Yarn and Cotton Wool mixed, wherein shall be wove in the Warp in the Selvage only through the Whole or any Part of the Length of the Piece, one or more blue Stripes of one or more Threads, under Penalty of Forfeiture, and £.10 per Piece by the Importer. French to have the Mark agreed on wove in each End of the Piece, admitted during the Treaty of Commerce until 10th May 1800.
Chocolate, ready made.
Cocoa Paste.
Coin (current), false or counterfeit, to be uttered.
Gold or Silver of Ireland.
Cut Work.
Embroidery.
Fringes of Thread or Silk.
Indian Corn or Maize.
Malt, made of Barley, Beer or Bigg, of Indian Corn or Maize, of Oats, Rye, or Wheat.
Pease, ground.
Rye, ground.
Wire, Card Wire or Iron Wire for making of Wool Cards.

(451)

Goods prohibited to be imported and used in Great Britain.

Bone Lace of Silk, made in any Foreign Parts; and Thread Lace made in France, except during the Treaty of Commerce until the 10th May 1800.
Brass, Work made thereof.
Brocade, of Gold or Silver.
Copper, Work made thereof.
East India wrought Silks, Bengals, and Stuffs mixed with Silk or Herbas of the Manufacture of Persia, China, or East Indies; and Calicos painted, printed, or dyed there.
Embroidery.
Fringe, Gold, &c.
Gloves and Mits of Leather or Silk.
Gold or Silver Thread Lace, Fringe, or Work made of Copper, Brass, or any inferior Metal, or Gold or Silver Wire or Plate, Embroidery, or Gold or Silver Brocade.
Lace, of Gold or Silk; Thread Lace made in France, except until 10th May 1800, by the Treaty of Commerce.
Leather, Foreign, cut into Shapes for Gloves or Mits.
Mits of Leather or Silk.
Needlework of Silk or Thread, except East India upon Muslins.
Popish Agni Dei, Crosses, Pictures, Beads, or such other superstitious Things.
Popish Primers, Ladies Psalters, Manuals, Rosaries, Catechisms, Missals, Breviaries, Portals, Legends, and Lives of Saints in any Language, and other superstitious Books in the British Tongue.
Silk Ribbands, Laces, and Girdles.
wrought, except Italian Crapes or Tiffanies from Italy.
Silver Thread Lace, &c. as Gold Thread Lace, &c. before mentioned.
Stockings, Silk.
Stuffs mixed with Silk or Herba.
Tobacco Stalks.
Velvets.

(452)

TABLE K.

Goods prohibited to be imported for Sale.

Artificial Flowers made of Silk.
Bits.
Cards for Wool.
Cattle, great Sheep, Swine, Beef, Pork (except Bacon), Mutton, or Lamb; except six Hundred Head yearly from the Isle of Man into the Port of Chester or Members thereof, viz. Lancaster, Liverpool, Poulton, Aberconway, Beaumaris, and Carnarvon.
But Cattle and salted Provisions of and from Ireland may be imported Duty free, and Beastials from the Isle of Man by the Inhabitants thereof, also Cattle See the Note after Alderney in Table A.
Cauls made of Silk.
Chapes.
Cheese from Ireland.
Coin, false or counterfeit.
Daggers.
Dagger Blades.
Girdles.
Gloves (other than Leather or Silk, which cannot be imported and used in Great Britain.)
Handles for Knives.
Harness for Girdles, and Horse Harness.
Hilts.
Knives.
Leather Laces. Points.
Pork.
Provisions, see Cattle.
Pummels.
Rapiers.
Ribbands of Silk only, or mixed with other Materials.
Saddles, except French, until 10th May 1800.
Scabbards and Sheaths for Knives.
Silk, wrought by itself, or with any other Stuff, in Ribbands, Laces, Girdles, Corses, Cauls, Corses of Tissue, or Points.
Spirits, from the British Plantations in America in Casks less than 60 Gallons, except for private Use.

from Guernsey, Jersey, Alderney, and Sark, by the Inhabitants thereof.

Locks.
Lockets.
Mutton.
Pins.

Stirrups.
Swine, fee Cattle.
Wire, Card Wire or Iron Wire for making of Wool Cards.

Goods prohibited to be imported for Sale, without Licence from his Majesty.

Ammunition.   Arms.   Gunpowder.   War, Utensils of.

Goods prohibited to be imported for Sale by any Persons, except made and wrought in Ireland, or taken upon the Seas, or wrecked.

Andirons.
Balls, Tennis.
Basons, counterfeit.
Bells, viz. Sacring Bells.
Blanch Iron Thread, called White Wire.
Bodkins.
Bosses for Bridles.
Brushes.
Buskins.
Candlesticks, hanging.
Caps, Woollen.
Cards, Playing.
Cards, for Wool.
Caskets.
Chaffing Balls or Dishes.
Cheffinen.
Cloths, Woollen, except French admitted by the Commercial Treaty until 10th May 1800.
Combs.
Corses.
Daggers.
Dice.
Dripping Pans.
Ewers.
Forcers.
Fringes of Silk and Thread.
Furs tawed, viz. Armin, Badger, Bear, Beaver, Calabar, Cat,

TABLE K.

Goods prohibited to be imported for Sale by any Persons, except made and wrought in Ireland, or taken upon the Seas, or wrecked.

Fitch, Fox, Leopard, Martin, or Martron, Mink, Mole, Otter, Ounce, Sable, Wolf, and Wolvering, or any other Kinds of Furs not originally rated as Skins.
Galley Tiles. See painted Wares.
Girdles.
Goloches, or Corks.
Gridirons.
Hammers.
Harness, pertaining to Saddles.
for Girdles of Iron, Latten, Steel, Tin, or Alkmine.
Hats.
Iron Thread, called White Wire.
Leather, any Thing wrought of tawed Leather.
Locks.
Needles, called Pack Needles.
Painted Wares, except Paper and Pictures, and Earthen Ware the Manufacture of Europe, other than Galley Tiles.
Pattens.
Pinfons.
Points.
Purses.
Rapiers.
Razors.
Ribbands.
Rings of Copper or Latten gilt, for Curtains.
Sheaths.
Sheers, for Taylors.
Shoes.
Silk embroidered and Silk twined.
Spurs.
Stirrups.
Tires of Silk or Gold.
Tongs, viz. Fire Tongs.
White Wire.
Wire of Iron, viz. Card Wire, and all Sorts of Iron Wire smaller than fine fine; and Superfine and Wool Cards, or any other Wares made of Iron Wire.
Woollen Caps.
Woollen Cloths, or old Drapery;

Knives, called Wood Knives.
Laces, of Thread or Gold.
Ladles.
Saddles.
Scissars.
Scummers.

except French of the Manufacture of the European Dominions of the French King until the 10th May 1800.

Goods prohibited to be imported for Sale, by Strangers, or Aliens.

Andirons.
Bells of any Sort, except Hawks Bells.
Bits.
Blade Smiths, } any Wares pertaining to them.
Black Smiths, }
Boots.
Broaches, or Spits.
Bottle Makers, any Wares pertaining to them.
Buckles for Shoes.
Candlesticks, hanging.
Iron standing.
Card Makers, any Wares pertaining to them.

Chaffing Dishes.
Chains.
Clasps for Gowns.
Cloths, painted.
Copper Smiths, any Wares pertaining to them.
Cupboards.
Cutlers, any Wares pertaining to them.
Forcers.
Forks, called Fire Forks.
Founders, any Wares pertaining to them.
Girdlers, any Wares pertaining to them.

Girdles.
Glass, painted.
Glovers, any Wares pertaining to them.
Goldbeaten, in Papers for Painters.
Gold Bearers, any Wares pertaining to them.
Grates.
Gridirons.
Hangers.
Harness, wrought for Girdles.
called Horse Harness.
Hinges and Garnets.
Horners, any Wares pertaining to them.

TABLE K.

Goods prohibited to be imported for Sale, by Strangers, or Aliens.

Horns, for Lanthorns.
Hurers, any Wares pertaining to them.
Images, painted.
Joiners, any Wares pertaining to them.
Iron, Ware.
Keys.
Knives.
Laces.
Latten, Ware.
Lavers, hanging.
Locks, called Stock Locks.
Lorimers, any Wares pertaining to them.
Nails of Latten, with Iron Shanks.
Painters,
Pinners,
Point Makers, } any Wares pertaining to them.
Purfers,
Pins.
Points.
Pouches.
Purses.
Rings, for Curtains.
Sadlers, any Wares pertaining to them.
Saddles.
Saddle Trees.
Scissars.
Sheers, for Taylors.
Silver (beaten), in Papers for Painters.
Spits.
Spoons of Tin or Lead.
Spurriers, any Wares pertaining to them.
Spurs.
Stirrups.
Stock Locks.
Stops, called Holy Water Stops.
Taylors Sheers.
Tongs.
Turnets.
Weavers, and
Wire Mongers, } any Wares pertaining to them.
Wool Cards, except Roan Cards.

Goods prohibited to be imported, except in particular Weights, Packages, &c. or under other Restrictions.

Aqua Vitæ, except in Ships belonging to Great Britain or Ireland, or of the same Country with the Goods, of 100 Tons Burthen, and in Casks not less than 60 Gallons each.

Ashes, Pot, from any Places, except in Ships belonging to Great Britain or Ireland, or of the same Country with the Goods.

Beef, except from the Isle of Man by the Inhabitants thereof, according to the Regulations of the 5 Geo. III. Chap. 43. into any lawful Port of Great Britain, and except Irish Beef into any Part of Great Britain.

Boards, except in Ships belonging to Great Britain or Ireland, or of the same Country with the Goods.

Brandy, in Casks containing less than 100 Gallons each, or in Ships less than 100 Tons, in any Case except in Ships belonging to Great Britain or Ireland, or of the same Country with the Goods.

Cambricks and French Lawns, except in British or French built Ships legally navigated and owned, and in Bales, &c. covered with Sackcloth or Canvas, containing 100 whole Pieces, or 200 Demy Pieces.

Cambricks and French Lawns, or Lawn from Ireland, until the Importation there shall be prohibited.

Candles, Soap, and Starch, or Hair Powder made of Starch, or which may serve for the same Uses as Starch, in any Package less than 224 Pounds Weight net.

Coffee, in Ships not above 50 Tons, and in Packages less than 112 Pounds net.

Coin, viz. light or base Coin, exceeding £.5.

Corn or Grain, except in Ships belonging to Great Britain or Ireland, or of the same Country with the Goods.

Currants (Turkey), except in British built Ships, or Ships of the Country with the Goods, and any

TABLE K.

Goods prohibited to be imported, except in particular Weights, Packages, &c. or under other Restrictions.

Currants in any Packages containing less than 5 Hundred Weight net.

Deal Boards from the Netherlands or Germany, except Deal Boards of the Growth of Germany, imported from thence by British in British built Ships.

Figs, except in Ships belonging to Great Britain or Ireland, or of the same Country with the Goods, and Turkey Figs except in British built Ships, or of the same Country with the Goods.

Fish, flat or fresh, in Foreign Ships, taken by or bought of Foreigners, except Eels, Stock Fish, Anchovies, Sturgeon, Botargo, Caveat, Lobsters, and Turbots.

Flax, except in Ships of Great Britain or Ireland, or of the Built of the same Country with the Goods.

Oil (Olive), except in Ships belonging to Great Britain or Ireland, or of the Built of the same Country as the Goods.

Packet Boats, any Goods or Merchandise therein except by Licence of the Commissioners of the Customs.

Pepper, except into the Port of London.

Pitch, except in Ships belonging to Great Britain or Ireland, or in Ships of the Built of the same Country as the Goods.

Prunes, except in Ships belonging to Great Britain or Ireland, or in Ships of the Built of the same Country as the Goods.

Raisins, except in Ships belonging to Great Britain or Ireland, or in Ships of the Built of the same Country as the Goods.

Rosin, the like.

Geneva, in Casks containing less than 100 Gallons, or in Ships less than 100 Tons, except two Gallons for each Seaman, if no other Spirits or Wine for their Use.

Hair Powder, made of Starch, except in Packages containing each 224 Pounds Weight net.

Hats or Bonnets of Baft, Straw, Chip, Cane, or Horse Hair, except in Bales or Tubs containing 75 Dozen each, and

Plaiting, or other Materials for making such Hats, except in Packages containing each 224 Pounds Weight net; thus into London only, and in Ships exceeding 50 Tons Burthen.

Isle of Man; Brandy, Rum, Strong Waters or Spirits, not to be imported from thence.

Masts, except in Ships belonging to Great Britain or Ireland, or of the Built of the same Country with the Goods.

Oak Bark, when the Price of Hatch Bark is under ten Pounds per Load, or Oak Bark in the Rinds under two Pounds ten Shillings the Load.

Rum, except in Casks that will contain 60 Gallons each,

if regularly imported from the British Dominions in America in small Casks for private Use the Commissioners may admit it to Entry.

Sail Cloth or Canvas from Ireland, except in entire Bolts or Pieces.

Salt, except in Ships of 40 Tons Burthen, or otherwise than in Bulk, except for the Ship's Provisions.

of Great Britain or Ireland, or other Salt coming from Ireland, or the Isle of Man, except for the Ship's Provisions, or taken in to cure Fish at Sea.

from any Place except in Ships belonging to Great Britain or Ireland, or in Ships of the Built of the same Country as the Goods.

Silk, thrown, except directly from Italy, Sicily, or the Kingdom of Naples, legally imported. raw Turkey, except from Ports in the Do-

TABLE K.

Goods prohibited to be imported, except in particular Weights, Packages, &c. or under other Restrictions.

Snuff, except in Packages containing each 450 lb. Weight net, and in Ships of 120 Tons Burthen.

Soap, except in Packages containing each 224 lb. Weight net.

Spice imported by Licence, except as follows, Cinnamon in Bales containing each 70 lb. Weight net, Nutmegs, Cloves, or Mace in Casks containing 300 lb. Weight net, or upwards.

Spirits of any Kind, except in Casks that will contain 100 Gallons each, and in Ships of 100 Tons Burthen on Forfeiture of the Ship and Goods, but Rum of the British Plantations and Arrack from any Part of Europe except by Licence of the Commissioners of the Customs.

Tobacco, except in Casks or other Packages containing each 450 lb. Weight net, and in Ships of 120 Tons Burthen, nor from any other Place than the Plantations of Spain or Portugal, from the British Plantations in America, from the United States of America, or from Ireland, the Growth thereof respectively, although the same may have formerly been exported from hence.

Turkey Goods, or of the Dominions of the Grand Seignior, except in British built Ships, or in Ships of the Built of the Country of which they are the Growth, &c.

Vinegar, except in British built Ships, or in Ships of the Built of the Country of which it is the Produce, &c.

Whalebone, cut (except in Fins).

Wines, except in British Ships, or in Ships the minions of the Grand Signior, legally imported.

may be imported in Casks that will contain 60 Gallons each; and Rum in smaller Casks for private Use, the Commissioners of the Customs may admit to Entry.

Starch, or Hair Powder made of Starch, or which may serve for the same Uses as Starch, except in Packages containing each 224 lb. Weight net.

Sugar, except in Ships belonging to Great Britain or Ireland, or of the Built of the Country of which it is the Growth.

Tar, from any Place except in British Ships, or in Ships of the Built of the Country of which it is the Produce.

Tea, only from the Place of its Growth, though formerly exported from hence, except by Licence of the Lords of the Treasury in case the East India Company do not supply the Market in British built Ships.

Timber, except in British Ships, or in Ships of the Built of the Country of which it is the Growth.

Built of the Country of which it is the Produce.

Spanish, Portugal, and French, except in Hogsheads, unless for private Use, and in Ships of 60 Tons Burthen. from any Place in Ships of less Burthen than 60 Tons.

in Flasks, or Bottles, or Vessels containing less than 25 Gallons, except French Wines in Bottles in Packages containing three Dozen Bottles each, until the 10th May 1800, and except Wines of the Dominions of the Great Duke of Tuscany, in open Flasks, or of Turkey, or any other Part of the Levant Sea, in the Manner as heretofore usually imported.

N. B. Two Gallons per Man, of Wine and Spirits, are allowed for the Ship's Use for each Seaman in Ships of any Country or any Tonnage.

TABLE K.

Goods prohibited to be exported.

Bell Metal.

Boxes, for Clocks or Watches, without the Movements, &c.

Brafs Metal.

Bullion, unlefs a Certificate from the Court of Lord Mayor and Aldermen of London is produced to the Commiffioners of the Cuftoms that it is Foreign, and not molten from Coin of this Realm, or Clippings thereof; nor from Plate wrought in this Kingdom.

Cafes, for Clocks and Watches of any Metal without the Movements, &c.

Clocks, without the Movements made fit for Ufe with the Maker's Name.

Coin of Gold and Silver without the King's Licence (except Foreign Coin upon Entry; or any other Coin into Ireland.)

Copper, except made of Britifh Ore.

port of the Mafter of the Ship, Mariners, Paffengers, &c. or for the Ufe of Cattle, Live Stock, or other Animals on board, or for victualling or providing his Majefty's Ships of War, &c. or for victualling or providing any of his Majefty's Forces, Forts, or Garrifons, Beans to the Britifh Forts, Cafles, or Factories in Africa, or for the Ufe of Britifh Ships trading on that Coaft which have been ufually fupplied from Great Britain, Corn Coaftwife upon the Security required by Law (except from a Port where the Exportation is not allowed at the Time of fhipping to any other Port of Great Britain from whence it may be exported), and except as mentioned in Tables L and G.

Dial Plates, for Clocks or Watches without the Movements, &c.

(463)

Corn, of any Sort, or Malt, Biscuit, Meal, or Flour made therefrom, except under the Regulations and Restrictions of the 31 Geo. III. Chap. 30.
viz. Wheat, or Meal, Flour, Malt, Bread or Biscuit made of Wheat when Wheat is at or above per Quarter 46s.
Rye, Pease, or Beans, or Meal, Flour, Bread, or Biscuit made of Rye, Pease, or Beans, when Rye, Pease, or Beans are at or above per Quarter 30s.
Barley, Beer or Bigg, or Meal, Flour, Malt, Bread, or Biscuit, made of Barley, Beer or Bigg, when Barley, Beer or Bigg are at or above per Quarter 23s.
Oats, or Meal, Malt, Bread, or Biscuit made of Oats, when Oats are at or above per Quarter 15s.
Foreign Corn of any Sort imported and not warehoused, or Malt, Meal, Flour or Biscuit made therefrom, except so much as shall be necessary for the Sustenance, Diet, and Sup-

Frames or Engines for Knitting of Stockings.
Fullers Earth, or Scouring Clay.
Gunpowder, when the Price exceeds £.5 per Barrel, or prohibited by Proclamation.
Hides, of Ox, Steer, Cow, Bull, or Calf, except Calves Skins dressed without the Hair, unless for the Ship's Use, not exceeding six raw Hides, and three tanned Hides.
Horns, British, unwrought.
Isle of Man, wrought Silks, Bengals, Stuffs mixed with Silk or Herba of the Manufacture of Persia, China, or East Indies; Calicos painted, dyed, printed, or stained there, Cambricks, or French Lawns may not be exported to the Isle of Man.
Lambs, alive.
Latten.
Metal, Brass, Copper, Latten, Bell Metal, Pan Metal, Gun Metal, Shruff Metal (except Lead and Tin, and Copper, and Mundick Metal, made of British Ore, and Foreign Copper in Bars.)
Morlings.
Rams, alive.

(464)

TABLE K.

Goods prohibited to be exported.

Scouring Clay.
Sheep, alive.
Shortlings.
Silver, molten, except marked at Goldsmiths' Hall, and by Certificate, &c. as in Bullion.
Tallow.
Tea, to Ireland, or the British Plantations, except in the original Package.
Thrumbs.
Tobacco Pipe Clay, except to the British Sugar Colonies in the West Indies, until 24th June 1792, &c.
Tools or Utensils, Machines, Engines, Press Paper, Implements, or any Model or Plan thereof, in the Cotton, Linen, Silk or Woollen Manufactures may not be shipped unless to be directly landed again in Great Britain or Ireland.
Articles, or any Model or Models of any of the beforementioned Utensils, Implements, and Machines, or any Part thereof, and all Sorts of Utensils, Engines, or Machines used in the boring of Cannon, or any Sort of Artillery, or any Parts thereof; Presses of all Sorts called Cutting-out Presses, Beds and Punches to be used therewith; Piercing Presses of all Sorts, Beds and Punches to be used therewith, either in Parts or Pieces, or fitted together; Scoring or Shading Engines, Presses for Horn Buttons, Dies for Horn Buttons, rolled Metal with Silver thereon, Parts of Buttons not fitted up into Buttons, or in an unfinished State; Engines for Chafing, Stocks for casting Buckles, Buttons, or Rings; Die-sinking Tools of all Sorts, Engines for

(465)

not to be collected together to be conveyed by open Sea to any Place except to Great Britain; but not to extend to Wool Cards or Stock Cards, not exceeding in Value 4s. per Pair, and Spinners Cards not exceeding 1s. 6d. per Pair, exported to any British Colony in America.

viz. Hand Stamps, Dog Head Stamps, Pulley Stamps, Hammers and Anvils for Stamps, Rollers, either plain, grooved, or of any other Form or Denomination, of cast Iron, wrought Iron, or Steel, for the rolling of Iron, or any Sort of Metals, and Frames, Beds, Pillars, Screws, Pinions, Utensil thereunto belonging; Rollers, Slitters, Frames, Beds, Pillars, and Screws, for Slitting Mills; Presses of all Sorts in Iron, Steel, or other Metals, which are used with a Screw exceeding one Inch and a Half in Diameter, or any Parts of these several making Button Shanks, Laps of all Sorts, Tools for Pinching of Glass, Engines for covering of Whips, Bars of Metal covered with Gold or Silver, Burnishing Stones commonly called Blood Stones, either in the rough State or finished for Use; Wire Moulds for making Paper; Wheels made of Metal, Stone, or Wood, for cutting, roughing, smoothing, polishing, and engraving Glass; Purcellas, Pincers, Sheers, and Pipes used in blowing Glass; Potters Wheels and Potters Laths for plain, round, and for Engine-turning Tools used by Sadlers, Harness Makers, and Bridle Makers, namely, Cattle Strainers, Side Strainers, Point Strainers, Creasing Irons, Screw Creasers, Wheel Irons, Seat Irons, Pricking Irons, Bolstering Irons, Clams, and Head Knives (except to Ireland).

Watches, without the Movements fit for Use, with the Maker's Name.

H h

TABLE K.

Goods prohibited to be exported.

Wool, Sheep, Wool Fells, Mortlings, Shortlings, Yarn made of Wool, Wool Flocks, Fullers Earth, Fulling Clay, and Tobacco Pipe Clay, except the latter to the British Sugar Colonies in the West Indies until 24th June 1792, &c.

Coverlids, Waddings, or other Manufactures of Wool slightly worked or put up together, so as they may be reduced to Wool and used as Wool again; or Mattresses or Beds stuffed with combed Wool, or Wool fit for combing.

Woollen Yarn.
Worsted.

British Hare Skins, or Parts or Pieces thereof, British Hare Wool, British Coney Wool; undressed or untawed British Coney Skins, or Parts or Pieces thereof.

TABLE L.

The Quantities of CORN, and other Articles, that may be exported in one Year to certain Places, for the Sustenance and Use of the Inhabitants thereof, from certain Ports, by the 31 Geo. III. Chap. 30.

To what Place.	From what Port.	Corn, and other Articles.	Quantity. Quarters.	Quantity. Tons.
Gibraltar.	London,	Wheat, Wheat Meal, or Flour, Rye, Barley, or Malt, or Pease, not exceeding in the Whole	2,500	
Guernsey, Jersey, and Alderney.	Southampton,	Wheat, Wheat Meal, or Flour, Rye, Barley, or Malt, or Bread, Biscuit, or Pease, not exceeding in the Whole	9,800	
Isle of Man.	Whitehaven, Liverpool, Kirkcudbright,	Wheat, Wheat Meal, or Flour, Barley, Oats, not exceeding Ditto Ditto Ditto Ditto Ditto	1,000 1,000 500	
St. Helena, Bencoolen, and the Company's Settlements in the East Indies.	Great Britain, by the East India Company,	Wheat, Wheat Meal, Flour, Rye, Barley, or Malt, not exceeding in the Whole	1,500	

TABLE L.

The Quantities of CORN, and other Articles, that may be exported in one Year to certain Places, for the Suſtenance and Uſe of the Inhabitants thereof, from certain Ports, by the 31 Geo. III. Chap. 30.

To what Place.	From what Port.	Corn, and other Articles.	Quantity. Quarters.	Quantity. Tons.
The Britiſh Forts, Caſtles, or Factories, in Africa.	By the Committee of the Company of Merchants trading to Africa,	Wheat, Flour, not exceeding — Biſcuit, not exceeding —		33 15
His Majeſty's Sugar Colonies in the Weſt Indies, in which the Bahama and Bermuda, or Somer Iſlands, are included.	From ſuch Ports, and in ſuch Proportions to each Iſland reſpectively, and in ſuch Proportions in each and every three Months as ſhall be directed by the Lords of his Majeſty's Privy Council, appointed for the Conſideration of all Matters relating to Trade and Foreign Plantations.	Barley Beans Oats Oat Meal Peaſe Rye Wheat Wheat Flour Biſcuit Grotts	5,000 20,000 25,000 4,000 500 1,000	600 3,220 950 25

The Bay of Honduras, or Coast of Yucatan, for the Sustenance and Use of the British Settlers there.	From such Ports as shall be directed by the Lords of his Majesty's Privy Council, appointed for the Consideration of all Matters relating to Trade and Foreign Plantations,	Flour, not exceeding — — —	115	250
		Bifcuit — — — —		50
		Peafe — — — —		20
		Oat Meal — — —		20
		Barley — — — —		20
Hudson's Bay, for the Benefit of the Hudson's Bay Company, and their Servants refiding there.	London,	Wheat Meal or Flour, not exceeding — — — —	260	40
		Oats, Oat Meal, Grotts, Barley, Peafe, Beans, Malt, and Bifcuit, not exceeding — —		
Newfoundland.	London,	Peafe — — — —	500	500
		Bifcuit — — — —		64
		Flour — — — —		
	Bristol,	Peafe — — — —	450	500
		Bifcuit — — — —		48
		Flour — — — —		

TABLE L.

The Quantities of CORN, and other Articles, that may be exported in one Year to certain Places, for the Sustenance and Use of the Inhabitants thereof, from certain Ports, by the 31 Geo. III. Chap. 30.

To what Place.	From what Port.	Corn, and other Articles.	Quantity. Quarters.	Tons.
Newfoundland.	Poole,	Pease	1,300	
		Biscuit		1,400
		Flour		400
	Dartmouth,	Pease	850	
		Biscuit		850
		Flour		240
	Topsham and Tingmouth, in the Whole from both Places,	Pease	1,200	
		Biscuit		900
		Flour		240
	Liverpool,	Pease	280	
		Biscuit		300
		Flour		48
	Weymouth,	Pease	240	
		Biscuit		120
		Flour		32
	Plymouth,	Pease	200	
		Biscuit		200
		Flour		40

Chester,	{ Pease Biscuit Flour	- - - - - - - - -	- - - - - -	- - - - - -	240 	200 48
Port Glasgow and Greenock, in the Whole from both Places,	{ Pease Biscuit	- - - - - -	- - - -	- - - -	100 	150
Barnstaple,	{ Pease Biscuit Flour	- - - - - - - - -	- - - - - -	- - - - - -	150 	150 64
Southampton,	{ Pease or Flour Biscuit	- - - - - -	- - - -	- - - -	300 	150
Cowes	{ Pease or Flour Biscuit	- - - - - -	- - - -	- - - -	300 	120
London,	{ Pease Biscuit Flour	- - - - - - - - -	- - - - - -	- - - - - -	600 	400 48
Bristol,	{ Pease Biscuit Flour	- - - - - - - - -	- - - - - -	- - - - - -	400 	350 32
Poole,	{ Pease Biscuit Flour	- - - - - - - - -	- - - - - -	- - - - - -	200 	200 32

Nova Scotia.

TABLE L.

The Quantities of CORN, and other Articles, that may be exported in one Year to certain Places, for the Sustenance and Use of the Inhabitants thereof, from certain Ports, by the 31 Geo. III. Chap. 30.

To what Place.	From what Port.	Corn, and other Articles.	Quantity. Quarters.	Tons.
Nova Scotia.	Dartmouth,	Pease	300	
		Biscuit		300
		Flour		48
	Topsham and Tingmouth, in the Whole from both Places,	Pease	400	
		Biscuit		400
		Flour		48
	Plymouth,	Pease	300	
		Biscuit		300
		Flour		40
	London,	Pease	500	
		Biscuit		400
		Flour		80
	Bristol,	Pease	400	
		Biscuit		300
		Flour		32

(473)

Bay Chaleur.	Poole, { Peafe / Bifcuit / Flour	200	200 / 48
	Dartmouth, { Peafe / Bifcuit / Flour	300	300 / 48
	Topfham and Tingmouth, in the Whole from both Places, { Peafe / Bifcuit / Flour	400	400 / 48
	Plymouth, { Peafe / Bifcuit / Flour	300	300 / 30
Labrador.	London, { Peafe / Bifcuit / Flour	500	400 / 32
	Briftol, { Peafe / Bifcuit / Flour	400	300 / 32
	Poole, { Peafe / Bifcuit / Flour	200	200 / 32

TABLE L.

The Quantities of CORN, and other Articles, that may be exported in one Year to certain Places, for the Sustenance and Use of the Inhabitants thereof, from certain Ports, by the 31 Geo. III. Chap. 30.

To what Place.	From what Port.	Corn, and other Articles.	Quantity. Quarters.	Tons.
Labrador,	Dartmouth,	{ Pease	300	
		Biscuit		300
		Flour		56
	Topsham and Tingmouth, in the Whole from both Places,	{ Pease	400	
		Biscuit		400
		Flour		48
	Plymouth,	{ Pease	200	
		Biscuit		300
		Flour		30
Portugal, or elsewhere.	From Kirkwall, under such Limitations and Restrictions as shall be made by the Lords of his Majesty's Privy Council, appointed for the Consideration of all Matters relating to Trade and Foreign Plantations,	{ Beer or Bigg, the Growth of the Islands of Orkney	5,000	

In the foregoing Table, fifty-six Pounds Avoirdupois of Wheat Meal, and forty-five Pounds Avoirdupois of Wheat Flour, is to be deemed equal to every Bushel of unground Wheat; and twenty-two Pounds Avoirdupois of Oat Meal shall be deemed equal to every Bushel of unground Oats.

In Cases of Exigency, his Majesty in Council may allow further Quantities to be exported, not exceeding in one Year five Thousand Quarters of each of the several Sorts of Corn unground, and two Thousand Quarters of each of the several Sorts of ground Corn. Any Sort of Corn may be exported from Great Britain to Ireland, after it has been notified in the London Gazette that such Sorts of Corn are prohibited to be exported from Ireland, Security being first given during such Prohibition or Embargo, that the same shall be carried to the Port or Place in Ireland.

TITLES OF DRUGS

Which are not frequently imported explained, and in what Countries they are produced.

Acacia, a Gum found in Egypt.
Acorus, a sweet Plant, produced in Europe.
Agaric, a Fungus growing on Larch Trees, found in the Levant, and in Europe.
Agnus Castus, a Plant of Europe.
Alumen Plume, Alum.
Ameos Seeds, suppose it should be Semen Ammi, Seeds of Bishopsweed, a Plant of Egypt and Europe.
Ammoni Seeds, the Bastard Stone Parsley, a Plant of Europe.
Angelica, a Plant of Europe.
Aristolochia, Birthwort, a Plant of Europe.
Asarum Roots, a Plant of Europe and the Levant.
Aspalthus, suppose it to be Asphaltus, the same as Bitumen Judaicum, found in Egypt and in the Dead Sea; Aspalthum is Rose Wood.
Auriculæ Judæ, Jews Ears, a Fungus of the Elder Tree.
Baccæ Alkakengi, Alkekengi, Winter Cherry, a Plant of Europe.
Balaustium, Wild Pomegranate Flowers, the Growth of Europe.
Bdellium, an East India Gum.
Ben-album, the Nut of a Tree, the Growth of East India and of America.
Bitumen Judaicum, found in Egypt and the Dead Sea.
Bolus Verus, the Produce of Europe, Asia, and Africa.

Calamus, sweet scented Flag, a Plant of Europe.
Capita Papaverum, the Poppy, a Plant of Europe.
Carlina, Thistle, a Plant of Europe.
Carpo Balsamum, the Fruit of the Balsam of Gilead, the Growth of Europe, America, &c.
Carrabe, or Succinum, rough Amber, found in Europe, chiefly in Germany.
Carthamus Seeds, Safflower, the Produce of Egypt and Germany.
Cerusia, white Lead, the Produce and Manufacture of Europe.
Cetrarch, Spleenwort or Miltwaste, a Plant of Europe.
Chamæpitys, Groundpine, a Plant of Europe.
Chelæ Cancrocrum, Crabbs Claws, the Produce of Europe.
Cinnabaris Nativa, Red Ore, the Produce of Europe, and Asia.
Ciperus, Galangal, a Plant of Europe.
Citraga, suppose it to be Cretago, Services, the Fruit of a Tree in Europe.
Colophonia, hard Rosin, Colophony, the Residium of common Turpentine.
Cortex Simarouba, the Bark of a Tree produced in Guiana, South America.
Costus Dulcis, a Root from East India.
Cubebs, dried Berries of an Ash Colour from East India.
Cuscuta, suppose it to be Cursuta, Dodder, a Root of the Gentian Tribe, Growth of Europe.
Cyclamen, or Panis Porcinus, a Plant of Europe.
Daucus Creticus, Candy Carrot, a Plant of the Levant and Europe.
Diptamus Leaves, suppose it to be Dictamnus, Dittany, a Plant of Europe.
Doronicum, Leopards Bane, a Plant of Germany and Europe,

Eboris Rasuræ, Shavings of Ivory.
Epithymum, Dodder of Thyme, a Plant of Europe and Asia.
Fechia Brugiata, Fechia Ashes.
Folium Indiæ, Indian Spikenard.
Grana Tinctorum, Seeds of Madder, the Growth of Germany, and Europe.
Granadilla Peruviana, Palma Christi, or Castor Bean of Peru, South America and West Indies.
Gum Curannæ, the Produce of New Spain, America.
Gum Hederæ, the Gum of the Yew Tree, produced in the Levant.
Gum Sarcocolla, the Produce of Persia, and Arabia, Asia.
Hermodactilus, a Root of the Produce of Turkey.
Hypocistis, produced from the Root of the Cestus or Rock Rose, the Growth of Europe and Asia.
Jujubes, a half dried Fruit of the Plum kind, the Growth of Europe.
Labdanum or Lapadonum, a resinous Juice of a Plant, the Growth of Europe and Asia.
Lapis Hæmatitis, Blood Stone, the Produce of Europe.
Hyacinthi,
Judaicus, } obsolete, and not to be found in the Materia Medica.
Magnetis,
Nephriticus, obsolete, but there is an American Tree called Nephritic.
Ostiocolla, a Fossil Substance found in Germany and other Parts of Europe.
Rubinus,
Sapphirus, } obsolete, and not to be found in the Materia Medica.
Smaragdus,

Spongiæ, the Produce of Europe and Asia.
Topagæ, obsolete, and not in the Materia Medica.
Tutiæ, an Ore of Zinck the Produce of Persia, Asia.
Litharge, a Scum which rises in trying Silver or Lead.
Lyntiscus, or Xylobalsamum, the Wood of the Tree that produces Balsam, the Growth of America, or Asia.
Mechoacana, the Root of the American Convolvulus, the Growth of Mexico.
Millium Solis, a Plant called Gromwell, the Growth of Europe.
Mirobolanus, a Fruit of the Plum kind, the Growth of Asia.
Nardus Celtica, or Spica Romana, Celtic Nard, a Species of Valerian, the Growth of Europe.
Nux de Ben, the Growth of Asia and America.
 Cupressi, the Growth of Europe.
 Indica, the Growth of Asia.
Oleum Carii, Oil of Carraway, the Growth and Manufacture of Europe.
 Petroleum, Rock Oil, the Growth of Europe.
Polypodium, the Roots of Polypody, the Growth of Europe.
Polium Montanum, the Leaves and Tops of the Mountain Poley, the Growth of Europe and Asia.
Pompholix, a Metallic Powder, of the Species of Tutty, but lighter, the Produce of Europe and Asia.
Psyllium, Fleawort, of the Plantain kind, the Growth of Europe.
Radix Bistortæ, the Root of Snakeweed, the Growth of Europe.
 Cassuminar, suppose it to be Casumunar, the Root of a Plant the Growth of Asia.
 Enulæ Campanæ, the Root of Elecampane, the Growth of Europe.

Radix Fistulæ, the Root of Spurge, the Growth of Europe.
Mei Athamantici, the Root of Spignel or Bauklmoney, the Growth of Europe.
Phu, the Root of Valerian, the Growth of Europe.
Scorcionera, suppose it to be Scorzonera, the Root of Vipers Grafs, the Growth of Europe.
Seneca, suppose it to be Senecio, the Root of Groundsel, the Growth of Europe.
Tormentillæ, the Root of Tormentil or Septfoil, the Growth of Europe.
Scincus Marinus, Skink, an amphibious Animal of the Lizard Kind, the Produce of Africa.
Scordium, the Leaves of Water Germander, a Plant the Growth of Europe.
Sebestines, a Fruit of Syria, not unlike the Damascus Prunes, the Growth of Asia.
Seler Montanus, suppose it to be Siler Montanum, Hartswort, the Growth of Europe.
Squinanthem, a sweet Rush, the Growth of Europe.
Stavesacre, the Seeds of the Plant are the Parts used as a Drug, the Growth of Europe.
Stechados, suppose it to be Storchas, the Flowering Tops of Lavender, the Growth of Europe.
Thlaspii Semen, Mustard Seeds, the Growth of Europe.
Tornsal, the Drippings of Red Wine on Rags, used as a Dye.
Turbith, the Bark Part of a Root of a Species of Convolvulus, the Growth of Asia.
Viscus Quercinus, the Leaves and Branches of Misseltoe; it should be Viscus Quernus, the Growth of Europe.
Umber, an Earth found in Silver Mines.
Ungulæ Alcis, the Hoofs of Elks, the Produce of America.
Zedoaria, the Root of an Indian Plant, the Growth of America.

To elucidate more particularly the Importation and Exportation of CORN and GRAIN, the Reader is defired to obferve, that

From and after the 17th November, 1791, the Importation and Exportation of the feveral Sorts of Corn and Grain within the feveral Diftricts, are to be regulated by the aggregate average Prices of Corn and Grain fold within the fix Weeks preceding the hereaftermentioned Dates in every Year, taken and tranfmitted by the Infpectors of Corn Returns in the feveral Diftricts, to the chief Officers of the Ports or Places of Importation or Exportation; viz. within feven Days after the 15th February, the 15th May, the 15th Auguft, and 15th November; a Copy of which is to be hung up in fome public Place in each of the feveral Cuftomhoufes, to which all Perfons may refort: Thefe Averages are to determine the feveral Duties payable upon the Importation of Corn and Grain, and are to govern the Exportation thereof, until otherwife altered by fubfequent new Averages in like Manner put up.

ERRATA.

Page 55, line 1, *after* Almonds, Bitter, *read* the Hundred Weight.
87, line 2 from Bottom, *read*, All Foreign Corn delivered in the Port of London is subject to a further Duty of 2d. per Last of ten Quarters, to be paid to the Corn Inspector.
163, after the Article Pitch, *insert*, N. B. Nine Pounds Weight of Pitch is deemed a Gallon.
198, line 5 from Bottom, Galley Tiles, except made in Ireland, *read*, except made and wrought in Ireland.
221, lines 2 and 3 from Bottom, *for* { British Ship, *read*, British built Ship. Foreign built Ship, *read*, Foreign Ship.
233, line 3 from Bottom, *for* Broom and Cant Spars, *read*, Boom and Cant Spars.
246, in the Note after Coals, *for* Chap. 4. *read*, Chap. 41.
314, the N. B. so charged by 28 Geo. III. Chap. 37. relates to the three Distinctions of Skins dressed in Oil which follow the N. B.
350, line 4 from Bottom, *for* Chap. 36, *read*, Chap. 26.
358, line 7, Linens, Stuffs, &c. printed, painted, or dyed, *read*, printed, stained, painted, or dyed.
362, Bottom line, *for* shall have paid, *read*, shall have *been* paid.
395, *for* Acts of Frauds, *read*, Act of Frauds.
450, Table I, after Indian Corn or Maize, *read*, Malt made thereof, and for the Importation of Indian Corn or Maize, see the Regulations in Table A. Also for the several Articles heretofore prohibited, which are permitted to be imported from France, being French European Manufacture or Produce, until 10th May 1800, see Table C, as there enumerated.
458, Table K, Deal Boards from the Netherlands, &c. to be omitted, as they may be imported from any Part of Europe in British built Ships, or in Ships of the Built of the same Country as the Goods, being properly navigated.
478, *for* Gum Curannæ, *read*, Gum Carannæ.

To be pasted to the Errata at the Back of Page 481.

Page 70, if exported to any Parts or Places beyond the Seas (except to Africa or the British Colonies or Plantations in America), if the said Goods shall have been printed, stained, or dyed in this kingdom, *read* (except to the British Colonies or Plantations in America), *and see* the same Article right printed under Linen, Page 139. 406, *for* † * Currants the Hundred Weight, 1*d. read*, † * Currants, the Hundred Weight, 2*d*.

TABLE ... the ...cks thereof allowed upon Exp...

DRAWBACKS OF CUSTO...

Portugal ...nd ...		European French, and other Wines, except those enumerated.						...		
...tish Colony in America.		If exported to any British Colony in America, or any British Settlement in the East Indies.			If exported to any other Place.			If exported to any British ...		
Drawbacks					of			Custo...		
1	$6\frac{2}{3}$	$3\frac{2}{3}$	0	2	4	0	1	$11\frac{1}{2}$	0	
3	$1\frac{1}{3}$	$7\frac{1}{3}$	0	4	8	0	3	11	0	
4	8	11	0	7	0	0	5	$10\frac{1}{2}$	0	
6	$2\frac{2}{3}$	$2\frac{2}{3}$	0	9	4	0	7	10	0	1...
7	$9\frac{1}{3}$	$6\frac{1}{3}$	0	11	8	0	9	$9\frac{1}{2}$	0	1...
9	4	10	0	14	0	0	11	9	0	16
...	$10\frac{2}{3}$	$1\frac{2}{3}$	0	16	4	0	13	$8\frac{1}{2}$	0	18
2	$5\frac{1}{3}$	$5\frac{1}{3}$	0	18	8	0	15	8	1	1
4	0	9	1	1	0	0	17	$7\frac{1}{2}$	1	4
5	$6\frac{2}{3}$	$0\frac{2}{3}$	1	3	4	0	19	7	1	6
	$1\frac{1}{3}$	$4\frac{1}{3}$	1	5	8	1	1	$6\frac{1}{2}$	1	9
	8	8	1	8	0	1	3	6	1	12
	$2\frac{2}{3}$	$11\frac{2}{3}$	1	10	4	1	5	$5\frac{1}{2}$	1	14
	$9\frac{1}{3}$	$3\frac{1}{3}$	1	12	8	1	7	5	1	17
	4	7	1	15	0	1	9	$4\frac{1}{2}$	2	0
	$10\frac{2}{3}$	$10\frac{2}{3}$	1	17	4	1	11	4	2	2	8
	$5\frac{1}{3}$	$2\frac{1}{3}$	1	19	8	1	13	$3\frac{1}{2}$	2	5	4
	0	6	2	2	0	1	15	3	2	8	0
	$6\frac{2}{3}$	$9\frac{2}{3}$	2	4	4	1	17	$2\frac{1}{2}$	2	10	8
	$1\frac{1}{3}$	$1\frac{1}{3}$	2	6	8	1	19	2	2	13	4
$\frac{1}{12}$ of a	8	5	2	9	0	2	1	$1\frac{1}{2}$	2	16	0
$\frac{1}{9}$	$6\frac{2}{3}$	$6\frac{2}{3}$	3	5	4	2	14	10	3	14	8	3
$\frac{1}{7}$	0	2	4	4	0	3	10	6	4	16	0	4
$\frac{1}{6}$	4	2	10	4	18	0	4	2	3	5	12	0	4
$\frac{1}{4}$	0	4	3	7	7	0	6	3	$4\frac{1}{2}$	8	8	0	7
$\frac{1}{3}$	8	5	8	9	16	0	8	4	6	11	4	0	9	1
$\frac{1}{2}$	0	8	6	14	14	0	12	6	9	16	16	0	14
The	0	16	0	29	8	0	24	13	6	33	12	0	28	1

Kk

TABLE for the Duties of CUSTOMS upon WINE imported into LONDON, and the DRAWBACKS thereof allowed upon EXPORTATION.

		CUSTOMS.						DRAWBACKS OF CUSTOMS.					
		In British built Ships.			In Foreign Ships.			Portugal, Spanish and Madeirs.			European French, and other Wines, except those enumerated.		Rhenish, German, and Hungarian.
		Portugal, Spanish, and Madeira.	European French, and other Wines, except those enumerated.	Rhenish, German, and Hungarian.	Portugal, Spanish, and Madeira.	European French, and other Wines, except those enumerated.	Rhenish, German, and Hungarian.	If exported to any British Colony in America.		Plate.	If exported to any British Colony, or to any British Settlement in any place in the Indies.	If exported to any other Place.	If exported to any British Colony in America.	If exported to any other Place.
	Gallons.	Duty.	Duty.	Duty.	Duty.	Duty.	Duty.					of	Gallons.	
	On 1	0 1 6¼	0 2 4	0 2 8	0 1 9¼	0 2 8	0 3 0	0 1 6¼	0 7 3¼	Draw- backs	0 2 4	0 1 11¼	0 2 8	0
	2	0 3 1¼	0 4 8	0 5 4	0 3 6¼	0 5 4	0 6 0	0 3 1¼	0 2 7¼		0 4 8	0 3 11	0 5 4	0
	3	0 4 8	0 7 0	0 8 0	0 5 4	0 8 0	0 9 0	0 4 8	0 3 11		0 7 0	0 5 10¼	0 8 0	0 6
	4	0 6 2¼	0 9 4	0 10 8	0 7 1¼	0 10 8	0 12 0	0 6 2¼	0 5 2¼		0 9 4	0 7 10	0 10 8	0 9
	5	0 7 9¼	0 11 8	0 13 4	0 8 10¼	0 13 4	0 15 0	0 7 9¼	0 6 6¼		0 11 8	0 9 9¼	0 13 4	0 11
	6	0 9 4	0 14 0	0 16 0	0 10 8	0 16 0	0 18 0	0 9 4	0 7 10		0 14 0	0 11 9	0 16 0	0 13
	7	0 10 10¼	0 16 4	0 18 8	0 12 5¼	0 18 8	1 1 0	0 10 10¼	0 9 1¼		0 16 4	0 13 8¼	0 18 8	0 16
	8	0 12 5¼	0 18 8	1 1 4	0 14 2¼	1 1 4	1 4 0	0 12 5¼	0 10 5¼		0 18 8	0 15 8	1 1 4	0 18 4
	9	0 14 0	1 1 0	1 4 0	0 16 0	1 4 0	1 7 0	0 14 0	0 11 9		1 1 0	0 17 7¼	1 4 0	1 0 7
	10	0 15 6¼	1 3 4	1 6 8	0 17 9¼	1 6 8	1 10 0	0 15 6¼	0 13 0¼		1 3 4	0 19 7	1 6 8	1 2 11
	11	0 17 1¼	1 5 8	1 9 4	0 19 6¼	1 9 4	1 13 0	0 17 1¼	0 14 4¼		1 5 8	1 1 6¼	1 9 4	1 5 2
	12	0 18 8	1 8 0	1 12 0	1 1 4	1 12 0	1 16 0	0 18 8	0 15 8		1 8 0	1 3 6	1 12 0	1 7 6
	13	1 0 2¼	1 10 4	1 14 8	1 3 1¼	1 14 8	1 19 0	1 0 2¼	0 16 11¼		1 10 4	1 5 5¼	1 14 8	1 9 9
	14	1 1 9¼	1 12 8	1 17 4	1 4 10¼	1 17 4	2 2 0	1 1 9¼	0 18 3¼		1 12 8	1 7 5	1 17 4	2 12 1
	15	1 3 4	1 15 0	2 0 0	1 6 8	2 0 0	2 5 0	1 3 4	0 19 7		1 15 0	1 9 4¼	2 0 0	2 14 4
	16	1 4 10¼	1 17 4	2 2 8	1 8 5¼	2 2 8	2 8 0	1 4 10¼	1 0 10¼		1 17 4	1 11 4	2 2 8	1 16 8
	17	1 6 5¼	1 19 8	2 5 4	1 10 2¼	2 5 4	2 11 0	1 6 5¼	1 2 2¼		1 19 8	1 13 3¼	2 5 4	1 13 11
	18	1 8 0	2 2 0	2 8 0	1 12 0	2 8 0	2 14 0	1 8 0	1 3 6		2 2 0	1 15 3	2 8 0	2 1 2
	19	1 9 6¼	2 4 4	2 10 8	1 13 9¼	2 10 8	2 17 0	1 9 6¼	1 4 9¼		2 4 4	1 17 2¼	2 10 8	2 3 6
	20	1 11 1¼	2 6 8	2 13 4	1 15 6¼	2 13 4	3 0 0	1 11 1¼	1 6 1¼		2 6 8	1 19 2	2 13 4	2 5 10
¼ of a Tun.	21	1 12 8	2 9 0	2 16 0	1 17 4	2 16 0	3 3 0	1 12 8	1 7 5		2 9 0	2 1 1¼	2 16 0	2 8 1
⅛	28	2 3 6¼	3 5 4	3 14 8	2 9 9¼	3 14 8	4 4 0	2 3 6¼	1 16 6¼		3 5 4	2 14 10	3 14 8	3 4 2
⅛	36	2 16 0	4 4 0	4 16 0	3 4 0	4 16 0	5 8 0	2 16 0	2 7 0		4 4 0	3 10 6	4 16 0	4 2 6
½	42	3 5 4	4 18 0	5 12 0	3 14 8	5 12 0	6 6 0	3 5 4	2 14 10		4 18 0	4 2 3	5 12 0	4 16 3
⅝	63	4 18 0	7 7 0	8 8 0	5 12 0	8 8 0	9 9 0	4 18 0	4 2 3		7 7 0	6 3 4¼	8 8 0	7 4 4
¾	84	6 10 8	9 16 0	11 4 0	7 9 4	11 4 0	12 12 0	6 10 8	5 9 8		9 16 0	8 4 6	11 4 0	9 12 6
⅞	126	9 16 0	14 14 0	16 16 0	11 4 0	16 16 0	18 18 0	9 16 0	8 4 6		14 14 0	12 6 9	16 16 0	14 8 9
The Tun	252	19 12 0	29 8 0	33 12 0	22 8 0	33 12 0	37 16 0	19 12 0	16 9 0		29 8 0	24 13 6	33 12 0	28 17 6

DRAWBACKS OF CUSTOMS.

	European French, and other Wines, except those enumerated.		Rhenish, German, and Hungarian.	
	If exported to any British Colony in America, or any British Settlement in the East Indies.	If exported to any other Place.	If exported to any British Colony in America.	If exported to any other Place.
Drawbacks		of	Customs.	
1	0 2 0	0 1 7½	0 2 8	0 2 3½
2	0 4 0	0 3 3	0 5 4	0 4 7
3	0 6 0	0 4 10½	0 8 0	0 6 10½
4	0 8 0	0 6 6	0 10 8	0 9 2
5	0 10 0	0 8 1½	0 13 4	0 11 5½
6	0 12 0	0 9 9	0 16 0	0 13 9
7	0 14 0	0 11 4½	0 18 8	0 16 0½
8	0 16 0	0 13 0	1 1 4	0 18 4
9	0 18 0	0 14 7½	1 4 0	1 0 7½
10	1 0 0	0 16 3	1 6 8	1 2 11
11	1 2 0	0 17 10½	1 9 4	1 5 2½
0	1 4 0	0 19 6	1 12 0	1 7 6
1	1 6 0	1 1 1½	1 14 8	1 9 9½
2	1 8 0	1 2 9	1 17 4	1 12 1
3	1 10 0	1 4 4½	2 0 0	1 14 4½
4	1 12 0	1 6 0	2 2 8	1 16 8
5	1 14 0	1 7 7½	2 5 4	1 18 11½
6	1 16 0	1 9 3	2 8 0	2 1 3
7	1 18 0	1 10 10½	2 10 8	2 3 6½
8	2 0 0	1 12 6	2 13 4	2 5 10
9	2 2 0	1 14 1½	2 16 0	2 8 1½
4	2 16 0	2 5 6	3 14 8	3 4 2
0	3 12 0	2 18 6	4 16 0	4 2 6
6	4 4 0	3 8 3	5 12 0	4 16 3
3	6 6 0	5 2 4½	8 8 0	7 4 4½
0	8 8 0	6 16 6	11 4 0	9 12 6
6	12 12 0	10 4 9	16 16 0	14 8 9
3	25 4 0	20 9 6	33 12 0	28 17 6

L l

TABLE for the Duties of Customs [illegible] imported into any Port of [illegible] except London, and the [illegible] thereof allowed upon Exportation.

	Gallons.	CUSTOMS. In British built Ships. Portugal, Spanish, and Madeira. Duty.	In British built Ships. European French, and other Wines, except those enumerated. Duty.	In British built Ships. Rhenish, German, and Hungarian. Duty.	In Foreign Ships. Portugal, Spanish, and Madeira. Duty.	In Foreign Ships. European French, and other Wines, except those enumerated. Duty.	In Foreign Ships. Rhenish, German, and Hungarian. Duty.
	On 1	0 1 4	0 2 0	0 2 8	0 1 6⅔	0 2 4	0 3 0
	2	0 2 8	0 4 0	0 5 4	0 3 1⅓	0 4 8	0 6 0
	3	0 4 0	0 6 0	0 8 0	0 4 8	0 7 0	0 9 0
	4	0 5 4	0 8 0	0 10 8	0 6 2⅔	0 9 4	0 12 0
	5	0 6 8	0 10 0	0 13 4	0 7 9⅓	0 11 8	0 15 0
	6	0 8 0	0 12 0	0 16 0	0 9 4	0 14 0	0 18 0
	7	0 9 4	0 14 0	0 18 8	0 10 10⅔	0 16 4	1 1 0
	8	0 10 8	0 16 0	1 1 4	0 12 5⅓	0 18 8	1 4 0
	9	0 12 0	0 18 0	1 4 0	0 14 0	1 1 0	1 7 0
	10	0 13 4	1 0 0	1 6 8	0 15 6⅔	1 3 4	1 10 0
	11	0 14 8	1 2 0	1 9 4	0 17 1⅓	1 5 8	1 13 0
	12	0 16 0	1 4 0	1 12 0	0 18 8	1 8 0	1 16 0
	13	0 17 4	1 6 0	1 14 8	1 0 2⅔	1 10 4	1 19 0
	14	0 18 8	1 8 0	1 17 4	1 1 9⅓	1 12 8	2 2 0
	15	1 0 0	1 10 0	2 0 0	1 3 4	1 15 0	2 5 0
	16	1 1 4	1 12 0	2 2 8	1 4 10⅔	1 17 4	2 8 0
	17	1 2 8	1 14 0	2 5 4	1 6 5⅓	1 19 8	2 11 0
	18	1 4 0	1 16 0	2 8 0	1 8 0	2 2 0	2 14 0
	19	1 5 4	1 18 0	2 10 8	1 9 6⅔	2 4 4	2 17 0
	20	1 6 8	2 0 0	2 13 4	1 11 1⅓	2 6 8	3 0 0
1/12 of a Tun.	21	1 8 0	2 2 0	2 16 0	1 12 8	2 9 0	3 3 0
1/9	28	1 17 4	2 16 0	3 14 8	2 3 6⅔	3 5 4	4 4 0
1/7	36	2 8 0	3 12 0	4 16 0	2 16 0	4 4 0	5 8 0
1/6	42	2 16 0	4 4 0	5 12 0	3 5 4	4 18 0	6 6 0
1/4	63	4 4 0	6 6 0	8 8 0	4 18 0	7 7 0	9 9 0
1/3	84	5 12 0	8 8 0	11 4 0	6 10 8	9 16 0	12 12 0
1/2	126	8 8 0	12 12 0	16 16 0	9 16 0	14 14 0	18 18 0
The Tun	252	16 16 0	25 4 0	33 12 0	19 12 0	29 8 0	37 16 0

	Gallons.	DRAWBACKS OF CUSTOMS. Portugal, Spanish, and Madeira. If exported to any British Colony in America.	Portugal, Spanish, and Madeira. If exported to any other Place.	European French, and other Wines, except those enumerated. If exported to any British Colony in America, or any British Settlements in the East Indies.	European French, and other Wines, except those enumerated. If exported to any other Place.	Rhenish, German, and Hungarian. If exported to any British Colony in America.	Rhenish, German, and Hungarian. If exported to any other Place.
			Draw-	backs	of	Customs.	
	On 1	0 1 4	0 1 1	0 2 0	0 1 7½	0 2 8	0 2 3½
	2	0 2 8	0 2 2	0 4 0	0 3 3	0 5 4	0 4 7
	3	0 4 0	0 3 3	0 6 0	0 4 10½	0 8 0	0 6 10½
	4	0 5 4	0 4 4	0 8 0	0 6 6	0 10 8	0 9 2
	5	0 6 8	0 5 5	0 10 0	0 8 1½	0 13 4	0 11 5½
	6	0 8 0	0 6 6	0 12 0	0 9 9	0 16 0	0 13 9
	7	0 9 4	0 7 7	0 14 0	0 11 4½	0 18 8	0 16 0½
	8	0 10 8	0 8 8	0 16 0	0 13 0	1 1 4	0 18 4
	9	0 12 0	0 9 9	0 18 0	0 14 7½	1 4 0	1 0 7½
	10	0 13 4	0 10 10	1 0 0	0 16 3	1 6 8	1 2 11
	11	0 14 8	0 11 11	1 2 0	0 17 10½	1 9 4	1 5 2½
	12	0 16 0	0 13 0	1 4 0	0 19 6	1 12 0	1 7 6
	13	0 17 4	0 14 1	1 6 0	1 1 1½	1 14 8	1 9 9½
	14	0 18 8	0 15 2	1 8 0	1 2 9	1 17 4	1 12 1
	15	1 0 0	0 16 3	1 10 0	1 4 4½	2 0 0	1 14 4½
	16	1 1 4	0 17 4	1 12 0	1 6 0	2 2 8	1 16 8
	17	1 2 8	0 18 5	1 14 0	1 7 7½	2 5 4	1 18 11½
	18	1 4 0	0 19 6	1 16 0	1 9 3	2 8 0	2 1 3
	19	1 5 4	1 0 7	1 18 0	1 10 10½	2 10 8	2 3 6½
	20	1 6 8	1 1 8	2 0 0	1 12 6	2 13 4	2 5 10
1/12 of a Tun.	21	1 8 0	1 2 9	2 2 0	1 14 1½	2 16 0	2 8 1½
1/9	28	1 17 4	1 10 4	2 16 0	2 5 6	3 14 8	3 4 2
1/7	36	2 8 0	1 19 0	3 12 0	2 18 6	4 16 0	4 2 6
1/6	42	2 16 0	2 5 6	4 4 0	3 8 3	5 12 0	4 16 3
1/4	63	4 4 0	3 8 3	6 6 0	5 2 4½	8 8 0	7 4 4½
1/3	84	5 12 0	4 11 0	8 8 0	6 16 6	11 4 0	9 12 6
1/2	126	8 8 0	6 16 6	12 12 0	10 4 9	16 16 0	14 8 9
The Tun	252	16 16 0	13 13 0	25 4 0	20 9 6	33 12 0	28 17 6

L l

...rman, and Hungarian.				European French, and other Wines not enumerated.					
If exported to any British Settlement in the East Indies.			If exported to any other Place.		If exported to any British Colony or Plantation in America, or to any British Settlement in the East Indies.			If exported to any other Place.	
of			Excise.						
0	$9\frac{24}{63}$	0	0	$5\frac{24}{63}$	0	1	$1\frac{2}{3}$	0	0	$5\frac{24}{63}$
1	$6\frac{48}{63}$	0	0	$10\frac{48}{63}$	0	2	$3\frac{1}{3}$	0	0	$10\frac{48}{63}$
2	$4\frac{9}{63}$	0	1	$4\frac{9}{63}$	0	3	5	0	1	$4\frac{9}{63}$
3	$1\frac{33}{63}$	0	1	$9\frac{33}{63}$	0	4	$6\frac{2}{3}$	0	1	$9\frac{33}{63}$
3	$10\frac{57}{63}$	0	2	$2\frac{57}{63}$	0	5	$8\frac{1}{3}$	0	2	$2\frac{57}{63}$
4	$8\frac{18}{63}$	0	2	$8\frac{18}{63}$	0	6	10	0	2	$8\frac{18}{63}$
5	$5\frac{42}{63}$	0	3	$1\frac{42}{63}$	0	7	$11\frac{2}{3}$	0	3	$1\frac{42}{63}$
6	$3\frac{3}{63}$	0	3	$7\frac{3}{63}$	0	9	$1\frac{1}{3}$	0	3	$7\frac{3}{63}$
7	$0\frac{27}{63}$	0	4	$0\frac{27}{63}$	0	10	3	0	4	$0\frac{27}{63}$
7	$9\frac{51}{63}$	0	4	$5\frac{51}{63}$	0	11	$4\frac{2}{3}$	0	4	$5\frac{51}{63}$
8	$7\frac{12}{63}$	0	4	$11\frac{12}{63}$	0	12	$6\frac{1}{3}$	0	4	$11\frac{12}{63}$
9	$4\frac{36}{63}$	0	5	$4\frac{36}{63}$	0	13	8	0	5	$4\frac{36}{63}$
10	$1\frac{60}{63}$	0	5	$9\frac{60}{63}$	0	14	$9\frac{2}{3}$	0	5	$9\frac{60}{63}$
10	$11\frac{21}{63}$	0	6	$3\frac{21}{63}$	0	15	$11\frac{1}{3}$	0	6	$3\frac{21}{63}$
11	$8\frac{45}{63}$	0	6	$8\frac{45}{63}$	0	17	1	0	6	$8\frac{45}{63}$
12	$6\frac{6}{63}$	0	7	$2\frac{6}{63}$	0	18	$2\frac{2}{3}$	0	7	$2\frac{6}{63}$
13	$3\frac{30}{63}$	0	7	$7\frac{30}{63}$	0	19	$4\frac{1}{3}$	0	7	$7\frac{30}{63}$
14	$0\frac{54}{63}$	0	8	$0\frac{54}{63}$	1	0	6	0	8	$0\frac{54}{63}$
14	$10\frac{15}{63}$	0	8	$6\frac{15}{63}$	1	1	$7\frac{2}{3}$	0	8	$6\frac{15}{63}$
15	$7\frac{39}{63}$	0	8	$11\frac{39}{63}$	1	2	$9\frac{1}{3}$	0	8	$11\frac{39}{63}$
16	5	0	9	5	1	3	11	0	9	5
1	$10\frac{2}{3}$	0	12	$6\frac{2}{3}$	1	11	$10\frac{2}{3}$	0	12	$6\frac{2}{3}$
8	$1\frac{5}{7}$	0	16	$1\frac{5}{7}$	2	1	0	0	16	$1\frac{5}{7}$
12	10	0	18	10	2	7	10	0	18	10
9	3	1	8	3	3	11	9	1	8	3
5	8	1	17	8	4	15	8	1	17	8
18	6	2	16	6	7	3	6	2	16	6
17	0	5	13	0	14	7	0	5	13	0

TABLE fo[illegible] Port of [illegible]TAIN, and the D[illegible] allowed upon EXPORTATION.

	Gallons.	EXCISE. In any Ships. Portugal, Spanish, and Madeira. Duty.	EXCISE. In any Ships. Rhenish, French, and other Wines. Duty.	DRAWBACKS OF EXCISE. Portugal, Spanish, and Madeira. If exported to any British Colony or Plantation in America.	Portugal, Spanish, and Madeira. If exported to any British Settlement in the East Indies.	Portugal, Spanish, and Madeira. If exported to any other Place.	Rhenish, German, and Hungarian. If exported to any British Colony or Plantation in America.	Rhenish, German, and Hungarian. If exported to any British Settlement in the East Indies.	Rhenish, German, and Hungarian. If exported to any other Place.	European French, and other Wines not enumerated. If exported to any British Colony or Plantation in America, or to any British Settlement in the East Indies.	European French, and other Wines not enumerated. If exported to any other Place.
				Draw-	backs		of	Excise.			
	On 1	0 0 11 1/7	0 1 5	0 0 9 [illegible]	0 0 6 [illegible]	0 0 3 [illegible]	0 1 1 1/7	0 0 9 [illegible]	0 0 5 [illegible]	0 1 1 1/7	0 0 5 [illegible]
	2	0 1 10 2/7	0 2 10	0 1 6 [illegible]	0 1 0 [illegible]	0 0 7 [illegible]	0 2 3 [illegible]	0 1 6 [illegible]	0 0 10 [illegible]	0 2 3 [illegible]	0 0 10 [illegible]
	3	0 2 10	0 4 3	0 2 3 [illegible]	0 1 6 [illegible]	0 0 10 [illegible]	0 3 5	0 2 4 [illegible]	0 1 4 [illegible]	0 3 5	0 1 4 [illegible]
	4	0 3 9 [illegible]	0 5 8	0 3 0 [illegible]	0 2 1 [illegible]	0 1 2 [illegible]	0 4 6 [illegible]	0 3 1 [illegible]	0 1 9 [illegible]	0 4 6 [illegible]	0 1 9 [illegible]
	5	0 4 8 [illegible]	0 7 1	0 3 9 [illegible]	0 2 7 [illegible]	0 1 5 [illegible]	0 5 8 [illegible]	0 3 10 [illegible]	0 2 2 [illegible]	0 5 8 [illegible]	0 2 2 [illegible]
	6	0 5 8	0 8 6	0 4 6 [illegible]	0 3 1 [illegible]	0 1 9 [illegible]	0 6 10	0 4 8 [illegible]	0 2 8 [illegible]	0 6 10	0 2 8 [illegible]
	7	0 6 7 [illegible]	0 9 11	0 5 3 [illegible]	0 3 7 [illegible]	0 2 1 [illegible]	0 7 11 [illegible]	0 5 5 [illegible]	0 3 1 [illegible]	0 7 11 [illegible]	0 3 1 [illegible]
	8	0 7 6 [illegible]	0 11 4	0 6 0 [illegible]	0 4 2 [illegible]	0 2 4 [illegible]	0 9 1 [illegible]	0 6 3 [illegible]	0 3 7 [illegible]	0 9 1 [illegible]	0 3 7 [illegible]
	9	0 8 6	0 12 9	0 6 10	0 4 8 [illegible]	0 2 8 [illegible]	0 10 3	0 7 0 [illegible]	0 4 0 [illegible]	0 10 3	0 4 0 [illegible]
	10	0 9 5 [illegible]	0 14 2	0 7 7 [illegible]	0 5 2 [illegible]	0 2 11 [illegible]	0 11 4 [illegible]	0 7 9 [illegible]	0 4 5 [illegible]	0 11 4 [illegible]	0 4 5 [illegible]
	11	0 10 4 [illegible]	0 15 7	0 8 4 [illegible]	0 5 8 [illegible]	0 3 3 [illegible]	0 12 6 [illegible]	0 8 7 [illegible]	0 4 11 [illegible]	0 12 6 [illegible]	0 4 11 [illegible]
	12	0 11 4	0 17 0	0 9 1 [illegible]	0 6 3 [illegible]	0 3 7 [illegible]	0 13 8	0 9 4 [illegible]	0 5 4 [illegible]	0 13 8	0 5 4 [illegible]
	13	0 12 3 [illegible]	0 18 5	0 9 10 [illegible]	0 6 9 [illegible]	0 3 10 [illegible]	0 14 9 [illegible]	0 10 1 [illegible]	0 5 9 [illegible]	0 14 9 [illegible]	0 5 9 [illegible]
	14	0 13 2 [illegible]	0 19 10	0 10 7 [illegible]	0 7 3 [illegible]	0 4 2 [illegible]	0 15 11 [illegible]	0 10 11 [illegible]	0 6 3 [illegible]	0 15 11 [illegible]	0 6 3 [illegible]
	15	0 14 2	1 1 3	0 11 4 [illegible]	0 7 9 [illegible]	0 4 5 [illegible]	0 17 1	0 11 8 [illegible]	0 6 8 [illegible]	0 17 1	0 6 8 [illegible]
	16	0 15 1 [illegible]	1 2 8	0 12 1 [illegible]	0 8 4 [illegible]	0 4 9 [illegible]	0 18 2 [illegible]	0 12 6 [illegible]	0 7 2 [illegible]	0 18 2 [illegible]	0 7 2 [illegible]
	17	0 16 0 [illegible]	1 4 1	0 12 10 [illegible]	0 8 10 [illegible]	0 5 0 [illegible]	0 19 4 [illegible]	0 13 3 [illegible]	0 7 7 [illegible]	0 19 4 [illegible]	0 7 7 [illegible]
	18	0 17 0	1 5 6	0 13 8	0 9 4 [illegible]	0 5 4 [illegible]	1 0 6	0 14 0 [illegible]	0 8 0 [illegible]	1 0 6	0 8 0 [illegible]
	19	0 17 11 [illegible]	1 6 11	0 14 5 [illegible]	0 9 10 [illegible]	0 5 8 [illegible]	1 1 7 [illegible]	0 14 10 [illegible]	0 8 6 [illegible]	1 1 7 [illegible]	0 8 6 [illegible]
	20	0 18 10 [illegible]	1 8 4	0 15 2 [illegible]	0 10 5 [illegible]	0 5 11 [illegible]	1 2 9 [illegible]	0 15 7 [illegible]	0 8 11 [illegible]	1 2 9 [illegible]	0 8 11 [illegible]
1/12 of a Tun.	21	0 19 10	1 9 9	0 15 11 [illegible]	0 10 11 [illegible]	0 6 3 [illegible]	1 3 11	0 16 5	0 9 5	1 3 11	0 9 5
1/9	28	1 6 5 [illegible]	1 19 8	1 1 3 [illegible]	0 14 7 [illegible]	0 8 4 [illegible]	1 11 10 [illegible]	1 1 10 [illegible]	0 12 6 [illegible]	1 11 10 [illegible]	0 12 6 [illegible]
1/7	36	1 14 0	2 11 0	1 7 4	0 18 9 [illegible]	0 10 9 [illegible]	2 1 0	1 8 1 [illegible]	0 16 1 [illegible]	2 1 0	0 16 1 [illegible]
1/6	42	1 19 8	2 19 6	1 11 10 [illegible]	1 1 10 [illegible]	0 12 6 [illegible]	2 7 10	1 12 10	0 18 10	2 7 10	0 18 10
1/4	63	2 19 6	4 9 3	2 7 10	1 12 10	0 18 10	3 11 9	2 9 3	1 8 3	3 11 9	1 8 3
1/3	84	3 19 4	5 19 0	3 3 9 [illegible]	2 3 9 [illegible]	1 5 1 [illegible]	4 15 8	3 5 8	1 17 8	4 15 8	1 17 8
1/2	126	5 19 0	8 18 6	4 15 8	3 5 8	1 17 8	7 3 6	4 18 6	2 16 6	7 3 6	2 16 6
The Tun	252	11 18 0	17 17 0	9 11 4	6 11 4	3 15 4	14 7 0	9 17 0	5 13 0	14 7 0	5 13 0

www.ingramcontent.com/pod-product-compliance
Lightning Source LLC
Chambersburg PA
CBHW020832020526
44114CB00040B/564